The Jews of Moslem Spain

I

THE JEWS OF MOSLEM SPAIN

by

ELIYAHU ASHTOR

VOLUME 1

Translated from the Hebrew by
Aaron Klein and Jenny Machlowitz Klein

The Jewish Publication Society of America
PHILADELPHIA

Originally published in Hebrew by
Kiryat Sepher Ltd., Jerusalem
Maps by DESIGN KARTA, JERUSALEM

ISBN 0-8276-0017-8
Library of Congress catalog card number 73-14081
Manufactured in the United States of America
Designed by
Sol Calvin Cohen

The translation of this book into English
was made possible through a grant from

THE ADOLF AMRAM FUND

CONTENTS

LIST OF MAPS

The Jews of Moslem Spain

I

1

THE CONQUEST OF SPAIN

I

The story which we would like to tell in this book starts in 711 C.E. on the slopes of the promontory later known as Gibraltar.

It was a warm, pleasant spring evening thirty years after the mainland on the opposite shore had been conquered by the Arabs. The moon was still new and the night very dark. The pale gleam of the stars hardly broke through the clouds that scudded across the sky. No sound or movement was heard on the slope of the promontory, and the waves rolled up and broke on its shore as from time immemorial, covering the sea with white foam. The darkness enveloped the straits like a cloak which enwrapped the world. But a discerning eye could make out two dark masses which moved speedily to the other side of the promontory, and after a while it became apparent that these were two galleys. As they came nearer, they slackened their pace because of the many sharp rocks jutting out of the sea. The darkness hid the men who crowded these battered boats being driven to the western shore of the promontory. Everyone was silent. Even the oarsmen allowed themselves little movement.

With one strong pull they brought the first boat to a tiny

landing, and at once the passengers sprang out and quickly went ashore. They brought a few mules and containers filled with drinking water up with them. The second boat came near, and its passengers also alit. They mounted the mules, clinging three or four to a saddle, like clusters of grapes. They urged the mules on toward the crest of the hill, where their guides showed them a big cave in which they could easily hide during the day. The road was difficult and full of pitfalls, and the mules were almost brought to their knees.

At long last the column reached its destination; the men unloaded the burdens and took them into the cave. They began to chop down branches to fortify the mouth of the cave against any eventuality. While these men were thus engaged, three more ships came to the shore, and their passengers hurried to a nearby cave which they, too, began to fortify. At daybreak the two groups entered their caves and hid throughout the day. Meanwhile, the ships returned to the southern end of the straits from which they had come. The following day this scene was reenacted, without the inhabitants of the town near the landing being aware of what was happening. This time a few boats came in a group, and when the passengers had hurried ashore, they immediately returned that very night to bring additional groups of invaders. Again the men climbed up the slope of the hill and found shelter in hidden clefts of the rocks, remaining there throughout the day. Within less than four days a veritable army was gathered on the rock.

A man stepped forth from one of the last boats; by his bearing and demeanor it was evident that he was the leader of the invaders. His skull was large, his hair black, and his face swarthy; his expression was one of energy and strong will. He wore a cloak which fit his body tightly and was fastened from within. A large entourage stood about him and paid close heed to every word he spoke. When he reached the top of the hill, a stir went through the camp. He looked about him with a probing eye, then ordered the various groups to return to their places while he, together with his staff of officers, withdrew to a corner to plan strategy.

This huge-skulled man was Ṭāriḳ b. Ziyād, a high-ranking officer in the Arabic army. He was the manumitted slave of Mūsā b. Nuṣair, the Arab commander who had finally succeeded in subduing the western lands as far as the Atlantic coast. Ṭāriḳ, who commanded Mūsā's vanguard, had been appointed governor of the city of Tangiers and its environs. Because he was a man of great initiative and boundless ambition, however, he aspired to military ventures that would bring him fame and dominion. This officer dreamt of land conquests. As he daily gazed northward across the straits he saw a land, broad and rich, which fanned his ambitions. Fortune smiles upon the brave of heart and seemingly causes events that pave the way to his goals.

In those days a vestige of the Byzantine Empire still remained in the strip of land on the western end of North Africa, the city of Ceuta, which had not yet been taken by the Arabs. They besieged it in 708 and destroyed the surrounding area, but the fortified city held its own. The governor of the city was Julian, a Byzantine officer, an adventurer by nature and lacking a conscience, but very active and full of ideas. Realizing that help would not come from faraway Byzantium, he made contact with the Visigothic rulers of Spain and placed himself under their protection.

When he saw that the Arabs were extending their dominion over all of North Africa, however, he turned his back on the Visigoths and made peace with the Arabs. Furthermore, he even spurred them on to try for the conquest of Spain and promised them his aid. He had at his disposal a number of merchant vessels, as well as men who knew well southern Spain, its cities, and its regions. The Arabs hesitated about undertaking so dangerous and daring an adventure, but Julian persuaded them at least to make an attempt and see what would result. In 710 an exploratory invasion was mounted that was, in effect, but a predatory raid. Four hundred men, all Berbers of the Ghumāra tribe, commanded by one of their own tribesmen named Ṭarīf, landed on an island near the coast, near a city later named after him—Tarifa. From there they fanned out in raids throughout the area and returned laden with spoils to the shore on the other side of the straits.

Naturally, this success strengthened the claims of Julian, who had never ceased telling the Arabs how easy the conquest of Spain would be and how great the wealth that awaited the conquerers was. So the Arabs began to prepare a real invasion. Many of the Berbers, who had heard of his exploits, willingly joined the army of Ṭāriḳ, who had been appointed commander of the venture. Julian placed ships and scouts at their disposal, and at the end of April in 711, with Ṭāriḳ at their head, they crossed the straits.

This great country which the Moslems were invading seemed at first glance to be powerful and affluent, united and ruled by a strong hand; but this was only a superficial impression, comparable to the apparent serenity that prevailed in the land on the other side of the promontory on those nights when Ṭāriḳ and his men encamped on the Rock of Gibraltar. It was outwardly calm but seething within. The kingdom of the Visigoths, who ruled for hundreds of years over the Iberian peninsula, was in actuality torn asunder and divided. The many contradictory elements within the population constituted ever-widening divisions that continually grew stronger, until they threatened to destroy the entire social structure.

It is true that the Germanic rulers tried, with the passage of time, to heal the rift between them and their native-born subjects, who had accepted Roman culture. The same code of law applied to both Visigoth and Ibero-Roman alike. The tax burden which had laid heavily on the natives was lightened, and they began to take a distinguished role in the synods of the priesthood, whose ordinances, once sanctioned by the king, became the law of the land.

However, more serious than the political cleavage was the class rift which rent the populace and turned them into hostile camps. The nobles and their allies, the clergy, shamefully exploited the multitude of peasants and serfs. They literally robbed the poor man of his land. On the one hand, the masses had no interest in the existence of this tyrannical government; and on the other, when war came, they were called to serve in the army and were required to fight in behalf of their overlords.

Under these circumstances the Visigothic kingdom was liable to collapse whenever a stray blow befell it. This kingdom was rotten from within, and when a strong and daring enemy reached its gates it could not withstand the blow. Destiny decreed that at this very time the Arabic-Moslem Empire reached the acme of its power and spread to dimensions never before known. The caliphate spread from the banks of the Indus to the Atlantic Ocean; and the zeal of this new faith, the desire for dominion, and the aspiration for gain goaded its armies to additional ventures of conquest. The Visigothic kingdom was like a ripe fruit, ready to fall into their hands. Moreover, besides the class rifts which divided the inhabitants of the kingdom, there was also dissension among the ruling elements. In 633 it was decided that the succession to the Visigothic throne should be determined by election: that is, after the death of a king his successor should be determined by election. But the Visigothic kings of Spain did everything in their power to secure the crown for their sons or relatives. This led to quarrels and rebellions which undermined the foundations of the kingdom.

These dissensions reached their climax in 709, after the death of King Witiza. He left behind three sons who demanded the throne for their family. But the ruling class, especially the princes of the church, hated the House of Witiza, with the result that his widow and two of her sons were forced to flee Toledo, the capital of the kingdom, and find a refuge in the north. Then Roderick, the duke of the province of Betica, was chosen king of Spain. He was reputed to be a skillful commander, and the nobles among the dominant Visigoths and the clergy put great hopes in him. Akhila, Witiza's first-born, who was governor of a large province in the north of the kingdom, attempted to oppose Roderick by force of arms, but his army was defeated.

Realizing that armed victory alone was not enough, Roderick sought to attract to his side the supporters of the House of Witiza by various means. He gave them posts of command in his army and appointed them rulers over provinces. But his efforts were in vain. The enmity between the two factions was too great. Here, too, occurred the kind of event which can play so important a role in a people's destiny. The Witiza faction viewed any means as appropriate, and it was ready to negotiate with any group, in order to win the throne. They turned to the Franks in Gaul and called on them to intervene; they also negotiated with the Moslem rulers of North Africa and asked for their help. Akhila himself crossed the sea and appeared before the Arabic rulers of Morocco to plead with them to seat him on the throne of Spain. The intermediary, who interceded for the nobles of the House of Witiza with the Arabic rulers, was, of course, Julian, the governor of Ceuta. These men convinced the Arabs that when they invaded Spain, their supporters would arise everywhere and join forces with them. Thus Ṭāriḳ and his men prepared for what was to come with a sense of assurance.

The Moslem commander wasted no time in his camp on the rock that later bore his name, Djabal at-Tarik (Mount of Ṭāriḳ)—or, as the Europeans called it, Gibraltar. He advanced with his small forces northward and with no difficulty took the city of Carteya, at the northern end of the bay. Turning south he captured the city of Algeciras, which was a port and crossing point to the African coast, as it still is. This city became the base of the invading forces, and Ṭāriḳ turned over to Julian the responsibility for protecting it and for channeling supplies for his troops through it. After his conquest of Algeciras, Ṭāriḳ began to move northward.

Meanwhile, King Roderick set out against the invaders at the head of a strong army and before long arrived in Andalusia. Ṭāriḳ asked Mūsā b. Nuṣair, governor-general of North Africa, for reinforcements. At all events, when the two armies clashed on July 19, 711, on the shores of Lago de Janda, Ṭāriḳ had no more than twelve thousand men. But he won a splendid victory. Roderick himself was slain and his army dispersed. This battle sealed the fate of Spain for many centuries.

His victory over the Visigothic king strengthened the ambitions of the Moslem commander. Though his orders from Mūsā b. Nuṣair had been not to advance to the heart of Spain, Ṭāriḳ disregarded them and started a daring advance toward conquest. With his small army he drove through this large territory, where the militia of the Gothic army were stationed, an area that contained many fortified cities with well-trained garrisons. True, it was a matter of common sense and good military tactics not to delay, but to strike at the vanquished foe before it could renew its strength and array its forces again. No doubt he was also under pressure from the supporters of the House of Witiza, who had invited the Moslems to help them regain the throne in the first place. Their aim was to reach Toledo, the capital of the country, and with the aid of the Africans to set on the throne one of their own men. So Ṭāriḳ moved northward. Near the city of Écija the Gothic forces tested their fortunes of war on the battlefield and were again routed. The vanquished troops fled to Écija, which Ṭāriḳ then had to besiege for some time before it capitulated and fell into his hands.

Meanwhile, chaos spread throughout the kingdom. Everywhere the supporters of the House of Witiza bestirred themselves, and the peasants and serfs rose up. The Ibero-Roman populace felt that the time had come to vent their feelings upon the German despots. The ruling class was dumbfounded and overwhelmed. Here and there they attempted to gather their strength together and to oppose the invaders, but since they lacked a guiding hand and direction they accomplished nothing. Most of the nobles and the clergy fled to the north of the kingdom or beyond its borders to Gaul. On the other hand, Spanish inhabitants by the thousands joined the invaders. The ranks of Ṭāriḳ's army grew from day to day. They were joined by serfs who wanted to gain their freedom, by peasants who sought vengeance against the great landowners and wanted to get the land for themselves, and especially by followers of the House of Witiza.

II

A month after the battle near Lago de Janda a troop of horsemen approached Cordova, the principal city of the province of Betica. The troop, numbering about seven hundred men, was led by Mughīth ar-Rūmī, an Arabic officer trained in the court of the caliph in Damascus. As he came near the city, which spread along the northern bank of the Guadalquivir River and was surrounded by a strong wall, he pitched his tent in a thicket on the southern bank and began to explore the environs of the city to search out a vulnerable spot. Moslem warriors marched around the city, while the Gothic forces on the walls watched them closely. The city was tightly shut; no one came out and no one entered. The governor of the city and his men had decided to fight to the last drop of blood and to sell their lives dearly. They were followers of King Roderick, who had formerly been the governor of this region, and were faithful to him even after his death.

All the while, numbers of Jews remained shut up in their houses, impatiently awaiting the outcome. Unlike the Goths and the clergy, they did not fear the invaders who besieged the city, but instead set their hopes on them. For the Visigothic kings had oppressed them sorely and had treated them with extreme cruelty. What memories must have passed through the minds of the Cordovan Jews on those nights as they sat in their houses and heard the footsteps of the guards on the walls. . . .

The Jewish settlement on the Iberian peninsula was a very ancient one and in its early stages had prospered. Even after the Visigoths had established their rule over the land, the condition of the Jewish communities remained favorable for a long time. They earned their livelihood with dignity, and they fulfilled the laws of the Torah and observed its commandments without hindrance.

However, when the Visigothic rulers changed from Arianism to another form of Christianity, Catholicism, in 586, the situation of the Jews changed. A period of disturbances and persecutions began. The synods of the clergy that assembled from time to time in the capital determined the policy of the regime; as a result, at every council that convened, zealous bishops promulgated decrees against the Jews. For their part, the kings vied with the clergy and spurred them on to find ways and means to institute laws to eradicate Judaism from the land. Whether this came from sincere religious zeal or from the avarice with which they eyed the possessions of the Jews, kings and clergy were of one mind—to embitter the lives of the Jews and to provoke them to change their faith.

In 613 King Sisebut decreed that all the Jews must convert or leave the land. This edict was carried out; thousands were converted to Christianity and thousands left the country. Swintila, who succeeded Sisebut, annulled the edict of conversion, permitted converts to revert to the faith of their fathers, and allowed those who had gone into exile to return. But when King Sisenand came into power, he was inclined to be severe. The council that met in Toledo in 633 decided that the Jews who had become Christians as an outcome of the laws of Sisebut must remain Christians and should be carefully watched, lest they treat any of the laws of the church with disrespect. The king gave this his sanction.

A synod of the clergy in 638, known as the sixth Council of Toledo, decreed that the Visigoths should not tolerate any person who did not believe in Catholicism. It also declared that upon ascending the throne each king should be obliged to swear that he would carry out the laws against Judaism. At that time the ruler was Chintila, who fulfilled the wishes of the clergy. Thus it came about that many were compelled to become Christians and to sign the proclamations requiring their observance of Christian customs. But Chindaswinth, who succeeded Chintila, removed these restrictions. It appears that during his reign the converts returned to their faith and even the exiles came back to their places of habitation.

Chindaswinth's successor, Receswinth, was more zealous than all his predecessors, however, and a veritable oppressor of the Jews. He appeared before the eighth Council of Toledo, which met in 653, and proposed that it renew the decrees of the council of 633—namely, that the converts *must* adhere to their new faith and, moreover, that converts who continued with Jewish observances should be put to death at the hands of other converts. But all this was not enough for this zealot king. He enacted additional laws that would deny to unconverted Jews the possibility to practice their religion and would limit their civil rights.

In their despair, the Jews began to join forces with those who rebelled against the government. In the days of King Wamba, the Jews cooperated with the governor of the province, Nimes, who promised them religious freedom. After the rebellion was put down, the Jews were expelled from the city of Narbonne, which, together with a large area of southern Gaul, belonged to the kingdom of the Visigoths. Three months after ascending the throne King Ervig convened the twelfth Council of Toledo and urged it to use all possible means to extirpate the Jewish religion from Spain. Acting on his proposal, the council decreed that every Jew must convert within a year. It was also declared that the clergy should teach the Jews the tenets and practices of Christianity; converts were obligated to inform the authorities of the names of any former coreligionists who might transgress the laws of the church. Not only were Jews forced to become converted, but the civil rights of even these converts were limited.

King Egica followed a different line. Instead of converting Jews by force, he sought to end their stubborn resistance by means of special privileges, which he offered to converts who would consent to be faithful to Christian practice. He annulled the limitations on the rights of converts but passed stringent laws against Jews who clung to their faith. They were required to sell to the king's exchequer all servants, houses, and land which they had bought from Christians—all to be handed over to the clergy. The king also ordained that Jews were forbidden to trade with the Christian inhabitants of the Visigothic realm; nor were they to deal in commerce with foreign countries.

The very severity of these enactments is proof that they were not fully executed, and despite the decrees of kings and councils many Jews remained in Spain. Indeed, from the decisions of the councils we learn that Jews bribed the nobles who held the reins of government, and even the clergy themselves, not to enforce these laws strictly. Nevertheless, their plight worsened and they looked for a source of deliverance.

In 694 the Visigothic authorities unearthed a plot by the Jews who were preparing to overthrow the government. According to the Christian authorities, the Jews had joined forces with their coreligionists on the other side of the straits in North Africa and were planning a military invasion that would free them from their oppressors. The seventeenth Council of Toledo, which met at the end of that year, therefore determined to employ more stringent measures. All Jews were turned over to Christian masters as their slaves and were scattered throughout the kingdom. Their masters were obligated to insure that they would observe the practices of the church and to take an oath swearing that they would not set the Jews free. The council further decreed that children over the age of seven be taken from the Jews in order that they might be reared in the spirit of Christianity and married to Christians. Jewish properties were confiscated.

But once again the wheel of fortune took a favorable turn. King Witiza was a more lenient ruler, and the clergy hated him. Christian writers of the Middle Ages claim that he annulled the enactments of Egica. But with the ascent of Roderick, the zealots—that faction whose goal it was to obliterate Judaism from the soil of Spain—came into power.

Such were the memories that passed through the minds of the Jews of Cordova. With all their hearts they sided with the Moslems at the gates of the city, but they were powerless to act. Gothic soldiers stood between them and the African besiegers.

One night the skies became overcast and the rains came, followed by hail. The guards on the wall sought refuge from the weather and abandoned their rounds. The Africans took advantage of the darkness, crossing the river at a shallow point. The southern wall of the city was built some fifteen yards or less from the river's edge. When Mughīth's men arrived at the northern bank of the river, they hastened to a point where there was a breach in the upper level of the wall. A fig tree grew near the breach. Quickly they climbed the tree and sprang onto the wall. The first man drew the second one up after him, and within moments a group of men stood on the wall. Immediately they dropped down inside, fell on the surprised guards of the nearest gate, and slew them. They opened the gate, and through it, with drawn swords, streamed the forces of Mughīth.

Here and there an individual sought to resist—only to be beheaded. Most of the populace barred the doors of their houses and remained quietly within. However, the governor escaped with his forces to a church in the western quarter of the city and fortified himself inside. On the following morning, when the inhabitants of Cordova emerged from their houses into the streets of the city and saw that Mughīth had occupied the governor's palace, they felt the first taste of subjugation. The Jews of the city, on the other hand, exulted. This was the day they had hoped for. They immediately made contact with the Moslem officer, who mobilized them into his army and turned over to them the task of guarding the city.[1]

Mughīth established his forces within the city and lay siege to the church in which the Gothic governor of the city had taken refuge. It was a sturdy edifice, and the Christians within, who numbered about four hundred, defended themselves courageously. The siege lasted three months; then the Moslems succeeded in cutting off the water supply of the Christians, who were compelled to surrender. They were put to death. The governor attempted to flee but was caught and later taken to the caliph in Damascus.

The events at Cordova were repeated in other Spanish cities. Everywhere the Jews rose up and volunteered aid to the Moslems in their war of conquest. Arab chroniclers only relate what happened in the principal cities, but it is quite likely that the same thing occurred in smaller cities and in villages. An early Arabic historian relates that wherever the Moslems came upon Jews, they appointed them as a militia and left a few of their own soldiers with them; then the majority continued on their march of conquest.[2] Another Arabic historian, who (though writing at a later date) drew upon early and reliable sources, repeats these facts, but adds that where no Jews were available, the Moslems had to leave a greater number of their own forces.[3]

From these historical records it is evident that the aid of the Jews was highly important for the Moslems. Since Ṭāriḳ had to leave behind soldiers in cities he had already taken while sending ahead troops to conquer other cities, the vanguard of whose forces threatened his lines of communication, the Moslem commander's small forces grew ever smaller as he penetrated deep into the heart of the country. The cooperation of the Jews was very advantageous to him, since it enabled him to release some of his soldiers from guard duty in the conquered cities and to utilize them as an attacking force in new conquests. It is clear that here and there the Jews gave the invaders important information and also acted as spies—as did the followers of Witiza, who themselves came to the aid of Ṭāriḳ's forces wherever they went.

So it was that in many cities small groups of Moslems, with the aid of their allies, the partisans of the House of Witiza and the Jews, set up the new order. Moreover, because as many of the nobles and officials, the wealthy, and the clergy fled to the north of the country, large numbers of houses and much property were abandoned, and it is certain that the Jews and everyone who helped in the conquest took possession of them. But it was the desire for revenge that primarily motivated the Jews to help the armies of Ṭāriḳ. The Moslem invasion gave them the opportunity to repay their oppressors for the wrongs that had been perpetrated upon them and their forebears for many generations.

Having sent Mughīth ar-Rūmī to take Cordova after the conquest near Écija, Ṭāriḳ sent troops to the southeast regions of Spain, while he himself decided to push ahead in the direction of the country's capital, Toledo. The decision to send these troops to the mountainous areas of the south was a military necessity, for had the commander failed to do this, he would have left himself open to attack from the rear. Though he could not spare substantial forces for this undertaking and thus assure the conquest of all districts in this section of the peninsula, he could at least hope that his forces would pin down his opponents and lay the groundwork for eventual conquest. No doubt he also took into consideration that both the Jews and the followers of the House of Witiza would come to his aid. In this hope he was not disappointed.

When Ṭāriḳ's troops reached Málaga, the city was all but empty of people. Its inhabitants had fled and hidden in the hills; even its Jewish residents had left. One Moslem column penetrated to the valley of the Genil River and approached the capital city of that region, then called Illiberi. The majority of the soldiers who had conquered Málaga and its environs turned northward, joining the column that attacked Illiberi. The city's garrison and those of its inhabitants who supported them closed the gates and attempted to withstand the invaders, but their opposition was of short duration. The Moslems broke into the city and took it; following the pattern set in Cordova, the conquerors mobilized the Jews into the militia.[4]

At the same time Ṭāriḳ continued his march northward. The number of Berber soldiers who had accompanied him from overseas grew ever smaller. Not only was he obliged to leave behind small units in the conquered cities and to send others to take important areas, but many also fell in the two battles at the beginning of the march or were slain when they wandered too far away from the advancing columns. Here and there they were ambushed by remnants of the retreating Gothic army, which was on its way to the northern regions of Spain. The Moslem commander supplemented his ranks with auxiliaries from among the natives who joined him. Thus it became possible for him to penetrate into the *Meseta,* that high plateau which stretches across the center of the Iberian peninsula. The Moslem army first turned eastward to the region of Jaén; north of the city it crossed over the Guadalquivir and then, continuing its march over the hills of the Sierra Morena, penetrated to the heights of Montiel by way of the Roman road named after Hannibal, and finally turned northwest until it reached its destination, Toledo.

When Ṭāriḳ arrived at the capital of the country he received his reward. The daring and speed of his march so astounded the Goths that they gave no thought to defending their capital but fled while they could. All the government officials, the priests, the wealthy, and the officers left the city; only the commoners remained behind. Ṭāriḳ penetrated the city almost without resistance. Later Christian sources tell that the Jews opened the gates of the city, while the Christians gathered within the Church of Santa Leocadia, outside the city's walls. This has all the earmarks of a legend created by anti-Semites after the reconquest.[5] The Arabic chroniclers do not report this. But they do relate that in this city, too, the Moslems mounted a garrison from among the Jews.[6] So the tables were now turned. The Jews became the masters in the very city where the proud Visigoths had ruled and where church synods had gathered to promulgate severe edicts against them. How wonderful are the ways of history and the vagaries of Jewish fate!

The daring Moslem commander did not tarry overlong in Toledo.[7] To be sure, he did not lose sight of the treasures left behind by the elite and the wealthy in their palaces. In the few days of his stay in the city he seized whatever he could, and his officers did likewise. But meanwhile the summer passed and fall drew near, and Ṭāriḳ decided not to slow his march of conquest. He reasoned, correctly, that if he slackened his pressure on the Christians and gave them time to renew their strength, they would reassemble their forces in those areas of the peninsula not yet penetrated by the Moslems and would renew the war with greater energy. For this reason Ṭāriḳ gathered his troops and began a march northward in order to overtake those who were fleeing. First he turned northeast to Alcalá de Henares and Guadalajara; from there he turned in a more westerly direction, crossing the chain of mountains of the Sierra de Guadarrama by way of the Buitrago Pass, penetrating into the province of Burgos.

The Arab chroniclers relate that he arrived at a city which they called al-Mā'ida, "the City of the Table," for according to them Ṭāriḳ found there "Solomon's Table," namely, the table of the shewbread that had been in the Temple. From there, according to them, he continued his march to Amaya, north of Burgos, and took this city also.

Winter set in. The high mountains were covered with snow, the roads became hard for the army to negotiate, and the African forces of the Moslem commander, already wearied beyond measure, pressed him to return to Toledo. This march, too, was crowned with success. Generally speaking, the fortified cities that Ṭāriḳ passed through fell into his hands like overripe fruit. The spirit of the Goths was broken, especially since the followers of the House of Witiza continued to give support to the invaders. The Witiza faction were keenly disappointed, however; they had hoped that when Ṭāriḳ got to Toledo he would seat one of the princes of the House of Witiza on the throne. But their ties with the Moslems had gotten them in so deep that they could no longer backtrack. On the other hand, Ṭāriḳ and his officers acted with prudence. They did all they could to avoid antagonizing the natives. Officers of the Moslem army refrained from needless slaughter. The march of conquest was accomplished with relatively little bloodshed.

III

When Mūsā b. Nuṣair, the ruler of North Africa, heard of Ṭāriḳ's accomplishments, he was not only astonished but also greatly angered. He was a man possessed by many ambitions; he had already fulfilled a role in the political affairs of the

Near East, and later had succeeded in renewing Moslem rule in North Africa, establishing it on a firm foundation. If the Moslems were destined to conquer Spain, he, the commanding general of the Moslem forces in the West, strongly wanted both the praise and the wealth that awaited him there. Yet now his erstwhile underling had dared to disobey him and penetrate to the heart of Spain, though he had been ordered to remain close to the southern coast, and had even succeeded in conquering the capital of the country.

But it was not envy alone which motivated Mūsā b. Nuṣair —concern lest the venture end in failure also figured in his thinking. Was he not the one who had the ultimate responsibility to the caliph for whatever was done by his officers and all who were under his command? Despite his advanced years —he was nearly eighty—he decided to cross over into Spain himself and immediately began to make extensive preparations. Once again troops were gathered for an expedition across the straits, and within a few months they were fully equipped.

The new army headed by Mūsā numbered eighteen thousand men, almost all of them Arabs. He crossed the straits in June 712 and stepped upon Spanish soil at Algeciras. Mūsā chose a different path of conquest from Ṭāriḳ's. He turned to the western part of the peninsula, to those sections which Moslem armies had not yet reached. Medina-Sidonia and Carmona were the first cities to be conquered. Then Mūsā proceeded to Seville. This big city, like Toledo and other cities, had been deserted by its original rulers. After meeting token opposition, the main body of the army moved on to other points in the west, to Niebla and Béja, while the Moslem commander established his authority over the city. Mūsā b. Nuṣair did what Ṭāriḳ had done: though his forces were greater in number, he did not leave behind many Moslems in Seville; instead, he mobilized the Jews of the city and established a garrison from among them.[8] Thus Seville, the city of the renowned prince of the church Isidore, fell under the rule of the Jews. Who would have expected this?

After the conquest of Seville, Mūsā ascended the Sierra Morena mountains and advanced beyond Mérida. He passed near the city of Puente de Cantos, which fell to him without opposition. But when he reached Mérida a protracted siege began. Into this city were gathered many of the faithful supporters of the Visigothic rule, nobles and knights, Christian zealots who were not willing to submit to the invaders. The besieged fought valiantly and frustrated Moslem attempts to penetrate the city. Time and again they sallied forth from the city and struck at the Moslems. The siege lasted for months, through the winter of 712/713 and the spring which followed.

Meanwhile, calls for help reached the Arab commander from places where weak garrisons had been left behind. As the Moslem army moved farther away, the natives mustered their courage and attempted to regain the dominion which they had lost in the blink of an eye. At first, word reached the Arabic staff of uprisings in southeast Spain. The Jewish garrison in Illiberi asked for help. For this reason Mūsā b. Nuṣair sent his son 'Abdal'azīz with a few troops there. 'Abdal'azīz crushed the rebellion and spread the Moslem rule over the province of Murcia. The city of Murcia was not yet in existence at that time, but several cities such as Lorca, Alicante, and Orihuela did exist, and the Christian inhabitants were very numerous. In April 713 'Abdal'azīz vanquished the Visigothic ruler of this province, Theodemir, who dwelt in Orihuela.[9]

Meanwhile, the Christians of Seville rebelled. They were near the theater of war in Mérida, and when they found that Mūsā could not subdue the besieged Goths, rebellion erupted in the city. With the help of the nobles who had first fled to other cities, the people of Seville rose up and killed about eighty of the garrison's men, both Jews and Moslems, and the remainder fled to Mūsā's camp before Mérida. After 'Abdal-

'azīz succeeded in restoring order in the southeast, his father made him responsible for crushing the rebellion in Seville. Here, too, 'Abdal'azīz was successful and even took the city of Niebla, south of Seville; from there he penetrated to the plains on the Atlantic coast, conquering also the city of Béja. From Christian chronicles we may conclude that in this city also the Moslem commander settled a number of Jews, entrusting them with the task of guarding the city.[10] This occurred in the summer of 713. By this time Mérida was already in Moslem hands, having been subdued on the last day of June.

These are the last indications of cooperation between Ṭāriḳ, Mūsā, and the Jews of Spain. These brief references prompt certain questions, inasmuch as they reveal far less than they explain. Did the invaders mobilize the Jews into the garrison troops? Was the mobilization of the Jews into the garrison troops by the invaders preceded by negotiations? Did the Jews reach an actually binding agreement with the Arabs? Spanish historians argue that the Jews conspired with the Africans to turn the country over to them,[11] whereas an important Jewish historian calls this an "anti-Semitic legend."[12] There is no proof for such arguments, and indeed it must not be thought that this cooperation was initially the consequence of a formal understanding. The silence of the sources is in itself no proof, but it is hard to believe that the Moslems made a compact with a group of people who were not identified with a specific territory, had no fortunes, and were not one of the fighting factions prior to the invasion. However, the action itself is a historic fact which cannot be disputed, since more than half the inhabitants of Spain sided with the invaders.

Arabic chroniclers are silent about another matter that should be of great interest to us. They record the conditions relating to the capitulation of only one city: Mérida. But did not the inhabitants of other cities that submitted to the invaders without any opposition, or after only a brief resistance, receive a promise of specific privileges—such as that their property would remain in their possession and that they would be permitted to continue the observance of their form of worship? Arabic sources depict the march of conquest as a military enterprise only. But we must assume that agreements between the Arabs and the inhabitants of various cities on the Iberian peninsula were made in accordance with the practice which prevailed in Moslem wars of conquest in the Orient.

If such agreements were indeed reached, we must assume that they applied to Christians only but that as a matter of course the Jews, too, benefited from them, inasmuch as their legal status paralleled that of the Christians. Support for this conjecture can be found in the chronicle by the Arabic-Spanish historian of the tenth century ar-Rāzī, relating to the history of the Great Mosque of Cordova. Ar-Rāzī, who depends upon an earlier source, says that during the conquest of Spain the practice of the Arabs was similar to that of Khālid b. al-Walīd and Abū 'Ubaida in the conquest of Syria—the Christians were allowed to retain half the big churches, while the conquerors took for the Moslems the remaining half to be mosques; according to ar-Rāzī, they did the same in Cordova. From the ensuing narrative of this historian, it is apparent that this was a formal understanding.[13]

While the old chronicles are more vague than explicit as to how the Moslems dealt with the inhabitants of the conquered cities, Christians and Jews alike, their accounts concerning the achievement of cooperation with the Jews is clear and detailed. As we learn from their accounts, the conquerors gathered the Jews into a given area in every locality. They transferred into the large cities those Jews who lived in their environs, concentrating them in one area there. This was a simple matter in those days, since many houses were left empty by the flight of the nobles and the wealthy; besides it was a matter of military necessity. The author of an ancient chronicle reports: "When Jews were found in a district, they were concentrated within its principal city." Another Arabic historian relates: "This became the fixed method of the conquerors: in every city that they took, they concentrated the Jews within its fortress."[14]

There is clear and unequivocal testimony from early Arabic historians as to the composition of the garrison forces. All accounts make it evident how important the nobles of the House of Witiza and their supporters among the Christian inhabitants of Spain were to the conquest of Spain. However, when the Arabic chroniclers tell about the establishment of Moslem rule in the conquered cities, they speak only of the mobilization of the Jews; they do not even mention that Christian natives such as the followers of the House of Witiza were incorporated into the standing army. This is not merely casual; the statement of the Arabic writers is really to be accepted. Most surely the conquerors did not want to depend upon the Christians or to place the government of important cities in their hands; instead, they preferred to graft onto the garrisons men of other nations. For thousands of years this had been a tried and true method among rulers of kingdoms composed of diversified nationals.

We have no information concerning other forms of aid the Jews rendered to the conquerors. But their mobilization into the garrisons speaks plainly and clearly. It emphasizes the special character of this Jewish community, which had no parallel in the history of other Diaspora communities. In other lands Jews generally defended themselves when attacked but took no active part in the wars of nations. This is a major principle in Jewish history in the Diaspora; occasional instances of Jewish participation in revolts only prove the rule. But military cooperation between the Jews and the Moslem conquerors was not unusual in Jewish life on the Iberian peninsula. Even in later generations the Jews of Spain did not refrain from girding themselves with swords and going off to battle. They were accustomed to participating in war and especially to defending the cities they inhabited.

What was the source of this trait? Did their prolonged stay in a land whose inhabitants had long been known to be warlike help them acquire this bent? Surely, it can only be attributed to their deep-rootedness and attachment to the soil. They dwelt in Spain even before the Goths arrived, and in the turbulent era of the predatory Germanic tribes, when the Roman Empire was crumbling and robber bands roamed everywhere, each person had to protect himself by force of arms.

But there were added reasons for the difference between the Jews of Spain and those of other lands, one being that Spanish Jews were not a stratum of foreign colonists but an indigenous element that adopted the customs of the other inhabitants of the land and lived according to their ways. An even more significant factor was their mode of life and their economic status. Many of the Jews of Spain were villagers whose livelihood depended upon agriculture and who, of necessity, had to defend their lives and property by force. There were also among them many craftsmen who earned their livelihood by the work of their hands. In other words, the character of the inhabitants of the land of which the Jews were an indigenous element, on the one hand, and their social structure, on the other, crystallized the warlike trait of the Jews of Spain. Thus a type of Jew who was singular in the history of Israel in the Diaspora was created. Whereas the Jews in most lands in the Moslem East and Christian Europe were a minority, tolerated, persecuted, and helpless, the Jews of the Iberian peninsula were proud and courageous, ready to draw the sword and seize the spear, to be on close terms with kings and nobles of the land. Such were the Jews of Spain for hundreds of years, and such were they when the Moslems invaded this land and conquered it.

Men of this caliber would seem to be fitting allies of a warring and conquering people, and indeed the cooperation between Jews and Moslems was consistently and steadily maintained until the end of the conquest.[15] True, the Arabic chroniclers do not mention the mobilization of the Jews into the garrison forces after the conquest of Mérida, but the reason for this is simple. In his other campaigns of conquest Mūsā b. Nuṣair traversed areas that were almost totally devoid of Jews, and the Arabic historians do not expatiate on the campaigns of Ṭāriḳ at that time because he was overshadowed by the coming of Mūsā to Spain.

After the occupation of Mérida, Mūsā b. Nuṣair proceeded to Toledo, where he met Ṭāriḳ and solemnly proclaimed the annexation of Spain to the caliphate. In the winter of 713/714 the Moslem generals planned further campaigns into the north of Spain, but when they embarked on them in the following spring, an envoy of the caliph appeared and called Mūsā back to the East. He returned in a triumphal match, but on his arrival in Damascus he was imprisoned until his death.

IV

Before leaving Spain, Mūsā b. Nuṣair had appointed his son ʿAbdalʿazīz governor of Spain. In trying to reconcile the Moslem invaders with the Christian population, ʿAbdalʿazīz provoked the hatred of the Arabs and was murdered by them. He was the first of a long series of *wālīs*, Arabic provincial governors. Most of them made great efforts to revamp the administration of the country that had been set up, and at the same time they tried to conquer more territories in the north, on both sides of the Pyrenees. However, all their efforts were in vain. Their attempts to put the administration on a sound foundation and to curb anarchy failed completely, and even their campaigns against the Christians were not successful. On the contrary, the Visigothic noble Pelagius could rally some hundreds of Christian zealots and found a little principality on the shores of the Gulf of Biscaya. That was the beginning of the kingdom of Asturias.

The Arabs who settled in Spain contained an intermingling of various groups who fought each other bitterly. These groups represented unions of Arab tribes held together, as related in their tradition, by their common origin. A distinctive feature among the Arabs had always been their particularism. Tribal loyalty took precedence over all else. This was a sacred obligation involving their honor. The history of the Arabs in their homeland was merely a series of intertribal wars. Two groups of tribes were especially conspicuous: the Yemenites in the south and the tribes of Ḳais in the north. Even after the Arabs had spread through all the lands of eastern Asia and around the Mediterranean Sea, these two tribes did not cease warring against each other, in Persia, Syria, and other lands.

The Omayyad caliphs, far from establishing peaceful relations among them, rather aggravated the situation. These caliphs made it a practice to support one of these tribal groups and to permit them to persecute their opponents. Thus when a caliph would give his support to the Ḳaisites, it was permissible for them to wreak havoc upon the Yemenites, imprison their leaders, confiscate their property, and even put them to death. When this caliph died and another caliph sympathetic to the Yemenites came to the throne, or if the caliph merely had a change of heart, the Yemenites could repay the Ḳaisites in kind. This was in essence the internal history of the Omayyad kingdom. The enmity was passed on from fathers to sons, and the instinct for revenge was highly developed among the Arabs. Men who had been born far from the Iberian peninsula and far from the center of the caliphal empire felt obligated to avenge acts by adversary tribes against their forebears in wars in the East that had occurred decades before. In Spain the intertribal wars were very severe, and the Yemenites and Ḳaisites fought each other to the bitter end.

But besides the Yemenites and the Ḳaisites, there were other groups who zealously looked after their own rights. With the army of Mūsā b. Nuṣair there came to Spain many Arabs from Medina, in Hedjaz, who had originally supported 'Abdallāh b. az-Zubair, the caliph who was the rival of the Omayyads. This faction hated the Arabs of Syria with a consummate hatred. In opposition to the Arabs were the Berbers, consumed with envy and full of bitterness. Although they had had a noteworthy share in the conquest of Spain, they were discriminated against by the Arabs when the land was apportioned, being given hilly areas whose produce was scant. They were a freedom-loving and warlike people who made their peace with the Arabic overlords only with great difficulty.

In time the competition between these factions became the axis of Spanish politics. Historians of Moslem Spain praise the memory of some energetic governors who did their utmost to uphold the unity of the big country and continued the invasions into Gaul. But all their efforts failed. Finally, a great revolt of the Berbers broke out which endangered the Moslem rule altogether.

The non-Arab natives did not become involved in the factional quarrels of the Moslems. But this does not mean that they stood to one side as though they had no interest in the matter. The attitudes of the two large factions among the Arabs toward the population of the conquered territories were dissimilar. To be sure, all the Arabs regarded the natives merely as cows for their milking. But apparently the Ḳaisites were more severe toward them. The Yemenites were more moderate, and, especially when the reins of government were in their hands, they looked with favor even upon the non-Arabs.[16] From this it can be inferred that the inhabitants of the conquered territories were generally sympathetic to the Yemenites and put their hopes in them. Even the Berbers preferred their rule to that of the Ḳaisites.

In those confused times the lot of the non-Moslems fluctuated with great speed. In the early years following the establishment of Moslem rule, their circumstances were favorable. The new rulers were not well versed in the conduct of orderly administration and needed the aid of the natives, both Christians and Jews. Indeed, this was the situation in all other lands conquered by the Arabs and in Spain. Thus it came about that the supervision of houses and estates—all the vast property that was deserted by the nobles and the wealthy who fled at the time of the conquest—was turned over to non-Moslems. There can be no doubt that the officers and overseers of property among both Christians and Jews reaped much benefit from their labor. The tension between the Moslem rulers and the Christians abated after a short period, during the rule of ʻAbdalʻazīz, the son of Mūsā b. Nuṣair. But the Jews also enjoyed religious freedom, which came to them suddenly—something which they had not even dreamt about these many years.

When news of the conquest of Spain by the Moslems spread throughout the breadth of North Africa, it stirred the hearts of Jewish communities everywhere. In these lands, especially in the cities of Morocco, dwelt many Jews who had fled Spain when the Visigothic kings persecuted them and daily issued new decrees against the Jewish faith. But many of them had been unable to adapt themselves to the conditions of life in the places where they had settled, for the differences in the economic and cultural level between Spain, a land with an age-old culture, and the lands of the Berbers were very marked. It is small wonder, therefore, that they yearned for the places from which they had been driven. Even the children of these exiles from Spain had heard much about that land and had turned hopefully toward it. This has always been a characteristic of emigrants and refugees.

When the great change in Spain became known, therefore,

many rose up and, taking courage, set forth to the port cities to sail across the sea and return to Spain. Thus began a wave of wandering that lasted a long while and, as time went on, became a veritable flood of emigration. This migration, about which there is little information in the historical sources, was the most important phenomenon in the history of the Jews of the Maghreb and the Mediterranean basin in general during this period. It was destined to result in gathering the great numbers of Jews in Spain, a settlement that numbered in the hundreds of thousands. But it is not only the outcome that gives clear testimony about this significant process; it also finds substantiation in the realities of history in general, as we meet it on the pages of the Arabic chronicles. In these writings we are told that with the Arabic rulers who were sent from the center of Arabic dominion in the East and in North Africa large groups of Arabs came to Spain. Just as al-Ḥurr, one of the rulers of Spain, brought with him a large retinue of Arabs from North Africa, from Kairawan, so also did his successor, as-Samḥ. He too reached Spain with fresh Arabic troops.

But in addition to the Arabs who came, there were the Berbers from all regions of North Africa, who migrated to Spain in order to acquire land or to serve in the army of the country that had just been conquered. Moreover, men of initiative and mere adventurers who hoped to benefit in the new province of the Islamic kingdom came: merchants, purveyors to the army, and the like. Thus a movement of migration to Spain followed in the wake of the conquest. Hence it was not just Jewish refugees from Spain who returned to the Iberian peninsula after the conquest; other Jews also took the wanderer's staff in hand and headed westward.

Jews who sojourned in the African coastal cities of the Mediterranean had good prospects of finding their livelihood in Spain. They already knew Latin from the days of Byzantine rule in the regions of Mauritania and had learned Arabic;

they were even on good terms with the Berbers. Moreover, they had the necessary qualities to become intermediaries between the new rulers of Spain, who had a great need for other people to act as administrators of the economy in the conquered state. Jewish immigration to Spain began in Morocco, which the Arabs called the "Far West," where the refugees from Visigothic Spain lived; later it encompassed the Jewish settlements in the other North African countries. At that time a veritable rage to migrate possessed the Jews of all these lands.

Until the Arabic conquest there had been a large settlement of Jews in Alexandria; according to Arabic historians, at the time of the conquest there were 40,000 Jews who were obliged to pay a poll tax, which indicates a community of at least 120,000 persons. One Arabic historian even says that many of the Alexandrian Jews fled before the conquest; according to him their number had reached 70,000.[17] To be sure, these numbers are exaggerated, but it is a historical fact that after the conquest the Jews of Alexandria continued to leave the city. A short time after the Arabic conquest, the Byzantines returned and took the city; then when the Arabs reconquered it in 645 they made a pogrom on its inhabitants. This episode probably speeded the process of migration. In any case, under Arabic rule Alexandria ceased to be an important community; but this does not mean that many Alexandrian Jews left for Fostat, since a big Jewish community did not develop there till several generations later. It is clear that because of commercial ties between Alexandria and the North African lands west of Egypt, more than a few Jews found refuge for themselves in those places.

When the Arabic commander, 'Uḳba b. Nāfi' founded the city of Kairawan in 670, many Jews went there from Egypt. Caliph 'Abdalmalik (685–705) asked his brother 'Abdal'azīz, the ruler of Egypt, to send a thousand Jewish or Coptic families to Kairawan, which became a focal point for the flourishing trade between Eastern and Western Islam that developed after the conquest of North Africa by the Arabs. Indeed, Arabic chronicles report that many Arabs migrated from Kairawan to Morocco and to Spain. It is rather likely that the Jews were caught up in this stream of migration. The Jewish migratory movement to Spain came in waves. The high and low points of this migratory stream understandably resulted from events in the originating countries of the migrants and from reports about the conditions of the Jews in Spain itself.

The honeymoon between the Moslem rulers of Spain and the inhabitants of the land did not last long. From the time that al-Ḥurr came to Spain as its ruler, new winds began to blow in the Moslem kingdom. The government increased the tax burden more and more, and within a short period both Christians and Jews suffered greatly under the rod of the oppressors and of the tax collectors, whose demands were endless. Whether they increased the poll tax or other fixed taxes, or whether they imposed upon them levies to maintain the army or for military expeditions, the yoke was very heavy, according to a Christian chronicler of the period. Even in the days of Mūsā b. Nuṣair, taxes were collected under much pressure.[18] Al-Ḥurr attempted to bring order to the collection of taxes, but he faced many obstacles. We are told that he was a despotic ruler, but we have no precise information as to the collection of taxes under his rule. Concerning another governor, ʻAnbasa, an Arab of the Ḳaisite tribe, this Christian chronicler relates that he taxed the Christians doubly.[19] It is likely that ʻAnbasa acted in the same manner toward the Jews, but the chronicler was concerned only with his coreligionists.

After ʻAnbasa, the caliph sent a Yemenite governor to Spain: Yaḥyā b. Salama al-Kalbī (726–728). As was characteristic of the Yemenites, he was more lenient. The Latin chronicle reports that this governor took back from the Moslems the monies that they had forced from the Christians and returned it to them.[20] Further on the chronicler says that the pressure of taxation in the reign of Caliph Hishām (724–743) was more burdensome than ever before.[21] And when he refers to the first period of the rule of the governor 'Abdalmalik b. Ḳaṭṭān, he reports that his officials drained the state of everything worthwhile; in fact, his deeds were worse than those of any governor who preceded him. Up to this time, he says, Spain was still a flourishing country despite all the catastrophes that had befallen it; then, however, it became impoverished and bereft of hope.[22]

The governor, 'Uḳba, ordered the tax rolls to be drawn up anew and collected the taxes energetically, thus filling the government's treasury.[23] Much depended on a proper listing of those who owed taxes, which provided cause for complaint on both sides. At times the names of people who owed taxes would be erased, yet at other times the names of people already dead would be listed in order to obligate their relatives or their fellow townsmen to pay their taxes. We learn from the anonymous Christian chronicler that one of the later governors ordered the listing drawn up anew, since it included names of many Christians who had long since died.[24] All these details have reference to the means employed by the governor-general of Moslem Spain, but we must not forget that the aides of the *wālīs*, the local governors and tax collectors of the provinces, also maltreated the Christians and Jews.

This pressure of taxation led many non-Moslems to be converted to the dominant religion, Islam; however, this was merely one of several reasons that prompted conversion and may not have been the main one. At all events, the weighty yoke of taxation made it plain to non-Moslems that they were destined to become second-class citizens, and this accelerated the conversion to Islam, which in any case would have been a natural concomitant of the conquest. When a new regime, religious or political, is established, there are always many who hasten to join its supporters. These are weak men, with no clear perception or strength of spirit, men who have not found fulfillment, men dissatisfied because they have not succeeded in life and lay the blame on the regime that has been overthrown, men who want to start afresh. In addition, there are all who are motivated by desire for honor or monetary gain and are prepared to betray all that they had once held sacred to achieve their aims.

At the outset of the Arabic rule in Spain there was no attempt to force non-Moslems to be converted. Indeed, in the early years of Arabic dominion, the Jews took advantage of the freedom afforded them by their close relations with the rulers and tried to make converts to *their* religion. Latin texts show that among the Christians, sects accepting Jewish tenets and commandments sprouted.[25]

In any case, the aforementioned reasons—the desire to be identified with the rulers, to derive benefit from the government, and to avoid heavy taxes—caused a trend toward conversion to Islam. This trend spread among all classes and continued for several decades. Many of these newly converted Moslems sought to act like Arabs in every respect. As was the custom in the Arabian peninsula from ancient times, these "neo-Arabs" sought to be counted as members of an Arab tribe, in order to come under its protecting aegis or invented for themselves a genealogy of pure Arabic lineage. All signs indicate that this trend to conversion to Islam was quite strong, but was relatively weaker among the Jews. We know of individuals and families who converted from Christianity to Islam and occupied important positions in the communal life of Moslem Spain at that time; however, we have no reports whatsoever of Jews doing likewise and thereby reaching eminent status among the Moslems.

Nonetheless, the change that occurred in the relations between the rulers and the non-Moslem communities resulted in a sharp reaction from the Jews which found expression in another way. The disappointment experienced by the Jews after the honeymoon period in their relations with the dominant Arabs was quite severe. It seemed to them that only yesterday freedom had been proclaimed for the dispersed Jews in the West and that henceforth they would be free men and perhaps even associates of the rulers. But instead the hope proved to be false, and all their illusions dissipated. It was plain to them that though their status had greatly improved, their new masters would not regard them as equals. Thus the groundwork was laid for a messianic movement that set off waves throughout all the Jewish communities in Spain and moved hearts to new hopes everywhere. This movement did not spring up in the Iberian peninsula, but rather in the Jewish settlements across the Mediterranean. This was a pan-Jewish movement, and the participation of the Jews of Spain was possible because in the wake of the conquest of Spain and its inclusion in the Moslem Empire, ties between Spanish Jews and other Jews in the Diaspora were renewed.

This messianic movement was nourished from two sources that were fundamentally different from each other. One was the antirabbinic current in Judaism, which took on different forms at various times but was active for many generations. Time and again there arose men who refused to accept the oral law and enactments of the rabbis, and claimed that Jews were obligated to perform only those commandments written in the Torah and no other.

A second factor that generated this movement was deeply rooted in Jewish existence from ancient days. This was the yearning for deliverance, the longing for redemption. From the time Israel was exiled from its land and lived in servitude in foreign lands, the soul of the nation thirsted for liberation, for the return to Zion, for a renewal of the past. The profound belief in the hearts of the people that in the fullness of time it would merit this gave it the strength to endure the heavy yoke of life in exile and gave it courage.

From time to time these yearnings hidden within their hearts would flare up into a mighty flame, into powerful movements that stirred all the communities of the Diaspora by their wondrous acts. Dreamers who wanted to speed the deliverance arose, leaders who failed and became designated in the history of the Jews as false Messiahs. When rumors of such a movement spread among the Jewish communities and men would whisper in remote corners of synagogues and houses of study, to prevent the secret from being spread abroad and becoming known to the gentiles, then impassioned youths and mature men alike would be ready to forsake their homes and cross over hill and dale, sea and desert to join the messenger, the would-be Messiah. Whenever such an ill-timed experiment ended in decided failure, many would refuse to believe it and would remain faithful to whoever had implanted hope in their hearts. Several of these "Messiahs" arrogated to themselves the right to alter the commandments and statutes of Judaism, mainly the enactments of the sages. Thus it came to pass that two streams—the antirabbinic and messianic—were brought into contact with each other.

About 721 there rose up in the province of Māridīn, in northern Mesopotamia, a man who claimed that he would bring about the redemption, return Israel to its land, and restore it to its ancient glory. This man, a Christian by birth, had been converted and, having studied the Scriptures diligently for some time, had become absorbed in religious fantasies. No doubt he was also influenced by the events of the time, especially the siege of Constantinople by the Arabs in 717. Christian sources of that era relate that he called himself Severa, a name that turns up somewhat later in one of the questions concerning this movement directed to the *gaon* Naṭrōnai bar Hilai, the head of the Academy of Sura. In this responsum the opinions and acts of this false Messiah are discussed. The "Messiah" would have permitted marriage forbidden by the sages, that is, relaxation of prohibitions enacted by the *sōf'rīm* (the early scribes). His disciples prepared the *k'tūbōt* (marriage contracts) and writs of divorcement in a manner differing from that prescribed by the sages. According to their opponents, they were indifferent to the laws of *nesekh,* in that they allowed non-Jews to come into contact with their wines, and they further charged them with disregard for the laws on *ṭ'rēfa* (ritually unclean food). Severa taught his disciples that work is permissible on the second day of a festival, which was, of course, proscribed by the sages for the Jews of the Diaspora. Moreover, they were accused of "not praying." This charge indicates, of course, that they had their own prayer service and did not recite the prayers established by the sages of the Talmud.

Severa apparently found many supporters in Syria and the Byzantine Empire. And according to a contemporary source, even in Spain many Jews were attracted by his doctrines. For Spanish Jews the essential point of the movement was its messianic aspirations. They joined it because they dreamt of the redemption of Israel. Whenever momentous events stirred the nations of the Diaspora and new governments were established, longings for redemption would well up within the Jews with greater urgency.

Jews who had beheld with their own eyes the great change in the fate of Spain dreamt of changes in the history of their own people, and were spiritually prepared for a messianic movement. The innovations in the law that Severa introduced were scarcely significant for them. The Talmud was hardly known to them at that time, and they had no place in their thinking for an antirabbinic movement. Therefore, when Spain received reports about Severa's movement, which promised to return Israel to its homeland, many of the Jews of Spain arose and, liquidating their affairs, crossed the sea to become partners in the grand achievement of redemption. Oppression by the rulers and the tax collectors, together with disappointment in the Arabic rule, had left their mark. These, too, prompted the Jews to leave the country, or at least affected them subconsciously.

But Severa's movement came to a very bad end. When the Moslems in Syria learned of the movement that had arisen among their Jewish populace, they imprisoned its leader. His disciples and followers sought to be readmitted into the Jewish fold, and Naṭrōnai Gaon was asked whether this required their immersion. Severa's Spanish adherents who had hastened to leave for Syria and Palestine had not even completed the sale of their possessions, and had left behind property and real estate. This provided a choice opportunity for the Moslem rulers, who sought ways to augment the government's treasury and to enrich themselves. The governor, 'Anbasa, gave instructions to confiscate this deserted property for the benefit of the state, with the result that much Jewish property reverted to the government exchequer. So ended this messianic movement.[26]

For the Jews the disappointment was great. They had to face the realities, adapting themselves to circumstances, and to continue bearing their burden. The obduracy of the Arabic rulers increased from year to year. Gone were the memories of the days when the Jews of Spain had aided the Arabs in the conquest of the land. In the eyes of the Arabs, the natives of the conquered lands were not equals, created, as they themselves were, in the image of God. The idea prevailed among them that there was only one single function for this subjugated mass: to enrich the Arabs, that great nation that had been called to rule.

But during the rule of the *wālīs* over Moslem Spain the Jews suffered not only from the burden of taxes; they suffered even more from their degradation. Arrogance and pride were conspicuous characteristics of the Arabs, as was their contempt for the weak. As long as they needed the Jews, they welcomed them; but once they had achieved their goal and could dispense with the help of the Jews, they discarded them as one does the unwanted peel of a fruit already eaten.

Such was always the fate of the Jews in exile—grease on the wheels of history. When a nation fights for its goals and needs help, it is prepared to take it from any people, living or dead, even one that at other times spreads fear and terror and evokes dissatisfaction and loathing. But once it achieves its goals and can without hindrance mold its life according to its own desires, then national pride waxes great, a pride which begets a militant spirit. This is a main motif in the history of the Jews in the Diaspora. Jewish communities in the Diaspora flourish and thrive within great empires that have as their base a collective association of various nations. As long as the dominant nation is compelled to reckon with smaller nations, the Jews have a place in their midst. Jewish communities have flourished in the Hellenistic world, which was based upon a syncretic culture in the caliphal empire in the East composed of Arabs, Persians, and other nationals; in Turkey, with its many peoples and religions; and in the United States of today. However, when the ruling nation can crystallize its mode of life according to its own inclinations, and its national consciousness becomes stronger, dominating its political and social life, then the lot of the Jews becomes hard. The decisive factor is then not the makeup of the populace, but rather the spirit that animates the state.

The predominant feature in the history of Spain in the days of the *wālīs* was overweening arrogance, the boastful pride of the Arabic nation and its various tribes. Actual disasters did not befall the Jews. Everything was in a state of chaos. Contradictory aims and influences abounded. Despite the worsening of the condition of the Spanish communities, the migration to the peninsula by the Jews of North Africa continued—for their condition there was far worse, owing to the Berber revolt and the virtual paralysis of normal economic life.

In Spain, too, the situation deteriorated. Relations among the various Moslem factions and groups worsened to the point where actual civil war broke out. The successes of the Berbers in Morocco compelled Caliph Hishām to mobilize a large force and send it to the Maghreb. This force was severely beaten by the rebels, and its vanguard fled to Ceuta, where the Berbers besieged it. The condition of the besieged became so desperate that they pleaded with the governor of Spain, 'Abdalmalik b. Ḳaṭṭān, to permit them to cross over to the Iberian peninsula. However, at that time the reins of government in Spain were in the hands of an Arabic faction which strongly hated the Syrians and feared their arrogance, a trait they had already displayed in the war in North Africa. The Spanish governor, therefore, put off their request.

Meanwhile, however, the danger engendered by the revolt of the Berbers against the Arab rulers of Spain increased; having no other alternative, 'Abdalmalik b. Ḳaṭṭān was forced to turn to the Syrians for help. In response, seven thousand Syrians crossed the straits, led by the army commander Baldj, an able and haughty officer. The Syrians defeated the Berbers, but were not satisfied with the status of an auxiliary force assigned them by 'Abdalmalik b. Ḳaṭṭān and refused to return to Ceuta. They drove 'Abdalmalik out of his palace and seated Baldj in his stead in September 741.

The Syrians were a consolidated group opposed to the Arabs, who had dwelt in Spain for some time and were called in Arabic *al-baladīyūn* (the locals). Thus another faction was added to the mosaic of political life in Moslem Spain, and the opposition of the Syrians to the *al-baladīyūn* beclouded for a time all other quarrels among them.

After setting Baldj on the governor's seat, the Syrians slew the aged 'Abdalmalik b. Ḳaṭṭān, hung his body on a cross, and on either side of him hung a dog and an ape. Thus did they treat a Spanish governor already well along in years.

The sons of 'Abdalmalik b. Ḳaṭṭān raised the flag of revolt, assembled a large force of Arabs and Berbers, and attacked the capital of the state. However, the Syrians were better soldiers and routed them in a battle fought in the vicinity of Cordova. But Baldj himself was mortally wounded. After his death in 742, the Syrians made Tha'laba b. Salāma governor of Spain. Once again the Medinese Arabs, together with the Berbers, revolted, and again they were defeated by the Syrians. Tha'laba returned to Cordova with thousands of captives and, prompted by blind rage, decided to humble them in the dust. He sold them to anyone who made the meanest offer. Thus one was bartered for a goat, another for a dog. Such were the circumstances of life in the days of the *wālīs.*

Soon Tha'laba was succeeded by another governor. But the long contest between the rival factions continued. The hatred between them was so great and the subversive activities so intense that they rendered the functioning of the central government quite impossible.

The disasters brought on by human beings were augmented by catastrophes resulting from natural causes. The year 750 saw the start of a drought which brought famine and pestilence in its wake. The famine was especially heavy in northern Spain, whose earth was the poorest and the most parched of any in that fruitful country, and the Berbers who had settled there left the country in droves. They were already weakened because of the revolts and the civil wars, and when the famine began to oppress them, on the one hand, and the Christians exploited the situation to attack them, on the other, they did not find the strength to resist and returned to their homeland, Morocco.

The departure of the Berbers and the evacuation of large

areas by the Moslem inhabitants enabled Alfonso I, the successor to Pelagius, to expand the borders of the Asturian kingdom, which hitherto had occupied a very small section of land. Thus Galicia was absorbed into this kingdom, as was a broad area that today is a part of northern Portugal. Alfonso came down from the Cantabrian hills and easily conquered the heights of León. The districts between Asturias and the Basque country all fell into his hands. Thus all the Spanish provinces north of the Duero River reverted to Christian rule forty years after the conquest of the Iberian peninsula by the Moslems. This broad area saw the destruction of Islam by fire and sword, and the Moslems who remained there were compelled to convert to Christianity. This was the outcome of prolonged civil war, of tribal and factional disputes that prevailed throughout Moslem Spain for such a long time.

But the Moslems learned nothing from this; nor did they recognize the signs that presaged evil. They remained unchanged. Once again civil war flared up. The Yemenites regained their strength and, with the aid of their allies from the tribe of Ḳuraish, besieged the city of Saragossa, which was governed by aṣ-Ṣumail, lieutenant of the governor-general of Spain. And once again the leaders of the Ḳaisites went throughout the provinces of Spain to arouse their compatriots to war.

2

THE FIRST OMAYYADS

I

While the Arabs in Spain were preoccupied with intertribal and factional wars and intrigues, and revolts brought the state to the brink of destruction, there wandered throughout North Africa a persecuted refugee who was destined in the fullness of time to bring about a change in Moslem history in the Iberian peninsula.

He was a young man, tall and slender, whose light-colored hair fell in curls from his forehead and was tied in locks at each of his temples. His face was thin, and he was blind in one eye. His gait was pleasing, even elegant, and generally he wore a white robe. His bearing showed him to have had a superior upbringing. He was courteous and used choice phrases in speech and could compose poetry extemporaneously. He was always attended by two or three servants, but his personal belongings were few; they were contained in a few chests loaded upon a mule, which was tied to a horse ridden by one of his servants. At times he would spend a few days in a village inn, and from time to time he would join a caravan, leaving it after having gone just a short distance, as though he really did not know his destination and was merely wandering along the roads.

This young man was ʿAbdarraḥmān, son of Muʿāwiya, a

prince of the House of Omayya, who had been saved from the catastrophe that had befallen his family when the Abbasids seized the reins of government of the Moslem Empire. The Abbasids were not content with merely taking over the government but were determined to extirpate the House of Omayya. Every Omayyad who was captured by their troops was killed and his body cast into the field, a prey to jackals and hyenas. No hiding place was secure for them. Ultimately the Abbasids employed a ruse, announcing an amnesty for the Omayyads. No harm would befall anyone who emerged from his hiding place—so they proclaimed publicly. More than seventy Omayyad princes fell into the trap laid for them. They gathered in one place, near Jaffa, and were slain to the last man.

One of the few who had no faith in the proclamation of amnesty was 'Abdarraḥmān, the grandson of Caliph Hishām. This youth, then only twenty, fled Syria with his brother Yaḥyā and found refuge in a villa on the banks of the Euphrates; but the police and the agents of the Abbasid caliph knew no rest and found them even there. At the last moment, when the hoofbeats of the horses of the Abbasid soldiers were within hearing, 'Abdarraḥmān fled and swam across the river. However, his brother, believing the soldiers' promises, turned back in midstream and was promptly slain. 'Abdarraḥmān decided to leave the Near East and to test his fortune in the provinces of North Africa. There were many circumstances to attract him there. In this portion of the Moslem Empire the rule of the Abbasids was not yet recognized, and therefore the path was clear for pretenders to the throne. Moreover, his mother was a Berber and he hoped to reap some advantage from the support of her tribe. After salvaging some jewels and money and being joined by two freed slaves of the House of Omayya, he went to Egypt and from there continued westward. At first he tarried in Barca but after a while went on to Tripolitana and to that province today known as Tunisia, then called Ifrīḳīya, which was a center of Arabic rule in North Africa.

'Abdarraḥmān's situation went from bad to worse. The little money he had at the start of his journey dwindled, and his hopes of finding sympathizers and allies who would be willing to put their lives in jeopardy for him faded. A time of despair and helplessness came. Nevertheless, the prophecy of his great-uncle Maslama never faded from his memory. He had singled out 'Abdarraḥmān to Caliph Hishām when 'Abdarraḥmān was yet a lad, declaring that though the House of Omayya was doomed to collapse, this lad would restore its dominion. However, as he contemplated his hopeless situation, he fell into despair. 'Abdarraḥmān reached Kairawan, the capital of North Africa, and was welcomed by the governor-general, 'Abdarraḥmān b. Ḥabīb al-Fihrī. This governor dreamt of the establishment of a kingdom of his own and, as was the custom at that time, consulted soothsayers to learn what the future held in store. One day a Jew told him that a prince named 'Abdarraḥmān who wore curls on each temple was destined to establish a dynasty that would rule over Africa. On hearing this, the governor reasoned that inasmuch as his own name was 'Abdarraḥmān and he governed all the lands from Egypt to Morocco, he needed only to grow hair over his forehead and then the prophecy would be fulfilled. The Jew replied that the prophecy did not concern him, since he was not of royal descent.

Some time passed. Then the young 'Abdarraḥmān appeared before him, and, on seeing his hair style, the governor recalled the prophecy and wanted him executed. But the Jew, who had once been an adherent of one of the Omayyad princes, intervened. He told the governor, "One of two things will happen: either this young man is not the one concerning whom I predicted, and you will be charged with a needless homicide; or else he is indeed the one whom a glorious future awaits and your efforts will be in vain." Thus the Jew saved the life of the Omayyad prince.[1]

At all events, the young 'Abdarraḥmān preferred to stay

away from this governor who hated the Omayyads. Once again he began a life of wandering. From time to time he sought refuge with a Berber tribe and would tarry with it awhile. He even attempted to gain friends and made connections that raised him to authority in one of the provinces. For this reason various opponents and foes rose against him, while at the same time the agents of the governor in Kairawan kept track of him. As a result he had to seek, time and again, new places of refuge. This roaming about went on for four years. Day and night he trudged along the caravan routes from district to district; through searing heat and sandstorms he traveled long distances or tarried at inns in the company of merchants among piles of their wares. And once again he was encompassed by despair.

At long last his wanderings took him to Morocco, to the Berber tribe of Nafza, to which his mother belonged. These Berbers occupied the coastal strip of the Mediterranean near the Straits of Gibraltar; while he was staying in this area the thought occurred to the wandering prince to try his fortune in the land on the other side of the straits. He had heard much about Spain and also knew about a large number of Omayyads who had settled there.

It was a well-established principle among Arabs that manumitted slaves and others who had become protégés of a distinguished family give it unwavering protection, both for them and their children after them. So 'Abdarraḥmān sent his servant, Badr, to Spain. The protégés received him favorably and promised him whatever help they could. They turned to aṣ-Ṣumail, the Ḳaisite chief, but he rejected their pleas. Having failed with the Ḳaisites, they turned to the Yemenites. Then 'Abdarraḥmān was invited to Spain. When he got there, in mid-August 755, he first stayed at the castle of Torrox, not far from Loja, on the banks of the Genil River. Yūsuf al-Fihrī, the governor of Spain, was at that time on a military expedition in the northern part of the country. Upon hearing of the plot devised against him by the Omayyad partisans and of the arrival in Spain of the young prince, he at once returned to Cordova in order to lead his forces against them and to nip the revolt in the bud. But his troops were weary and most of them deserted. Yūsuf therefore began negotiations with 'Abdarraḥmān. His emissaries promised 'Abdarraḥmān wealth and honor provided that he would forgo his ambitions to rule.

But Yūsuf did not achieve his goal even by this means, and by the end of the winter, hostilities broke out. With his supporters, 'Abdarraḥmān passed through the provinces of Málaga, Sidonia, and Seville, and everywhere he was joined by many. In March 756 he entered Seville and from there attacked Cordova. In mid-May, a battle was fought at the gates of the city, which culminated in the flight of Yūsuf and aṣ-Ṣumail. The troops of 'Abdarraḥmān entered the capital, and in the Great Mosque he was proclaimed ruler of Moslem Spain, having barely reached the age of twenty-six. Thus began the reign of 'Abdarraḥmān, the first of the Omayyad dynasty in Spain. He occupied the throne for thirty-two years (756-788).

The path of 'Abdarraḥmān I as king—or, as he and his successors were designated, emir—of Moslem Spain, was not strewn with roses. Arabic historians of the Middle Ages tell of many revolts which occurred throughout his rule. The Arabs, consumed by hatred and ridden by factionalism, plotted vengeance, since by their nature they abhorred a strong central government. A weak government based on intertribal agreements was more to their liking. 'Abdarrahmān I therefore had to establish his authority over them by force of arms. He was convinced that this was the only way to establish peace and order in Moslem Spain, and he devoted all his energies to this end. From time to time he personally went forth to battle against rebels of all sorts and subdued them. His was a despotic rule, and the Arabs of Spain obeyed him because he cast fear over them; but success shone upon him, and the manner of his rule became the pattern for his sons and heirs.

The supporters of the last *wālīs,* who had been evicted by ʻAbdarraḥmān, partisans of the Abbasids, disappointed Yemenites who had hoped to overcome the Ḳaisites with the help of the Omayyad—all revolted against him.

The long list of rebellions that ʻAbdarraḥmān I crushed is sufficient testimony to his character. It demonstrates his energy and stubbornness. He never lost his presence of mind and always knew how to adapt his actions to circumstances. He was a man of keen intellect and quick of thought. But he was also a tyrant, never retreating from any action that could prove beneficial to him. In his eyes, everything was permissible. He broke his promises, deceived his enemies, and hired killers. No doubt his bitter experiences had brought him to this. It is certain that he often did what he did "so that they might fear and learn." It cannot be doubted that a strong hand was needed to make order prevail in the kingdom; but in no way can it be said that the circumstances justified or engendered his tyranny. The young fugitive who had wandered throughout North Africa in the middle of the eighth century was the selfsame tyrant who occupied the throne toward its end. At first he was only a potential despot, but ultimately he became a despot in reality. He had inherited his despotic tendencies from his forebears and from his earliest days had an unchecked bent to rule. His character never changed; but his many disappointments increased his natural tendencies—especially his distrustful bent.

In his latter days ʻAbdarraḥmān I acted like a typical despot, remaining shut up in his palace, irritable and suspicious. His subjects hated him and kept away from him. Yet he did achieve his goal. He established for his family a new kingdom and set the pattern for it. His descendants, who were his successors, laid upon Moslem Spain a rule of fear, it being their opinion that this was the only way to teach the Arabs and the other subjects law and order.

There can be no doubt that the many military adventures, entailing expenditures of large sums, compelled 'Abdarraḥmān I to tax his subjects heavily, and it is likely that the burden of the non-Moslem elements was especially onerous.[2] However, from a practical standpoint, 'Abdarraḥmān I felt that it was to his advantage to foster good relations with Jews and Christians. It was the practice of many despots in the Middle Ages to place reliance on groups and individuals from whom nothing untoward could be expected, since they were very weak—without roots in the land and without hopes or aspirations of gaining dominance over it. 'Abdarraḥmān I felt more and more let down, particularly by the Arabs, and toward the end of his life he preferred non-Arabs, from whom he selected his close aides, giving them positions of importance.[3] Christians and Jews constituted a nonmilitary element, completely subdued and dependent upon the protection of others. 'Abdarraḥmān I was quite aware of this fact, and he treated these non-Moslem groups benevolently.

Toward the end of his reign he decided to enlarge the Great Mosque in Cordova, which had become too small to contain all the worshipers. This mosque was a part of a church, for when the Moslems took the city, the conquerors behaved here as elsewhere: they appropriated for themselves half of a big church, leaving the remaining half for the Christians and destroying all other churches. 'Abdarraḥmān I did not want to deprive the Christians of their share of the building and opened negotiations with them. They stood their ground, and the negotiations were prolonged. Ultimately the Christians agreed to sell their share of the church for 100,000 dinars, a very substantial sum in those days. They further won a concession: the destroyed churches outside the walls were to be rebuilt.[4]

The non-Moslem groups appreciated the benevolence of 'Abdarraḥmān I. It can be assumed that both Christians and Jews regarded favorably the protection the crown extended to them. The tribal wars that had preceded the reign of 'Abdarraḥmān I had been accompanied by violent and forced levies, and those elements among the populace who did not take an active part in these wars found them repugnant. It is quite revealing that Jews and Christians were not conspicuous and did not take part in the numerous rebellions that marked the reign of 'Abdarraḥmān I. This indicates their position. The very absence of any action can only mean in this instance that they sided with the government. The benefit derived by the government from this attitude was very considerable, inasmuch as the non-Moslem communities had ties with their coreligionists beyond the borders, especially the Christians, who were likely to be the intermediaries between the rebelling faction and the Christian forces outside the borders of Moslem Spain and hence had the potential to bring destruction on the Omayyad rulers.[5]

For the Jews of Moslem Spain, the rule of 'Abdarraḥmān I was an era of communal growth and development. After the government of 'Abdarraḥmān I was firmly established, immigration into Spain once again increased. When it became known that one of the Omayyads had succeeded in founding for himself a kingdom in Spain, the members of this family who had managed to survive and their relatives who had been his subordinates migrated there. To Spain came 'Abdalmalik b. 'Umar b. Marwān, Bishr b. 'Abdalmalik, Djuzay b. 'Abdal-'azīz and others, together with their sons and daughters. 'Abdarraḥmān I gave them positions and pensions and freed them from the obligation to pay taxes. Moreover, he encouraged the migration of his family and their followers to Spain. We even hear of his sending a mission to the East to invite his kinsmen and friends of the family to come to Spain under his aegis.

In his reign many Berbers also came to the Iberian peninsula, and he took them into his army as mercenaries, some even holding posts of eminence in his court. 'Abdarraḥmān I also mobilized into his forces serfs and mercenaries from among the Christian nations of southern Europe, who were known in Spain as "Slavs." As reported in Arabic sources, the number of these foreign soldiers reached forty thousand. The emir's militia also included blacks—Ethiopians. Thus people from many countries streamed into Spain, but mainly from North Africa.

There can be no doubt that this wave of immigration also swept with it many Jews. It was always the tendency of the Jews to migrate to areas of settlement, and such was the Iberian peninsula in the eighth century. The news of the improved circumstances of the Jews in Spain that came about with the establishment of the Omayyad regime had the effect of making Spain look more alluring to the Jewish migrants. Most of the Jews came from North Africa, but Jews from Syria also came to the West—to Ifrīḳīya (Tunisia), Morocco, and Spain. The very Jew who had saved the life of 'Abdarraḥmān I in Kairawan had first lived in Syria. But withal the full flow of migration from the Eastern countries to Spain had hardly yet begun. There were not then circumstances to impel large groups of Jews to leave for the West.

In those days the Jews of Spain lived peacefully, were on a friendly footing with other religious groups, and even spread their religious concepts. In 785 Pope Hadrian I requested of the Spanish bishops to restrain the spread of Jewish influence on their flocks.[6]

II

Hishām I, son of 'Abdarraḥmān I, succeeded his father and ruled for eight years (788–796). At the outset of his reign a war of succession erupted between him and his two brothers,

Sulaimān and 'Abdallāh. Sulaimān, the eldest, was the governor of Toledo, and Hishām had to lay siege to the city. Sulaimān escaped from the beleaguered city and continued the fighting in the east of Spain, but in the end Hishām bribed him with a large sum of money and he left Spain, as did his younger brother, 'Abdallāh. Later other quarrels broke out in the Ebro region, but they were easily put down. In a general way it may be said that Moslem Spain was tranquil during the reign of Hishām I. This enabled him to direct his forces against the Christians in the north.

In those days a long series of military ventures began, which the Moslems carried on for many generations against the Christian kingdoms in the north. Again and again Moslem troops moved toward the "land of fortresses," Old Castile, and toward the region of Álava, which is between the northern part of Old Castile and Navarre. Arabic accounts of these military ventures are for the most part very laconic. We are told that in such-and-such a year an invasion was mounted against the land of the fortresses, that the Moslems were victorious and slew many Christians. However, between these few dry lines of chronicle are hidden unceasing acts of blood and tears.

Generally, these invasions occurred in the spring. The Moslem soldiers invaded the Christian districts, fell upon tranquil villages, plundered whatever was of value, set fire to the produce in the fields, burnt the houses, killed all the men, and took the youths captive. The populace of northern Spain could expect disaster every spring and summer, and they lived in constant fear. Whenever the hoofbeat of cavalry was heard, everyone hid. But often the church sexton did not have time to warn the villagers by ringing the church bells, for the enemy had already penetrated to the center of town and begun his destructive work. In but a moment the cry of the wounded rent the air and flames burst from the rooftops. A shepherd might stand on a hilltop blowing his pipe, when suddenly horsemen in white garb would emerge; one would draw his sword and with a sweep of a powerful hand decapitate the shepherd; the flock would be brought to the village, where clouds of smoke billowed from houses and granaries. Such was life in Spain during this period.

Thus the hatred between the religious groups, so characteristic of this land, became deep-rooted and ultimately erupted into a mighty flame consuming those of the weakest religions, not Christians or Moslems. . . . But the Arabic chronicles make no mention of this. We only learn from them that the Moslem military expeditions in the days of Hishām I were crowned with success.

The Moslem hordes gained victories over the Christian armies and plundered their cities. In 793 the Moslems sent an expedition to Septimania, reaching the city of Narbonne, which had already returned to Christian rule. They set fire to the city and routed the troops of the duke of Toulouse in the vicinity of Carcassonne. But in the main the armies of Hishām I attacked those districts under the rule of the king of Asturias. In 794 the city of Oviedo was taken and despoiled, and in the following year Astorga. The second emir of the Omayyad dynasty in Spain invested much effort and money in these ventures because he was filled with an overwhelming desire for war against the Christians. He was very devout, clinging to his God wholeheartedly and fulfilling the commandments of his faith. He performed many good deeds and was very interested in theology.

During the rule of Hishām I the character of religious life in Moslem Spain was determined; this was especially important with regard to relationships between the Moslems and the non-Moslem communities—Jewish and Christian—especially with respect to their juridical status.

Hishām I encouraged pious Moslems to make the pilgrimage to Mecca, which was one of their most important precepts.

Moslem theologians who journeyed to Hedjaz came in contact with their colleagues in oriental countries and on returning to Spain recounted the achievements in the study of law and theology. Thus a spiritual-cultural link between Eastern and Western Islam was created.

In those days Mālik b. Anas (d. 795), the founder of one of the *madhhabs*, the schools of orthodox theology, taught in Medina. Some of the Spanish theologians who went to Hedjaz tarried in Medina and heard his lectures. His distinguished disciple was Yaḥyā b. Yaḥyā al-Laithī (d. 848). Mālik at first had been in sympathy with the family of 'Alī, who had attempted at various times to rebel against the Abbasids and to restore the caliphate to their family, which was descended from Mohammed. After becoming involved in one of these revolts, Mālik was given seventy lashes. Naturally he harbored hatred against the Abbasids, and when he was told about the pious Omayyad who had mounted the throne in Spain, he praised him enthusiastically.

The Spanish theologians reported this to Hishām; understandably, he was greatly pleased and began to show preference for Mālik's tenets over other tenets in Islamic law. Before long, the theology of Mālik was officially espoused throughout Islamic Spain. Once the Omayyad government had determined upon this, it became necessary for all the Moslem judges in Spain to become associated with these schools of law and to render decisions in accordance with their tenets. Moreover, the theologians were very influential and involved themselves in governmental affairs. Thus it came about that very much depended upon Mālik's juridico-theological standpoint.

In truth, differences among the four juridical schools of orthodox Islam are not great. They consist for the most part of customs and details especially relating to the fulfillment of various religious precepts. At all events, it is evident that of the systems of Islamic jurisprudence, Mālik's is distinguished by its conservatism and rigidity in matters of religion. While they are liberal in laws of matrimony, the Mālikites tend to strictness in matters of religion in the narrow sense of the word, for example, ritual and observance of the religious precepts. Followers of this school are zealots and are opposed to scholastic theology. They guard dogma strictly and will not hear of innovations. They incline to severity in whatever hurts Islamic faith and all that relates to juridic matters as those concerning the protected communities, Jew and Christian, under Islamic rule.

Eastern Islamic lands were dominated by schools of thought that held a more lenient view on these matters, or the state recognized a more liberal school—thus it was possible to bring a case dealing with a non-Moslem community before a more lenient judge of this school. For example, it was the custom to go before a judge of the Ḥanafite school whenever a question about the repair of a non-Moslem house of worship arose, for, in keeping with the principles of his thinking, such a judge would more likely grant the requested permission. This was not possible in Islamic Spain. There a strict school of thought that tolerated no deviation in law and judgment prevailed. The Moslem regime in Spain was thus far from liberal.

The dominance of the Mālikites over religious life in Moslem Spain had the potential for aggravating religious fanaticism and bringing about the persecution of Jews and Christians. However, for more than eight generations, until the end of Omayyad rule, the Jews of Moslem Spain were not persecuted. The government did not oppress them or make any decrees to harm them; nor did the populace rise up against them. This is unique in the history of the Jewish Diaspora, which usually consisted of a long line of evil decrees and calamities. There were epochs and lands in which the Jews flourished because they filled an essential economic function from which the majority derived their livelihood. But the fact that some Jews or even a group of Jews occupied an important economic function in Spain cannot explain the existence of a large Jewish settlement consisting of many communities in various districts throughout the land.

The tranquil circumstances of the Jews in Moslem Spain during the reign of the Omayyads must rather be understood as the result of the policies of this dynasty and of the political attitude demonstrated by the Jews. They comprised a group loyal to the government, a consolidated ethnic body having no secret relationships with factors outside the government that might frighten the Moslem rulers of the peninsula. The Omayyad government needed such elements, willingly depending upon them and supporting them. The goals of the Omayyads' enemies were centrifugally directed, and the welfare of the Jews required the existence of a strong central government.

A like situation existed in Egypt in the tenth century. The Fatimid dynasty relied, among others, on the Christians and Jews who were willing to cooperate with it, whereas the orthodox Moslems hated the dynasty, regarding it as representing Islamic heresy. Both in Egypt and in Spain there was a community of interest.

But the similarity of conditions of the Jews in Egypt and Spain was more apparent than real, for the conditions of rule of the Fatimids and the Omayyads of Spain differed. They were not at all analogous. The Omayyads in Spain could quite easily adopt varying policies, since they did not differ in religious matters from their subjects. They could, for example, foster fanaticism and pressure their subjects into persecuting religious minorities. Such had been the wont of kings and governments in different lands and times. Although Hishām I had a tendency toward fanaticism, however, he did not persecute the non-Moslems. Evidently, in accordance with family tradition, the Spanish Omayyads followed a line of tolerance and extended their protection to the Christians and Jews. Such was the way of this Moslem dynasty, though other dynasties—indeed, the majority—followed other paths.

III

The third of the Omayyad rulers, al-Ḥakam I (796–822), was strong, courageous, and energetic. He more closely resembled his grandfather, ʻAbdarraḥmān, than his father, Hishām. He set for himself the goal of preserving the integrity of his kingdom by any means and of maintaining his authority, not allowing anyone to interfere in matters of government. Such a king was truly needed in Moslem Spain at the opening of the ninth century, for within the state forces were at work that could bring about its disintegration. Like other Omayyads, al-Ḥakam I had to subdue the revolts of princes of the royal house and of governors and chieftains in various provinces. But the most dangerous insurrections were those in the populous towns of Toledo, Mérida, and Cordova itself. The suppression of these popular movements involved much bloodshed and the expulsion of many inhabitants from the Spanish capital.

Although disturbed by conspirators and rebels throughout his rule, al-Ḥakam I did not shrink from doing battle with the Christians in northern Spain. During his reign military ventures were also mounted against Alava, Old Castile, the Basque country, and Galicia. At times these expeditions were commanded by high-ranking officers, and at times al-Ḥakam himself would lead his army. Notwithstanding all this, the power of the Christians waxed during his time. The Franks penetrated the northeastern part of Spain and took the border district, the Spanish March, an area destined to protect southern France from Moslem invasions and to serve as a springboard for French advances into Spain itself. In 798 they conquered the area between Gerona and the Segre River, and in 801, after a two-year siege, they captured Barcelona. They also attempted to advance farther south, beyond Tortosa, but were forced to retreat.

Al-Ḥakam I and the details of his rule are fully and clearly portrayed in Arabic chronicles. He was an Arabic aristocrat, powerful and haughty, no doubt contemptuous of non-Arabs; yet because of considerations of state he was prepared to work together with those elements who were ready to extend a helping hand. He welcomed the neo-Moslems (that is, Spaniards who had converted to Islam), even though many Arabs regarded them as second-class citizens. These *muwalladūn* were among the closest subordinates of al-Ḥakam, and in his court "Slavs" and Berbers also were to be found. He gave the head of the Christian community of Cordova, Rabīʿ, the son of Theodulf, very important duties: he appointed him chief of the royal militia and overseer of taxes. Rabīʿ was not the only Christian to hold an important office in the government; indeed, there were many others like him. In similar fashion, there were also Jews who were the emir's close associates, performing various missions for him.[7]

But there was a great difference between the status of the Christians vis-à-vis the Omayyad ruler and that held by the Jews. Among the Christians there was a bloc that was prepared to cooperate with the emir and to be meshed into the Omayyad government in Spain, but others had a negative attitude toward it and schemed and plotted against it. The Christians in Mérida, for example, actively participated in an uprising against al-Ḥakam. On the other hand, the Jews were an element loyal to the Omayyads. They sought to find a shield and a shelter in the government of the emir, repaying it with loyalty and devotion. They took no part in attempts to undermine the government and rebel against it. They sought to avoid becoming caught up in the political vortex. Al-Hakam I and his subordinates valued highly the stand taken by the Jews and regarded them with approval.

In certain historical works we find information that sheds a clear light on the position of the Jews. Such information is contained in Arabic historical accounts of the "Revolt of the Suburb" in 818. One of the chief instigators among the theologians was Ṭālūt b. 'Abdaldjabbār, who had been a disciple of Mālik b. Anas in Medina. After the rebellion was crushed, the theologians, along with the other inhabitants of the suburbs of Cordova, were ordered to leave the town; but al-Ḥakam at least allowed them to remain inside the borders of Moslem Spain. Ṭālūt, who did not want to leave the city, disappeared, and for a year nothing was heard of him. He found refuge in the house of a Cordovan Jew and hid there all that time. The Jew treated him deferentially and provided for all his needs.

Eventually he tired of his stay with the Jew. He thanked the Jew profoundly and indicated that he intended to put up at the house of one of the senior officers of al-Ḥakam, who had once been his disciple and whom he would ask to intercede for him with the emir to grant him amnesty. His host cautioned him against taking so ill-considered a step and adjured him to drop the plan. The Jew assured him that no matter how long he tarried with him, his attitude toward him would remain unchanged. But Ṭālūt refused to listen. In the dark of night he went to the house of his former disciple. The latter went quickly to al-Ḥakam and revealed the matter to him.

The theologian was taken before the emir, who first addressed him harshly but later showed him clemency. Asked where he had kept himself all this time, Ṭālūt told his story. On hearing of the treachery of his official, al-Ḥakam became very angry and drove him from his presence. But he lauded the Jew who had treated the Moslem theologian so generously, even endangering himself, his family, and his property for one of another faith.

This tale, found in the writings of Arabic historians,[8] points up the fact that Jews were not involved in the political intrigues and schemings of the opponents of Omayyad rule. In this and in other tales[9] concerning Jews of that period, they are depicted sympathetically by Arabic historians. This also shows that they had been successfully dovetailed into the Spanish-Moslem state and held a position of esteem therein.

The loyal attitude of the Jewish populace toward the Omayyad government and the kindness with which the court treated the Jews—this mutuality in their relationship constitutes a prominent motif in the history of the Jews of Spain at that time. It becomes clearer and clearer with each detail about the Jews contained in the sources. Still another prime manifestation in the history of the Spanish Jews is the increase in the number of communities through immigration.

The migration of the Jews to Spain continued throughout the reign of Hishām I and his son, al-Ḥakam I, and, as in the days of the *wālīs* and of 'Abdarraḥmān I, was a phenomenon that paralleled Moslem migration to Spain. The migration of the Jews was a mere rivulet alongside the mighty flood of immigrants who poured forth in those days from North Africa and other lands into the Iberian peninsula. In the days of al-Ḥakam I, as in the days of his grandfather, descendants of the Omayyads who had been rescued from the clutches of the Abbasids and also their followers and protégés came to Spain. The Berbers, too, continued to cross the Straits of Gibraltar and hire themselves out to the armies of the Omayyads.

The Jews were not merely drawn into this stream but had special motives that prompted their migration to Spain. While Hishām I occupied the throne, to Morocco came one of 'Alī's descendants, who established a principality for himself. This was Idrīs I, founder of a Sherifite dynasty, which continued to exist in Morocco until the second half of the tenth century. In the few years of Idrīs I's reign in Morocco (788–793) he inflicted many calamities upon the Jews. He fought the Berber tribes who had converted to Judaism, compelling them to become Moslems. In 789 he attacked the Jews in the Tadla region and fought them again the following year. As a result of these actions by Idrīs I, many Jews and Berber converts to Judaism migrated to Spain. From Ifrīḳīya (Tunisia) a flow of migrants to Spain continued also, as we are told in a mid-ninth century Jewish source.[10]

At the other end of North Africa, in Egypt, where there had always been a big Jewish community, the condition of the populace steadily worsened under their Arab oppressors, and many of the Jewish inhabitants of the land of the Nile were prompted by these circumstances to migrate to the West. In the middle of the eighth century a series of revolts broke out as the result of burdensome taxation that lay heavily upon the natives. By the end of the eighth and the start of the ninth century these uprisings were very frequent, and in lower Egypt, in the Delta region, where a dense Jewish settlement existed, a move to rebellion began. In 811 a band of Spanish Moslems seized control of Alexandria and set up a reign of terror. These despotic masters, who brought ruin to the inhabitants of Alexandria, held out for sixteen years against the Abbasid government. As an outcome of these events, there no doubt poured forth a new wave of migration by Egyptian Jews to Kairawan and beyond it to Spain.

Naturally, not all the migrants remained in Spain. In lands that absorb immigrants there is a constant movement to and fro. Some migrants are not absorbed and return whence they came; some continue to wander on to other lands.

In 789 Idrīs I founded the city of Fez, which in time became one of the most important cities in the entire Moslem world. The city that Idrīs I founded stretched along the eastern bank of the Wadi Fez and was inhabited by Berbers. In 808 his son and successor, Idrīs II (803–824), built the part of Fez that is on the west bank and settled there Arab immigrants from Ifrīḳīya, who, for the most part, came from the chief city of North Africa, Kairawan. Idrīs himself moved to Fez, which became the capital of his kingdom. Men from Spain also went to Morocco to join Idrīs II and serve in his army. In 805, for example, a large band of Arab horsemen crossed the straits and joined Idrīs's army. Many of the inhabitants of the southern suburb of Cordova who had been expelled from the city after the revolt of 818 migrated to Morocco and settled in Fez.

Idrīs II welcomed these refugees with open arms and settled them in the part of the city built by his father, on the east bank of the wadi, thereafter known as the "bank of the Andalusians." The aim of the Sherifite ruler was clear. He was glad for the opportunity to give the city a more Arabic character and to be able to live in Arabic surroundings. A history of the fourteenth century relates that many Jews came with the stream of settlers to Fez. There is reason to think that quite a number of them were Moroccan Jews who had migrated to Spain and returned from there. Idrīs II placed the Jewish settlers in the northern section of the western part of the city. From the amount of the poll tax he imposed on them, as reported by Arabic historians, it can be concluded that the number of Jewish settlers was very large. But it is certain that the migrants from Spain constituted only a small portion of the large Jewish population of Fez.[11]

There were also Jews who wandered from Spain to the big country north of the Pyrenees. The Jews were then enjoying favorable conditions in the kingdom of the Franks. The important commercial enterprises were in their hands; it was they who supplied the royal court, the nobles, and the heads of the clergy with jewels, spices, and other precious articles from

Eastern lands. Since this trade brought them much profit, it is not surprising that Jewish merchants from Moslem Spain decided to go to Gaul. A Jewish inhabitant, Abraham of Saragossa, requested from Louis the Pious, the son and successor of Charlemagne, permission to settle in Gaul. In reply, the emperor instructed his officials, the judges, and the clergy of his kingdom to permit the Jew to carry on trade and to buy and sell slaves, to let him observe his religious practices unhindered, and to exempt him from taxes and imposts.[12]

IV

The first emirs of the Spanish Omayyad dynasty differed from each other in character, and naturally in the despotic rule which crystallized in Spain, following the pattern of oriental rulers, this fact had decisive importance in the political development of the kingdom. 'Abdarraḥmān II (822–852), the son and successor of al-Ḥakam I, was a person who tended to be influenced overmuch by his environment. He was not a warlike man, as his father had been, but rather preoccupied with matters of culture and art, poetry and literature, edifices and music. So favorable was the political situation during his reign that he could always follow his propensities. No great rebellions endangered the existence of his government, and in their wars with the Christian kingdoms to the north the Moslems were the victors.

The Arabic chroniclers describe the period of 'Abdarraḥmān II's reign as a quiet one in the annals of Moslem Spain, without any political upheavals. But in actuality strain existed in the land even in his days because of friction between the various groups and factions, and there was no lack of rebellions. For a considerable time civil war raged in the east of Spain between the Yemenites and the Arabs of the tribe of Muḍar, who originated in northern Arabia. To add to the concern, one of the Yemenite leaders professed devotion to the Abbasid caliph, and the government in Cordova did not succeed in calming the stirred-up emotions. So the conflicts continued from 822 to 829. In the south the Berbers rose up in 826 and again in 850. But these rebellions were quelled without undue effort.

Much more serious was the uprising in Toledo, whose inhabitants hated the Omayyad regime. It was headed by a simple laborer, Hāshim the blacksmith. He gathered armed bands and organized forays into the areas around the cities that were loyal to the government. Even after Hāshim was slain in a battle near the city of Daroca, the rebels continued their activities, and the government could not overcome them. In 834 the government forces laid siege to Toledo and had to abandon it. Toledo held out for seven years, but in 837 the forces of the government broke into the city and took it.

Yet another city, Mérida, gave the government no little trouble. As they had in the days of al-Ḥakam I, its inhabitants revolted during the rule of his son. In 828 they rose up and slew the governor of the city. In the following years 'Abdarraḥmān II himself took his forces against Mérida but did not achieve his purpose. In 830 the siege was renewed, and the city was subdued.

Arabic historians list the series of campaigns that the armies of Moslem Spain undertook during the long reign of 'Abdarraḥmān II. Like other Omayyads, he sent his troops time and again against the Christians in the north of the peninsula, into Catalonia, Old Castile, and Galicia. But they also had to fight against the Normans, who invaded Spain in 844. This invasion was only an interlude, however, and soon the Moslem armies continued their endless wars with the Christians in the north.

The activities of 'Abdarraḥmān II were, it would seem, very much like those of his forebears, but the similarity is only apparent. For in the meantime, the Omayyad kingdom of

Spain had established itself, and the effort which ʿAbdarraḥmān I and his descendants had put forth began to bear fruit. By the first half of the ninth century the Moslem-Spanish state had become one of the major powers in the Mediterranean basin. The permanence of the government, the successes of its armies, its geographic position, which made it a natural bridge between Christian Europe and Moslem Asia—all these factors increased its importance in international relations.

In 840 a mission from the Byzantine emperor came to Cordova and established diplomatic relations between the two powers that lay at the eastern and western ends of the Mediterranean Sea respectively, relations which continued into the tenth century. The Byzantines were deadly enemies of the Abbasid caliphs and wanted to incite the Omayyads of Spain against the Moslem princes of North Africa (who were vassals of the Abbasids) and thereby to disturb them and divert strength away from them.

No less conspicuous than the growing influence in international relations was the development of its governmental apparatus and cultural life. After the sudden invasion of Andalusia by the Normans, the Omayyad government began to improve its naval fleet and erected a shipyard in Seville. Moreover, a mint was established in Cordova in order to increase the money that would circulate among the people; for until this time it was very limited, a factor which hindered the development of commerce. In the days of ʿAbdarraḥmān II the income of the royal exchequer was very large, and this enabled him to build edifices of great magnificence. In one city he repaired the walls; in another he built a fortress; and it goes without saying that he built and enlarged mosques. During this emir's rule the influences of the Abbasid culture penetrated into Spain, a syncretic civilization in which Arabic-Moslem, Persian, and Hellenistic elements were joined. The royal court witnessed the introduction of ceremonies and celebrations that the Abbasids had revived after the manner of the former kings of Persia. The court of the Omayyad king at Cordova was at its grandest in those days, and the upper strata of Andalusian society strived to embellish it with gracious manners.

In this process a musician named Ziryāb, who had come to Spain from Irak at the beginning of the reign of ʻAbdar-raḥmān II, played an important part. It was his official function to play and sing before the emir, but in point of fact he also set the pattern of social living in Cordova. He showed the nobles in the capital how to dress, trim their hair, and prepare meals in good taste. A Jew of the court was involved in his coming to Spain.

This Babylonian musician had been compelled to leave Bagdad because he aroused the envy of his teacher and master. In consequence he migrated to the court of the Banū Aghlab, who ruled in Kairawan. Later he wrote to al-Ḥakam I, the Omayyad emir in Cordova, offering his services. When this letter reached Cordova, he was recommended by the Jew Abū 'n-Naṣr al-Manṣūr, who apparently was himself a musician at the court of al-Ḥakam I. (The Jewish artist evidently did not fear the competition of a distinguished colleague or suffer from the envy usually found among those of a like profession, especially artists, the very emotion which roused Ziryāb's master and coreligionist and forced him to flee his homeland.) The emir graciously accepted Ziryāb's proposal, inviting him to come promptly and offering him a considerable salary.

Ziryāb headed westward, crossed the Straits of Gibraltar, and landed in Spain at Algeciras; but when he arrived he learned that in the meantime al-Ḥakam I had died. The Babylonian musician considered returning to Africa, but al-Manṣūr, the Jew whom al-Ḥakam had sent to meet him, persuaded him with kind words to stay. The Jew then sent an urgent message posthaste to ʻAbdarrahmān II, describing to the new emir the greatness of Ziryāb's artistry and entreating him to do all that he could to keep the Iraki artist in Spain. 'Abdarraḥmān complied with his request. He sent Ziryāb a warm invitation and beautiful gifts and instructed government officials to help him and show him every courtesy until he arrived at Cordova.[13]

This account fits very well with other information concerning Jews to be found in Arabic writings depicting this period in the annals of Spain. Arabic writers do not mention Jews who were prominent in the government, but almost all the information about Jewish activities in their writings contains a common element: the Jews appear as loyal aides of the Arabic rulers, performing various and even important services, and the Jew is always presented in a favorable light.

'Abdarraḥmān II was a devout Moslem, and the influence of the theologians at his court was very strong. The most conspicuous among them was the Berber Yaḥyā b. Yaḥyā, who became the final arbiter in all matters of law and faith in Moslem Spain. The emir himself accepted all the rigors relating to personal conduct and the observance of Islamic precepts that Yaḥyā imposed on him. Moreover, all judges were appointed or dismissed in accordance with the wish of this theologian. 'Abdarraḥmān II tended toward actions that made his orthodoxy conspicuous, thereby finding favor with the zealous masses. When he held the post of regent during his father's last illness, Yaḥyā got him to agree to the execution of Rabī', the Christian commander of the royal militia. He also ordered the demolition of an inn in one of the city's suburbs, where Moslems liked to drink. But at all events he was not a zealot, and during his rule the non-Moslem communities enjoyed the freedom of worship and citizens' privileges that they had had earlier. Many Christians held posts in the government or in the service of the Arabic nobles.

Nevertheless, a change in the climate that enveloped the

non-Moslem communities did come about. Whereas at the outset of Arabic rule there were almost no theologians in Moslem Spain, now in the ninth century a highly influential class of Moslem clergy arose which involved itself powerfully in the life of the public. Among the Christians a strong tendency toward insubordination and active opposition to Moslem rule developed.

In Toledo and Mérida, the two cities which again and again rose up against the emirs of Cordova, there were large Christian communities that played an important part in these revolts. The Christians of Mérida even entered into conspiracies with Christian powers that had hostile relations with the Spanish-Moslem kingdom or even engaged in warfare with it. The Christian inhabitants of Mérida sent a letter to the French emperor, Louis the Pious, to inform him of their troubles under Moslem rule; in 828 they received from him a reply in which he promised to help them by means of military pressure applied from the direction of the Spanish March, which is in the northeast part of the peninsula. It seems that the people of Mérida were also in touch with agents of the king of Asturias, who was interested in stirring up confusion and rebellion within the Moslem kingdom.

The silence of the Arabic chronicles regarding the role of the Jews during the many revolts that shook the foundations of the Omayyad-Spanish state in the first half of the ninth century is very edifying. We hear of rebellions by Arab and Berber tribes, uprisings of Moslems of Spanish origin, and the revolt of cities, of the role of various social strata, of help extended to the rebels by Christians; but concerning the Jews no word is mentioned throughout all these events. This silence is proof that the Jews adopted a stance of reserve and nonintervention. They conducted themselves like their forebears in the first days of the Omayyad dynasty, whereas the Christians followed a different path. The Jews filled the role of an indigenous Spanish group supporting the Moslem rulers with complete loyalty. The court repaid them by maintaining good relations with them and encouraging all their actions. So it was that Moslem Spain became a state wherein Jews felt freer than in any other.

The Jewish attitude was viewed in terms of a severe crisis that developed in relations between the various religious groups in Moslem Spain in the middle of the ninth century. This crisis began as a clash between the Christians and Jews, the two "protected communities." The Jews and Christians hated each other. No doubt Jews remembered what the Christians had done to them when they were the dominant power; on the other hand, Christians told their children how the Jews had sided with the Moslems at the time of the conquest. During the time of 'Abdarraḥmān II, relations between the two groups became especially strained. This tension was the result of an uncommon episode in the annals of the Jews in the Diaspora; the story begins elsewhere, but in the main it takes place in Moslem Spain, where Jews lived as free men.

In those remote times it was the custom in European countries for young men who were thinkers and persons of ability to dedicate their lives to the church. This was the path followed by the sons of nobles who found it repugnant to be constantly embroiled in battle and strife without reason or a vision of a better day; and quite naturally it was also the course taken by men who came from the lower social strata, since it offered them the sole opportunity to rise on the social scale. At a very tender age the youths were entered in monastic schools and given monks' garb. The splendid pageantry of the church impressed them strongly; the ideals discussed with conviction by the teachers excited their enthusiasm.

But with maturity came skepticism. The pageantry became merely routine, the distance between teacher and disciple disappeared. Underneath the lofty phrases of the robed monks their ignorance was revealed, and their naked lust was brought into the open. Then gnawing doubts, nesting in the heart of the young cleric, would rack him. Once having lost faith in the masters, he began to doubt their teachings. He tried to stamp out these thoughts and to triumph over his skepticism by devout prayer, hoping doubt would forsake him and he would again acquire the assurance of unblemished faith. When priest and monk fell to their knees in the magnificent cathedrals shrouded in dimness, the air saturated with incense, while from a thousand mouths a mighty hymn of praise for their Messiah burst forth, accompanied by the sound of the organ, who knows how many thoughts of despair were silenced in those who had gone astray. But at times the doubts would prove too strong—not everyone could overcome or suppress his thoughts. Then heretics who had cast aside the monk's robe would emerge into the outside world.

One such man was Bodo, a German who lived in the first half of the ninth century. He came from a noble family in the south of Germany, but lived for many years in the land of the Franks across the Rhine. He received an excellent education and spent many years studying the branches of Christian theology and also the classics in the form in which they existed at the time. He joined the ranks of the clergy and advanced steadily within the church until he became priest at the court of Louis the Pious. He continued to progress, and success came his way.

But with the passage of time his faith began to waver. When he discussed religious subjects with men of learning and high-ranking persons, he became convinced that they held divergent views on important matters. This is readily understandable, for Christian theological learning in Western Europe in those days was not profound. But this thinking young man was confused and disappointed by the divergent opinions and evasive answers and the superficiality shown toward the weightiest matters. Even the moral level of the clergy made a sad impression on Bodo. A keen eye was hardly needed to note that beneath the mask of piety lay hidden men with strong appetites who found ways to satisfy them. On one hand they preached modesty and abstinence from worldly pleasures and deprecated carnal lust, while on the other they sought out honor and glory, and many were addicted to lewd practices.

It was then that Bodo came in contact with the Jews who frequented the court of the emperor, most of them being engaged in commerce. From them he got clear answers to his questions in matters of religion. His riven heart, plagued by doubts on the problem of the Trinity and the nature of Jesus —who according to Christian belief was both God and man— was greatly impressed with the simplicity of belief concerning God held by Jews. Gradually the thought came to him to turn his back on Christianity and to find salvation for his soul in the Jewish faith. To reach a decision on this matter was not easy; he sought to escape it, but time and again returned to it. In 837 he requested the emperor's permission to travel to Rome and visit the pope and to prostrate himself at the graves of the saints. The emperor granted him leave, saw to it that he went on his way provided with all necessities, and gave him many presents.

What Bodo did on leaving the court is not known. Whether he became greatly disappointed with the heads of the church on reaching Rome, or whether the whole matter of going to Rome was merely an alibi to get him away from the court and he never reached Rome, one thing is certain: the emperor's priest did not return from his journey but instead went to Moslem Spain and was converted to Judaism. The exact date of this conversion is known. It was in 838, during the celebration of the Ascension, which occurs forty days after Easter. It appears that it took place in Saragossa.[14]

When a priest changes his faith, especially a priest who holds a position of eminence, it is not a light matter. Since this act was likely to create a stir everywhere and held great danger for him, it is likely that he preferred to be converted in a non-Christian country; and in truth one source states that he became a Jew in Spain.[15] Inasmuch as Bodo dwelt in Saragossa after his conversion, it is most likely that this act took place there, a city that had a large Jewish community, rather than in one of the small towns whose Jewish inhabitants were not learned and with whom a man of his station would have nothing in common. When Bodo was circumcised he was given the name Eli'ezer.[16]

As was befitting a man of his lofty station, Bodo had embarked on his journey accompanied by an entourage of servants. After his conversion, he urged them to convert too, but they refused, and out of exasperation he sold them into slavery. One of his relatives, a nephew, however, heeded his request and was converted. Bodo himself, who was still a young man, took a wife from the Jewish women of Saragossa and joined the ranks of the Arabic army.[17] When the news of this reached Louis the Pious, it was so surprising to him that he could not believe it. Meanwhile, Bodo learned Hebrew and dedicated much of his time to acquiring a knowledge of the tenets of Israel, biblical commentaries, and laws.

Full of enthusiasm and strong in his new faith, as is customary in any convert, Bodo regarded it as his function to show the upright way to his former coreligionists. Both orally and in writing he began to make war on Christianity in various ways. In his writings he spoke of the coming of the Messiah, which in his view would occur soon and for whose appearance he hoped with all his heart. The leaders of the Christians in Moslem Spain grew alarmed; the conversion of a prominent priest could make an impression on their flock, and they especially feared the influence of his propaganda, inasmuch as for some time heretical ideas had been circulating.

At the end of the eighth century the Spanish church was rocked by a debate between Elipando (archbishop of Toledo) and Felix (bishop of Urgel) and their opponents. Elipando and Felix championed the theory of adoptionism, one of the theories designed to solve the complex problem of the nature of Jesus, a problem that occupied so many church councils and caused divisions within the church. Elipando and Felix taught that one must discriminate carefully between the human and the godly aspects of Jesus. He who was of woman born suffered on earth and it was he who was crucified, as distinct from the son of God who for a time adopted the form of a human. Jesus was the son of God not by nature but by adoption—hence the term adoptionism.

Theologians who opposed the two bishops saw in this aspect a fragmentation of the personality of their savior, the man-God who in their view was one and one only. They held that even in his human aspect Jesus was the true son of God. He was not man (*homo*), but God-man (*Deus-homo*). The theology of Elipando and Felix was apparently influenced by Islam, which finds the apotheosis of man born of woman repugnant. Leading spokesmen from among the Christian theologians in Western Europe arose against Elipando and Felix, and even the pope became directly involved and compelled Felix to recant. But the views preached by Elipando and Felix were not eradicated from among the Christians in Moslem Spain until the middle of the ninth century.

In 839 a council of the clergy met in Cordova to consider sectarians who opposed the worship of relics, changed the method of baptism, and expressed views of their own regarding marriage and the eating of meat. Opposition to the worship of relics was surely influenced by contact with the Moslems and Jews.[18]

Thus church heads in Andalusia had good reason to fear Bodo's propaganda, which was likely to cause confusion among the populace and weaken their faith, which was already wavering and was exposed to influences they did not view with favor. For this reason one of the finest intellects in the Christian camp rose up to fight in its behalf against Bodo: Paulus Alvaro, one of the leaders of the Christians in Cordova. One of the ironies of history was that this Christian spokesman, who rose to do battle with the German priest who had become a Jew, was himself of Jewish derivation, apparently a descendant of those Jews who were forced to be converted to Christianity during the rule of the Visigoths.[19]

Alvaro was a scion of a wealthy family and throughout his life never had to worry about a livelihood. Possessed of outstanding abilities, he devoted himself to his studies diligently. Among the teachers who had a marked influence upon him one is mentioned especially: the abbot Spera-in-Deo, who had written a polemic against Islam. Alvaro did not become a priest, but he wrote in behalf of the church, producing works on Christian ethics and epistles to the heads of the Spanish church of his day and even trying his hand at poetry. Actually, his writing shows more learning than independence of thought. At all events, he had much influence on the Christians in Cordova and throughout Andalusia, because of both his social status and his literary activities.

A literary debate developed between Bodo and Alvaro, an exchange of letters in Latin that lasted for some time and stirred much excitement among Jews and Christians alike. The time of the debate is known because Alvaro says in one of his letters that he wrote this particular letter in 840.[20] Bodo's letters were not preserved, for a Christian reader who despised the arguments against Christianity destroyed the manuscript. But from Alvaro's replies and arguments one can infer the arguments of Bodo. He cited the rabbinic sages and commented on the Bible from the Christian viewpoint. Alvaro's style is artificial, in keeping with the style of his times. He adorned his writing with information gleaned from the classics and tried to show off his learning. His arguments are hackneyed and unoriginal. Alvaro opened his polemic with an appeal to Bodo that contained forced expressions of Christian love and exaggerated humility. This style annoyed Bodo-Eliezer, who was, even without this provocation, imbued with zeal. He attacked Alvaro personally, accusing him, among other things, of being mercenary. Then Alvaro became angry and he turned on his opponent quite sharply.

In his first letter to Eliezer[21] and in all the others Alvaro tries to prove that Jesus is the Messiah for whom the Jews have waited, and for proof he cites verses from the Bible which Christian polemicists have used throughout the centuries. In Jacob's blessing (Genesis 49:10) we find the words: "The sceptre shall not depart from Judah,/Nor the ruler's staff from between his feet,/As long as men come to Shiloh;/And unto him shall the obedience of peoples be." Yet, says Alvaro, in our times Israel has neither a Temple nor a king—whence it can be inferred that Jesus is Shiloh the Messiah.

The prophet Hosea says (3:4–5): "For the children of Israel shall sit solitary many days without king, and without prince, and without sacrifice, and without pillar, and without ephod or teraphim." These kings, the Christian writer explains, are the kings of the days of the second Temple, who were not of the seed of David, but nobles, as is implied by the words of the prophet. At all events, we find that until the time of Jesus, the Jews had their own rule.

Alvaro also cites the words of Daniel (9:26): "An anointed one [shall] be cut off, and be no more; and the people of a prince that shall come shall destroy the city and the sanctuary," and maintains that all this was fulfilled in Jesus, inasmuch as the city of Jerusalem was destroyed after his death.

Finally, Alvaro attempts to prove that the time of Jesus is alluded to in our Scriptures. He cites Leviticus (23:15): "And ye shall count unto you from the morrow after the day of rest, from the day that ye brought the sheaf of the waving; seven weeks shall there be complete." Alvaro gives the following interpretation: And you shall count unto you seven weeks of years, or forty-nine years.[22] "A week" in the Scriptures indicates seven years. Daniel prophesies (9:25) that the Messiah will come when seventy weeks are complete, which means 490 years, the time that elapsed between the days of Daniel and the coming of Jesus, according to Alvaro.

Bodo replied in a letter in which he contradicted the interpretation of Alvaro, such as that "week" means seven years. He made his own reckonings of the time when the Messiah was to come based partly on Daniel 12:12: "Happy is he that waiteth, and cometh to the thousand three hundred and five and thirty days." Bodo held that by his reckoning the Messiah would come in twenty-seven years. He tried also to prove by other means that Jesus was not the intended Messiah. He points out that his sufferings, such as his death on the cross, are not properly appropriate for the savior-redeemer.

Alvaro opened his second letter to Bodo with the complaint that Bodo's mode of writing contains a desecration of the Name and complains that Bodo insulted him and his ancestors. After this beginning, Alvaro again cites verses from the Scriptures which, according to him, deal with Jesus. The prophet Zechariah (11:12) mentions thirty pieces of silver, which in his view were the ones paid for Jesus. Isaiah 7:14 predicts: "The young woman [virgin] shall conceive, and bear a son." Alvaro further cites a verse out of the Wisdom of Solomon, insisting that the Jews removed the Wisdom of Solomon from the Scriptures because of this verse and proscribed the reading of it. Generally speaking, Alvaro holds, the Jews erased from the Scriptures or in some manner falsified those verses which speak of Jesus. In Deuteronomy 21:23 they added the word God ("for he that is hanged is a reproach unto God") in order to imply a reference to Jesus (that is, the crucified God, God whom they had crucified), for nowhere else in the Scriptures is the name of God appended to a curse. As to Bodo's reckoning of the "end," Alvaro argues that from the words of Josephus it can be inferred that he regarded the destruction of Jerusalem as the one Daniel had said would come in the days of the Messiah.

Bodo's answer hinged on the topic "Israel the Chosen People." This people received the Torah on Mount Sinai and keeps its statutes and judgments. Its mission is to bring salvation to the world through keeping the laws and statutes of the Torah, for without them there can be no redemption. The converted writer quotes Isaiah 40:15: "Behold, the nations are as a drop of a bucket,/And are counted as the small dust of the balance"; and Isaiah 60:2: "For, behold, darkness shall cover the earth,/And gross darkness the peoples;/But upon thee the Lord will arise,/And His glory shall be seen upon thee"; and Psalms 147:20: "He hath not dealt so with any nation;/And as for His ordinances, they have not known them." The Christians do not observe the commandments of the Torah; hence there is no salvation in their religion. Further on Bodo attacked the belief in the Trinity and based his view on Jeremiah 17:5: "Thus saith the Lord:/Cursed is the man that trusteth in man."

In the third and longest of his letters to Bodo, Alvaro seeks to prove that the Christians are the true people of Israel, the chosen community. From the very prophecy of Isaiah on which Bodo leans, it can be concluded that God has rejected the Jews. We read ahead in the text (Isaiah 40:17): "All the nations are as nothing before Him;/They are accounted by Him as things of nought, and vanity"; the Jews too are included in this principle.

As for Bodo's opinion on the observance of the Torah's commandments, Alvaro answers this with a quotation from Isaiah 43:18–19: "Remember ye not the former things,/Neither consider the things of old./Behold, I will do a new thing;/Now shall it spring forth." From the prophet's words we learn that the Jews were also given the new statutes. It is further stated there: "I will even make a way in the wilderness,/And rivers in the desert." The "way" refers to Jesus, according to John 14:6. Isaiah's prophecy was fulfilled in the acts of Jesus, who taught the nations of the world the laws of God.

Bodo's contention that only the Jews are chosen is contradicted, says Alvaro, by a verse of the prophet Malachi (1:11): "For from the rising of the sun even unto the going down of the same/My name is great among the nations;/And in every place offerings are presented unto My name,/Even pure oblations;/For My name is great among the nations,/Saith the Lord of hosts." In this quotation the Christian writer dwells on the phrase "among the nations"—that is, non-Jews.

As for Bodo's view that the royal House of David would endure forever, Alvaro maintains that this refers to the kingship of Jesus. In 2 Samuel 7:12–13 we read: "When thy days are fulfilled, and thou shalt sleep with thy fathers, I will set up thy seed after thee, that shall proceed out of thy body, and I will establish his kingdom. He shall build a house for My name, and I will establish the throne of his kingdom for ever." As is his wont, Alvaro distorts the meaning of the words, asking how a descendant could arise from David after his death and arguing that since this is impossible, it must mean that the seed of David who will build the Lord's house and whose kingdom will be established is none other than Jesus.

After attempting to contradict Bodo's arguments, Alvaro returns to his favorite method: selecting verses in the Scriptures which, according to Christian thinking, speak of their Messiah. Among others he cites Jeremiah 5:11, Isaiah 60:6, Psalms 22:28. In Isaiah 49:5, Alvaro finds proof for the doctrine of "incarnation," which is the very foundation of Christian theology. The prophet proclaims: "And now saith the Lord/That formed me from the womb to be His servant." Alvaro's contention is that this verse refers to Jesus, explaining it homiletically: through his mother (womb), Jesus is the servant; through his father, he is God. He holds that it is idle for Bodo to inveigh against him, in that he put his trust in a man ("Cursed is the man that trusteth in man"), seeing that Jesus is God. He defends the Trinity doctrine, stating that Christians do not believe in three gods but in one, for the three are one. In support of the doctrine of the Trinity he cites, among other sources, Genesis 1:26: "And God said: 'Let us make man in our image, after our likeness,' " and Isaiah 6:3: "And one called unto another, and said:/Holy, holy, holy, is the Lord of hosts"; he therefore maintains that the three are one.

Alvaro explains the matter of the conception as stemming from the Holy Ghost, and holds that this is not contrary to the idea of the holiness of God. Jesus' death on the cross is not a reproach but an honor. At the close of the letter the Christian writer cites many verses from the prophets to prove that the Jews wait in vain for salvation, for the prayer will not be heard, even as was reiterated by the prophets.

Of two more letters, one from Bodo and one from Alvaro, only a few lines remain. Among other things, Bodo contended that his adversary reveals nothing new but instead gleans from Christian writers who preceded him.

Over and above the theological arguments, the two disputants also voiced many insults and invectives. Bodo-Eliezer wrote that he forsook a faith that was deceitful, inferior, and despised; Alvaro charged the proselyte with conversion for the pleasures of the flesh. Naturally, passions were inflamed in both camps. These letters were destined for the general populace; they were read and spread by Jews and Christians throughout the cities of Spain. Moreover, the fact of Bodo's conversion created a stir in the whole Christian world. They could not accept in silence this desertion of his faith by a priest of the French emperor's court.

Amulo, the archbishop of Lyons, exploited this incident by

composing a screed steeped in venom. In his treatise, *Against the Jews*, the prince of the church writes that many Christians do not realize how dangerous contact with the Jews can be—even for theologians. His intent, he states, is to show how one should conduct oneself in this matter in consonance with the tenets of the church. He refers to the laws of the Christian emperor of Rome, the opinions of the church fathers, and the enactments of the popes. The Bodo incident, so widely discussed in clerical circles, serves him as an example. He avers that such an incident has never happened before. The emperor's priest has been led astray by Jews, who enticed him with blandishments of Satan himself—so much so that he has forsaken the palace of the emperor, the land of his birth, and his parents to join the Jews of Spain. Amulo describes Bodo for his readers as "sitting each day in Satan's houses of worship, bearded, and married and profaning the name of the Nazarene and his church, even as do all the Jews."[23]

In Spain itself this polemic did not remain within the confines of a literary debate. The Jewish leaders saw this an an opportunity to attack the Christians, to make them odious to the Moslems and impress the ruling powers. They intended to take as much advantage of the conversion of the distinguished priest as possible. Bodo-Eliezer proclaimed his views denigrating Christianity before the ruling powers, incited to this course by the Jewish leaders. Later he went to Cordova, the capital of the Spanish-Moslem kingdom, where he continued his propaganda. According to the Christians, the convert proposed that the Moslem government compel the Christians, on pain of death, to forsake their faith and become Jews or Moslems.

In 847 the Christians sent a letter to Karl the Bald, emperor of the Franks, and to the bishops throughout his kingdom, requesting the emperor to demand that the emir in Cordova turn Bodo over to him.[24] This is the last detail known to us about the priest who converted and riveted upon himself the eyes of the populace of Moslem Spain for a period of ten years.

The dispute with the convert Bodo-Eliezer was one of the incidents that aroused the ire of those Christians in the Omayyad kingdom who could not adapt themselves to Moslem rule. Despite the tolerance of the emirs, the Christians were experiencing the bitter taste of being a religious group that was subservient to the rule of another. This taste was all the more bitter since the Christians had once been the rulers in this selfsame land, and the majestic edifices in every city of Spain bore silent witness to the splendor of the dominance of the church in days gone by. The Moslem masses began to demonstrate signs of fanatic zeal and at every opportunity would taunt the Christian clergy.

To be sure, this distress and the embitterment caused by subsequent status did not prevail among all Christians. The greater majority meshed themselves into the life of the country, just as the Jews had. They adopted the Arabic language and Arabic customs and strove to imitate them in every respect, except that they held fast to their faith. But a small minority of zealots, mainly priests and monks, would not make their peace with Moslem rule, and it was they who, at the end of the reign of 'Abdarraḥmān II, provoked a severe crisis in the relations between the Christians and Moslems, a crisis which also engulfed the Jews.

These priests and monks, who exaggerated the situation, considered themselves degraded and downtrodden by the ruling powers and the Moslem masses. For this reason and also because they regarded with utter contempt the dominant faith, which they did not hold in esteem or want to recognize, these zealots felt themselves to be superior and exalted. To them it seemed that they were being persecuted because of their superiority. A mystic fervor welled up within them, a mood which did not reckon with realities.

This faction was led by Eulogius, who was cloaked in blind zeal. He was a disciple of the abbot Spera-in-Deo and a friend of Alvaro's. Eulogius preached to his fellow Christians to foster

Latin-Christian culture and not grovel before the Moslems; he endeavored with all his power to rouse in them the feeling that their religion was superior. He dashed from church to church and from monastery to monastery stirring up and inspiring his hearers.

The zealous priests who had read the lives of the saints of the church, the adored martyrs, and deemed to be themselves superior human beings, began to dream of self-sacrifice as the pinnacle of life. In order to achieve a halo of sanctity, they appeared before Moslem courts and publicly reviled the dominant faith and the memory of Mohammed. In accordance with the strict sense of the law, Moslem judges should have sentenced them to death, which was what the Christian zealots desired. The judges and the authorities sought to avoid bloodshed that might inflame passions and tried to persuade the zealots to recant, but their efforts were in vain; to their chagrin, they were forced to execute the Christians.

Moreover, yet another factor was involved. The tranquil atmosphere that had prevailed in the relationships between the various communities and the many mixed marriages between Moslems and Christians had from time to time resulted in the conversion of someone who had been reared as a Moslem to Christianity, the faith of his father or mother. Moslem authorities shut their eyes, even though according to their law this was the severest of transgressions, one which called for the death sentence. As an outcome of this mystic awakening at the end of the 840s, these apostates began to proclaim their conversion publicly, in order to earn the crown of martyrdom. The authorities acted with leniency and asked the converts to return to the right path—to no avail. In the end they had to carry out the law and put them to death.

So the number of those executed grew; the funeral processions of the martyrs made their way through the streets, and the fervent preachers made their eulogies. Thus the atmosphere of religious zealotry that was characteristic of Spain for several centuries was created.

This movement started in the capital of the kingdom, Cordova, the center of attention of all Spain. Hence the concern of the government waxed ever stronger, but despite this the number of those who perished grew apace.

This state of affairs began in 850. In a debate with Moslems a priest called Perfectus had insulted the memory of Mohammed and had been executed. Somewhat later a Christian merchant got into an argument with his competitors, who accused him of swearing by the life of their prophet in order to praise his wares and attract customers. The Christian merchant became excited and shouted that he would never again swear by Mohammed, adding that he who did so should be accursed. He was flogged and led through the streets mounted backward on a donkey. In 851 the situation worsened. A monk named Isaac came before a Moslem court, reviled the memory of Mohammed, and invited the judge to become a Christian. He was executed. Two days later a Christian soldier of the militia did the same thing. He was beheaded. This was on a Friday in June. On the following Sunday two monks and four priests stationed themselves before a Moslem judge, reviled Mohammed, and were executed. During July two other priests and a monk did the selfsame thing and paid for it with their lives.

Naturally, this aroused a great furor in the capital of Spain. The acts of these Christian zealots became the subject of conversation for all the inhabitants of the city. Among the Christians themselves confusion reigned. The majority feared that the zealots would bring catastrophe upon them. The authorities, who wanted to cool down tempers, imprisoned the chief instigators, among whom was Eulogius. But even in prison Eulogius continued his activities. He found there two young women: one had been reared as a Moslem but had appeared before a Moslem court to avow her Christian faith; her companion was a nun who wanted to die for her religious beliefs. Eulogius encouraged the two women not to recant; they withstood the appeals of the Moslems and were executed. Later the leaders of the zealots were released from prison by the authorities, in the hope that the excitement would die down. Their hopes proved vain.

In 852 the chain of self-destruction for the glorification of their religion continued. At the beginning of the year two churchmen reviled the memory of Mohammed and were executed. In the middle of the year a rich convert and his wife, a relative and his wife, and a monk who had come from Palestine to gather alms in Spain were all put to death. During August two more monks were added to the list of zealots who sacrificed their lives in this manner.

Thus the atmosphere in Cordova became ever heavier. Both Christians and Moslems were aroused and angry. The Jews kept to themselves and did not become involved. But before long the face of the matter took on a new guise.

3

CHAOS IN MOSLEM SPAIN

I

The sun shone high in the heavens, and its rays shed light and warmth over the peninsula; nevertheless, the Great Mosque of Cordova was shrouded in shadow and a chill could be felt from its thick walls. Whoever entered the broad expanse of its prayer hall instantly forgot the world without, for he found himself in a maze of tall decorated columns. These numerous columns—which stood on no bases, as though they grew out of the earth—were adorned with sculptured and carved capitals that were joined at the top with arches of hewn stone and vari-colored bricks or even bedecked with ornate Arabic script. They stood close to one another and were so numerous that the eye could not take them all in, as in a dense forest. But in the middle of this hall there was a broadening out in the columns, and there one could see a recess that showed the direction to Mecca, to which all Moslems turn in prayer.

It was Friday, near noon, and the thousands of the faithful who were gathered for festive worship stood thronged among the columns, all garbed in their beautiful white robes but bare-foot, as was their custom in their houses of prayer. Their hearts were directed to the omnipotent God and to Mohammed, His prophet, and their persons were directed to the recess, which they called *miḥrāb*. In a mighty voice they proclaimed as one, "God is great," bowed to the ground until their hands touched the floor, and then arose, lifting their hands heavenward. After this they knelt and touched the ground with their foreheads. Again they arose and continued to pray half sitting, half kneeling and again they prostrated themselves. Row by row they stooped on the stone floor, their headdresses pushed back, so that if one had looked inside at that moment he would have seen white mounds which entirely filled the hall. The ceremony had almost come to an end, for they had already come to the last of the four segments of the Friday prayer.

The worship proceeded in exemplary fashion until all at once silence fell upon the congregants, and the recitation of the benedictions and the verses of the Koran was interrupted. A voice resounded through the space, urging the worshipers to forsake their faith, to profane that which they held sacred, and to prefer that which they had despised. It was the voice of a Christian monk who had penetrated the mosque in order to preach to the Moslems and to turn them away from their prophet. The preaching voice sounded strange, for this old monk was a eunuch. (A second monk who stood beside him to encourage him was also a eunuch.) Such an incident—the profanation of the dominant faith in the Great Mosque and in the presence of thousands—had never before happened; the entire congregation stood dumbfounded. But it quickly bestirred itself; those nearest the monks seized them and, being consumed with anger, might have torn them to pieces, had not the judge of Cordova, who was the leader of the service in the Great Mosque, approached and restrained them.

The monks who had reviled the name of Mohammed were removed from the hall, and the prayer concluded with great excitement. But on the same day a trial was held; it was of but short duration. Both monks were condemned to death. First, their hands and feet were cut off, then their heads were severed, and what remained of their bodies was hung in a public place. This happened on September 16, 852. Only a day before two Christian zealots had reviled Islam and its prophet in order to attain martyrdom. The emotional pitch in the capital of Spain reached its peak.

The Omayyad government became frightened by the acts of the Christian zealots and determined to take steps to calm inflamed emotions and to deter outbreaks. It was decided to call, without delay, an assembly of the priests of all the cities of the kingdom, in order to get the ordained heads of the church to prohibit their flocks from following the zealots. The government adopted this method knowing full well that many Christians were opposed to this zealot sect and desired with all their hearts to establish normal relationships with their Moslem neighbors. However, the bishops who assembled for a council in Cordova at the invitation of the government did not dare condemn the zealots in explicit terms, and contented themselves with warning their fellow Christians not to destroy themselves in order to sanctify their faith. They refrained from pronouncing judgment against those already condemned to death because of their actions, on whose heads the zealots had put a crown of martyrdom. The council's decisions were thus ambiguous, and the bishops' pronouncements were of no avail.

Meanwhile, the emir, 'Abdarraḥmān II, died, and his son, Muḥammad I (852–886), succeeded him. This new king of Moslem Spain took a stronger position against the Christians. He was even more under the influence of Moslem theologians than his father had been and was determined to crush this mystic movement among the Christians, which could lead to dire consequences. Immediately after the council, an order was issued to imprison the leaders of the zealots and those bishops who regarded them favorably, thereby encouraging them. The leaders of the zealot sect went into hiding, but some were caught and imprisoned, among them Saul, the bishop of

Cordova. At the same time, the Christians were dismissed from the militia and pressure was put upon Christian government officials to forsake their religion and become Moslems.

The employment of Christians and Jews as officials in the service of Moslem governments had always roused the ire of the Moslem zealots, who saw in this a degradation of their religion. They argued that the appointment of Christians and Jews to government posts signified the placing of authority over the faithful into the hands of infidels—all the more so because in the view of Moslem theologians it was permissible for non-Moslems to live in a Moslem state only if they were inferior in status. On the other hand, in all Moslem lands Christians and Jews supplied a great number of educated men who ably carried on the administration of the government, to the extent that the Moslem rulers could not dispense with their services. At times they would yield to the demands of the devout of their faith and dismiss the non-Moslem officials. This was the procedure of Moslem kings who desired to attract to their camp those theologians who exercised great influence, or rulers who were apprehensive of alliances between non-Moslems officials and other powers in which their coreligionists dominated. However, by and large, after a short time elapsed their positions would be restored to the non-Moslems. In some countries, such as Egypt, the non-Moslems had complete control over the machinery of government, and there were times when they did not allow a Moslem to set foot in certain departments.

The demand for dismissal of non-Moslem officials became one of the important slogans of the Moslem zealots, and the struggle for status in the service of the government ran like a scarlet thread throughout the history of the Jews and Christians in Islamic lands. According to Arabic writers of the Middle Ages, 'Umar I (634–644) had forbidden the employment of non-Moslem officials. Caliph 'Umar II (717–720) apparently attempted to dismiss these officials and turned to the provincial governors in this matter; but even if his directive was implemented, it was merely a passing phenomenon. Throughout the days of the Omayyads the offices of the caliph's government were conducted by non-Moslem officials.

With the rise of the devout Abbasid dynasty the situation changed, especially since in the meantime a stratum of educated Moslems had flourished. The first caliph who was diligent in dismissing non-Moslems was al-Mutawakkil. This was in the year 235 of the *hidjra* (849/850 C.E.), precisely at the time the Cordovan Omayyad oppression of Christian officials began.

This represented a significant change in the history of Moslem Spain. The fact is that in this country Christian as well as Jewish officials apparently played an important role throughout the eighth and the first half of the ninth century without any enemies arising to oppose their status or threaten them with dire consequences. Even Muḥammad I did not employ severe measures against the non-Moslem officials, and stories told by Christian writers concerning his restrictive measures are exaggerations and readily refuted.[1] In general, Christians and Jews were put into the same category whenever the ire of the devout in any Moslem country was aroused against non-Moslem officials, even though their intention was mainly to get rid of the Christian officials, who were more numerous and seemed to constitute more of a threat. At times Arabic chroniclers speak of the dismissal of the "Christian officials," and we may add "and their colleagues, the Jews, who suffered because of them"; however, there can be no doubt that in this case the Omayyad ruler did not include the Jews. Muḥammad also embraced the political tolerance characteristic of the Omayyad dynasty to the extent he thought it feasible.

The government oppressed the Christians in yet another fashion. It aggravated the yoke of taxation that they had to bear, which was already burdensome enough. Christian writers relate that Muḥammad I also ordered the destruction of the churches built during Moslem rule and those structures added during this period to the older churches. The question of non-Moslem houses of worship was one of the chief problems in the complex of relationships between the Moslems and the non-Moslem communities under their dominion. Although Muḥammad I published a decree to destroy the new places of worship, he was only carrying out Moslem law forbidding construction of non-Moslem houses of worship within his domain. According to Christian sources, in complying with this decree the Moslems also destroyed churches that had been erected many generations before, but even here they exaggerate greatly.

It appears that in actuality the Moslems destroyed only one convent, that of Tabanos, near Cordova, which happened in the second half of 854. This convent had served as a center for Christian zealots.[2] We cannot refer to this as a persecution of Christians. The Moslem government was merely trying to restore the rule of order: the Christian zealots had stirred up unrest in the capital, therefore measures had to be taken against them. The stronger faction among the Christians, which feared the results of the zealots' activity, sided at all times with the government. This faction feared that the Moslems would identify them, the moderates, with the zealots and that they would suffer material losses as well as the loss of positions and income. This stratum included, of course, the wealthy and the government officials and all those who were more concerned with this world than with the next. The more consistent of this faction converted to the dominant faith.

However, Eulogius and his followers did not despair. They continued their propaganda. Fanatic monks appeared before the Moslem judges, insulted the memory of the prophet of Islam, and were executed. Finally, Eulogius himself met this fate in 859. To be sure, when the movement had lost its leader, it ebbed. But the fanaticism that had aroused Eulogius was not extinguished.

Christian zealots continued to vaunt the superiority of Latin-Christian culture and to make light of Arab-Moslem culture, while in their heart of hearts they dreamt of the day when the proud grandeur of the Moslems would be brought low and the yoke of their dominion would be removed from their necks. Even more than they disliked the Moslems, the zealots hated the Christian moderates who cooperated with the Moslem authorities. The majority of the moderate faction acted with discernment. They realized the necessity to adapt themselves to circumstances, inasmuch as this would make it possible for Christians to pursue normal lives, as individuals and as a community.

But there were some among them who were avid of honor, who pursued wealth and sought close ties with the ruling powers. One such was Servando, who was designated head of the Christian community of Cordova and who, with the authority of the government, collected heavy taxes from his fellow Christians. A relative, Hostegesis, was bishop of Málaga; of him it was said that he used the alms contributed by the Christians to give presents to the nobles and awarded priestly preferments for a price. Hostegesis had both many supporters and many enemies—especially after he began to make public his theological opinions. To avoid being identified with a pantheistic outlook, Hostegesis taught that only the Lord's spirit is manifest throughout the whole universe. Against this his opponents could not argue at all, for at the very worst he had stated that the spirit of the Lord is *necessarily* manifest in all things. Hostegesis also expressed the opinion that Mary had carried Jesus in her heart, not in her womb.

Such statements elicited many complaints from pious Christians, and those who possessed the ability to express their views in writing rose up to dispute him. This faction was headed up by an abbot, Samson, a cleric in the church where Eulogius had once served as priest. But like the fanatics who had condemned Hostegesis and his opinions, the bishop of

Málaga (who had meanwhile come to Cordova) also accused Samson of sectarianism and impiety. Samson put his principal views in writing, his "credo," as it were, which he presented to the council of bishops of Andalusia that met at Cordova in 862. The council discussed the theological questions seriously and, under pressure from Hostegesis, condemned Samson. The bishops decided to dismiss him from the priesthood; they excommunicated him, and imposed exile from Cordova on him.

But the design of Hostegesis and his colleagues was nullified. Some bishops who had not participated in the council held that the principles of Samson were correct, and some who had taken part in the assembly of the clergy changed their minds. Moreover, Valentius, the bishop of Cordova, annulled the council's decree; and since the clergy and the church community in which Samson officiated had decided to appoint him head of its clergy, the bishop confirmed their choice.

These steps naturally enraged Hostegesis and Servando. Nor did they sit idly by; in 863 they convened a new council at Cordova in order to reaffirm the decisions of the earlier clerical assembly. Hostegesis's opponents, the leaders of the fanatical faction, did not dare appear at this meeting to voice their objections, knowing full well that Hostegesis and Servando had acted with the knowledge and support of the government, inasmuch as they had promised to wring additional taxes from the Christians. A discernible number of the invited therefore absented themselves from the council, and when notable men among the Christians in the city were looked for to seat them in the assembly, it was discovered that they had left the city. Hostegesis and his followers were thus compelled, in order to maintain the council, to include in it Moslems and Jews.[3] Matters had indeed gone quite far. The tables were now turned. At the very assemblies that had formerly enacted oppressive legislation against the Jews, now, in the middle of the ninth century, Jews sat and decided what the correct tenets of Christianity were and what was needed for the welfare of the church!

This episode illustrates the consistency with which the Jews of Spain followed the course they had set for themselves. They tied their destiny to Moslem dominion and stood by it in all areas of life as loyal aides. In that era their loyalty was conspicuous, in contrast to the sabotage the Christians practiced and the provocation indulged in by the zealot faction in Cordova; it stands to reason that their loyalty earned them a large measure of appreciation at the royal court.

In general, Omayyad rule in Spain was marked by its tolerance toward non-Moslems. It is likely that this tolerance was in essence deliberate and planned. Even emirs who were surrounded by theologians (*faḳīhs*) and sought to demonstrate their piety at every opportunity refrained from oppressing non-Moslems. This was apparently the result of the tradition of the Omayyad dynasty and the awareness that in Spain, where the Arab population was sparse, restraint and an effort to bring together and even merge the various ethnic elements must prevail. It is evident that of the two motives, the first took precedence, for other paths were available, such as the establishment of a large army of mercenaries from among the Berbers and the Spaniards to that point where numerical equality would prevail for both groups.

At all events, the Omayyads chose the path of restraint and understanding in respect to non-Moslems; however, they were not shown understanding by all segments of the non-Moslem population in the kingdom. Various factions of Christians negotiated with their coreligionists on the other side of the border, seeking aid from their kings while at the same time provoking their rulers and causing disturbance in the realm; the result was that they profited in lesser degree from the tolerant attitude of the Omayyad government. The Jews, who were wholeheartedly loyal to the rulers, derived much benefit from this attitude.

It goes without saying that the council which assembled in 863 at Cordova, wherein Christians, Moslems, and Jews took part, was very docile, acquiescing in all that Hostegesis and Servando demanded. The bishop of Málaga propounded his views on Christian theology to the gathering, and the council affirmed them as correct tenets of the Christian church. It was also decided to dismiss Valentius as bishop of Cordova. Once again the moderates had the upper hand and the fanatics were rendered powerless. Samson left Cordova to find refuge in the city of Martos, where in 864 he wrote his treatise *Apologeticus,* which narrates in detail this entire episode.[4]

II

In the space of seven generations, the Spanish branch of the Omayyads provided a line of kings of varied talents, each in his own way. Even Muḥammad I was a distinguished ruler. Characterized by a keen mind and initiative, he personally supervised all the administrative affairs of the government. The responsibilities he carried were heavy, for in his day a Spanish nationalist revolutionary movement spread throughout all the provinces of the land that could have crumbled the Omayyad kingdom and completely destroyed the entire Moslem rule in the Iberian peninsula. It must be understood that national consciousness in that era was a matter of sentiment alone, with no clear discernment and no crystallized designs.

The insurgent movement, which quickly turned to armed rebellion, developed from the disgruntlement of native Spaniards and their progeny with Arabic oppression. The mass of *muwalladūn,* Moslems of Spanish origin, complained at the slight they endured from the Arabs. The arrogance of the Arabs offended the honor of the rich merchants and men of property. The wrath of the peasants was aroused by the oppression of the Arab landowners, who laid heavy taxes upon them. The artisans in the towns suffered on all sides. This movement therefore involved many classes: townspeople and farmers, landowners and laborers. The rebellion was especially dangerous because one of its manifest characteristics was the tie between the various rebel groups and the Christian kings of Asturias, the archenemies of the Omayyad kings. At first this was revealed merely as agitation expressing itself in isolated uprisings, but with passing time it grew ever stronger, until it became a powerful movement sweeping along with it almost all Spanish classes and bringing to the Moslem kingdom a state of chaos.

Immediately after Muḥammad I began his reign, the city of Toledo rebelled against him. The inhabitants of the revolting city made forays against the nearby regions, growing stronger and stronger. The city of Calatrava was abandoned by the militia. The troops from Toledo penetrated the valley of the Guadalquivir, vanquishing the Omayyad forces near the city of Andújar. However, the Omayyad returned blow for blow. He gathered a strong force, attacked Toledo, and routed the rebels near the city, who had been augmented by auxiliaries of the king of Asturias. The defeat which the men of Toledo suffered in this battle, in June 854, was severe. Nevertheless, the armies of the government could not break through into the city itself, and two years later they besieged the city without success. In 858 Muḥammad I himself laid siege to the city, and this time its inhabitants surrendered to him—that is, they recognized him as their sovereign ruler. The operation of the city's government remained in the hands of the inhabitants. In the 870s the people of Toledo endeavored to nullify even this dependence, but when the emir of Cordova appeared before the city in 873 with a large army, they reconsidered; they promised to pay him taxes and gave him hostages.

Even in other provinces of Spain, governors and influential chieftains revolted against the government of Cordova and became virtually independent princes. The family of the Banū Ḳasī founded a big principality in the provinces which later became known as the kingdom of Aragon. 'Abdarraḥmān b. Marwān founded a principality in the western part of Omayyad Spain, with Mérida as its capital. Both the Banū Ḳasī and Ibn Marwān, who were of Christian origin, entered into relations with the Christian rulers of northern Spain.

However, even more menacing than the revolts in Toledo, the Ebro Valley, and the west was the rebellion that broke out in Andalusia in the last days of Muḥammad I. What happened there was all the more serious because this was the most important province, the heartland of the Spanish-Moslem kingdom, both because in it was located the capital city and because of the density of its Arab settlement. This uprising also frightened the royal court because of the dauntless man who initiated it. 'Umar b. Ḥafṣūn was a member of an affluent family of *muwalladūn* that lived in the province of Ronda. From the days of his youth he could not adapt himself to a normal civilian mode of life, and in 880 he gathered around him a band of armed men, initiating the kind of guerrilla warfare typical of civil wars in Spain. The fortress of Bobastro in the valley of the Guadalhorce River, which is in the north of the province of Málaga, served as his base of operations. From there he organized raids, which at first were mere depredations. He attacked caravans of merchants and made onslaughts on rich estates of Arab landholders in the lowlands between Campilios and Cordova, took whatever spoils he could, and returned to his base.

The activities of Ibn Ḥafṣūn aroused great joy among the populace of the province of Málaga, most of whom were *muwalladūn*; many poor peasants would come to him for a loan. Youths who had nothing worthwhile to look forward to within the prevailing order, irreligious men, and in general reckless and irresponsible fellows soon filled the ranks of Ibn Ḥafṣūn's band.

From the first moment Ibn Ḥafṣūn emphasized the anti-Arab character of his movement. He never harmed the peasants among the *muwalladūn*. On the contrary, he began to stir them up against the Arabic rulers, who, according to him, drained their very lifeblood. He explained to them that he intended to bring them deliverance and to free them from the oppressive yoke the foreign conquerors had laid upon them. In 883 the emir's army that had besieged Bobastro forced him to surrender, and he was sent to Cordova and put into the Omayyad army. But after a year he fled to Bobastro and began his rebellious activities anew. With redoubled energy he turned to the peasants, spurring them to rise up against their Arab overlords and to support him in his struggle with the Omayyad government. Fortune smiled on him, and he conquered a number of fortresses in that region; these became the nucleus for the independent government over a wide area of southern Spain that was later to come into being.

Thus the area over which the Omayyad emir ruled in the north, west, and south shrank more and more. Nevertheless, the Omayyad kingdom in the days of Muḥammad I was still a rich one, with a very large income. And the military power of the emir was also considerable. In 859 the Normans appeared on the shores of Spain and fell upon Algeciras and then on Murcia, but this was no more than a mere episode, changing nothing in the course of diplomacy or the balance of power.

The Omayyad government was engaged, as always, in a never-ending struggle with the Christian kingdoms in northern Spain. In spite of the trouble that the many uprisings gave it, the emir's government still had sufficient power to carry on this war, which it viewed as its chief obligation—indeed, as a holy war. These military ventures against the Christians were not always undertaken directly by the armies of the government. Rather, it was the vassal princes, especially the Banū Ḳasī from the Ebro region, who performed an important function in this war, whether they fought their Christian neighbors on their own initiative or because they were requested by the emir of Cordova to invade their territory.

Thus in the days of Muḥammad I the Iberian peninsula was in the grip of endless military campaigns. Again and again the emir's armies invaded the Spanish kingdoms to the north, and the troops of the king of Asturias attacked the border districts of Moslem Spain. Within the Omayyad kingdom the government troops fought stubbornly with the various rebels. Everywhere one saw armed bodies of soldiers; rumor followed rumor.

With the country in such an inflamed state, no group within the populace could stay aloof. Each group pinned its hopes for a better and easier life on the success of one of the warring armies, and anybody who was hot-tempered and physically fit enough himself took up arms and joined the fighting. The Jews who dwelt in the Spanish cities were among those who took a definite stand in the bitter struggles between the Moslems vis-à-vis the Christians and between the Arabs and the *muwalladūn*. They too gave their blessings to the armies whose success they desired, helping them actively in various ways. Their position in the war between the armies of the emir of Cordova and the Christian kingdoms to the north could have only one meaning: they supported the Moslems wholeheartedly. They were convinced that despite the pride of the Arab rulers and rigid Moslem legislation with regard to the status of non-Moslems inside their borders, their position in Moslem Spain was immeasurably better than it had once been under Visigothic rule—so they had been told by their elders.

To be sure, in deciding whose victory was more likely to improve the status of the Jews and Judaism and whose victory would result in hardship for them, they did not have to ask their elders to repeat stories handed down from their forebears concerning those remote days when the Visigothic kings ruled Spain. They had only to note what was happening in their own time in the Christian kingdoms in northern Spain. Extreme fanaticism raged unrestrained. The kings of Asturias did not tolerate Moslems within their borders. Moslem theologians who were captured by Christian soldiers were slain out of hand, and such Moslems who remained in their kingdom were compelled to become Christians. The routes followed by Christian armies in their campaigns were marked by mosques that had been put to the torch. At the same time, the Christian rulers bitterly persecuted anyone suspected of heresy and burned alive men and women who were reputed to be witches. Great indeed was the difference in the attitude toward other religious groups exhibited in the Omayyad kingdom and that of the Christians in the north. For this reason the Jews of Spain congratulated the Moslem armies on their triumphs and helped them as much as they could.

A trustworthy Christian source tells of the aid given by the Jews of Barcelona to the Moslem army that had come to besiege the city. This was one of the last attempts by the Moslems to reconquer this important city, which had been wrested from them at the beginning of that century. According to the Christian chronicler this occurred in 852. Arabic chronicles, which do not mention the Jews in this instance, speak of a number of campaigns against the Spanish March that were undertaken at this time. An Arabic historian writes that in the campaign of 850 many prisoners and much booty were taken and that the Moslem armies returned without suffering any losses.[5]

In 856 the Moslems again invaded the Spanish March. Mūsā b. Mūsā, who was asked by the emir of Cordova to undertake an expedition there, penetrated into Catalonia, reaching the vicinity of Barcelona and taking the fortress of Tarega, which lay between Lérida and the chief city of the March.[6]

A third campaign was undertaken, according to Arabic chroniclers, in 861. They relate that strong forces participated in the military action in that year, for the count of Barcelona asked for aid from the Franks, who sent him auxiliary troops. The Moslems also were given reinforcements. An Arabic writer recounts that in this campaign the Moslems laid siege to Barcelona, taking its suburbs and two turrets in the wall of the city.[7] Inasmuch as the aforementioned Latin chronicler died at the beginning of April 861, and military exploits would, of course, take place in the summer, it is impossible that he was writing about this campaign; he must have been referring to the hostilities of 856, or to an even earlier campaign. There is only a difference of two years between the date he gives (852) and the one given by the Arabic historian (850). But the Arabic source does not state that in 850 the Moslems reached Barcelona.[8] The Latin chronicler is able to relate that the Moslems penetrated to Barcelona because of treacherous action by the Jews of that city, and he adds that they killed nearly all the Christian inhabitants, destroyed the houses, and retreated without any losses.[9]

Whether Jews in the Moslem army conspired with their fellow Jews in the beleaguered city, or whether the Jews of Barcelona remembered what they had heard their parents tell of the favorable conditions they enjoyed under Moslem rule and in consequence helped the Moslems penetrate the city, the fact speaks for itself and clearly indicates the feelings of the Spanish Jew of that age. To evaluate this incident properly one must bear in mind that the attitude of the courts of the Spanish March to the Jews was surely much better in those days than that shown them by the Asturian kings.

The alternative confronting the Jews in consequence of the rebellions in various sections of the Spanish-Moslem kingdom was quite difficult. For a long period the Jews very consistently supported the existence of a unified and central government and were careful not to be drawn into conspiracies and uprisings against the emirs of Cordova. But during the rule of Muḥammad I they could not maintain this stand unwaveringly. In their secret heart they no doubt leaned as before toward the side of the Omayyad government, which promised its peaceful citizens security of life and property and protection against the willful actions of local officials and governors.

There was yet another consideration. A characteristic phenomenon marking the rebellions that shook the Spanish-Moslem kingdom in the ninth century was the growth of the influence of the Mozarabs, the Christians within the borders of Islamic rule. Their power grew steadily, and they endeavored to supplant the *muwalladūn,* the Spaniards who had converted to Christianity. The pacts that the rebels made with the Asturian kings naturally strengthened the influence of the Christians in the provinces under control of the rebels. Some of the nobles who had rebelled against the emir vacillated—for example, the Banū Ḳasī who had become Christians. But the strength and the perseverance of the rebels were great, and the prime concern of the Jews perforce had to be that relations with their neighbors should be proper. Since the main source of their livelihood came from their immediate environment and their fellow townsmen, the establishment of good-neighborly relationships was more important than speculative considerations.

The city of Toledo became independent at the outset of the reign of Muḥammad I and preserved its independence for eighty years. Inside the city factional disorders occurred, but the Jews no doubt were implored to show loyalty to the local governing authority. The Banū Ḳasī who held sway over the provinces of Aragon in the ninth century appear to have benefited from strong support among the populace. There is no doubt that the Jews in this region also cooperated with these feudal lords.

III

In the final days of Muḥammad I the breakup of the Spanish-Moslem kingdom went forward with great celerity. This was the result of a process that extended over a long time. The Spanish nationalist rebel movement, which was nourished by the dissatisfaction of the native Spaniards and their wrath over the attitude of the Arabs toward them, gradually flourished and grew—underground, as it were—and erupted forcefully in the 870s. The proud Arabic aristocracy, which abhorred strong monarchic government, took advantage of this opportunity to rid itself of the royal yoke. In those provinces where there was a large Arab population their leaders did all in their power to establish a government by tribal heads, to which they were accustomed from time immemorial. However, there was no unity among the Arabs, for the Ḳaisite tribes and the Yemenites had not yet forgotten their ancient rivalries. When the *muwalladūn* and the Arabs revolted everywhere and each man was preoccupied with his own concerns, the Berbers did not sit idly by. They too tried to snatch a share of the disintegrating kingdom. Thus Moslem Spain sank into chaos. Each person acted as he pleased, and the strongest prevailed. Stout-hearted captains and heads of tribes held sway over cities and fortresses, and the peace-loving citizenry was compelled to support their armies and finance their wars.

After the death of Muḥammad I, his son, al-Mundhir, who was of outstanding ability, ruled. He was courageous and active—a ruler noble in spirit who captivated all hearts. Arabic historians heap praises upon him and maintain that if he had lived longer, he would have crushed all the rebellions. But it was his ill fate to rule in Cordova for but two years (886–888). During his short reign he turned his energies mainly toward crushing the uprising initiated by 'Umar b. Ḥafṣūn. In 888 the government forces under the personal command of al Mundhir attacked him. The emir besieged the city of Archidona until it surrendered and conquered many fortresses in that province. After this he attacked the chief fortress of Ibn Ḥafṣūn, at Bobastro, and laid siege to it. The plight of the besieged became severe, and the emir's supporters already hoped to succeed in destroying the nest of the rebels.

But Ibn Ḥafṣūn tricked them. He entered into negotiations for surrender and promised to leave the fortress and to go to Cordova; when the parties had reached an understanding, he asked for a large number of beasts of burden. But when the emir sent him the animals, he kept them and shut the gates of Bobastro in the emir's face. Meanwhile, his forces had already scattered in the belief that the siege had been successfully terminated. Al-Mundhir wanted to recall the troops and continue the siege, but before he had time to fulfill his vow to take the fortress, he himself fell a victim. In the camp outside Bobastro he was poisoned by a doctor hired by his brother 'Abdallāh.

In this unsavory manner did 'Abdallāh come to the throne at Cordova, occupying it for twenty-four years (888–912). Al-Mundhir was not the only blood relation to be killed at his command. He murdered two more brothers and two sons. 'Abdallāh was of a suspicious nature and made his reckonings cold-bloodedly, being altogether without moral restraints. Yet combined with this was his piety; he diligently prayed and read the Koran often and was meticulous in the performance of acts of worship. It cannot be denied that he possessed an instinct for government. When he began to rule, the state of the Omayyad kingdom was at its lowest. Everywhere new rebellions erupted, province after province stopped paying taxes, and funds that remained in the treasury from better times were quickly expended; the emir lacked the power to maintain a large army. 'Abdallāh adopted a policy of vacillation whose purpose was to gain time and wait until the storm blew over. Having no other choice, he made his peace with the situation; regarding the rebels as his loyal vassals, he endeavored to keep the governors of the various provinces of Moslem Spain apart, inciting them against each other so that they would not unite to oppose him. Military campaigns by the government forces in his time had the collection of taxes as their main goal.

As depicted in the pages of the chronicles, this emir surely did not attract men to him, but in the last analysis he did fulfill his objectives. With the passage of time the various rebels grew weary, and the path was cleared for the reestablishment of the monarchy on a firm foundation.

When Arabic historians of the late Middle Ages come to the period of the reign of Emir 'Abdallāh and find a wealth of information in their sources about various rebels who controlled the provinces of Spain, they become confused, giving us primarily lists of names of rebels and the areas over which they held sway. No doubt such a review is bound to present some sort of a picture of the condition prevailing in the government at that time. However, the nobles and officers who spread their dominion over cities and provinces, heads of tribes and parties who fought each other—all were overshadowed by 'Umar b. Ḥafṣūn.

When 'Abdallāh ruled in his brother's stead and the rebel movement spread throughout the length and breadth of Spain, 'Umar b. Ḥafṣūn reached the acme of his influence. His heroic exploits acquired for him a great reputation, and all the *muwalladūn* regarded him as their true leader. He cast fear and terror into the Arabs in the palaces of Cordova. Mothers told their infants about the chief of the brigands, ugly of face and possessing a bulbous nose, who lurked in waiting for his victims with drawn sword. Even the preachers in the mosques, who exhorted their listeners to repent of their wrongdoing and admonished them to beware of God's wrath, did not fail to mention the terrible anger of 'Umar b. Ḥafṣūn. His forces grew very powerful and spread over all the provinces of Andalusia like the mighty waters of a river which rises out of its bed and overflows its banks.

But this courageous commander acted without any clear aim, changing his goal from time to time. There were times when he proposed to the Abbasid caliphs that he act as their deputy in Spain; at other times he would enter into discussions with the Christian king of Asturias; again he would reach a compromise with Emir 'Abdallāh and recognize his overlordship. On another occasion he sought to make a compact with the rebels everywhere in Spain, for example, with the Banū Ḳasī. Ultimately the absence of any clear destination brought him to grief and caused his movement to fail.

But in the early years of Emir 'Abdallāh's reign, he was the uncrowned king of Andalusia, from Algeciras to Murcia. His depredations carried him from the villages and farms in the valley of the Guadalquivir to the gates of the capital. In the district of Priego his loyal ally Sa'īd b. Mastana held sway, and most of the fortified areas in the province of Jaén were controlled by his faithful associates. In 889 he captured the city of Écija, and the menace to Cordova grew larger than ever. The weak emir girded his strength, gathered whatever forces he could, regulars and irregulars, and attacked 'Umar b. Ḥafṣūn. Although the number of rebels was twice as large as the army of 'Abdallāh and though they were trained for war and experienced in battle, the unexpected happened: Ibn Ḥafṣūn was defeated near the capital in May 891.

'Abdallāh exploited his victory by penetrating into those provinces that had formerly accepted the authority of 'Umar b. Ḥafṣūn, and the cities of Écija, Archidona, Elvira, and Jaén opened their gates to him. It is true that in the following year Ibn Ḥafṣūn succeeded in conquering three of these cities —Archidona, Elvira, and Jaén—but his path of conquest was checked. Before long he had lost Elvira, while 'Abdallāh waxed stronger and began to assemble his forces. Then 'Umar b. Ḥafṣūn took the decisive step of his life: he changed his faith. Having been a Moslem, he became a Christian.

In essence this was a protest on the part of a Spanish patriot who wanted to draw a line between himself and the alien rulers who professed the faith of Islam. At the same time we can assume that the link binding Ibn Ḥafṣūn to Islam never was very strong and that his heart opened to various influences and persuasions. In any case, his family, his household, and his aides all became Christians.

When his conversion to Christianity became known, the fight against him turned into a holy war, a *djihād*. Some of his supporters, who though *muwalladūn* were nevertheless loyal Moslems, deserted him, and the *faḳīh*s urged their coreligionists to fight him to the bitter end. Henceforth a change occurred in the struggle between the emir and the rebels. The forces of the emir became the attackers. In the last ten years of 'Abdallāh's rule a campaign was launched each year against southern Andalusia, and success shone upon the emir. In 903 Jaén was taken, and one after another cities and fortresses in that area fell into the hands of the emir's forces.

In the provinces of Andalusia south of Guadalquivir there were more Jews than in any other province of Spain. In the many cities and towns of this part of the country the Jewish settlement was very old, and during the days of the first Omayyad rulers the number of communities increased. When the rebel bands and the government troops began to traverse the roads, everyone was challenged: Are you on our side or that of our foes? The segment of the population that was of Spanish origin, whether Moslem or Christian, sided overwhelmingly with 'Umar b. Ḥafṣūn. With all their hearts and with all their might the *muwalladūn* supported the rebel chief who, from time to time, would sally forth from his aerie, Bobastro, to wreak vengeance upon the Arabs. The *muwalladūn* of Granada pinned their hopes upon him after suffering a severe defeat at the hands of the Arabs in their vicinity. There were, to be sure, many among them who supported the emir, but the nationalists were stronger.

Even the Mozarabs in the capital blessed the weapons of 'Umar b. Ḥafṣūn, and a band of youths from their midst joined his forces. Their leader was the son of Servando, who in the days of Muḥammad I had been the leader of the moderate Christians who cooperated with the government. In 890 this group fled Cordova and entrenched itself in the fortress of Poley which is known today as Aguilar, south of the capital. The fortress of Poley served 'Umar b. Ḥafṣūn as an observation post, and the Mozarabs of Cordova fanned out from there to the surrounding areas of the capital each day, plundering and murdering in the villages.

The Jewish stand was the reverse of this. By and large the *muwalladūn* nobles were easygoing toward their subjects; they enforced order within their domain, set up an efficient administration, and were concerned with the welfare of all the inhabitants. As we learn from the Arabic chroniclers, the inhabitants of the eastern and southwestern portions of Spain were very satisfied with the rule of the *muwalladūn* nobles, and the Jews were most likely no exception in this matter and gave them their affection. But their position regarding 'Umar b. Ḥafṣūn was different from their attitude to the other rebel princes. Even before the Andalusian rebel chieftain had converted to Christianity he had been suspected of leaning toward Christianity, inasmuch as bands of Christians were conspicuous among his troops. When Emir 'Abdallāh defeated him in 891, he sentenced his Christian captives to death. The rebellion of 'Umar b. Ḥafṣūn was pictured by the emir's supporters as an armed uprising against Islam, and there is no question that the Jews had no interest in supporting such a movement. The prospect of the renewal of a Christian government in the plains of Andalusia frightened them. Even though they endured much from Arab arrogance, they knew that what awaited them from Christian rule, as exemplified by the Christian kingdoms in the northern part of the peninsula, could be much worse. One must not compare conditions at the end of the ninth century with those of the eleventh century, for by that time the Christian kingdoms were more humane, and even non-Christians could live under favorable conditions.

However, it was not only the religious aspect that decided the position the Jews took. The rebellion of 'Umar b. Ḥafṣūn was superimposed upon the socioeconomic revolt of the petty farmers of Spanish origin, the tenant farmers and the agricultural laborers. Ibn Ḥafṣūn incited them against their masters, urging them not to pay rent or give up any of their produce. This is clear from the comments of the Arabic chroniclers. 'Umar b. Ḥafṣūn was a mortal foe of the landowners, who were mainly Arabs.

Not only did his propaganda cause upheavals and disturbances in agricultural production, but it also created upsets in the marketing process. The landowners, who made a living from marketing their agricultural products, were no doubt interested in seeing that the big market of Cordova remained open, but the forays by Ibn Ḥafṣūn and the spread of his dominion cut off any trade with Cordova. The interests of the merchants and manufacturers, too, required that the large economic unit of which Cordova was the focal point should not be harmed. From this it can be inferred that the Jews, among whom there were many merchants and manufacturers, would not be interested in supporting Ibn Ḥafṣūn.

At the beginning of 891 the emir's situation seemed hopeless to his supporters. Almost all the cities of Andalusia south of Cordova were held by 'Umar b. Ḥafṣūn. When Écija was captured, it became the seat of his general staff. The towns of

Estera and Ossuna, south of Écija, were taken by him. Baena, southeast of Cordova, also fell into his hands.

One city remained faithful to the emir's rule—Lucena, whose population was mainly Jewish. At first glance, the city's plight was desperate, inasmuch as the Mozarabs of Cordova had gotten a foothold in Poley, twenty kilometers west of the city. One day early in spring several hundred rebel soldiers appeared before the walls of Lucena, some on mules and others afoot, and laid siege to the city. Many wore chain armor and iron helmets but many others wore only the ordinary dress of the Andalusian farmers: a heavy fur cloak.

Ibn Ḥafṣūn's men did not surround the city on all sides but took up positions opposite only a part of the wall, at a distance of several hundred meters. At first they showed no signs of action; they remained quiescent for an entire day. But on the second night, in the third watch, when the inhabitants of the city slept the sleep of the righteous, the men of Ibn Ḥafṣūn broke forth from their camp and quickly drew near the wall, threw many sacks filled with sand into the moat to enable them to come up to the wall itself, set ladders upon them, and endeavored to scale the wall. But the guards on the wall were alert. Some began throwing huge stones on the attackers; others called out reinforcements, and before long the attempt to surprise the inhabitants and take the city by storm came to naught.

The following day Ibn Ḥafṣūn's men began to assemble siege instruments from parts they had brought with them in their carts; they also installed movable protecting shields (mantelets) beneath which they could approach the walls of the beleaguered city. They set up two large catapults, and these devices shook the city from afar. These machines consisted of a beam tied by ropes to two poles with a sling at the end. When the ends were suddenly released, the stone in the sling was flung forcefully for a distance. At the same time archers bearing large bows came up under the protection of the shields; they shot javelins and arrows four times larger than the usual arrow. For many hours they shot at the inhabitants of the city who stood on the wall, but the defenders did not lose heart. They were prepared for a siege. Young and old took part in the defense. All the males could be found on the walls and turrets, raining down stones and arrows upon the attackers—especially flaming arrows that set the mantelets afire.

Meanwhile, Ibn Ḥafṣūn's troops began to use the weapon known as a ram. This was a very large tree trunk that was held fast with iron chains to beams which were at its sides. Tens of men pulled it as far back as possible; when they let go it sprang forward with great force and struck the city walls. This machine, too, was covered with a mantelet, and as the attackers strove to bring it close to the wall to effect a breach, the defenders sought to set fire to the mantelet, without which the ram could not be operated. The defenders performed their task ably and succeeded in setting fire to the mantelets beneath which the bowmen were making an assault, but they could not destroy the mantelet over the ram. In the end they achieved their goal in a different way; they destroyed the ram itself. When it was brought close to the wall they threw wooden beams from above; these spread out, forklike, and became entangled in the ram, which was then set afire.

So the days went by, with the men of 'Umar b. Ḥafṣūn making no progress at all. They then tried to break into the city by an unusual method. They built a new ram, and very early one morning they put it in operation at one of the gates, hoping to unhinge it. But here too they failed. Two days later the rebel troops, under cover of night, tied up their belongings, loaded them on their wagons and beasts of burden, and disappeared. The Jewish city of Lucena was saved from the clutches of 'Umar b. Ḥafṣūn. Some weeks later he was severely defeated in battle with Emir 'Abdallāh.[10]

The suffering that the civilian population had to endure as a result of the rebellions and the ensuing military campaigns was no doubt great. The rebels fought each other, and in Andalusia itself the Omayyad government was able to muster enough strength to send troops on punitive expeditions against the rebels. In sum, cities changed rulers repeatedly; they were besieged and their inhabitants split into factions that fought each other fiercely. Entire areas in Andalusian cities went up in flames, and their inhabitants were left without a roof over their heads.

Both the rebels and the emir's forces had one desire in common—to extort taxes or "contributions" from the populace. In a reliable Hebrew document written in Cordova in the middle of the tenth century, we are told how the Jews were oppressed in those times by tax collectors appointed by the government.[11] It is no wonder that under these circumstances many of the inhabitants took the wanderer's staff in hand and left the land, riven asunder by factional strife, to seek a more tranquil place in which to build a home. Inasmuch as the Jewish population of Andalusia was large, it is natural that among these migrants were a considerable number of Jews.

Understandably, many returned to North Africa, where their forebears had come from. An Arabic source tells of a young Spanish Jew (this source does not give his name) who wandered at that time to Kairawan, the largest city in North Africa at that time, and attained there a position of eminence. He became the court physician of Ziyādatallāh III, the last of the Aghlabid dynasty (903–909). Ziyādatallāh had previously invited Isḥāḳ b. 'Imrān from Irak, assuring him, among other things, that whenever he wanted to leave the country, no obstacle would be placed in his way. But in time he lost favor with the king. Ziyādatallāh had been stricken with asthma, and Isḥāḳ b. 'Imrān stringently forbade him to eat certain foods. The Spanish Jewish doctor appeared on the scene just at this time, and he allowed the king to partake of the foods against which he had been warned by the Babylonian physician. The upshot was that the king commanded that Isḥāḳ be put to death.[12]

At this time Jews from Spain began to appear in southern Italy. *The Scroll of Aḥīma'aṣ*, which tells the story of an Italian Jewish family of that era, mentions a Spanish Jew who went to the city of Gaeta, an important port city on the west coast of southern Italy.[13]

The temporary disintegration of the Spanish-Moslem kingdom at the end of the ninth century and the confusion into which the government sank for a full generation held some important consequences for the Jewish community. During the reign of the first Omayyads the Jewish community increased, in consequence of the Jewish immigration that streamed into Spain from North Africa and the East. Large Jewish communities came into existence in the important cities, especially in southern Spain. When the Omayyad kingdom disintegrated and was followed by small principalities, their chief cities, where the rulers lived, became the focal points of economic and cultural life. New economic units were established, and the princes who ruled the districts and provinces endeavored to expand their capitals and attract inhabitants to them. For instance, Badajoz, which in the middle of the ninth century was a small settlement, became an important city under the rule of Ibn Marwān. Daroca and Calatayud began to develop after the Omayyad government decided to expand the power of the Tudjīb family (so that they would be a source of competition to the Banū Ḳasī) and turned those cities over to them.

The ninth century witnessed the establishment in Moslem Spain of several new cities that developed favorably, such as Murcia and Almería. The Omayyad government also concerned itself with the settlement of locations that it held to be of strategic importance. When the Omayyad government disintegrated, the importance of these cities was not diminished; on the contrary, they became independent centers for the territory surrounding them. From the beginning the Jews tended to migrate to new cities, and when a series of revolts and civil wars started, and the numerous military campaigns resulted in much suffering on the part of the population, many Jews uprooted themselves and resettled in other cities, especially in new cities and in those cities that had become the capitals of small principalities. Thus it came about in the history of Spanish Jewry that the period of numerical growth was replaced by a period of dispersal, with new communities being founded where there had previously been no Jews at all.

Yet another important change in the demographic circumstances of Spanish Jewry took place at that time.

From the first days of the Omayyad kingdom in Spain the migration of Christian Mozarabs had proceeded from the Moslem area to the Christian principalities in the north of the peninsula. At times this process was strong and at times it was weak, but it never came to a full halt. Monks and priests wandered to Asturias and the Spanish March, establishing monasteries there and serving as priests in high ecclesiastical posts. In the middle of the ninth century, during a severe crisis in Moslem and Christian relations resulting from the mystic movement that existed in Cordova, the process of migration grew apace. Many of the clergy fled to the north. However, the abundance of information concerning the migration of the priests from the Moslem south to the Christian north could lead us into error by distorting the true picture of this migration. Side by side with abbots and bishops, about whom the Latin chroniclers who were their colleagues inform us, roamed a mass of unknowns—peasants and artisans—who poured into the boundaries of Christian authority.

In the second half of the ninth century the Asturian kings

began a comprehensive program of colonization. They wanted to settle those areas in their kingdom that had been vacated on being conquered, now abandoned by the Moslems. They therefore encouraged their coreligionists in the Moslem portion of the peninsula to come and settle in the unpopulated cities and villages. Thus the population within the Christian region was increased—especially by the Mozarabs, who brought to the north, which was poor and lacking in culture, the achievements of Islamic civilization, a cultural level which was far superior to that of the Christians.[14]

Ordoño I (850–866) resettled the cities of Amaya, León, Astorga, and Tùy. He rebuilt their walls and erected gates. A Christian source explicitly states that he settled there people who came from Moslem areas.[15] King Alfonso III (866–910) wrought exceedingly great achievements for the areas under his suzerainty. He resettled the north of what is modern Portugal, the districts between Porto and Tùy. The nobles of his kingdom followed in his footsteps. Between 882 and 884 Diego Rodriguez, prince of Castile, founded the city of Burgos. In 893 Zamora was rebuilt. An Arab-Moslem source tells us that the city was reconstructed by Mozarabs who had migrated there from Toledo.[16] About 899 Simancas, on the banks of the Duero River, was settled. During the rule of Emir 'Abdallāh, when Spain was sunk in a state of chaos, the stream of migrants grew. It is certain that at this time many Christian peasants moved from Moslem territories to Christian principalities in the north, and the migration of the clergy continued through the second half of the ninth into the beginning of the tenth century.[17]

Jews, too, were swept into this migratory movement. The attitude of the inhabitants and the governments of Asturias and Castile was as hostile as it had always been, and the environment into which the immigrants were cast was oppressive. Christians in the north were zealous for their faith and found themselves in a constant state of war with the Moslems. Both sides regarded this animosity as a holy war—except for the Christians this was a battle of life or death, for the area they controlled was smaller and every summer they could expect an invasion by Moslem forces, who laid waste their cities and villages and turned them into heaps of ruins. It is not surprising that their religious zeal and the hate in their hearts flamed. The numerous monasteries erected during that period in the mountains of Asturias and Galicia contained hundreds of monks, who inspired the men of the army and set ablaze the fires of hatred. When the kingdom of Asturias was established and the territories that became its nucleus were captured, it is certain that all Jews whom the Christians chanced upon were slain.[18]

But necessity overcame all hidebound conceptions. The populations of Asturias, León, Castile, and Navarre were an amalgam of nobles and peasants, and the urban stratum was very sparse. In the courts of the nobles a need was felt for skilled artisans who were expert in their craft, like the Mozarab migrants who had come from the Moslem south but not in sufficient numbers. For this reason the rulers of the Christian principalities gradually became reconciled to the existence of those Jews who remained in conquered settlements and who infiltrated into the borders of their dominion. Even the authorities of the church recognized that the settling of areas empty of people demanded a tolerant attitude toward the Jews. On the other hand, there were in the large Jewish community in the Omayyad kingdom bold young men, expert craftsmen, who were ready to test their fortune in an alien environment, as well as merchants with initiative. These men followed in the steps of the Mozarabs and found in the Christian principalities a source of prosperous livelihoods. Many of them lived in the courts of the nobles and enjoyed their protection. Juridically their status was that of servants of the princes and lords.[19] In documents of that time concerning the Christian principalities, mention is made of Jews who acquired land and houses, of course, but only on rare occasions are artisans mentioned; though perhaps more numerous, they had not reached the stage of being able to acquire land.

The number of Jews in northern Spain did not become great in those days, but all signs indicate that by the end of the ninth century a migratory movement had begun that resulted in the establishment of many communities. In León there was a Jewish community from the beginning of the tenth century. A document from 905 mentions a rich Jew named Habaz who converted to Christianity, even becoming a monk.[20] In the tenth century the number of Jewish names appearing in documents of the city of León is relatively large, and among them is a considerable percentage of Arabic names: Abu'l-Ḳāsim (in 926), Sulaimān (951), Sa'dūn (973), 'Azīz (977), Sayyida (980), Yūsuf (998), and others. There is not always an indication alongside these names marking their bearers as Jewish, but it is almost a certainty.[21] Jews even lived in Coimbra, now a part of Portugal. A document of the year 900 speaks of Jewish property in one of the suburbs, including houses and vineyards.[22] In the ninth century, Sahagún, southeast of León, developed as a small settlement near the renowned church, and in 905 Alfonso III founded a monastery there.

In various documents of the tenth century Jewish names are mentioned among that city's inhabitants. In 933 a man named Abuharun sold two houses to the monastery. In a document of 943 a man named Moisen appears; Ebrahem is mentioned in 947, and Yūsuf in 955.[23] Although there is nothing positive in this, it is quite probable that Jews are referred to. Jews also settled in Old Castile during this period. When the count of Castile, García Fernandez granted privileges to the inhabitants of Castrojeriz in 974, he also fixed the status of the Jews in it.[24] For the Jewish communities in the Christian kingdoms of northern Spain, the tenth century was a period of continuous growth.

In the beginning of the eleventh century the Jews of the kingdom of León constituted an important urban element, as is demonstrated by the decisions of the council that met in its capital in 1020.[25] Documents preserved from that period show clearly that they possessed property, such as vineyards. The Arabic names by which many Jews within the borders of Christian authority are called point to their origin.[26] Their names prove that they came from Moslem sectors, where they spoke Arabic. We thus learn that parallel to the Mozarab migration, there flowed, from the beginning of the latter half of the ninth century and as a consequence of conditions then prevailing in the Spanish-Moslem kingdom, a stream of migrants to the Christian principalities in the north of the peninsula. This migration laid the foundation for that large Jewish community in Christian Spain that was destined to fill so important a role in the history of the Jews.

4

RELIGIOUS LIFE IN THE NINTH CENTURY

Notwithstanding changes and vicissitudes, the Jewish community of Spain continued to develop uninterruptedly during the first two centuries of Arabic rule. Progress and growth were evident in all things. Not only did the number of Spanish Jews, both as individuals and as communities, increase from generation to generation, but their cultural level also mounted ever higher. Spanish Jewry did not live by bread alone, nor did its thoughts turn solely on earning a livelihood. In every community, especially in the large ones, there were scholars who dedicated their time to the study of Torah and were well versed in Jewish law and its meaning. While Spanish communities were cut off from the Jewish way of life during the Arabic conquest, by the tenth century they had reached the stage of conducting themselves strictly in accordance with talmudic law, and many were quite well versed in all its branches.

Spanish Jewry shared fully in all that happened throughout the Diaspora and took an active part in the entire life of the nation. This was an outcome of educational attainment, which began shortly after the changes brought about by the establishment of an Arabic kingdom on the Iberian peninsula occurred, a process that continued throughout the entire eighth and ninth centuries.

I

In the period before the Arabic conquest of Spain, the Jews of the peninsula were not only severely persecuted by the clergy and Visigothic kings, but also cut off from Jewry elsewhere. Because of the political barriers between the Visigothic kingdom, on the one hand, and the Byzantine Empire and the Arabic domain, on the other, Jews could neither move about freely nor maintain permanent ties with the center of Jewish life in the Near East, where rabbinic law had achieved its most crystallized state.

During the last generation of Visigothic rule the situation worsened considerably. The government proclaimed that Judaism was a religion without legal standing, and the Jews, in consequence, could observe the commandments of the Torah only in clandestine fashion. It is not surprising that knowledge of Jewish law constantly waned.

But after the triumphant campaigns of Ṭārik̦ b. Ziyād and Mūsā b. Nuṣair, the Jews of Spain attained freedom, becoming subjects of a vast empire that also included all the countries of North Africa, Palestine, and Babylonia, together with their numerous communities. Regular communications were established between all these countries, and there were no obstacles to prevent the free movement of Jews from land to land or to keep them from making contact with their brethren everywhere.

When the first upheaval resulting from the war of conquest had died down and life resumed its normal course, the Spanish Jews planned to develop programs for the education of their children in the spirit of traditional Judaism and to shake off the state of isolation in which they had existed hitherto.

In those days the Talmud was already the recognized legal code for all Jews, and therefore the Spanish Jews endeavored first and foremost to acquire texts of the Gemara that would be thoroughly correct. Naturally, they turned to the great academies in Babylonia, which were renowned throughout the Diaspora as the most important centers of Torah and scholarship. The heads of communities asked merchants to bring copies of the Gemara from Babylonia or sent special messengers to the Near East to bring back the desired books. (The Moslems of Andalusia acted similarly. In the early days of Arabic rule in the Iberian peninsula they, too, required spiritual sustenance from the Near East, the cradle of Islamic culture, and therefore they sent messengers and whole delegations to acquire books from there.)

In those days, rich and notable Jews contributed funds for the acquisition of Mishnayot and Gemarot, for this was regarded as a religious duty and a very meritorious act. The Jews of Spain were especially interested in books that were carefully edited, because they were not well versed in Aramaic, the language in which the Talmud was written, and every corruption in the manuscript presented the student with manifold difficulties. Hence great care was taken to obtain texts that had been copied with exactitude; indeed, in later generations, Spanish copies of the Gemara were famous for the correctness of their text. The great scholars of the thirteenth century placed their reliance upon "an old Spanish text edited in the academy of the *g'ōnīm*" or "edited texts that came from Spain."[1]

A high premium was placed upon oral learning in those days, so Spanish Moslems sent their talented youth to study from the *'ulamā* (Moslem theologians and scholars) in Hedjaz and Egypt. But the number of students who went from Jewish communities in Spain to the academies in the East was apparently meager. In the last quarter of the eighth century, however, a teacher of considerable prominence came to Andalusia from Babylonia, who, by instructing the Jews, propagated the knowledge of the Gemara. This man had come to Spain because he had been a candidate for the office of exilarch, the head of Babylonian Jewry; his candidacy having failed, he could not bear to remain in the land of his birth. His name was Naṭrōnai bar Ḥabībae,[2] and he was a scion of the exilarch's family, which traced its family tree back to the Davidic dynasty and the kings of Judah. The high office of exilarch was then occupied by Judah b. Isaac, also known as Zakkai b. Ahūnai.

In 771, four years after Judah b. Isaac became the exilarch, a man named Malka bar Aḥa was elected head of the Academy of Pumbedita. Malka decided to dismiss the exilarch from his post, appointing in his stead Naṭrōnai bar Ḥabībae, who not only enjoyed ancestral merit (namely, his ties with the House of David), but was in his own right an estimable person. In his youth he had been a disciple of Y'hūdai, the head of the renowned Academy of Sura, becoming an illustrious scholar.[3] Among the Babylonian Jews there was a faction that agreed with the views of Malka and joined forces with him; thus he put his scheme into effect, proclaiming Naṭrōnai to be the exilarch.

But the majority of the community leaders, and particularly the scholars of the academies, would not acquiesce in this change. They met, reaffirmed the exilarch, Judah b. Isaac, in his post, dismissed Malka from his office, and chose a new head of the academy. This happened in 773. Malka and his faction did not give up but prepared to resume the controversy; however, a short time later Malka died. Naṭrōnai then reached the conclusion that he could no longer hope to attain the office of exilarch.

Disappointed and full of resentment, he left Babylonia and set out on the road to the remote land at the other end of the Mediterranean Sea, where, according to reports reaching him, a large Jewish community had sprung up. He went to Spain, where he was received with great honors, and at the request of the community leaders and scholars he taught them about the more involved problems of the halakha. The name of this illustrious teacher was not forgotten by the Andalusian Jews, and later generations told how the expelled exilarch came to the Jews of Spain and set the Talmud down in writing for them as he knew it—by heart.[4]

Thenceforth there were to be found many Jews in Spain who could find their way at their pleasure in the problems of the Talmud. In the large communities of Andalusia there were schools where youths and adults met for the study of Gemara. Some sources maintain that the study of the Torah never ceased in Spain.[5] These comments may be somewhat exaggerated, but as regards this period, the eighth and ninth centuries of the Common Era, this testimony may be considered valid. One writer tells us that although in those generations the Spanish Jews were not really great scholars, they engaged in lively discussion over the problems in the Gemara.[6] It was not only scholars whose occupation was the study of Torah that fixed a time for study, but also laymen, who were encumbered by family responsibilities and preoccupied with the need to earn a living. These laymen made it a practice to study especially on the Sabbath, as an early source informs us.[7]

Even in those early days of Judeo-Arabic culture in Andalusia one can perceive the scientific goal that is characteristic of the spiritual life of the Jews of Spain in every generation. In their study of the Gemara, too, the striving for exactitude and system is conspicuous. Spanish Jews sought an explanation for every obscure phrase in the Gemara and tried to remove from their books every segment of inexact text. According to an authentic source, in the middle of the ninth century they applied to the head of the Academy of Pumbedita, Palṭoi bar Abaye (842–858), requesting him to set down in writing a

"Talmud together with its interpretation," and he fulfilled their request.[8] There is almost no doubt that the *gaon* was not asked to write a commentary on the entire Talmud for the Jews of Spain; more likely the request was for fixing the correct text of various phrases and the clarification of difficult segments.

This appeal to the *gaon* of Pumbedita was one of many, for it was customary for the Jews of Spain of that era to apply to the heads of the great academies of Sura and Pumbedita whenever they were faced with questions or doubts in matters of faith and law. In those days the heads of these two academies, both of whom bore the title *gaon*, filled the role of spiritual leaders for all Jewry. Students came not only from Babylonia but also from other countries to study at these academies, spending many years there in the study of the Gemara. Moreover, instruction was only one activity of the *g'ōnīm*; they also performed other important functions. They wrote codes of law in which they summarized the legal discussions in the Gemara and also gave decisions on religious or legal problems that were brought before them, always in accordance with talmudic law, tradition, and their own reasoning.

The changes in circumstance wrought by the passage of time required them to modify talmudic laws on occasion, interpreting them in harmony with the new situation. For this reason the scholars of the academies headed by the *g'ōnīm* would meet to institute enactments that often modified the law as found in the Gemara. The interpretations the *g'ōnīm* gave to the Gemara and their decisions and regulations were accepted by all Jewish communities everywhere as statutes and judgments from which none might deviate. The Jews of the Diaspora accepted the authority of the Babylonian *g'ōnīm* because they recognized their supremacy in knowledge of the Torah and their authority. The academies of Babylonia were steeped in hoary tradition; in them the Babylonian Talmud had been created. Who could, therefore, possess greater authority to interpret it than the heads of these academies?

The acceptance of their authority by all Jewish communities enabled the *g'ōnīm* to fulfill a historic mission. By their activity as teachers and authorities in legal matters they preserved the nation, which had no state of its own, from schisms and disintegration and at the same time gave it a constitution. The Babylonian Talmud performed this function; the Palestinian Talmud was pushed aside. Jews who had formerly belonged to the Roman Empire received their religious instruction over many centuries from the Jewish settlement in Palestine; but after the edicts promulgated against the Jews by the Byzantines toward the end of their rule over Palestine, the Jews of the old fatherland grew weak and could no longer compete with Babylonian Jewry, which surpassed them in every aspect. Furthermore, the conquest of Palestine by the Arabs broke the normal ties between the Jewish settlement in that land and Jews who remained outside the Arab Empire, weakening the influence of the Palestinian Talmud even more. On the other hand, the Jewish community in Babylonia grew stronger in consequence of the establishment of Arabic rule. The new rulers recognized the autonomous organization of Babylonian Jewry, and the exilarch, who in the days of the Abbasid dynasty had gone to live in Bagdad, represented for the caliph Jews in all the lands under Arabic dominion.

Of the two large academies in Sura and Pumbedita, the former enjoyed the special patronage of the exilarch and in time came to excel its rival. The Academy of Sura began to flourish in the middle of the eighth century when Y'hūdai was called to head it. He and the *g'ōnīm* who succeeded him raised the level of study in the academy, and they and their disciples wrote various books of laws and other treatises dealing with matters of faith and justice. Not until the middle of the ninth century could the Academy of Pumbedita equal that of Sura. Matters took on a different complexion with the appointment of Palṭoi bar Abaye as head of the Academy of Pumbedita. Thereafter the number of students at Pumbedita increased steadily, until within a period of some fifty years it overshadowed Sura.

The maintenance of teachers and officers of the academy and the support of needy students called for large sums of money, and the academies derived these sums from two types of sources. They and the exilarch divided the provinces of Irak and Persia into three zones called *r'shūyōt* (spheres of control), and each academy appointed judges for its own zone and collected taxes therein. The academies also derived income from communities in other lands not under their jurisdiction. They received from them taxes termed *p'sīḳōt* (voluntary contributions) and *ḥumashīm* ("fifths"), as well as donations on stated occasions.[9]

Jewish communities throughout the Diaspora would send letters to the *g'ōnīm* in Babylonia and set before them questions concerning various matters; writing the responsa to these questions became one of the most important functions of the *g'ōnīm*. The heads of the Babylonian academies were gratified with the increasing number of questions, since these appeals demonstrated a recognition of their authority; besides, the questioners were wont to send, together with the questions, donations that lightened the heavy financial burden they bore. In time the circle of those asking the questions expanded to encompass the entire Diaspora, while the responsa themselves became more comprehensive. Many of the responsa of the early *g'ōnīm* were short; however, in a later period the *g'ōnīm* answered in minute detail, their answers growing ever longer and at times becoming whole books.

If the question presented to them dealt with a matter of principle or was very complex, they would defer the reply, usually until all the scholars of the academies assembled, as was their custom, in the month of Adar, when they could debate the question and how best to answer it. There were times when the answer could not be held up, however, since the messenger was ready to leave or for some other reason. Copies of the responsa remained at the academy, and if at some later time a question was asked dealing with the same subject, the *gaon* indicated in his responsum what had been the earlier reply. This was their practice even if the first question had come from another community. In such an instance they directed the questioners to those who had already received the first answer, for it was their presumption that the reply had been carefully preserved. The *g'ōnīm* were able to do this because the responsa which they sent to various lands were there gathered and put into collections and also because intercommunication in the days of the caliphs was secure and travelers abounded.

Of the many Jewish communities that fostered connections with the Babylonian academies, the numerous communities of North Africa were preeminent. The fact that most of the responsa which have been preserved were intended for these communities bears the strongest witness to the fact that their ties with the Babylonian academies were very close. At that time the Jews of North Africa were not only a large settlement numerically, but also stood on a high level culturally. In the large communities there were academies where distinguished scholars taught; a substantial number of students attended them. The most prominent among these communities was Kairawan, which throughout this period was an important political, economic, and cultural center. But the communities of Gabès, Tlemcen, Sidjilmāsa, and Fez were also renowned as centers for the study of Torah. These Jewish settlements contained not only scholars who confined their study to the Torah, but also intellectuals who delved deeply into the study of the Hebrew language and problems in philosophy.

Both of them regarded the *g'ōnīm* of Babylonia as their spiritual leaders.

From the middle of the seventh century, in the time of the *gaon* Y'hūdai, it was the practice to send questions to the Academy of Sura, and from the time of the *gaon* Palṭoi they entered into correspondence with the Academy of Pumbedita. They turned to the *g'ōnīm* of Babylonia not only in regard to halakhic (legal) matters but also with all kinds of other questions and problems; the *g'ōnīm* responded at length, in a manner befitting scholars. There were many ties between the communities of North Africa and the Jews of Spain, particularly since a substantial part of Spanish Jewry had its origins in North Africa. For this reason the influence of North African learned rabbis on the Jews of Spain in those times was very strong, and it was they who transmitted to Spain the lore of the Torah they had received from the Babylonian academies.

In the eighth century and the first half of the ninth century the rabbis of North Africa held, from every aspect, the role of intermediaries between the Babylonian academies and the Jews of Spain, which constituted a new settlement in the Judeo-Arabic world. (For the Moslems, too, Spain was a new settlement, and their venerable judges were no doubt accustomed to turn to their learned theologians and mentors in the Near East.) Whenever a Spanish-Jewish community wanted to present a question to one of the Babylonian academies, it would send its missive to Kairawan, where official representatives of the academies were located. They would accept the documents and the funds on behalf of the academies and relay them to their destination. In most instances, the documents would be sent from Kairawan to Fostat, to the "functionary of the academy," as this representative was designated; from there they would be relayed, by way of Palestine and Syria, to Babylonia.

Whenever one of the Andalusian communities received,

from the *g'ōnīm,* responsa to questions that had been addressed to them, much interest was aroused. The reading of the responsa was essentially a ceremonial occasion. When the missive from a *gaon* arrived, the heads of the community and the learned rabbis of the city would be invited to be present at the reading.

Toward the end of the summer of a year early in the 850s, the city of Lucena received a long epistle from the head of the Academy of Sura, which contained replies to several questions sent to him one and a half years before. In the late afternoon some ten elders were waiting in the synagogue in the center of the city; they were seated on a mattress near the wall, while opposite them sat a group of young men on mats spread on the floor with their feet doubled up under them. In one corner sat the messenger, holding in his hand a securely tied bundle wrapped in linen. This messenger, whose profession it was to transmit epistles and missives, had come from Fostat, having already delivered several letters to merchants in Kairawan and Sidjilmāsa. His bags still held letters for men in Cordova, and he was prepared to leave the next day without delay.

The heat was oppressive, as is usual during the summer in Andalusia, inducing an air of lassitude. From time to time, the conversation, which was being carried on in a lazy fashion, would come to a halt. The hall of the synagogue, which was on the ground floor, was not large, its walls were whitewashed and bright, and the door, which faced the courtyard, was wide open. Gradually, the heads of the community, having disengaged themselves from their occupations, entered, kissed the *m'zuzah,* approached the elders—the teachers of the academy, greeted them with the blessing of peace, and took their seats also.

When the hall was full, one of the elders took the packet from the messenger, and at a signal an attendant approached and opened it very carefully with a knife. Meanwhile, a low table had been brought in, upon which all the papers in the packet were placed. The elder and two of his companions bent over the documents and began reading them aloud. From time to time they would translate some of the Aramaic words into Arabic so that everyone could understand them. From the expression on the faces of the community leaders it was evident that, in spite of the explanations, they had not gotten the sense of the matter, but they nevertheless sat motionless in their places. The eyes of the elders, though dimmed by age, would light up when a response to a halakhic question, over which they had argued very much, was read. The reading was done hurriedly, this being only the first reading; a more careful perusal of the responsa would come later.

Meanwhile, the shadows lengthened and the sun began to set. But though the reading of the responsa was not yet completed, they all stood up as one of them began to chant, in a throaty and somewhat hoarse voice, the afternoon prayer: *"Ashrē yōsh'vē bēt'khā."*

Even though the arrival of these responsa was an occasion for great joy, there was no novelty in the matter, inasmuch as the Jews of Andalusia had been in constant touch with the academies of Babylonia for several decades. From the beginning of the ninth century they used to send questions to the *g'ōnīm* and receive answers from them. Nevertheless, whenever a reply did arrive they made it an occasion for joy, as though it was happening to them for the first time.

At first they engaged in correspondence only with the Academy of Sura. At the beginning of the ninth century they came into contact with Jacob bar Mordecai ha-Kōhēn, who served as head of the Academy of Sura for fourteen years. This *gaon* was renowned for his lenient interpretation of various laws, and when the Jews of Spain received a decision from him on a question of *ṭ'rēfōt* (forbidden foods or vessels) they placed their reliance on him. The Jews of Kairawan, however, were more stringent in this regard.[10]

Quite different in character was Ṣaddōḳ bar Rav Ashi, who occupied the office of *gaon* for two years at the beginning of 820s. He inclined toward stringency and also had another prominent trait: he taught in an independent manner, established new interpretations, and initiated new enactments when he thought they were needed, these being then accepted and approved by the rabbis. The Jews of Spain addressed questions to him also,[11] as they did later to Kōhēn Ṣedeḳ bar Abūmai, who headed the Academy of Sura in the 840s. This *gaon* is mentioned several times in halakhic literature in connection with a comprehensive judgment on the order of the prayer service, a matter on which the Jews of Spain also received instruction from him.[12]

The Spanish Jews likewise maintained contact with his successor, Sar Shālōm ben Bōaz, who also served in the 840s. This *gaon,* who left behind many responsa, was from many aspects a very interesting person. He sought to refrain from imposing severe decrees upon the nation and demanded that an attitude of honesty be maintained toward members of other faiths. Even in the manner of his writing he differed from the other *g'ōnīm.* Because they regarded themselves as mentors to all Jewry, they employed a style of decree and command in their responsa, whereas Sar Shālōm addressed those who questioned him in gentle terms, informing them as to the practice of the Babylonian academies, and leaving it to them to decide on their course of action. The Spanish communities received responsa from him on several questions.[13]

Naṭrōnai bar Hilai succeeded Sar Shālōm at Sura. He filled an important role in the religious development of Spanish Jewry as a result of the many responsa he sent them. At the time of his accession to the gaonate, Naṭrōnai was already well along in years, but he was still in full vigor and strength, as is indicated by the large number of responsa ascribed to him. Naṭrōnai served as head of the academy for eight years (849–857), during which the academy reached the acme of its greatness, so that questions were directed to it from all parts of the Diaspora.

Naṭrōnai was not an innovator; in most of his responsa he repeats the words of the Gemara, neither adding anything nor taking a decisive stand on the various opinions found there. On the other hand, he did not employ the amalgam of Hebrew and Aramaic used until then by the *g'ōnīm* and also was apparently the first to write in Arabic. Among the responsa he sent the Jews of Spain there is an interesting judgment relating to their occupation with agriculture,[14] commentaries on the tractate Shabbat,[15] and several decisions on matters of liturgy.[16] Because of the many responsa the Jews of Spain received from Naṭrōnai, they regarded him as their teacher par excellence in halakha; and a folk tale was circulated that told how he came to Spain by miraculous means, taught the Jews halakha, and returned to Babylonia.[17]

After the death of Naṭrōnai a break apparently occurred in the contacts of the Andalusian communities and the Academy of Sura. Naṭrōnai was succeeded by 'Amram bar Sheshna (858–871). This *gaon* had an extensive correspondence with the Jews of Barcelona, where the most important community in Christian Spain was located; but there is no information on any responsa being sent by him to the Jews of Andalusia.[18] The next *gaon* of Sura was Naḥshōn bar Ṣaddōḳ (872–880), whose literary fame rests on a treatise that he wrote concerning the Jewish calendar, *'Iggūl*. The Jews of Moslem Spain maintained a correspondence with him.[19]

In the second half of the ninth century, the Jews of Spain established strong ties with the Academy of Pumbedita. The first among the *g'ōnīm* of Pumbedita with whom they engaged in extensive correspondence was Palṭoi bar Abaye, a forceful and energetic person. He did much to raise the prestige of the Torah and to strengthen religious observance among the Jewish communities; but most especially he labored indefatigably for his academy. His responsa were brief, and at times he would adduce no proof for his decisions, which reflected his forceful character.[20] In the next fourteen years after Palṭoi's death four scholars held the office of *gaon* at Pumbedita; these achieved little, either because of intramural quarrels within the academy or because of their demise shortly after their appointment to office.

But in 872 Ṣemaḥ, the son of Palṭoi, who was one of the most distinguished among the *g'ōnīm* of the ninth century, was chosen head of Pumbedita. He occupied his post for nineteen years, and during this long period sent many responsa to the Diaspora. It was his practice to explain carefully his opinions in his responsa; he did not find it sufficient merely to cite the Gemara, but also rendered the content of the segment, adding his own commentary. Ṣemaḥ had a grasp of lay culture, also knew Persian, and was the author of a talmudical lexicon (*'ārūkh*) arranged alphabetically. In the 880s he was regarded as the leading rabbi of his generation, and everyone sang his praises. The Jews of Spain addressed many questions to him. His grandson reported that in his time the Jews of Spain sent to the Academy of Pumbedita "so many portions of the entire Talmud whose purport was doubtful to them, that there were not enough donkeys to carry them."[21] The Jews of Andalusia also corresponded with Ṭōbh, the son of Ṣemaḥ, during whose term of office he was president of the court at the academy.[22]

Since the various communities directed their queries to the *g'ōnīm* in Babylonia, each one independently, it occasionally happened that two communities asked the same question. But they were not wont to present a similar question to the heads of the two great academies of Babylonia. The *g'ōnīm* themselves did not want this to happen from a just concern that the rendering of two dissimilar decisions where the same question was involved could cause disputes to arise both between the academies and the communities that presented the question.[23] There were, indeed, occasions when those asking the question were dissatisfied with the reply sent them and would write to the responding *gaon* asking for a clarification of obscure points. The questions that the Jews of Spain addressed to the *g'ōnīm* dealt with matters permitted and matters forbidden, laws concerning the Sabbath, and laws relating to forbidden foods. Often they would request of the *g'ōnīm* explanations for portions of the Gemara. These questions constituted the majority of those brought to the attention of the *g'ōnīm.*

Among the list of questions coming to the *g'ōnīm* from other countries, there appear also questions involving commentary on the Scriptures, such as difficulties in chronology. This type of question is absent from the queries of the Spanish communities. But the Andalusian communities did send to the *g'ōnīm* in Babylonia questions dealing with human relationships. In a responsum to questions addressed to him by the community of Lucena, Naṭrōnai Gaon explains that it is forbidden to buy commodities for the purpose of speculating in them and raising the prices, or to demand a higher price in a transaction involving credit, since this is held to be interest. In another responsum the *gaon* speaks about the flogging of children at school; he questions whether this method should be employed in education.[24]

In judicial matters, however, they turned to the *g'ōnīm* only on rare occasions, because in disputes involving money it was difficult to postpone the decision long enough for the decision to arrive from faraway Babylonia. The *g'ōnīm* themselves did not want to be turned to in such matters from distant lands.[25] Many questions revolve around the order of the prayers and their formulation—for weekdays, Sabbaths, and holidays—and around rules governing the reading of the Torah and the organization of the synagogue. Naṭrōnai sent the Jews of Lucena a formulary of the one hundred benedictions to be recited daily.[26] At a later date his successor, 'Amram, sent to Spain a prayer book containing the complete formulation of the prayers. This book of prayer was sent to Barcelona;[27] however, it contained many decisions concerning daily prayer enunciated by Naṭrōnai, and these are apparently responsa that he had sent to the Andalusian communities.[28]

With the questions the Jews of Spain sent along contributions for the maintenance of the academies, though they would have supported them in any event. In the missives of the Babylonian *g'ōnīm* of the middle of the tenth century, there is mention of "contributions, donations, and 'fifths' [*ḥumashīm*]," which were sent to the Academies of Sura and Pumbedita,[29] and a twelfth-century Spanish-Jewish writer tells of "the fixed contributions to the academies that came from Spain."[30] All these sums would be turned over to a representative of the academy in Kairawan.[31] When the flow of these contributions ceased, the *g'ōnīm* began to complain bitterly, reminding the leaders of the Spanish communities of the desirable practice of their forebears.

As the Jews of Spain corresponded voluminously with the *g'ōnīm* and were guided by them in well-reasoned responsa and commentaries on sections and extracts of the Gemara, the level of studies and learning in their numerous schools rose. By the middle of the ninth century they were already well versed in all branches of the halakha, and even the *g'ōnīm* themselves were well aware of this. In their replies to questions addressed to them from Spain, the *g'ōnīm* employed honorific language, as is befitting for distinguished scholars, even though they were not wont at this time to heap praises or bestow encomia.[32] By now Spain could boast of scholars who were renowned for their knowledge, brilliant in expounding the halakha, and able to stand on their own feet without need for constant guidance. The scholars of the Andalusian communities knew how to adapt the laws of the Gemara to life's evolving circumstances on their own and how to formulate enactments appropriate to them. In the responsum of one of the *g'ōnīm* there is mention of a Spanish scholar, Pinḥās, who made an enactment relating to the setting up of an *'ērūbh* on Passover. The *gaon* agrees with his formulation and praises it.[33]

Among the Spanish scholars of the ninth century, one, El'āzār b. Samuel, who was born at the start of the century and was an inhabitant of Lucena, achieved fame. This El'āzār was a man of learning who had gained a reputation for erudition and profundity. Various communities in Spain addressed questions to him, and he responded with detailed decisions.[34] At the same time El'āzār corresponded with the Babylonian *g'ōnīm,* putting to them questions in halakha. He sent many questions to Naṭrōnai, the head of the Academy of Sura,[35] but with respect to one question—if one has a son by one's maidservant, is he freed from the obligation of *yibbūm* (the levirate marriage)—El'āzār wrote both to Naṭrōnai and to Palṭoi, the head of the Academy of Pumbedita.[36]

The exchange of letters alone did not satisfy him, and he was seized with a desire to know the scholars of the academies face to face and to discuss halakhic principles with them. Therefore, he girded his loins and went forth to faraway Babylonia. On the way he passed through Kairawan and, his fame having preceded him, was welcomed by this large community with great honor. The Jews of Kairawan asked him to take a sum of money designated for the Academy of Sura, and he complied. Naṭrōnai recalled the service rendered by El'āzār to the scholars of the academy and was grateful to him for having made it possible for them to pay the debts with which the academy was encumbered.[37]

El'āzār remained in Babylonia, making his residence in Sura. He dwelt there for many decades, having gone to Sura during the days of Naṭrōnai bar Hilai, and was still there in the days of the *gaon* Naḥshōn bar Ṣaddōḳ.[38] During these many years he participated in the activities of the academy in study and discussion, and therefore his name is mentioned frequently in the writings of the *g'ōnīm* of subsequent generations.

His personality left a deep impression on the scholars of the academy, for here was a scholar coming from afar, a scholar who was as well versed in the Gemara as if he had been a member of one of the old g'ōnic families born and bred in academic circles. He could clarify for them matters referred to in the Mishna and the Gemara of which they had no knowledge, such as references to European coins,[39] spices,[40] and fish.[41] Once they knew El'āzār personally and were aware of the vast reaches of his knowledge, they bestowed upon him the title of *resh kalla*, one of the honorary titles of the academy granted only to the select few.[42]

El'āzār was concerned with all questions about Judaism, and the Karaite movement in particular aroused his interest. He studied their writings diligently, something not customary for the scholars of the academies, who abhorred such works. Thus when Naṭrōnai wanted to express his opposition to the view of Anan, the founder of Karaism, he depended upon El'āzār, who had read Anan's *Book of Commandments* (*Sefer ha-miṣvōt*).[43]

The pursuits of this scholar are reliable witness to the strong ties existing between the scholars of Spain and the academies of Babylonia, as well as the heights they had attained in their learning. The relationships which developed at that time between the scholars of Spain and the spiritual center in Babylonia expressed themselves in yet another way.

Among the judges and especially among the scholars, for whom study of the Torah was an avocation and whose spare time was limited, the need for codes of law to sum up the discussions in the Gemara and relieve them from poring over entire sections that at times were difficult to understand had been felt for a long time. The *g'ōnīm* and those close to them did not look favorably upon the tendency to employ such "abridgments," especially since the students began to study them and not the Gemara. Yet they could not hide from the needs of the majority of the people, and therefore they themselves wrote such works.

The most outstanding of these codes was the compilation called *Ha-Halakhōt ha-g'dōlōt* written by Shim'ōn Kayyara about 825. He came from Basra, was educated in the Academy of Sura, and was numbered among its scholars. He used as an important source *Halakhōt r'sūḳōt,* the teachings and decisions of Y'hūdai Gaon which had been written down by his disciples as he uttered them. He depended as well upon the *Sh'iltōt* (Homiletical Questions) of Aḥa Gaon, which were also composed in the middle of the eighth century, and *The Book of Deeds* from Palestine. Besides these works he introduced into this compendium the teachings of the early *g'ōnīm.*[44]

His book was very popular with the scholars throughout the Diaspora in two editions that differ in many respects. The main edition, and apparently the closest to the original version as it came from the author's hand, spread during the Middle Ages among the scholars of France and Germany.[45] But of even greater circulation in the days of the early scholars was another edition called by them the "Great Halakhōt of Spain."[46] This edition has both omissions and many additions as compared with the other edition, the addenda consisting largely of g'ōnic responsa, among them being material from some of the *g'ōnīm* of the middle of the ninth century and the first half of the tenth. The last *gaon* whose decisions were added was Ṣemaḥ bar Palṭoi (d. 890). From the wording of the addenda (for example, "And he sent . . . that the halakha is according to so and so" and the like) we may infer that this edition was edited in a country that had constant dealings with the Babylonian *g'ōnīm*: either North Africa or Spain. But whether edited in Kairawan or in one of the cities of Andalusia,[47] it served the scholars of Spain, inasmuch as they had no knowledge of the first edition. It was this text, which reached northern France in the twelfth century and Germany in the thirteenth, that was known as the "Great Halakhōt of Spain" because it had come from there and because the Spanish scholars depended upon it for study and legal decisions.

Compared to the close ties between the Spanish communities and the academies of Babylonia, which were manifested clearly in various ways, the influence of the Jewish population in Palestine upon them was small. To be sure, there were indeed mutual relationships between the Jews of Spain and the communities in Palestine. In common with the other Diaspora communities, the Jews of Spain gave aid to the impoverished settlement there, especially to the learned rabbis who, after the establishment of Arab rule, renewed their educational activities and endeavored to reestablish a religio-spiritual center in Palestine whose influence would emanate to Jewish communities throughout the Diaspora. But the Palestinian Talmud never won acceptance from Spanish Jewry; they studied the laws in the Babylonian Talmud and the decisions of the *g'ōnīm* of Babylonia. On the other hand, they esteemed highly the Palestinian scholars who devoted themselves to the study of the Scriptures, the Masoretes who concerned themselves with the vocalization and annotation of the text. Spanish-Hebraic sources of the tenth century mention "Spanish and Tiberian scriptural texts of early recension";[48] and a Hebrew grammarian living in Spain in the eleventh century mentions having an accurate Jerusalem Bible.[49]

But generally speaking there is no recognizable spiritual influence from the Palestinian communities upon Spanish Jewry. In Italy, France, and Germany, the Jews accepted the midrash and the *piyyūṭ* (liturgical poetry) stemming from Palestine, and these became so popular among them that their own scholars composed *midrāshīm* and *piyyūṭīm* in the Palestinian manner. But this cultural influence is nowhere evident among the Jews of Spain. They followed Babylonian Jewry in every respect, and even imitated them in the pronunciation of Hebrew.[50]

From a cultural aspect the Jewish settlement of Spain was, in a sense, a colony of Babylonian Jewry. The Babylonian Talmud put its stamp on their religio-spiritual life in that era. By the ninth century the study of the halakha was the principal occupation of the Spanish scholars. But this one-sidedness also reflected the emotional needs of Spanish Jewry. It was linked with the circumstances of their lives. The majority of individuals constituting the communities of Spain, whose workaday preoccupation was to make a living, were intermingled with the Spanish-Moslem society, whose chief identifying trait was a feeling of hauteur and animosity toward other ethnic groups. These social relationships created within the Jews a tendency to segregate themselves spiritually and emotionally, and to stress in their consciousness and way of life within their own circles that which differentiated them from their neighbors. This was the reaction of Jews throughout the Diaspora whenever religio-national hatred waxed strong and non-Jews regarded them with arrogance.

The reaction of Spanish Jewry—this spiritual introversion—was typical of the way of life of all Jews in the Diaspora. The selfsame Jew who six days a week heard the cries of Arab shopkeepers, the Berbers and *muwalladūn* (who were involved in a struggle with each other), and who heard the slanders of all these groups directed at the Jews, really enjoyed the moments during the Sabbath when he listened in the synagogue to the scholars expounding the laws of the Gemara, whose sole intent it was to surround the Jewish people with a protective hedge. The singlemindedness of Spanish Jewry was also tied to the status of Arabic culture in Spain. All instruction among Arabs in Spain was at that time concentrated in their religious laws. There had not yet arisen among them talented poets who could stimulate others to emulate them; nor had they begun to cultivate a knowledge of the various sciences. Hence no one within the Moslem environment could induce Jewish intellectuals to stray from their path and occupy themselves with subjects other than the laws of the Gemara.

II

For many generations Spanish Jewry was reared in the spirit of the Talmud. The masters of the halakha within the large communities sought to infuse their disciples with an awareness that the oral law, as it is summed up in the Babylonian Talmud, is *the* religion of the Jew in its purest form. They trained the members of their communities in a religio-national discipline, of which the first rule was obedience to the teachings of Babylonian *g'ōnīm*. The simple folk honored the scholars, as was befitting for spiritual leaders and authoritative teachers; and the scholars themselves, whose sole preoccupation was the halakha, spent their days and nights in schools and synagogues. In the academies of Lucena and Barcelona they delved into the tractates 'Erūbhīn, N'dārīm, and Y'bhāmōt and debated heatedly over the laws of impurity as expounded by Ḥanīna, called "the principal of the priests." Earnest and exacting scholars immersed themselves in the sea of the Talmud, engaged in casuistry, and discovered new interpretations and brought up problems. Those discussions were the very essence of their lives.

But not all the scholars devoted themselves to casuistry. While some debated the words of Rabba and Abaye, there were others who perused the folk tales in the Gemara, which would follow passages of halakha; the tales, legends, and succinct allusions that they found in the yellowed pages drew them more than the dry halakha and stirred their imagination.

There were many who did not find satisfaction in all the enactments propounded by the scholars of the academies. These men felt that the salvation of Israel did not lie in the many restrictions with which the scholars hedged the *miṣvōt* about. They held that those *miṣvōt* and enactments really thrust aside religious feeling and drained it of its vitality. For them the aim of talmudic legislation was to strengthen Judaism in alien lands, to make possible an accommodation with life in the Diaspora; whereas in the folk tales and legends—especially in the homilies—they found a thousand allusions to the termination of the exile, which was sure to come and which could be hastened by prayer and good deeds.

The more burdensome the yoke of the non-Jews upon the dispersed nation, the stronger grew the longing for redemption, the yearning for the return to Zion and for a life of peace in the ancestral land. This hope never dimmed and, in the dark days of oppression and persecution, indeed did strengthen their spirits. Throughout the generations, the hopes of the Jews for redemption were fed especially by tales concerning the Ten Tribes, who, according to legend, lived a life of freedom in a faraway land. Indeed, since the fall of the Roman Empire there had been repeated invasions by nations and tribes, large and small, which poured forth from the plains of Asia to the lands circling the Mediterranean Sea and set up new kingdoms. Why—so went their thinking—should not the stories found in the Apocrypha and the *midrāshīm* prove to be true, so that in due time the Lost Tribes would appear and emancipate their brethren oppressed by the yoke of the gentiles?

Thus in every generation many could be found whose ears were attuned to catch any report and whose hearts were ready to believe messengers of good tidings. The ground was prepared for preachers and visionaries. And indeed at the close of the ninth century C.E. a Jew who came from distant lands appeared in Andalusia, a scholar who could tell tales, great and marvelous, about the Ten Tribes and whose words left an indelible impression upon that generation.

He called himself Eldad, stating that he was a member of one of the tribes, which lived in freedom "beyond the River Kush." But his odd name had been of his own selection, and there was no truth to his tales about the land of his birth. He was, in fact, born in Babylonia. He was reared there in an environment permeated by Jewish culture. In his youth he was a disciple of distinguished teachers, and he himself became an outstanding scholar. However, though he was quite at home with talmudic halakha, he was most particularly interested in the folk tales and meditated upon the homilies, the parables, and allusions contained in them. After devoting much of his time to studies he began to deal in commerce. Eventually he left Irak and settled in the southern part of the Arabian peninsula, where the arteries of two branches of international trade in that era crossed each other. Each year ships from India, bearing precious cargoes of spices designated for Egypt and North Africa, would reach the cities of southern Arabia and the Red Sea ports. These ports also served as important way stations for the slave trade: blacks who were captured on the African continent and sold in Irak to work there on the large agricultural estates.

For many years the man who called himself Eldad lived in this portion of the Arabian peninsula where the vast trade routes met; he was successful in his dealings and became rich. But despite his multifarious business dealings and his success in buying and selling, he never forgot what he had learned when still young—the many tales about the kingdom of Israel and its ancient glory, and the promises of salvation in the future. He had acquired wealth but was far from happy. How could he, a man of fine sensitivity, be content when time and again he heard the scornful words that the Moslems insolently hurled at the Jews, who, having neither kingdom nor government, had to endure the yoke of non-Jews. The burden of exile grew more onerous from generation to generation. Even the Arab kingdom, which had earlier been favorable to the Jews, now began to oppress and humiliate them. Sadly and frequently, he mulled over these thoughts.

But from time to time he would hear reports about Jews living in far-off lands, Jews who enjoyed freedom. Travelers passing through Persia would tell about Jewish tribes living somewhere north of the Persian Gulf. The Jewish tribes of Hedjaz had not yet been destroyed; some of them clung to their faith, and even in the latter days of the Middle Ages the report was abroad that free Jews remained there who from time to time made depredations upon the Arabs, particularly those making the pilgrimage to Mecca. These stories were in part false rumors, but the reports that frequently reached Eldad about Jews in the mountains of Ethiopia had a basis in fact. Naturally, he listened eagerly to the tales of seafarers and merchant wayfarers, and he would press them to tell him more and more. But though he was interested in those free Jews, the Moslem merchants from whom he got these reports were not at all interested. They recounted to him what they had heard incidentally or casually. Their accounts were truncated and contradictory.

At all events, it was his opinion that what he heard on all sides could not be mere figments, and he continued his inquiry and investigation into the matter. Gradually an image of Jewish life in Ethiopia formed in his mind. Finally, luck was with him and he met some of these tribesmen who had been brought as slaves to Arab ports and redeemed by Jewish merchants. For hours Eldad sat with them, querying them sevenfold regarding their customs and way of life; whatever they told him in their broken Arabic he set down in writing. What they told him was balm to his soul. But their narratives not only provoked his wonder; they also reminded him of much that he had read in folk tales in his youth.

The Jews of Ethiopia were indeed a branch of Israel that had become separated from the main body of the nation in a much earlier era. It was a settlement in a faraway land that had lost contact with the other bodies of the nation. As a result, it was completely forgotten in many lands, and only the Jews of Egypt and southern Arabia were aware of its existence. They also knew that it had neither the Mishna nor the Talmud, but observed the commandments of the Torah in their own peculiar way. The first Jews in Ethiopia came from Egypt, and their religious outlook was influenced by the priests of the House of Onias, who had offered sacrifices upon Egyptian soil. Later Jews who were of direct Jewish descent or proselytes arrived there from southern Arabia. These intermarried with the Abyssinian tribe of Agau, many of whom became Jewish converts. From this tribe they acquired the language they came to speak and various customs.

When the Abyssinians became converts to Christianity, the break between Abyssianian Jews (known as Falashas) and Jewish groups elsewhere became complete, and the Christian faith began to exert an influence upon their way of life. Like the Egyptian Jews in the days of the Ptolemies, they had priests who offered up "sacrifices" of baked fine flour, and, like the Christians, they confessed to a priest before death. They also acquired the practice of baptizing their children from the Christians and together with the Abyssinian Christians began to celebrate some holidays. Like them they abolished the rights of the firstborn in matters of inheritance.[51] In the matter of Sabbath observance they conducted themselves like the Karaites and did not light candles on the Sabbath eve. They took their Sabbath laws and other laws from one of the books of the Apocrypha, *The Book of Jubilees,* which they regarded as sacred.

Apart from their religion, there was no difference between the Abyssinian Jews and their neighbors. Like them they were bellicose and for many generations carried on warfare with the Christian kings. They had their own kings and government, and according to various sources at the end of the ninth century the Falashas gained hegemony over the whole of Abyssinia, establishing from among them a dynasty of emperors.[52] This occurred near the time when the Babylonian Jewish merchant Eldad was living in southern Arabia and gathering information on the independent tribes of Israel.

The information reaching him convinced Eldad that no tribe had departed from Judah and that there did indeed exist a Jewish kingdom having a mighty army and waging warfare with might and main against its neighbors and observing the ancient statutes of the Torah. When these matters became clarified for him, he got the notion to leave his city and go among the dispersed Jews who groaned under gentile rule to bring them the good tidings concerning these independent tribes. He was of the opinion that the news of the existence of these tribes would give them the courage and strength to endure the heavy yoke of life in exile and perhaps stir them to deeds that would hasten the redemption—so he thought.[53]

To carry out the mission he had imposed on himself properly and to make the desirable impression, he believed that he must appear as one of the independent Abyssinian Jews. Having heard that some of them count themselves members of the tribe of Dan, he decided to claim to belong to that tribe; he called himself Eldad the son of Maḥlī the Danite and created for himself a genealogy going back to the progenitor of the tribe. Understandably, his first impulse was to go to Babylonia, whose Jewish community was numerically the largest and also was the religio-spiritual center for all Jewry.

In about 880 C.E. Eldad left the city in which he lived and set out for Irak, but along the way he was beset with uncertainty. Though much time had elapsed since he left Babylonia and he was now well on in years and his appearance altered, he was apprehensive that he would be recognized and that people, knowing him to be a deceiver, would not give his tidings credence. On reaching Babylonia he did not go before the heads of the community to tell his story nor did he show himself in the large academies. He was no doubt afraid of the reaction his words would provoke. But while he was in a city far from the academies he revealed a small part of his tidings, and his words roused much amazement. Eldad told them about the independent Jews beyond the rivers of Abyssinia and spoke of their customs, which differed from those of the Babylonian Jews.[54] But even there he did not expatiate on his story; instead, he hastened to leave the country.

Nevertheless, though he did not have the courage to divulge the matter for which he had gone to Babylonia, he did not discard his notion; instead, there came over him a stronger awareness that he had to fulfill his mission. Therefore, after a short time he went to Egypt; there he gained a greater degree of courage. He told the people that he had been taken prisoner by savage cannibals but had managed to escape, found a log floating on the Nile, got hold of it, and reached Egypt on it. He claimed to have sold the log and become rich with the money he got.[55] But since many Babylonian Jews lived in Egypt he became apprehensive, and after a short while he left as he had come.[56]

His notion had become an idée fixe, however, giving him no rest. After struggling with his many perplexities, he decided to go to a place far from Irak and there divulge his secret thoughts. Meanwhile, he could weigh and evaluate the impression his veiled hints had made in Irak and Egypt; he hoped that he would benefit from his experience in those lands.

Eldad next appeared in Kairawan, the most important community in all the lands of the Muslim West, a city full of scholars. On arriving there, he spoke only Hebrew, saying that this was his native tongue and the language spoken by all the free Jews of Ethiopia. He maintained that the knew no other tongue and endeavored to speak in biblical Hebrew. Naturally, this was not easy for him, especially since he wanted his speech to have the quality of ancient Hebrew. He therefore used words of rare occurrence, employed the causative verb form extensively, and at times imparted to Hebrew words an extraordinary sense or even spoke words entirely unknown. Since he had lived for several decades in an Arabic environment and thought in that language, he would at times use idioms carried over from Arabic or even employ actual Arabic words.[57]

The Jews of Kairawan were amazed and began to put this strange traveler to the test. They made a list of the uncommon and unknown words that he used, and after some days had passed, they asked him once more for their meaning, to convince themselves that he was familiar with these expressions; he passed the test.

Meanwhile, Eldad lectured in public, telling his story about the independent Jewish tribes. He claimed to come from "Havilah, where there is gold" (Genesis 2:11) and related that in Abyssinia four tribes dwelt: the tribes of Dan, Naphtali, Gad, and Asher. The Danites had left the land of Israel in the days of Jeroboam the son of Nebat, and had reached Ethiopia by way of Egypt; the tribes of Napthali, Gad, and Asher arrived there much later. In Ethiopia they were fruitful, multiplied, and became wealthy, and now, went his account, they sowed and reaped and had orchards and vineyards in great number. These tribes were constantly waging war against the Abyssinian kings. Each tribe would fight for three months, bringing booty to their king, whose name was Adiel (or Uzziel); he would apportion it. The four tribes lived according to the laws of the Torah and could execute the four means of capital punishment prescribed by Jewish law.

In the land of Ḥavīla the Levites also dwelt, who, when in

Babylonia, refused to sing the Lord's song in a foreign land at the demand of the Chaldeans and were then taken miraculously to that place. The river Sambaṭyōn separated them from the four tribes; its waters flowed swiftly, hurling huge stones. The Levites were isolated behind the river, unable to enter or leave, but they kept in touch with the four tribes by means of carrier pigeons.

There was some truth in Eldad's account[58] concerning the free Jews in Abyssinia—but the story about the Levites was an utter fabrication. Generally speaking, he told a composite of truth and fiction. This was the wont of most travelers in those days, except that Eldad had an ulterior motive in spreading his fabrications. He repeated in his tale an old legend about the fate of the Levites that he had found in folkloristic accounts woven around chapter 137 in the Book of Psalms. Even the river Sambaṭyōn is mentioned in midrashic literature, and non-Jewish writers of olden times also knew about it.[59]

Eldad also told an engrossing story about his journey to Kairawan from the land of the four tribes. His words had a twofold purpose. Wanting to explain why the free tribes did not come to the aid of their brothers who were being oppressed by the Arabs, he told them that no road existed from their land to the countries bordering upon the Mediterranean and that he himself reached them unintentionally by a chain of extraordinary occurrences. He inserted into his travel story information about the other tribes of Israel that had been exiled by the Assyrians and continued to live in various parts of the world in freedom and independence. This tale was a conglomerate of all the reports that had reached him over many years.

Eldad said that he had gone forth with a Jew from the tribe of Asher to engage in trade; when the ship in which they sailed foundered, he and his companion held fast to a board until they reached a Negro people who were cannibals. They slew and ate his companion, and he himself was delivered from their hands when they were themselves attacked by other savages who took him captive. He tarried with these people a long time, until they took him to the land of Sin, where he met a Jew of the tribe of Issachar, who redeemed him and took him to his country.

The tribe of Issachar—according to Eldad's account—dwelt in the mountains at the rim of the Persian Gulf. For their livelihood they raised sheep and cattle. The tribe of Zebulun dwelt in the mountains of Paran reaching to the Euphrates River; they dealt in trade and commerce. The tribe of Reuben dwelt nearby, and at times the three tribes would combine to make war against their neighbors. These tribes obeyed the laws of the Torah and its statutes, maintaining among other things the four methods of capital punishment; they also had the Mishna and Talmud. The tribe of Ephraim and half the tribe of Manasseh lived on the Arabian peninsula, not far from the cities of Mecca and Medina. But the tribe of Simeon and the other half of the tribe of Manasseh dwelt in the remote north, where they held sway over their neighbors and twenty-five kingdoms who were their slaves and did their work.[60]

Eldad realized the anomaly that inhered in his account of the tribes of Israel in Ethiopia, separated in part from the entire nation before the destruction of the first Temple, and maintaining the Mosaic law without the oral law that gives a detailed commentary on the commandments. He therefore stated that they had their own Talmud, entirely composed in Hebrew, which had no discussion at all but merely the tradition as submitted by Joshua bin Nun. He told the scholars of Kairawan that he had brought with him a portion of this Talmud: the part having the laws pertaining to the slaughter of animals (*sh'ḥīṭā*) and the laws dealing with nonkosher food.

It is plain that he wanted to report to the scholars of the academies of North Africa those practices of the Falashas that did not differ sharply from the official Jewish position. Had he reported that there are Falasha hermits who castrate themselves and the like, they would instantly have said that these tribes were not Jews at all. And how strong their protest would have been had he reported about the calendar of the Falashas and their festivals! But there was nothing in the differences relating to animal slaughter that could affect any principles of faith; and in general the development of practices relating to this subject had not reached a conclusive stage in that era.

The ritual laws that Eldad mentioned to the rabbis of Kairawan were, of course, figments of his own imagination, but they were nevertheless similar to the practices of the Falashas, as these had been reported to him by various people. The remainder were laws and customs that had been discarded over the years but that a scholar such as Eldad would have knowledge of.[61] The most conspicuous element in Eldad's laws was the principle that every effort must be made to drain all the blood out of a slaughtered animal. According to Eldad's law, the legs of an animal, which had been first tied, should be loosed immediately after the application of the slaughter knife, so that by its kicking action the animal would draw the blood from its limbs. This extra strictness with regard to drainage of the animal's blood was the singular concern of those factions in Israel which, for their part, viewed even ordinary slaughter as having sanctity, since they even offered sacrifices outside the limits of the Temple Mount; whereas the position of the official body of Jewry was that there was a sharp distinction between the offering of sacrifices and ordinary animal slaughter, for which they allowed concessions.

The Falashas, having acquired their customs from the priests of the House of Onias, did their slaughtering in the courtyards of their synagogues, and in this respect acted in accordance with the principles mentioned by Eldad.[62] The rabbis set down no fixed rule regarding the age of the slaughterer (*shōḥēṭ*), whereas the Karaites required that he be at least thirteen years old; but in Eldad's rules the age was set at eighteen.[63] The juridical schools of thought followed by the majority of the Moslems, on the other hand, did not fix a specific age for a slaughterer. Eldad's raising of the age of the slaughterer did not, therefore, stem from the influence of Moslem environment.[64]

Generally speaking, Eldad's rules of slaughter resembled those of the Karaites rather than those of the Rabbanites; on the other hand, this mysterious traveler reported on laws concerning forbidden foods to the rabbis of Kairawan, who had no such body of laws whatsoever. To be sure, even in the matter of food whose consumption is either forbidden or permitted, there was an important difference in Eldad's rules as compared with the prohibitions accepted among Jews in general. According to Eldad it cannot be inferred that the verse "Thou shalt not seethe a kid in its mother's milk" (Exodus 23:19) constitutes a general prohibition against eating meat together with milk, but the verse should rather be interpreted liberally; and indeed, the Falashas know nothing about this prohibition.[65]

The scholars of Kairawan were surprised and amazed, and as it was their wont in all matters of doubt or religious problems to turn to the head of the Babylonian academies, they did so on this occasion. They rushed a missive to the *gaon* Ṣemaḥ bar Ḥayyīm, the head of the Academy of Sura, in which they reported Eldad's account of the four independent tribes of Abyssinia and a résumé of his body of laws, and asked for an opinion.[66] They also set down in writing Eldad's tale of his travels and distributed it to other communities of North Africa.[67]

Ṣemaḥ sent back an unequivocal and well-reasoned reply. In his opening remarks he wrote that he had already heard about Eldad, for in about 880 a man named Isaac bar Simḥa had met him.[68] He gave proof that there was no contradiction between the accepted tradition and Eldad's account that the tribe of

Dan had wandered to Ethiopia before the exile of the other tribes. Even the report concerning the Levites going from Babylonia to Ethiopia and living on the other side of the river Sambaṭyōn was credible, wrote the *gaon*. As to the differences between Eldad's version of the laws and those practiced by the Jews generally, Ṣemaḥ pointed to the fact that the Gemara abounds in differences of opinion among the scholars; and he also added that perhaps Eldad had erred and forgotten some things on account of the tribulations that had befallen him during his wanderings.[69]

From the *gaon's* viewpoint, Eldad's version of the laws constituted a support for normative Judaism as against the Karaites, since it proved that even a stray and isolated segment of the Jewish people depended upon oral law that greatly resembled the oral law of the rabbis. But more important, there was encouragement in the message of Eldad, and most likely it was for this reason that the *gaon* hastened to justify his words to the people of Kairawan.

When the reply from the *gaon* was received in Kairawan, esteem for Eldad mounted among all people, and even those who had previously been skeptical of his reports now accepted them as true. Eldad himself drew encouragement from his success and decided to continue his journey. But he still remained hesitant and cautious, preferring to visit communities in those provinces that the Arabs included under the name "Midwest" (today's Algeria) and the "Far West," now known as Morocco. His chief goal was Spain, however, inasmuch as, aside from Babylonia, it was regarded in those days as the land with the most important Jewish settlement.

In 883 Eldad sent a letter to the Jews of Spain to inform them of his coming and to transmit the events of his life to them,[70] and then started on his way. He first visited all the important communities of the Maghreb, and everywhere he told his story in expensive detail. One place he visited was Ṭāhort, the capital of the principality of the Banū Rustum and an important center of trade, in which a large Jewish community existed. In this city he met the grammarian Judah b. Ḳuraish, author of a number of treatises. Naturally the grammarian was happy to chance upon a Jew of the Ten Tribes who claimed he knew no language other than Hebrew. He queried him extensively, listing the uncommon locutions he heard from Eldad and employing them to explain difficult words in the Scriptures.[71]

When Eldad the Danite reached Andalusia he was welcomed with honor. Here too he spoke in public, and the report that he gave in biblical Hebrew aroused much interest among the learned and the unlearned alike. Achieving success and acquiring greater self-assurance, he began to embellish his story and add various details. Thus whereas in Kairawan he had stated that in the "Talmud" of the four tribes no name except that of Joshua bin Nun is mentioned, in Spain he added the name of the judge Othniel b. Kenaz, putting it thus: Othniel b. Kenaz received the tradition from Joshua, who received it from Moses, who received it from God.[72]

But his audiences did not pay close heed to the expansions and modifications in his report; indeed, the more he spoke, the more they enjoyed hearing him. When the tanned, gray-haired old man, wearing a long beard, would stand in the courtyard of the synagogue and speak about the tribes in Ethiopia, the hearts of his listeners were full of joy and beat with pride. His words made a strong impression and aroused much excitement. For a long time his report was the subject for discussion and comment, and the majority of the Andalusian Jews did not cast any doubt upon the tidings he brought. Their joy was doubly great, for they could now have a retort to the Moslems and Christians when reproached by them because the scepter had departed from Judah. Eldad accomplished a great deal while in Spain. He even brought to the Jews there a "Hymn of Unity" composed by the Levites on the other side of the river Sambaṭyōn.[73]

However, his stay in the Iberian peninsula was not of long

duration, and after having visited several important communities he left the country and returned to the Near East. He fully recognized that he would have to fulfill the main object of his mission, to bring good tidings and encouragement, among the Jews of Babylonia. His successes in Kairawan and Spain inspired him with the courage to return there. After a long journey he finally reached his homeland, and this time was emboldened to appear at the Academy of Sura. There he lectured on the subject of release from vows, also revealing that he possessed the "Talmud" of the four tribes. But on being asked to produce the volume so that a copy could be made of it, he had misgivings and claimed that he had to resume his journey. Once again he was overcome with timidity while in Babylonia.[74]

So this old man disappeared never to be seen again. He came like a meteor, but his message was never forgotten; and when men gathered in the synagogues of Toledo and Cordova on Sabbaths and festivals, they retold the words of Eldad for many decades.

5

ḤASDAI IBN SHAPRŪṬ

I

The weakening of the ties between the Jews of Spain and the Babylonian academies that began at the end of the ninth and the start of the tenth century was no doubt linked to the political state in which the Iberian peninsula found itself in that era. The disintegration of the Omayyad kingdom and the sprouting up of minuscule princedoms that were constantly at war with each other naturally interfered with the flourishing of the Jewish communities and the fostering of their cultural values. These Andalusian communities, which sprang up anew with the Moslem conquest of Spain and the establishment of Omayyad rule, had hardly become firmly established and still were in the process of becoming rooted. Many communities were founded in the ninth century and, being small and weak, required assistance. The fighting among the various princes, meantime, was very savage; they showed no mercy to the cities or their inhabitants, who suffered fearfully.

But all that changed completely in the second decade of the tenth century. The new ruler of Cordova, 'Abdarraḥmān III, succeeded in reuniting Moslem Spain. This was not the sequel of a series of successful campaigns only; it resulted from a very clever policy. 'Abdarraḥmān III conceived the idea of reconciling the followers of the different religions and the members of the various ethnic groups who lived under his scepter, and of blending them more or less into one nation. When he had reestablished the unity of the old Omayyad kingdom, he assumed, in 929, the title of caliph and the surname an-Nāṣir li-dīn Allāh—"he who gives victory to Allah's creed." He embarked on a very active foreign policy and launched new wars with the Christians in northern Spain. But on the other hand peace prevailed within his kingdom, and a new flourishing of the Spanish economy set in. Industries enjoyed unheard-of prosperity, and commercial relations with other Mediterranean countries were intense.

In the middle of the tenth century, Moslem Spain was a strong military power and a very wealthy state. The fixed revenues of the royal exchequer were large and enabled the caliph to erect a new capital city near Cordova. This new city, whose construction was started in 936, was called Madīnat az-Zahrā. Since it was designed to symbolize the splendor of the Omayyad kingdom, the caliph spared neither means nor money to attract outstanding craftsmen to his project and to procure the most precious building materials from every available source. The administration in both the central and provincial governments was very efficient during his rule. In essence it was the caliph's distinction that he himself was so thoroughly consistent in all he did. The very length of his rule added stability to the renewed Omayyad monarchy; he reigned almost fifty years: from 912 till his death in 961.

As was the practice of many mighty oriental despots, he himself conducted the affairs of the government. At first he was aided by a prime minister, or *ḥādjib*, but after the death of Mūsā b. Ḥudair in 932 he did not appoint anyone in his place. Moreover, 'Abdarraḥmān III endeavored to base his rule on the collaboration of the various national groups within his kingdom: Arabs, Berbers, and descendants of the Ibero-Spanish population. Naturally, many of the important posts at the royal court, in the army, and in the civil administration were held by noble Arab families, such as the Banū Abī 'Abda, Banū Ḥudair, and Banū Shuhaid. Nevertheless, Berber families appear in the lists of nobles and high officials also.

Alongside them, holding eminent positions, was a group of courtiers not of Spanish descent at all but recently come to the Iberian peninsula. These were slaves bought by the Omayyad ruler to serve in various posts at the royal court. Such was the custom of Moslem rulers in both the East and the West. In keeping with the practice of Moslem despots, 'Abdarraḥmān an-Nāṣir deliberately changed those holding office at frequent intervals, but it is evident that in his last days the bondsmen known as Slavs (*Ṣaḳāliba*), because they came from East European lands, waxed in power. Just as 'Abdarraḥmān III drew unto himself men of various national origins almost as a matter of course, he also welcomed the service of non-Moslems.

'Abdarraḥmān III was distinguished for his tolerance insofar as matters of faith were concerned. To be sure, he observed the practices of his religion, but he was far from being a zealot. There is no doubt that this enlightened ruler was the most tolerant of all the Omayyads who ruled in Cordova. The chronicles of his reign include no information of any harm befalling non-Moslem communities. This matter is all the more conspicuous in light of the information about the Jews' lot in other countries, whether Islamic or Christian, on the rim of the Mediterranean basin in that era. By the middle of the ninth century Jews and Christians throughout the lands of the Abbasid caliphate were required to mark their garments with a distinct sign, and at the start of the tenth century this offensive law had been reenacted by Caliph al-Muḳtadir. He also ordered anew the dismissal of non-Moslem officials from government service. The rulers of the Islamic countries in the East found many other ways to oppress the religious minorities and embitter their lives.

To evaluate properly the difference between the condition of the Jews in Moslem Spain and that of the Jews in the other Moslem lands and endeavor to ascertain the causes for it, we must not forget that the juridical school of thought dominating Islamic Spain, the Mālikite school, was in this regard one of the strictest. We should therefore give credit for the absence of persecutions to that great ruler, who left his mark on his own generation and the one that followed.

After the great difficulties of the first days of his rule, 'Abdarraḥmān III kept faith with the policy of tolerance that was so characteristic of the Omayyad dynasty, but so very different from the policy that most Moslem dynasties adopted toward any religious minority. When he ascended the throne, Andalusia was immersed in a struggle between those supporting the emirate of Cordova and those supporting 'Umar b. Ḥafṣūn, with both sides viewing it as a religious struggle. 'Abdarraḥmān III also held this view of the struggle with 'Umar b. Ḥafṣūn. He wanted to attract to his side the *muwalladūn,* the Spaniards who had converted to Islam; he therefore was very stern toward the Christian soldiers of 'Umar b. Ḥafṣūn, and sought to cast dread into the hearts of the Mozarabs, so that they would desist from their support of an archrebel.[1] The beginning of 'Abdarraḥmān's reign also witnessed the renewal of the suicide-martyrs.[2]

But the placatory spirit demonstrated by 'Abdarraḥmān after he had subdued the rebels in southern Andalusia accomplished its purpose. Gradually the Omayyad ruler won the loyalty of the non-Moslem populace, and even the very observant Christians were grateful to him for the security they enjoyed under his rule. And the Jews benefited from 'Abdarraḥmān's policy even more than the Christians. In a state that comprised varied ethnic and religious elements and whose rule was enlightened and far from fanatical, which sought to bring together the different elements in the population without forcing the smaller groups to assimilate with the larger ones—in such a state the Jews of the Diaspora found their place and their communities flourished. In those days Moslem Spain was a multinational state and did not bear a clearly defined religious stamp; therefore its rule did not endanger the existence of a minority, national or religious. On the contrary, the Omayyad government depended upon a variety of groups. Loyalty and ability in achievement fixed the status of individuals and of groups, and in these traits the Jews were outstanding. Therefore, their lot under the rule of the first Omayyad caliph was a happy one, and it was not long before a Jew rose to high office at the royal court.

II

In the 940s there rose into the ascendant in the skies of Andalusia the star of a court Jew. Moslems and Jews alike spoke in whispers, saying that this Jew was one of the caliph's favorites and had it within his power to help or harm. At first there was nothing outstanding about this Jewish courtier, but as time passed the caliph gave him important assignments and then his name became well known.

He was a member of a Jewish family from Jaén, an important city in eastern Andalusia. The family's name was Ibn Shaprūṭ. The courtier's father, whose name was Isaac b. Ezra Ibn Shaprūṭ, had left the city of his forefathers and gone to the capital of Moslem Spain, Cordova.[3] Isaac Ibn Shaprūṭ was a wealthy man known for his piety. He was devoted to the Jewish faith with all his soul and might. Among many benevolent deeds he established a synagogue in his new city of residence. He was also interested in literary matters, a benefactor giving generous support to scholars and writers who devoted their lives to the Torah and to literature.[4]

In about 910 a son was born to him whom he named Ḥasdai.

Of course such a father would give a son an excellent education. The youth was taught the Scriptures and other traditional subjects by good teachers; but even though he evinced unusual abilities while still young, he seemed to show no penchant for these subjects. Apparently he did not become a distinguished Torah scholar. As a lad he showed a proclivity for languages and had a good knowledge of Arabic, both written and spoken. He also studied Latin with Christian teachers, members of the Mozarab clergy of Cordova. Besides these two languages, he knew, as did the majority of Andalusians, Romance, a dialect that evolved from a late form of Latin and was to become the language of the Spaniards. At that time Romance was spoken not only by the Mozarabs but also by many Moslems, descendants of Spaniards and mixed families.

The strongest desire of the maturing youth was the study of medicine, to which he devoted all his intellectual energies. Day and night he studied diligently the books on medicine which Arab doctors in the Near East had written, books which contained the essence of the medical lore of the Greeks as translated by oriental Christians in the ninth century.

The youthful Ḥasdai was outstanding not only for his ability and diligence, but also most particularly for his character. He had that quality that is precious above all others: he knew how to get along with people, was pleasant to everyone, and won their trust. He actually took people's hearts captive. He was very bright, and each word he uttered was measured and properly reasoned out. He was also ambitious and had already decided to succeed and become famous. He was not concerned about the welfare of the masses, but rather sought for himself happiness, success, and wealth. Ḥasdai believed in himself, in his ability, and in his future.

The youth became a man and progressed consistently. Although his contemporaries were married by now and involved in family matters, Ḥasdai Ibn Shaprūṭ remained a bachelor.

In a letter written to him in the 940s, the wish is expressed that he acquire a wife, "a lovely and graceful bride, one proper for him, to be a help to him and give him children and grandchildren, who would occupy themselves with that which is more precious than pearls" (meaning the Torah).[5] There can be no other reason for his remaining single than Ḥasdai's desire to devote all his time to advancement in the honorable profession of medicine and not to take the responsibilities of marriage upon himself.

Before many years had passed, he had acquired fame in Cordova as a distinguished practitioner of medicine. His cures were successful and his praise on everyone's lips.[6] He was known especially for a discovery he made. From ancient days doctors had sought to put together a miracle drug that would be effective against a large variety of ills and especially against various poisons. People for many generations, until the nineteenth century, believed that if they could succeed in compounding such a remedy properly, it could be used successfully against snakebites and poisons, stomach ailments and asthma, jaundice and myopia, impotence, the plague, and other epidemic diseases. In the early part of the first century B.C.E. a king, Mithridates Eupator, first discovered a remedy known as theriaca. Later Andromachus of Crete, who was Emperor Nero's doctor, developed a wonder drug compounded from sixty-one elements. This remedy became famous throughout the world, and in the second century C.E. the Roman government produced it for their own use. But with the passing of time the secret formula of this precious compound was lost, and the doctors labored mightily to rediscover it. Arabic doctors, who called this wonder drug *fārūḳ*, and Jewish doctors, who called it "the savior," did a lot of research, and men of wealth, especially nobles, put at their disposal the necessary financial and material means. Among the substances required for this compound the doctors of the Middle Ages numbered opium, snake's flesh properly boiled, and various spices. Maimonides wrote a treatise concerning theriaca, wherein he describes the effort put forth by the vizier, al-Ḳādī al-Fāḍil, who sought by divers means to get the elements needed in compounding theriaca from distant lands.

One day Ḥasdai Ibn Shaprūṭ reported that he had succeeded in rediscovering the secret and in compounding theriaca.[7] It is no wonder that so successful and noted a physician was summoned to serve at the royal court. Thus it came to pass that Ḥasdai first set foot in the palace of 'Abdarraḥmān. This was at the beginning of the 940s, when Ḥasdai was still young, being not much over thirty years old.[8] He was not the only physician appointed to the royal household, for it was the custom of Moslem caliphs in the Middle Ages to employ several doctors and seek their counsel when necessary. Near the royal court at Cordova an actual medical service was set up composed of the caliph's physicians.[9]

Success shone upon Ḥasdai in his new field of endeavor. Even on the slippery ground of the royal court. Ḥasdai made his way skillfully and wisely. His calm speech and pleasant ways made a good impression, and when conversations took place between him and the caliph that dealt with matters other than health, the caliph noted his great intelligence and willingly gave him his ear. 'Abdarraḥmān III appointed some physicians to administrative posts,[10] among them the Jewish physician. He turned over to him the management of the department of customs.[11] This was an important office inasmuch as the duty collected from the ships coming to Spain and departing from it constituted an important source of revenue for the royal exchequer.[12] Nevertheless, the caliph did not elevate Ḥasdai to the level of finance minister, or, as such ministers were called in those days in the Moslem Kingdom of Spain, *khāzin*. The only explanation can be that the practical ruler was careful not to elevate a Jew too high so as not to provoke the wrath of the Moslems. 'Abdarraḥmān III was too circumspect to disregard the feelings of his subjects, who were zealous in their faith.[13]

On the other hand, the caliph put Ḥasdai Ibn Shaprūṭ at the head of the Jewish settlement in his kingdom and gave him the authority to settle the affairs of the communities as he saw fit. Among the Jews he was known by the title of *nāsī* (prince).[14] By virtue of the authority and status of his office he was able to defend individuals or whole communities against harm when enemies arose to trouble them. He was able to rescue a Jew whom the tax collectors had set upon to rob; and when he interceded for another to ask that he might be given a post in the service of the government, his words did not go unheeded.

After the manner of nobles and high government officials he bestowed alms upon the needy with a generous hand, and for this reason Abū Yūsuf, as he was popularly called, received praise, and the fame of his deeds was spread throughout all the communities of Spain. In the view of the Jews of Spain it was not for his own merit or for his ability that Ḥasdai Ibn Shaprūṭ reached his high station; rather, it was in their behalf that he won the appointment. It was their opinion that his designation and success were the act of Providence, which exercised a protective care over the Jews even under the yoke of gentile nations in alien lands. Thinkers developed this notion and propagated it, so that it became a commonly held view. One of the Hebrew poets living in Moslem Spain in that era even gave it poetical expression.[15]

III

In his new office as director of customs Ḥasdai Ibn Shaprūṭ was also very successful, and the esteem in which the caliph held him went ever higher. From time to time he would be asked to give an opinion on a variety of matters that disturbed the caliph's peace of mind, and the advice he gave was regarded with favor. Inasmuch as Ḥasdai knew Latin very well and this was the language the Christian kingdoms in northern Spain used in their negotiations with the caliph, he began to require Ḥasdai's aid at more and more frequent intervals whenever a situation involving a knowledge of Latin arose. In those days there was no minister of foreign affairs at the court of Cordova; it was the caliph himself who dealt with matters concerning other governments and who settled all affairs at his own discretion. He would place responsibility for a mission or negotiations on this or that officer. At all events, it was more congenial for him to be able to consult with a courtier who was not suspected of rebellious tendencies, but rather was as pliable as clay in the hands of the potter.

There were many contacts between the court of the Omayyad caliph and the other countries on the rim of the Mediterranean. Even as troops of soldiers crossed the border of the Duero River in either direction, which happened almost annually, negotiations would also be in progress between the royal courts of León and Pamplona and the government of the caliph—and at times even missives from vassal nobles of Christian kings who were conspiring against their masters. Local rulers in the Moroccan and Algerian provinces would send messengers to the caliph requesting his aid, moral and financial, in their struggle with the Fatimids and transmitting information about intrigues fabricated in utter secrecy in various oases. Any reply that was made called for the highest degree of sagacity.

Even the great kingdoms of Christian Europe would send emissaries to the court of the caliph seeking his intervention when the subject appeared to be important to them. In consequence, Cordova was a center of diplomatic activity tied by threads to many lands. Dealing with these affairs took up much time on the caliph's part, and in time occupation with them came to be one of the important responsibilities of his aide and advisor, Ḥasdai Ibn Shaprūṭ.

At the close of the 940s diplomatic ties were renewed between the Byzantine Empire and the Omayyad kingdom of Spain, and Ḥasdai took an active part in these negotiations. More than one hundred years had passed since ties between these two governments had first been established. Throughout this long period the Omayyad kingdom of Spain had gone downhill because of rebellions and was not a state that the Byzantine emperor deemed worthy of friendship. However, in the middle of the tenth century a change occurred, and Moslem Spain once again became a strong power. The ruler in Constantinople at this time was Constantine VII, also called Constantinos Porphyrogenetos (945–959), a scholar and author who was very much interested in festive ceremonies and in protocol dealing with the reception of diplomatic missions; he had even written a treatise on this subject. During his reign the Byzantine Empire waxed stronger and hoped to regain large areas in the Near East that it had lost.

But this was the very time that the Fatimids were establishing their kingdom in North Africa. Their powerful war fleets cast dread throughout the shores of the Mediterranean Sea, and their armies began to raid areas under Byzantine rule.[16] The Fatimids, who had not yet conquered Egypt, were regarded by the experienced and far-seeing Byzantines as a potentially dangerous enemy. Since they were aware of the history of relations between the Fatimids and the Omayyads of Spain, Constantinos VII decided to initiate negotiations with the caliph in faraway Cordova. In 947 he sent a eunuch named Salemon to the capital of Moslem Spain with the suggestion that the caliph send a mission to Constantinople to negotiate a treaty of friendship. 'Abdarraḥmān complied with this suggestion, and while Salemon continued on to Germany to carry out a similar mission there, the Omayyad caliph prepared a delegation to depart for Constantinople.

In the summer of 948 the delegation, headed by a Christian

cleric, Hishām b. Kulaib, set sail and reached its destination in peace. After tarrying some days to rest from the rigors of the journey, the delegation received a festive welcome at the emperor's palace on October 24. The emperor, on his part, decided to send a delegation to Cordova in response to the caliph's invitation. At the head of this delegation he placed one of his courtiers, Stephanos, who held the posts of *ostiarius* and *nifsestiarius*—chief of protocol for welcoming visitors and emperor's chamberlain, who ministered to his personal wants.

The Byzantine mission set sail in the spring of 949 in three ships that were accompanied by the Byzantine fleet, which was going out to do battle with the Moslem rulers of the isle of Crete. In August the Byzantines reached the port of Pechina, and when the caliph was informed of this, he sent one of his courtiers, Yaḥyā b. Muḥammad Ibn al-Laith, to accompany them to the capital. The arrival of this mission was regarded as a signal honor by the caliph, who did all he could to give them a reception worthy of the representatives of a great power. When they reached the outskirts of Cordova a military parade was arranged in their honor, and when they came into the city itself they were housed in Munyat an-Naṣr, the palace of the crown prince. The caliph himself, who was then in Madīnat az-Zahrā, returned to welcome the mission in his palace at Cordova.

On the day designated for the reception, September 8, the palace was decorated, especially the portico called "al-Madjlis ab-Zāhir," where the caliph sat on the royal throne and received the emissaries. The Byzantines handed him a *chrysobull,* a royal epistle in Greek, written on blue parchment in gold letters. This parchment, in the form of a scroll, contained a page on which the gifts sent by the emperor were listed. On the missive itself was a seal of gold of considerable weight, on one side of which was a picture of Jesus and on the other a likeness of the emperor and his son. The scroll—so goes the admiring account by Arabic chroniclers—was inside a silver box adorned with engravings and topped with a cover of gold. They also report that many poets and writers were commanded to compose poems and orations to recite during the welcome, to embellish the occasion, but most of them became frightened when they beheld the multitude of distinguished people, the resplendent garb, and the decorated hall.[17]

Of the mission itself (that is, what the emissaries transmitted orally, aside from the document containing the pact), or the emperor's proposals and the outcome of the discussions between the ambassadors and the caliph, or the role of Ḥasdai Ibn Shaprūṭ—of all these matters, the Arabic chroniclers tell little. One of the Arabic historians speaks of a treaty of friendship between the two governments as a result of the emperor's action.

On the other hand, some of the chroniclers do mention a number of the gifts brought by the emperor's emissaries. As was befitting a ruler as scholarly as Constantinos, he sent the caliph rare books. One was a history by a Spanish author of the fifth century, Orosius, who wrote it in Latin, and another was a manuscript of Dioscorides' *De Materia Medica* in the original Greek. Its author, Pedanios Dioscorides from Ainzerba, who lived in the second half of the first century C.E., summarized the attainments of Greek pharmacology, also adding a great deal from his own experience. His book, in which he mentions more than six hundred plants, oils, and stones which could be used for medicinal purposes, became *the* textbook on pharmacology for fifteen hundred years. It was translated into Arabic in the middle of the ninth century in Bagdad by a group of Christian translators upon whom the Abbasid caliphs imposed the duty of translating the classical works of Greek literature. The translation of this book had been undertaken by Stephen the son of Basil, and the leader of the group, the renowned physician Ḥunain b. Isḥāḳ, examined the translation and made emendations therein. But the two could not explain a substantial number of plant names mentioned in the work of the Greek physician.[18] Nevertheless, their translation circulated among all Arabic-speaking lands, and physicians depended upon it until the middle of the tenth century.

The manuscript that the emperor sent to Cordova was illuminated with beautiful designs and aroused wonder; but it also made for difficulty. For among the Christians in Moslem Spain there were none who knew Greek, and in consequence the book was likely to remain unopened in the caliph's library like an unturned stone. Therefore the caliph asked the emperor to send him a person who knew Greek and Latin and who would teach some of his people Greek so that they would be able to translate books from that language. The emperor, responding to his request, sent a monk named Nicholas. He arrived at Cordova in 340 A.H. (951/952 C.E.) and began his work. As reported by an Arabic physician who lived in Spain in the second half of the tenth century, there were at the time in Cordova several physicians who were interested in the translation project, but the greatest degree of interest was shown by Ḥasdai Ibn Shaprūṭ. For one thing, there stirred in him anew a desire to increase his knowledge and steep himself in research, a field in which he was outstanding in his youth; and for another, he wanted to demonstrate his prowess to the caliph in order to buttress his standing. And he knew well how much the caliph esteemed this activity. With youthful energy Ḥasdai set to work translating, with Nicholas, the names of those remedies hitherto not understood by the Arabs, and in particular coordinating the translation with the correct idiomatic usage in Arabic Spain.[19] It need hardly be said that the regard in which the caliph held him increased greatly with this display of versatility.

But even while Ḥasdai applied himself diligently to scholarly pursuits, he was not permitted to be free of diplomatic affairs.

Not only was the caliph absorbed in relations with the Christian kingdoms of northern Spain and with the princes of Morocco, for which he sought the advice of Ḥasdai, but he had also become diplomatically involved in a serious way with a mighty power not bordering upon his kingdom, one with which he seemingly had no dealings. In the negotiations between the caliph and representatives of this power Ḥasdai filled an important role.

That involvement had resulted from the activities of Spanish robber bands, which undermined the security of the shores of France and its neighbors. In the 890s a large group of robbers had settled on La Garde-Freinet in the bay of Saint-Tropez in Provence. From there they organized predatory raids on the continent—throughout all the provinces of southern France to the lofty Alps. They set ambushes in the mountain passes for pilgrims on their way to Rome and other wayfarers and attacked wealthy monasteries; and the more they succeeded in their depredations, the bolder they grew. Their swift-moving bands penetrated to remote valleys in the Alps, reaching the cantons of Switzerland. In 939 they raided the eastern monastery of Saint Gall, one of the wealthiest in alpine lands.

Matters came to such a pass that Otto I, king of Germany (936–973) decided to intervene. Otto I stood guard to protect the interests of Christianity everywhere and labored arduously to spread his faith throughout eastern Germany; obviously he would not sit by idly while bands of Spanish Moslems invaded the territories under his rule. The provinces that suffered most from the forays of those brigands belonged to the kingdom of Burgundy, which encompassed a large part of what is now western France and western Switzerland, to which Provence was annexed after 948. When Rudolf II, king of Burgundy, died in 937, the king of Germany placed Rudolf's young son Conrad under his aegis, and Conrad began to act as regent of Burgundy. This was done to prevent Hugo, the king of Italy, from seizing control of it; such a move would have created a large kingdom encompassing Italy and western France to the Rhine. The eastern provinces of Switzerland belonged to the German duchy of Swabia, but important districts had been given to bishops, such as the bishop of Chur, who was related to Otto I.

It was thus a matter of great importance that the German ruler take effective measures for the defense of Burgundy and Switzerland; he therefore sent an emissary to the caliph at Cordova asking him to put an end to the depredations. 'Abdarraḥmān reacted by sending a mission of his own to the court of the German ruler in 950. This mission was headed by a Mozarab bishop who was received with great honor, but when the letter he took to the ruler was perused, it was found to hold contumelious utterances against Christianity. Naturally, this was regarded as a searing insult, and the king, who was very mindful of his honor, was strongly offended. But he did not rush into penning his reply or sending the embassy home. Meanwhile, Otto I went to Italy in 951, but he was compelled to return because a revolt had broken out in Germany; in consequence he did not find the time opportune for giving his attention to the matter. So the mission tarried in Germany, and in the meantime the bishop who headed it died.

Finally, in 953 Otto I decided to return the caliph's embassy. When Adalbero, bishop of Metz, one of his loyal supporters, appeared at the court, he asked him to find among the clergy in his province someone who would take upon himself a perilous mission—for since Otto had determined to reply to the insults in kind, the undertaking involved the possibility of danger. The bishop turned to Eginoldus, the abbot of the monastery of Gorze, requesting that he choose from the monks two who would go to Spain. One of the two selected by Eginoldus became mad with fear, and the prior of the monastery, Johannes, volunteered to carry out the assignment.

This priest was himself one of the founders of the monastery and accomplished great things for the church in the tenth century. He was a member of a noble family that lived in Vendier in the district of Pont-à-Mousson. Having since the days of his youth been drawn to the life of a monk, he went to Italy and sojourned for a time among the Benedictines on Monte Cassino. On returning to his homeland he made a number of friends. Bishop Adalbero gave them the monastery at Gorze, which then stood in ruins. Johannes and his colleagues preached in behalf of the betterment of the life of the monks, and were indeed successful in permeating the monasteries with a new spirit and in provoking a stimulating movement in their own land and in the neighboring provinces. Johannes was therefore regarded as one of the great reformers in the Benedictine order. His journey to Spain as emissary of King Otto I was an important episode in his life, and it is described in detail in the biography written by Johannes the abbot of Saint Arnulf's monastery in Metz, who had received the details directly from Johannes of Gorze.

The German king assigned to his brother Brun, chancellor of the kingdom and later archbishop of Cologne, the task of drafting a letter to the caliph that would contain harsh expressions directed against Islam; but he also prepared, in keeping with the accepted practice of those days, a number of gifts for his emissary to present to the caliph. Johannes was joined by another monk from his monastery, the deacon Garamanus, and a man from the city of Verdun named Ermenhard, most likely a merchant who had already been to Spain. In addition, he was accompanied by the caliph's emissaries, who had not yet returned, and also by two Jews, Saul and Joseph.

At the beginning of the summer they went to Lyons, where they took a boat and sailed on the Rhône to the seacoast. From there they continued their journey overland. On reaching Barcelona, which together with its surrounding areas was then an independent Christian dukedom, they tarried for one month.

At the end of autumn in 953 they arrived at Cordova, where they were accommodated in a very beautiful villa. But though the Moslem authorities concerned themselves with making them comfortable, they showed no haste to arrange an official welcome, and when the emissaries complained about this, they were put off repeatedly. At long last they were reminded with some asperity that the German king had not returned the caliph's mission until three years had gone by. Later the representatives of the caliph appeared and inquired about the purpose of their mission, but the emissaries refused to divulge anything, stating that they had permission to transmit their king's message to no one but the caliph himself.

The caliph's men then tried to intimidate them, telling them that the death penalty awaited them because of the missive they brought with them. In this fashion they sought to indicate to the emissaries that the contents of the missive were already known to them. And in fact, when the emissaries reached Tortosa they had given the letter to a man who had returned to Spain with them, having been in the entourage of the Mozarab bishop, the caliph's emissary who had died in Germany. This man had told them of his fear that some calamity might befall them and that, in consequence, he would return without a reply from the king of Germany. He had reached Cordova before them, and possibly it was from him that they learned something about the contents of the missive.

The caliph himself was somewhat confused, not knowing how to proceed. On one hand he was apprehensive that the letter might contain slanderous references to Islam, and against an insult to his faith he could not act with restraint; on the other hand, Otto I was a powerful ruler, and the military campaigns of Charlemagne in Spain were scarcely forgotten. The caliph therefore decided to turn to Ḥasdai Ibn Shaprūṭ and lay upon him the responsibility of negotiating with the emissaries of the German king, his chief function being to extract from them clear and authentic information about the contents of the missive.

Ḥasdai employed all his diplomatic skill to achieve his end. Since it was known that Johannes of Gorze was the leader of the emissaries and that the letter was in his possession, Ḥasdai addressed himself principally to him and sought to win his trust. He began his conversation by speaking with a soothing tongue to allay Johannes's anxiety, telling him no harm awaited him and that he and his companions would be sent back to their homeland with honor. Ḥasdai expatiated on the customs of the Moslems and explained how the emissaries were to conduct themselves. He pointed out that in Spain it was customary to report promptly to the caliph on any important matter, concealing nothing from him. At the same time he did not omit mentioning that the Moslems fulfill their laws under all circumstances. This was a transparent hint that the caliph would be obliged to execute the emissaries if the missive did contain offensive references concerning Mohammed and his faith. But Ḥasdai slurred over this observation in the course of his remarks.

The conversations between the Jewish courtier and the fanatical monk went on for a long while before Ḥasdai touched upon the subject proper: he asked Johannes for the contents of the missive. When Johannes vacillated about replying, Ḥasdai assured him that he would keep the answer a secret and would even give him counsel. Johannes again replied that it was his responsibility to give the missive and the gifts to the caliph himself and to no other. But he finally was unable to resist Ḥasdai's coaxing and informed him of the contents of the letter. Then Ḥasdai said—so reported Johannes—that it was dangerous to present himself before the caliph with such a missive. "Be cautious in your answers to the messengers he sends you. I have no doubt that you know about this stringent law. There is, therefore, a need for caution so that you escape from this danger." Having succeeded in this fashion in extracting from Johannes his secret, he went his way, leaving matters in the hands of others.

But then a long interruption in the negotiations with the envoys of Otto I occurred. It was only after some months had passed that the Mozarab bishop from Cordova came and proposed that they not submit the missive to the caliph. The Spanish bishop endeavored to convince them that they should adapt themselves to circumstances, even as the Mozarabs who lived under Moslem rule were doing. But Johannes of Gorze angrily rejected his suggestion and his reasoning. No matter how much the Mozarab bishop urged him to refrain from needlessly angering the caliph, Johannes would not change his stand.

The year 954 ended and 955 began without the mission of Otto I having been received by the caliph. During this long interval the envoys remained isolated in the villa, having no contact with anyone and being allowed to go to a nearby church accompanied by guards only on Sundays and Christian holidays.

One day as Johannes went to the church he was given a letter informing him that if the caliph were compelled to execute him, he would do the same to all Christians in his kingdom, and their blood would be upon Johannes's head. But Johannes could bring much benefit to the Mozarabs if he would modify his position, that is, yield on the matter of giving up the missive. For if he did indeed surrender it, the caliph would fulfill any request he made on behalf of the Mozarabs. Whereupon the fanatical monk replied that even if his limbs were cut from his body he had no fear and would not change his course. As for the Christians in Spain, in the reply to the letter which Johannes sent to the royal court at Cordova, he mentioned the biblical episode concerning Haman, whose counsel came to naught. Finally, the caliph sent a messenger to inquire from him what, in his opinion, should be done to escape the predicament. Johannes advised that the caliph send a mission of his own to the king of Germany to ask him for new instructions.

The caliph accepted his suggestion, but ran into the difficulty of finding a person who would be willing to undertake the mission, which seemed fraught with danger. After he had made many promises to anyone who would volunteer, Rabī' b. Zaid, a cultured Mozarab who was an official in the service of the government and knew Arabic and Latin well, offered himself. He received his reward forthwith: although he was not even a priest, he was appointed bishop of Elvira.

In June 955 he started out on his journey, reaching the monastery of Gorze in ten weeks. He was warmly welcomed there and later received an invitation from Bishop Adalbero. He stayed in Metz during autumn and winter and in mid-spring of 956, he, together with the bishop and the abbot of Gorze, went to Frankfurt; in March they were received by the king. Otto I praised the devotion of Johannes, but decided to write a more restrained missive and to instruct Johannes to conceal the earlier one. To be sure, reasons of state dictated the change in his stand. For some time now he had initiated diplomatic moves looking to the subjugation of Italy, and he expected this diplomacy to involve him with the Byzantine Empire, which held a part of southern Italy. He therefore preferred not to turn the Omayyad caliph into an enemy, for if that resulted, the caliph would be brought closer to the Byzantine Empire and collaborate with it against him. For this reason he instructed Johannes not only to negotiate with the caliph in the matter of the Saracen robber bands in Provence, but also to propose a treaty of peace and friendship with him.

The king gave the new missive with the additional instructions to a man named Dudo, who came from Verdun. Without any delay Dudo and Rabī' b. Zaid started out for Spain, reaching Cordova in June. After they turned the new instructions over to Johannes, a welcome was arranged and official negotiations started; but just what the caliph's reply was to the appeal of the king of Germany is unknown, because the last portion of the biography of Johannes of Gorze is either fragmentary or lost or may never have been completed.[20] At any rate, Johannes returned safely to his monastery and was even raised to the position of abbot. The meeting with Ḥasdai Ibn Shaprūṭ made a powerful impression upon him and his associates, and to his last day he would relate to anyone willing to listen that never had he met a person as wise and alert as this Jew.[21]

In the very year in which the dispute between the court of the caliph and the king of Germany and his envoys ended, Ḥasdai was given a very important diplomatic mission to another Christian king.

The raids made by the armed bands of the caliph beyond the northern boundaries of his kingdom occurred more frequently after the death of the king of León, Ramiro II, in 950. In July 955 the Moslem forces attacked a fortress in Castile, a vassal dukedom of the kingdom of León; the outcome of these encounters resulted in heavy losses to the Christians. To be sure, Ordoño III, the new king of León, reacted with a raid on the region of the Atlantic coast, which was under the caliph's rule. But although Fernán González, count of Castile, won a victory over the Moslems near the fortress of San Esteban de Gormaz, Ordoño was of the opinion that it was to his advantage to terminate the fighting. In consequence, he sent envoys to Cordova in 955, proposing a truce to the caliph.

'Abdarraḥmān was inclined to welcome the suggestion, for he had determined to strike a severe blow to the Fatimids and their adherents in North Africa; but to do this he needed to be free of concern for the northern borders of his kingdom.

For this reason he decided in 956 to send a mission to the court of the king of León in order to fix the terms of the pact. He appointed two envoys to go to León: Muḥammad b. Ḥusain and Ḥasdai Ibn Shaprūṭ. In most instances such a pact would include the requirement to relinquish to the caliph a number of border fortresses or the demolition of some fortifications.

The negotiations in León were quickly ended, and the caliph's two envoys, accompanied by envoys from the Christian king, returned with a draft of the pact. The terms were satisfactory to the caliph, but inasmuch as he was well along in years and now made it a practice to train his son, al-Ḥakam, the crown prince, in the art of government, he called on him for his opinion. Since al-Ḥakam agreed to the proposed terms, the pact was signed, and the envoys of the Christian king returned to their land.[22] The duke of Castile, following the lead of the king of León, also made an armistice with the caliph, and all the involved parties thought they had succeeded in bringing peace to Spain. At all events the caliph hoped that for a while he would not be troubled by new crises in his relations with the Christian kings in northern Spain. But this hope very soon proved to be false.

King Ordoño III died in the spring of 957[23] and was succeeded by his brother, Sancho I, who, like Ordoño, was a son of Ramiro II, but by his second wife. Sancho's mother was the princess of Navarre, Teresa, the sister of García, king of Navarre. The new king of León refused to honor the pact that had been made between Ordoño III and the caliph, and therefore in the summer of 957 a new Moslem invasion of the kingdom of León was initiated.[24]

In the meantime, opposition to Sancho arose among the nobles of León, his opponents claiming that he was disqualified from ruling because of his health. He was very fat, and his enemies alleged that as a result his reason had dimmed. They conspired against him, attracting to their side Fernán González, prince of Castile, and in the spring of 958 they dethroned him. The conspirators placed another prince of the royal house on the throne, Ordoño IV, while Sancho departed for Pamplona, where his uncle, García, ruled.

The deposition of Sancho naturally provoked much anger in the capital of Navarre, the widowed Queen Toda, the mother of King García and the deposed Sancho's grandmother, being especially irked by it. Toda was a very forceful princess with a craving for power. When her husband died in 926 and her son was a minor, she had ruled in his stead, and even after he reached maturity her name appeared with his on many documents. When disputes erupted within the kingdom of Navarre, she would sit in judgment with her son, and in time of war she would go forth to battle. The impulse for dominion was so overpowering in this woman that she was prepared to make any sacrifice and to perform extraordinary deeds to put her grandson back on his throne. The most urgent matter, in her view, was the need to cure Sancho's obesity, so that his appearance would not provoke laughter. To her great distress, there were no distinguished physicians in Pamplona or in the other provinces of Christian Spain who could heal him.

But a mere cure would not suffice. It was clear to the queen that the armies of Navarre were too weak to impose her will on the nobles of León and Castile. The nobles of Navarre with whom she took counsel told her plainly that if she was indeed determined to return her grandson, come what might, to the throne of León, then it was incumbent upon her to turn to the caliph at Cordova and seek his help. He would be able to send one of the outstanding physicians from Cordova—so they stated—with plenty of troops under his authority who were prepared at all times to invade León.

This counsel was trustworthy, but it was difficult for Toda to accept it, for who had fought against the Moslems as she had? More than once she had gone forth at the head of the army to the battlefront, and she had even been present on the field during the celebrated Battle of Simancas. But her desire was too overpowering. She sent envoys to Cordova and asked for help from the caliph. Upon hearing the words of the envoys, the caliph was surprised, but he did not express his thoughts. He understood at once that these were good tidings for him and that now there was an opportunity to set upon the throne of León a prince who would do his bidding. The caliph determined to exploit to the full the situation of Sancho and his grandmother, but for this he required a skilled diplomat who would go to Pamplona and play upon the heart of the aged queen. For this delicate mission 'Abdarraḥmān could think of no more fitting person than Ḥasdai Ibn Shaprūṭ.

After receiving his instructions Ḥasdai left with all speed for Pamplona in order to forestall any change of heart by Toda. On reaching the capital of Navarre he presented himself as the physician and envoy of the caliph and explained to the aged queen that it would be better to treat her grandson at Cordova, where he would have at hand whatever he needed and consequently a better chance for a successful cure. At the same time he reported that the caliph was ready to accede to her request and send an army to León; however, on this matter it was desirable that he hold conversations with Sancho and herself in person. Therefore he requested that she and Sancho both come to the capital of Andalusia.

This was a proposal the likes of which had never been heard in the capital of a Christian kingdom. To be sure, the first reaction was one of shock; but Ḥasdai's diplomatic skill came to his aid. He knew how to convince and persuade Toda with assertions that seemed reasonable to her; he played upon those weaknesses in her makeup of which he was aware and pictured to her the splendor that awaited her family upon the successful termination of the negotiations.

The queen experienced much soul-searching. Mixed feelings struggled within her: she was overwhelmed with shame at the need to appear at the court of the caliph as a suppliant for his aid, but she was also possessed of a powerful desire to restore the royal crown to her grandson. In the end the impulse to regain the crown for her grandson triumphed. Toda accepted Ḥasdai's suggestion, and in the autumn of that very year, 958, she and her grandson Sancho, with a large retinue of priests and nobles, departed for Cordova.

This visit by royalty was unheard of and aroused excitement throughout Spain. For the aged caliph it was no small satisfaction to see before him as a suppliant the haughty queen and the son of Ramiro II, who had defeated him at Simancas. As the Moslems of Andalusia saw it, this visit symbolized the greatness of the caliphate, which had humbled the Christians into the dust. But the Jews of Cordova and all through Andalusia also exulted no little, for in their eyes this visit was first and foremost the personal achievement of Ḥasdai Ibn Shaprūṭ. Their emotions even found expression in verses composed for this event by one of the Jewish poets of that era.

At the festive reception arranged for this occasion, only courteous phrases found utterance; the real negotiations started later. But these conversations were not protracted. Sancho promised to give the caliph ten fortresses if he would indeed help him gain back his authority over the kingdom of León. On her part, Toda promised to send the army of Navarre to attack Castile at the very time the Moslem forces were invading León, and thereby confront Fernán González (who led the conspirators against Sancho) with a troublesome distraction.

Meanwhile, the physicians treated Sancho, and before long he became as lean and alert as he had once been. In the spring of 959 the forces of 'Abdarraḥmān, who brought Sancho along with them, penetrated into León, and Ordoño IV fled to Asturias. The city of León, the capital of the Christian kingdom, held out for a while. But in the second half of 960 it too fell into Sancho's hands.

The task which Ḥasdai had begun was now fully completed.[25]

IV

Ḥasdai Ibn Shaprūṭ went on from success to success. The Lord gave him favor and grace in the eyes of the caliph, and he found contentment over the years. Nevertheless, he was well aware that his glory was without substance. It is true and certain that the standing of all the courtiers and nobles depended solely upon the will of the caliph, who at any given moment could elevate or humble as he pleased. To be sure, no one at the royal court of Cordova considered anything other than his own welfare and personal good and ephemeral pleasures. Religious ideals, or indeed any others, were not fostered in this circle. Nor can it be said that the status of a member of the clan of Ibn Abī 'Abda or the Banū Ḥudair was better entrenched than that of Ḥasdai, since it was the main goal of the caliph to weaken the authority of the Arab aristocrats. But the very essence of opposition existing between the Arabs and those of Berber origin, and between these two groups and the "Slavs," resulted in the members of one group joining forces against another—whereas Ḥasdai stood alone. An atmosphere of intrigues enveloped him and he was well aware that his enemies were substantial in number.

Though the caliph appreciated his great ability and devotion to the interests of the kingdom, his eminence was a thorn in the flesh of many devout Moslems among the populace.

The masses in Cordova disliked members of other faiths. Not only were the Spanish theologians followers of the Mālikite school, which was very uncompromising in religious matters, sowing seeds of hatred in the hearts of the masses against the "impious," but the scene that repeated itself time and again—of troops going forth to a holy war against the Christians—poisoned the atmosphere and set aflame the fires of fanaticism. Yet it was not hostility and zeal alone that stirred the hearts of the masses; there was also contempt for anyone who did not believe in Mohammed's mission. A Moslem believed with a perfect faith in his own superiority, which was his due because of his religious belief. He was permeated with an awareness that it had fallen to his lot to dominate members of other faiths, who could live in areas of Moslem domination on the condition that they be humbled and their honor trampled in the dust. Hence they were unwilling to become reconciled to the fact that the caliph had exalted a Jew from the dustheap and bestowed upon him so much honor.

Neither the caliph nor Ḥasdai could disregard the feelings of the masses. The caliph refrained from granting his Jewish courtier the title or official status that he merited in terms of his functions; and Ḥasdai, for his part, never forgot that his status depended on the caliph's favor in greater measure than did the status of the other courtiers; more than once he found himself weighed down by these gloomy thoughts. At times the populace would give vent to its suppressed wrath. The celebrated philosopher Ibn Rushd relates that one day a fanatical theologian, addressing the caliph before a multitude of Cordovan inhabitants, heatedly remarked, "As for the prophet for whose sake alone you are given honor, this one [the Jew] says of him that he is a liar."[26]

But within the walls of his palace the caliph continued to bestow upon Ḥasdai signs of esteem and affection, and to demonstrate to him that he did not share these hostile sentiments. Not only did he assign him important tasks, but Ḥasdai actually became an intimate and one of his favorites—or, as they were designated in Cordova at the time, the "special ones." From time to time, this circle of high officers who held the important positions were invited by the caliph to a gathering of his companions, and on such occasions Ḥasdai, whom they called Abū Yūsuf, would also be present.

V

No matter how wrapped up he was in the governmental affairs of the kingdom of ʻAbdarraḥmān III, Ḥasdai Ibn Shaprūṭ never forgot his origin. On the contrary, he endeavored with all his power to exploit the opportunities given him to do good for his people wherever they were. He was, as it were, trying to prove that he was worthy of the high status with which the Lord had favored him. It is as if he regarded himself as one having an obligation toward his oppressed brethren. Ḥasdai—and other Jewish courtiers who came later resembled him in this respect—did not sever himself from his people but was always with them, at least in spirit. He was concerned for the welfare of Jewish communities throughout the Diaspora, doing all he could to revive the fallen House of David and restore its former glory. It is certain that he maintained ties with the impoverished communities that still remained in Palestine.[27] Similarly, he came into contact with the Jews of Irak. It would seem that he sent a letter to Dōsa, the son of Saadya Gaon. Dōsa was but a lad when his renowned father died; but with the passage of time he acquired fame as a scholar, and various communities addressed inquiries to him on matters of faith and law. At the request of Ḥasdai, he sent him the biography of his father, which he had especially written.[28]

Ḥasdai was not content merely to have Jews in various countries get in touch with him and transmit reports on their condition by correspondence. He also sent emissaries to the communities in lands near and far.

In a letter sent him by one community in southern Italy we

are told of the contacts Ḥasdai made with the Jews in that country. The beginning of this letter, as it has come down to us, is defective. But apparently not much more is missing than the inscription. The members of that community ask to be forgiven by the recipient of the letter for the delay in writing, especially since it is in response to his appeal to them for information. They had good reason for the delay. They relate that the Jewish communities of southern Italy had endured severe religious persecution. According to their account, the government banned the sacred books and prohibited scholars from occupying themselves with study of them. Government troops searched for the rabbis to force conversion upon them and wanted to destroy the sacred books. Scholars were arrested, severely tortured, and the sacred books were burned.

The persecution started in the city from which the letter was sent, and the Jews there had just enough time to warn the community of Otranto. There the sacred books were concealed, but two scholars, Rabbi Isaiah and Rabbi M'naḥem, and their disciple Rabbi Eliah committed suicide lest conversion be forced upon them against their will. A subordinate of the recipient of the letter, Samuel, who tarried at that time among the communities of southern Italy to fulfill a mission for him, made a stern comment. Farther on the letter relates that Samuel had had with him missives for the recipient of the letter but had lost them. The persecution itself, according to the letter, lasted for two days only, after which the wrath of the authorities subsided. The authors of the letter list the rabbis and scholars who escaped persecution in their city and in Otranto, and they close by heaping blessings and good wishes upon the recipient of the letter.[29]

The Hebrew style of the missive is the prevailing style of writing among the Jews of southern Italy in those days. However, not only is the address missing in the letter and the name of the person to whom it was sent not mentioned, but it also lacks the name of the city and country from which it was sent, as well as the date. But on the very page that contains the letter, right after its last lines another letter starts, written by "Rabbi Judah ben Jacob of Rome, of blessed memory to Rabbi Ḥasdai, may he rest in paradise." From this we can conclude that we have here a collection of copies of letters written by Ḥasdai Ibn Shaprūṭ and written by others to him. The honorifics addressed to the recipient of the letter are quite compatible with his status. He is designated "leader" and the like.

The decree of which the letter speaks was no doubt one of those decrees against the Jews promulgated by the Byzantine Empire, and we know from Christian sources that the Byzantine emperor Romanos I Lekapenos, who reigned from 919 to 944, persecuted the Jews and wanted them to convert to Christianity or leave the borders of his dominion. This emperor humiliated the church greatly by appointing one of his sons, who was still a boy, as patriarch of Constantinople; on the other hand, probably to appease the masses, he caused pressure to be put upon people of other faiths, such as the Armenians, in order to bring them over to the Orthodox Church. No doubt he also put pressure on the Jews. There is an old Jewish saying: "Whoever causes trouble to the Jews becomes a leader." Those rulers from under whose feet the ground was being cut sought to reinforce their position by oppressing the Jews.

Information concerning the persecution of the Jews by Romanos Lekapenos has been preserved, gleaned from various sources that confirm each other. An assembly of the clergy in 932 at Erfurt, Germany, received from the Christian patriarch of Jerusalem a missive that had been delivered by the patriarch of Constantinople to Rome, from where it had been sent on to Germany. That missive gave an account of a dispute between the Christians and the Jews in Jerusalem: the Jews had sought by offers of money to attract the Moslem rulers to their side, but a miracle had occurred at the Holy Sepulchre, after which all the Jews across the sea had become Christians. The missive ended with the demand that all Jews in Christian Europe be compelled to convert to Christianity or leave Christian lands.[30] About this time the authorities of the government and the church of Venice, the doge Peter Candiano and the patriarch Marinus, wrote a letter to the king of Germany, Henry I (918–936), in which the incident that occurred in Jerusalem is also reported. The letter goes on to say that at the request of the patriarch of Jerusalem, the Byzantine emperor gave instructions requiring all the Jews in his domain to become Christians, but that the Jews had converted voluntarily after hearing about the miracle in Jerusalem. This letter calls upon the king of Germany also to give the Jews in his kingdom the choice of conversion to Christianity or departure from his domain.[31]

The account of the events in Jerusalem in those letters was of course distorted, but it is a fact that in the middle of the tenth century there was much tension between the Jews and Christians in Jerusalem. The Christian-Arab writer Yaḥyā b. Sa'īd tells about disturbances occurring in the city at the end of May 966. During the week preceding the Christian festival of Pentecost the multitudes fell upon the Christians; entered the Church of the Holy Sepulchre, the church atop Mount Zion, and a third church, and wrought havoc in them. Then they slew the patriarch. The Christian writer relates that the Jews outdid the Moslems.[32] This deed occurred several years after the events mentioned in those letters; perhaps it was an act of retaliation by the Jews, who saw an opportunity to even an old score with the Christians. But the Byzantine government did indeed promulgate a decree against the Jews at the very time that the letters were sent from Jerusalem and Italy to Germany. In an apocalypse called *The Vision of Daniel,* written in Byzantium, there is an account of a Byzantine emperor who gave the Jews the choice of conversion to Christianity or exile. From the words preceding this passage it is patent that the emperor referred to is Romanos I Lekapenos.[33]

The decree against the Jews in the part of southern Italy that belonged to Byzantium, concerning which the missive of that Italian community reports to Ḥasdai Ibn Shaprūṭ,[34] was only one of the steps taken by the Byzantine authorities from time to time to fulfill the decree of the emperor, at least ostensibly. This was a punitive act implemented a long time after the promulgation of the original decree in the 930s. As for the letter to Ḥasdai, it was no doubt written some twelve or fourteen years after this.[35] Among other matters, the letter mentions Abraham ben Jehoshaphat as one of the scholars who was saved and it also says of him that he was previously the rabbi of the community of Oria, which was "dispersed." Now, Arabic chronicles tell of several Moslem incursions and attacks from Sicily onto the Italian mainland. One of these incursions took place in 925 under the leadership of Abū Aḥmad Dja'far b. 'Ubaid, and some of the Arabic historians report that on this occasion Taranto was taken and Otranto besieged. However, some Arabic sources recount as one of the important episodes of this campaign the conquest of the city of Oria, where, according to their report, the Moslems effected a fearful slaughter, putting six thousand to the sword and taking into captivity the rest of the inhabitants, who numbered ten thousand.[36] The renowned Jewish physician Shabb'tai Donnolo relates that ten scholars were killed on that occasion; he himself was taken captive and redeemed when he was twelve years old.[37]

Less than two years after this attack, the Moslems returned and invaded Calabria, with the result that the inhabitants of these regions had no respite in which to repair their ravaged places. Oria itself remained in ruins for decades. We know from the chronicles of the family of Rabbi Sh'faṭya, which were written in the eleventh century by Aḥima'aṣ, that the community of Oria was dispersed to various places.[38] There is no doubt that the authors of the letter to Ḥasdai had this event in mind when they spoke of Oria the "dispersed."[39]

The Jews in the Byzantine sector of southern Italy who sent this letter to Ḥasdai made no request of him. They merely recounted the persecutions that they had endured. However, the Jewish courtier at Cordova who was concerned for the welfare of Jews everywhere gave thought to the means whereby he could help them and prevent the Byzantine rulers from attacking them anew. The opportunity for this presented itself a few years later, in 948, when the caliph's envoys went forth to Emperor Constantine VII. Ḥasdai sent two letters with these envoys to the royal court at Constantinople. These letters have come down to us in a Hebrew text, and there are grounds for believing that they were originally written in Hebrew. Apparently Ḥasdai requested permission from the caliph to take advantage of this opportunity to act on behalf of the Jews under Byzantine rule, and the caliph granted his request on the condition that it would be done in Ḥasdai's name. The caliph neither could nor desired to appear as the defender of the Jews and thereby become involved in the affairs of the Christian government, but he had no objection to steps being taken in this direction by Ḥasdai. To point up the fact that the requests came from the Jewish courtier, it was therefore agreed that the letters be written in Hebrew.[40]

In international relations at that time it was customary for anyone sending diplomatic correspondence to write in his own tongue, it being assumed that the recipients of the document would have expert translators at their disposal. No complete copies of the letters Ḥasdai wrote to Constantinople have come down to us; we merely have fragments whose texts are themselves defective. The language of the two letters is that employed in liturgical poetry, and in some of the metaphors, the style of Ḥasdai's Hebrew amanuensis, as we know it from his writings, can be detected.[41]

One of the letters is addressed to a noblewoman. Ḥasdai requests that she graciously act in behalf of the Jews of her empire and protect them from further oppression. The writer speaks of them as "the surviving remnant of the Jewish community which is among you," and he pleads that they not be coerced into doing anything against their will. He puts forth a specific suggestion: that the recipient of the letter take the Jews under her aegis and appoint one of her subordinates to deal with their affairs. To give added weight to his words, Ḥasdai mentions that he can do good for the Christians living in Spain and that he is in fact already doing this. Naturally, the letter contains flattering words concerning the noblewoman, as well as the emperor. But anyone perusing this missive will admit that it is very cleverly put together. In all the lands ringing the Mediterranean Sea in those times there circulated a report about the extraordinary prince who occupied the throne in Constantinople and was wholeheartedly concerned with the writing of books; no doubt this report had reached Ḥasdai. He therefore stressed that "men of understanding and knowledge" have no greater concern than that the remembrance of them be perpetuated; and he makes it clear that the rulers of Byzantium will indeed merit this if they comply with his request. Though these observations are included in the letter addressed to the noblewoman, they are really intended for the emperor.

The second letter is directed to the emperor himself. He is addressed as "king," for this was the true designation of the Byzantine ruler (basileus), whereas his authorities of a lower rank bore the appellation "caesar." In a general way the letter is written with scrupulous concern for diplomatic usage. According to Byzantine ceremonial rules, the envoys of foreign powers had to address the emperor with the phrase "great and exalted basileus [king]," and in Ḥasdai's letter we read: "the great king exalted on high." This is a literal translation of the Greek words. Ḥasdai informs the emperor in an obiter dictum that the missive he had sent to the caliph had given him much joy. Unfortunately, this letter is mutilated and faulty from the very beginning, and except for this piece of information and the customary honorifics nothing can be salvaged from it.[42]

The name of the noblewoman to whom the first letter was directed is not mentioned in the fragment that has come down to us. Nor are there any titles in those lines preserved in the fragment available to us; but trustworthy Byzantine historians report that in the days when that emperor, who was both scholar and author, occupied the throne in Constantinople, his wife, Helena, involved herself vigorously in the affairs of the empire. Helena was the daughter of Romanos Lekapenos, who kept Constantine VII from the throne and endeavored to establish a new dynasty. In order to seize the reins of government, while he was still the admiral of the fleet Romanos's first step had been to marry off his daughter to Constantine. Romanos's reign lasted twenty-six years.

After he was overthrown and sent into exile by his sons, and they themselves were driven out by Constantine, who finally became the supreme ruler of Byzantium, Romanos's daughter, the wife of Constantine, still remained on the throne. This woman inherited from her father her strong passion for dominion and glory. While her husband applied himself diligently to writing books, Helena appointed officers and nobles, in collaboration with Basilios, a bastard begotten by Romanos; needless to say, she did not do this without an ulterior motive.[43] Inasmuch as she dealt with governmental matters over an extended period of time, it would seem that Ḥasdai addressed his letter to her.[44]

During the reign of Constantinos Porphyrogenetos the pressure upon the Jews was eased so that they could observe their faith secretly. Ḥasdai no doubt heard of this from Salemon, who came to Cordova in 947. At all events, he did not want to forgo the opportunity to intercede for them, but from the formulation of the letters we can deduce that he did not have in mind the Jews throughout the Byzantine Empire, but rather communities in a specific area. After speaking about the "surviving remnant in your midst," he elaborates and clarifies his statement: "their scholars, who have survived capture and duress." Based on its linguistic structure in Hebrew, this last term probably should read "siege." This must accordingly be a reference to the communities that experienced captivity and siege, namely, the Jews of southern Italy, the community of Oria the "dispersed," the Jews of Otranto, and other cities in that region. It was to them that Ḥasdai referred.[45] He wanted the Byzantine court to give special consideration to those communities that suffered so greatly because of the incursions of the Fatimid armies, which were inimical to Byzantium and Spain alike. He requested that these communities be treated leniently in the matter of their faith. This plea was thus the outcome of the letter dispatched to Ḥasdai by the Jews of southern Italy some years previously.[46]

Having taken this action in behalf of the Jews under Byzantine rule, Ḥasdai now endeavored to do what he could to help the Jews in the south of France. To be sure, the name France did not yet apply to the southern provinces of ancient Gaul, nor were they united within the political framework of the central and northern provinces of this large country. In the first half of the tenth century, until 947, the southern region of this state was a separate kingdom—a vassal state of the large German kingdom.

But no matter who the king of this land might be, the Jews, who had inhabited the land from ancient times, were wasting away under the yoke of the gentiles and were being severely oppressed by the clergy to the full extent of its power. In the city of Toulouse a Jew had to appear on the eve of Easter at the gate of the cathedral and offer thirty pounds of wax for candles to be lit in the church. The bishop would stand at the gate, and when the Jew had presented his offering, the cleric would strike him on the cheek. This was an annual occurrence; once the bishop gave the Jew such a strong blow that he died.[47] In this manner the Christians of Toulouse sought to remind the Jews of the incident of the thirty pieces of silver for which, according to the Gospels, Judas Iscariot betrayed their savior.

This matter is dealt with in a Hebrew letter that is incomplete and lacking an inscription, its style testifying that it was written a long time ago, before the era of the Crusades. The senders of the letter relate that representatives of the communities of the region had gathered together and that three men had arrived who had previously frequented the house of the letter's recipient. The names of these Jews were Saul, Joseph, and Judah. Saul and Joseph are known to us as those of the Jews who accompanied the messengers of King Otto I to Cordova in 953, and it is reasonable to assume that on their way back they tarried in southern France and held conversations with the Jewish communities located in its cities. They are referred to in the letter as "our great ones," that is, important Gallic Jews who were known to the writers of the letter. In all likelihood they are to be counted among those wealthy French Jews who for a long time constituted the merchant class; they supplied the royal court and the nobles with those products of the Orient for which they craved and maintained a steady contact with Moslem Spain. From the letter remaining with us it appears that they related to the Provençal Jews many tales regarding the splendor of the man to whom the letter was directed and who bore the appellation "prince of Israel." This was no doubt Ḥasdai Ibn Shaprūṭ.

The letter mentions that "Samuel the faithful," the messenger of the letter's recipient, had reached its authors. This messenger of Ḥasdai is also referred to in the letter sent him from southern Italy. Samuel had gone there to make contact with the Jewish communities and to ascertain their condition; in that letter he is also referred to as "Samuel the faithful." Apparently this is not a name but an appellative indicating his function. Here the Hebrew word for "faithful" means "representative," a translation of the Arabic term *wakīl.*

According to the account in the letter from Provence, Samuel asked them what they would like to have done in their behalf by the man who sent him; whereupon they took counsel and decided to request that he endeavor to abolish the humiliating custom in Toulouse on the eve of Easter. Samuel told them—so they report—that for the person who sent him, this would not be at all difficult. Thus far goes the text of the letter.[48] Whether Ḥasdai did indeed take any measures at all in this matter, we do not know. But if he did make an attempt, he was not successful. For about 150 years thereafter the Christians of Toulouse continued to humiliate the Jews in the manner described in this letter.

VI

These faded epistolary fragments and the brief items of information found in Arabic sources regarding the life of Ḥasdai all tell of deeds through which he became prominent and acquired fame. But concerning those bitter moments that overtook the Jewish courtier at the court of the caliph, of the hours he spent recounting to himself the tale of insults heaped on him by the despotic caliph, who in his old age had become drunk with his success and was inclined to make somewhat light of the opinions of his aides, of the times when Ḥasdai would remember the provocations given him by the Arab nobles—on all these we will seek in vain for any hint in historical sources. But such moments when anguish would well up in him and Ḥasdai took stock of what it meant to be a Jewish courtier were surely not few. Even this Jewish courtier, of lofty station and resplendent attire, bore within himself his cup of sorrows. In his bitterness he would wrathfully swear that if he were certain of the existence of those Jewish tribes who were said to live in independence far from nations Christian or Moslem, he would disregard all the honors and all the glory—which was only illusory—and would wear his feet out trudging over mountains and through deserts until he joined his free brethren.

Such thoughts would occur to him because in that generation, as in the preceding and later generations, Jews everywhere were convinced that there was a place in the world where their brethren lived in freedom and independence, without any alien yoke to oppress them. The Jews in Moslem and Christian lands saw themselves as that part of the nation which was subjugated, whereas another part enjoyed self-rule. The more imaginative among them always nursed in their hearts the impulse to unite with the free Jews. Thus it was that Ḥasdai remembered what he had heard about Eldad the Danite, tales which the elders of his generation were wont to repeat. He had also heard from merchants who wandered afar in northern lands reports that verified these tales. Those merchants who went to Slavic countries, bringing slaves back from there, had heard reports of a Jewish kingdom far off in the East. They told of a nation called Khazars who inhabited the coast of a sea named for them. However, it was difficult to know the thing for a certainty, for these merchants reported what they had learned merely from hearsay.

Ḥasdai doggedly pursued these reports until his interest became public knowledge. The Arabic geographer Ibn Ḥauḳal, who states that he reached Andalusia in the summer of 948, gives us geographical details on the location of the land of the Khazars, which he learned from Ḥasdai Ibn Shaprūṭ. He reports that Ḥasdai was well versed in matters relating to that land because he himself had been there and had met with its kings and nobles. The Arabic geographer set this observation down on back of one of the maps in his treatise, apparently long after his visit to Spain, when his memories of his stay there had grown somewhat dim. Ḥasdai never was in that faraway land, but it is likely that Ibn Ḥauḳal met him in Cordova and got from him the information he had received from merchants. Ḥasdai probably also told him of his efforts to make contact with that kingdom.[49] Ḥasdai also inquired about the Khazars from envoys of various kings who arrived at the court of the caliph; from them he got, bit by bit, additional details that combined to give a clearer picture.

The Khazar kingdom was indeed a large and powerful state at that time, and its king and nobles all were Jews. They were a tribe from the Turkish family of nations, which had arrived, as part of a powerful stream of immigration by the Turks between 570 and 580, at the plains of southern Russia. Their number was not large, but they annexed to their ranks many of the peoples who dwelt in the vast plains between the Caspian Sea and the Caucasus Mountains, and succeeded in establishing an enduring kingdom. The Khazars were tent-dwellers who wandered from place to place. Band by band they moved annually from summer encampment to winter encampment.

These camps also served as centers of mobilization for military expeditions. They were a people fond of war and ready at any moment to fall upon their neighbors. In 627 they co-operated with the Byzantine emperor Heraclios when he invaded the Sassanid kingdom of Persia. At first they were under the sovereignty of the Khāgāns of the vast Turkish Empire that was established at that time in eastern Asia; but when this empire fell apart, they became independent under the leadership of their own khans who, it seems, belonged to the same family of Turkish kings that produced Genghis Khan.[50] In the seventh century they succeeded in spreading to the West and extending their rule to the Sea of Azov and the Crimean peninsula, where the Byzantines held sway. They then came into contact with the Byzantine culture and the Christian religion.

At that time important cities grew up in their land. Near the fixed sites where their camps were pitched during certain seasons of the year, large settlements of merchants arose who supplied them with assorted products from other lands, especially manufactured goods. These merchants were mainly Moslems from Khwārizm and from its neighboring provinces, and through them the religion of Islam was spread among the Khazars. But Judaism too spread in Khazaria; particularly after the issuance of suppressive edicts against the Jews by the Byzantine emperor Leon the Isaurian in 723, Jews arrived there in considerable numbers.

The continuous propaganda carried on by members of the monotheistic faiths among the Khazars, who until now had practiced a simple form of shamanism, brought up the problem of a change of faith and the adoption of one of those faiths as the state religion. Since the representatives of the Christian faith were also the agents of the Byzantine Empire and the acceptance of Islam was tied in with the acceptance of the rule of the caliph, it seemed to the leaders of the Khazar state that Judaism was more desirable than those other faiths. Thus it came about that in the first third of the eighth century they became converted to Judaism. Theirs was not the normative Judaism current in those days, but rather a form of Mosaic belief. They erected a tent for a tabernacle and offered up sacrifices. Their conversion was very superficial, and before long little remained of it. In the biography of Saint Ibo, who visited their country around 780, there is no mention of the Khazars' being Jews.[51]

During all this time they fought fiercely in the lands of the Caucasus. From the time that the Moslems appeared there in the middle of the seventh century, there was a series of wars between them and the Khazars. In 685 the Khazars invaded Armenia, and in 717 they invaded Azerbaidjan. From 722 on, the fighting between them and the Moslems was incessant. In 737 they mounted a successful invasion that penetrated as far as Ardebil and won a mighty victory in a fierce battle with the Moslems. They reached the environs of Mosul but finally were beaten back. In 737 the Moslems launched an expedition against the Khazars and, according to their account, subjugated them and forced them to accept the Mohammedan faith. In connection with this military venture there is no mention of Jews being there; this can be taken as a sign that their conversion was already almost forgotten.

The Khazars speedily regained their strength and in 762 again invaded the borders of the caliphate. In an invasion mounted in 799 they reached Ispahan in the east and Mosul in the west, returning with a large number of captives. It is worth noting, according to the historian Ibn al-Athīr, that in this invasion not only were the Moslems attacked but also the "client group," which indicates that their conversion had not yet become complete.[52]

The Khazar kingdom was thus at that time a significant military power feared by all its neighbors. But shortly after this war their Jewish consciousness became stronger, and they began to observe Jewish precepts. To be sure, many Moslems and Christians remained among them, and these enjoyed equal rights, being able to worship as they pleased. But whereas the Khazars acted on the principle of quid pro quo, the Abbasid caliphs and the Byzantine emperors maltreated their Jewish subjects. At all events, the Jewish people had not enjoyed such power for centuries, and it is small wonder that their deeds were reported in every land.

Until the middle of the ninth century the Khazars held sway over the plains of southern Russia, from the Caspian Sea in the east to the Dnieper in the west, and it appears that at certain periods they spread their dominion even beyond, toward the Far East to the steppes of eastern Asia and westward to the river Sereth. As large part of the Crimean peninsula also came under their rule. They succeeded in establishing their mastery over the Slavic tribes who sojourned in the Russian forests north of the great steppes; these peoples became their tributaries.

However, in the second half of the ninth century the Normans, who were later to give Russia its name, took control, first of Novgorod and some years later, in 862, of Kiev, and forced the Khazars out of the areas near these cities. At the end of the ninth century the barbaric Pechenegs rebelled against Khazar rule, and the struggle with them required great efforts. But even after losing large provinces in the north and the west, the Khazars were still a powerful nation in the tenth century. Emperor Constantinos Porphyrogenetos pictures them as dangerous enemies of the Byzantine Empire, but from the instructions that he includes in one of his treatises dealing with diplomatic protocol between his government and that of the Khazars, it is evident that great honor was accorded to their kings.[53]

As additional information about the might of the Khazars came to Ḥasdai's attention, his eagerness to make contact grew, and he sought daily for ways to achieve this. When an envoy of the Byzantine emperor reached Cordova in 947, Ḥasdai questioned him cautiously regarding the Khazars, for he was well aware of the hatred of the Greeks for the Jews. Even though the envoy, as is befitting a diplomat, was restrained in his replies, Ḥasdai understood from their tenor that he had not heard false reports. The envoy told him of the ties that existed between Byzantium and the Khazar kingdom, such as those involving trade and commerce, and gave him information on the distance between the two countries.

On hearing these things, Ḥasdai calculated that it would be very easy to reach the Khazars from Constantinople, and he therefore became determined to act. He assigned to a person of experience named Isaac bar Nathan the task of joining the envoys of the caliph who were about to depart for the court at Constantinople, from which he was to proceed on his journey to Khazaria by sea. Ḥasdai gave him a letter and gifts for the Khazar king and furnished him with a good sum of money and whatever else he might need for so long a journey; he also provided some people to accompany him.[54]

But of course Isaac bar Nathan could not arrange to sail on the Black Sea without the permission and assistance of the Byzantine emperor. Now, in that letter to the Byzantine queen in which Ḥasdai had interceded for the Jews of southern Italy, there is mention of a second request. The part of the letter dealing with this request is not legible, but at the end of the page can be made out these words: ". . . the land of the Khazars" and on the reverse side of that page, where the letter continues, we find: ". . . one of the ships of the King's fleet . . . he and the men who accompany him. . . ."[55] In this letter, then, Ḥasdai requested the queen for permission for Isaac bar Nathan to sail in a Byzantine ship to the land of the Khazars. If we are to take the words of this letter in their simple meaning, he apparently requested that his envoy be carried on a ship of the royal navy so that he would not have to make his way in a mercantile vessel, which touches many ports for the sake of trade.

Isaac bar Nathan left for Constantinople, together with the Spanish emissaries, in the summer of 948 and presented his missives and Ḥasdai's gifts to the imperial couple. But the

Byzantine emperor did not comply with Ḥasdai's request. The welfare of his empire necessitated the isolation of Khazaria, and especially the prevention of any contact between it and Mediterranean powers, just as this later became the principle of the successors of Byzantium vis-à-vis Russia.

Nevertheless, it was not convenient for the emperor to gainsay the request of the Jewish noble, who was a person of influence at the court of the Omayyad caliph, especially when he had just established ties with the caliph. The Byzantine rulers therefore told Ḥasdai's envoys that the roads were bad because of troop movements, and, it being winter, they claimed that the sea was too stormy to venture upon it. Eventually they sent them back to Spain, with the caliph's emissaries placing in their keeping a letter containing these excuses.[56] The venture thus ended in failure.

But during the months when Isaac bar Nathan stayed in Constantinople he met a Jew from the Khazar kingdom. This man was apparently in the service of the Khazar ruler or one of his favorites, and he was also an erudite person. It would seem that Isaac bar Nathan asked him to put in writing whatever he knew of Khazar history, their conversion, and their relationships with the neighboring states. This Jew complied with his request and produced an essay written in the form of a missive to Ḥasdai Ibn Shaprūṭ. This work has not come down to us in its entirety, but a large fragment of it is extant. This fragment does not have either the beginning or the end of the essay, but it does mention "your emissaries who came from Constantinople," and these are no doubt the envoys of Ḥasdai: Isaac bar Nathan and his associates; for at that time there was no noble or important personage among the Jews capable of sending such a mission and showing so great an interest in the Khazars except Ḥasdai Ibn Shaprūṭ. The missive was written by the Khazar Jew in Greek, which was at that time the language of culture and diplomacy in all the lands ringing the Black Sea.

This letter is mentioned by Y'hūda al-Barcelōnī, a distinguished talmudic scholar who lived in Spain and in the first decade of the twelfth century wrote the treatise *Sefer ha-'ittim* (Book of the Times). This book is the first part of a big halakhic work, and regarding the halakha in the tractate Z'bhāḥīm 116b that "it is forbidden to help non-Jews or to perform a service for them in these times with respect to the offering of a sacrifice," the author seeks to clarify whether it is even permissible for a Jew to instruct a gentile on how to perform a sacrifice for the sake of heaven. Here he mentions the Khazars, most likely because he had heard that they offered up sacrifices and of the attempt by Ḥasdai to make contact with them. He goes on to say: "We have come upon a text that a Jew wrote in his own tongue in Constantinople concerning the kings of Constantinople and King Aaron and also about the wars between certain gentile kings and King Joseph b. Aaron."[57]

This is, of course, the treatise of the Khazar Jew.[58] The essential portion of that fragment of the treatise which has been preserved is the account of the wars fought by the Khazars. The Hebrew phrase *mi-malkhē Ḳosṭanṭīnōpōli* offers some difficulty (since it means "*from* the kings of Constantinople"), but its intended meaning is undoubtedly (as if the phrase read "*'al malkhē*" etc.) "*concerning* the kings of Constantinople."[59] The author of this work[60] drew from various sources and perused many books,[61] and therefore his report is of great value.

In the first part of this treatise, which we do not possess, it is apparently reported that the Khazars were originally idolaters, until at one time or other they—either all or only some of them—became converted. But as time passed, their Judaism was almost completely obliterated from their minds. Yet from the earliest times, Jews who had suffered from the oppression of the gentiles fled to them and were very cordially received by them. They began to take part in the affairs of the state like the other inhabitants and accompanied them in battle. They intermarried and abandoned their national heritage, except that all of them circumcised their sons and some of them kept the Sabbath.

In those days there was no king in the land of the Khazars, but when one of the nobles would markedly distinguish himself in warfare, they would appoint him as a high-ranking commander. One of the Jews was thus appointed commander in chief over all their forces. This Jew had a wife named Seraḥ who urged him to observe all the precepts of Judaism, and he heeded her request. Moreover, he influenced other nobles in this direction. The change that took place among the leaders of the Khazar people became known among the neighboring countries, provoking the Moslems and Christians to such anger that they sent envoys to the Khazars to try to deflect them from their course.

The aforementioned noble decided to arrange a disputation among theologians of the three faiths. He invited Greek clerics and Moslem theologians and Jewish scholars from the neighboring countries. After the Greek clerics, the Moslem theologians, and the representatives of the Jews had debated among themselves, the Khazar nobles ordered brought before them sacred books from a cave in the valley of Tizul. These were the Scriptures, and the manner in which the Jews interpreted them convinced the Khazars that the Jewish religion is the true faith. This disputation made a powerful impression. Descendants of Jews who had immigrated to Khazaria and had ceased observing the precepts of their faith now repented, and so did the Khazars who had earlier accepted Judaism. After these events, many Jews from Babylonia, Persia, and the Byzantine Empire arrived in the country and became the Khazars' teachers. The Khazars then made the Jewish commander their king, changing his name to Sabriel, and they also chose one of the rabbis to be their judge.

King Sabriel feared that the judaizing of the Khazars would prompt their neighbors to unite their forces against them and make war on them. He therefore made peace with the Alans, hitherto the traditional foes of the Khazars. So they lived in peace with their neighbors until the days of King Benjamin. During his reign the neighbors of the Khazars did make a pact and unite to make war upon them, except for the king of the Alans, who fought on their side. In this war the Khazars were victorious. Both King Benjamin and the Alans won great victories. In the days of King Aaron the Byzantines persuaded the Alans to attack the Khazars, but this time also the Khazars were victorious. The Khazar king took the king of the Alans captive and forced him to enter into a treaty of friendship with him and to have his daughter marry the Khazar ruler's son, Joseph.

When Joseph occupied the throne, the Byzantine emperor, Romanos, began to persecute the Jews in his empire, whereupon the Khazars wreaked vengeance upon the Christians within their borders, putting many to death. Romanos sent many gifts to the duke of the Russians and persuaded him to attack the Khazars. He responded to the instigation, began a war, and conquered the city of Samkari[62] when its governor, Ḥashmōnai, was absent. Then the commander Bolshaṣī,[63] whose Hebrew name was Pesaḥ, went forth to attack the cities of Romanos; he captured three of them, putting their inhabitants to the sword. He besieged one city, but a powerful Byzantine force defended it fiercely, and the Khazars lost ninety men. But in the end Bolshaṣī prevailed over it, and the city paid him tribute. He spared its inhabitants, but all the Russians found there were slain.

Having been victorious over the Byzantines, he attacked the Russians, overcoming them too and compelling their duke to wage war against the Byzantines. The Russians besieged Constantinople for four months but could not take the city. The besieged employed Greek fire, causing many fatalities among the Russians. The Russian duke felt so humiliated that he did not return to his country but went to Persia, where he died. His country then came under the dominion of the Khazars.

Thus far goes the historical portion of the letter written by the Khazar Jew, that is, the fragment that has been preserved. In the last portion, which is fragmentary, the author gives several details about the land of the Khazars. Among other things he mentions that between Khazaria and Constantinople lies a distance of nine days' travel by sea and twenty-eight days' travel by land.

When this letter reached Ḥasdai Ibn Shaprūṭ, he must have read the information therein with the greatest interest, since all this was new to him. The Jewish courtier was naturally unable to investigate its veracity and had to accept it for what it was. We who peruse this letter one thousand years after it was written also find it of great interest, but we have it in our power to investigate the reliability of the information it contains.

The Khazar Jew depicted the conversion to Ḥasdai as a customary act of religious propaganda, without the addition of any miraculous elements, whereas among the votaries of other faiths it was customary in the Middle Ages to so characterize it. The detail concerning the cave wherein the sacred books were placed was not a literary ornamentation invented by the author, for it is also mentioned by Judah Halevi in his book *Ha-Kūzarī* (The Khazar).[64] According to the author of the letter, the judges who were chosen after the conversion were called *khāgān*; this is undoubtedly an error, for their kings were called *khāgān* or *khāḳān*. To be sure, it is possible that we have here a copyist's error rather than one by the author himself. But the historic reliability of the letter will be tested mainly by the veracity of the description of relations between the Khazars and their neighbors.

The author speaks of the Alans as dangerous neighbors of the Khazars, and various writers do indeed give us information that confirms his observations. The Alans were an Iranian tribe that had occupied the steppes of southern Russia for hundreds of years before the coming of the Khazars,[65] and at the time that the Khazars were founding their kingdom, the Alans were still one of the powerful peoples in the region north of the Black Sea. Alongside them dwelt the Asians who were related to them from the standpoint of origin; the author of the letter to Ḥasdai also mentions these people. Emperor Constantinos Porphyrogenetos, in his treatise on the conduct of the Byzantine government, claims that it was particularly easy for the Alans to make war on the Khazars. Inasmuch as nine of the Khazar provinces that supplied most of life's necessities were close to the Alans, these were especially dangerous to them.[66]

The war between the Khazars and the Russians and the siege of Constantinople by the Russians took place, according to this letter, when King Joseph ruled in Khazaria and Emperor Romanos reigned in Constantinople. According to the anonymous author of the letter, these occurrences resulted because of the persecution of the Jews by Emperor Romanos. This is, of course, Romanos I Lekapenos, who is known from other sources as a foe of the Jews. A contemporary, the Arabic historian al-Mas'ūdī, apparently alludes to the influence of the persecution of the Jews by Emperor Romanos I Lekapenos on the relations between the Khazars and the Byzantine Empire. He reports on the persecution of the Jews in the Byzantine Empire and adds that as a result of it many Jews fled to Khazaria.[67] To be sure, he does not mention the date of this persecution.

In any event, according to the Greek chronicles the siege of Constantinople occurred in the last years of the reign of Romanos I, in 941. According to the account in the Greek chronicles, as well as in other sources,[68] a huge Russian fleet (the number of vessels given is ten thousand) appeared at the beginning of June and laid siege to the city. But in September, after the Russians suffered a number of defeats and most of their ships were destroyed, they retreated. Regarding the time of the siege and the development of events there is no contradiction between the letter of the Khazar Jew and the Christian sources. In the letter of the Khazar Jew, the Russian prince who headed their forces then is called Oleg. But according to the famous Russian chronicle, Oleg was dead by 912, and in 941 his successor, Igor, was ruler. Was the Russian prince who besieged Constantinople in 941 another Oleg? Or did Oleg's successors perhaps take as a cognomen the name of this great prince? It would be simplest to assume that the author of the letter had put the name Oleg instead of that of Igor, who actually ruled in 941.[69]

The account of the demise of the Russian prince, as we find it in our letter, is consistent with what we know from other sources, even though our anonymous author was not precise. According to Moslem, Armenian, and Syrian writers, a huge Russian armada ventured into the Caspian Sea and attacked its southern coast. According to them, this venture terminated in a severe defeat, and the Russian prince was among those slain. Apparently this was Igor, who hoped, by a successful campaign in Persia, to improve the poor impression his defeat at the gates of Constantinople had made.[70] The report in the letter regarding the pressure put upon the Russians by the Khazars to besiege Constantinople also seemingly receives authentication from the text of the peace treaty between the Byzantines and the Russians in 944. That treaty gives a detailed account of relations with the Khazars, and in its beginning there is mention of "Satan, who hates the good," who caused the breach of the peace between the Byzantines and the Russians. This is a reference to the Khazars.[71]

Except for the confusion regarding the titles of the rulers

(judges) we do not find in the letter of the anonymous Jew anything to tarnish its reliability. Whatever is written in this document could indeed have been penned by a Khazar Jew in 940. But Y'hūda al-Barcelōnī speaks of a letter written by a Jew in Constantinople in his own tongue, Greek; however, the fragment we possess was written in biblical Hebrew with an admixture of some rabbinic phraseology. The only manuscript of this fragment was written—in the opinion of the renowned scholar who discovered it—in the twelfth century or perhaps at an earlier time.[72] But the very fact that Y'hūda al-Barcelōnī speaks of a letter which describes, in the main, wars between the Khazars and the Byzantines, and the fact that the author of our letter addresses himself to a Jewish noble who sent envoys to Constantinople, point clearly to the identicalness of the two letters.

However, the Hebrew text (which, as we have said, contains nothing that could not have been written by a Jew in the middle of the tenth century) proves in many details that it is nothing other than a translation, and perhaps a somewhat adapted translation done in the later Middle Ages, possibly by a Jew who was familiar with the Italian language. Thus he calls his people "Qazars," whereas the Byzantines spell it "Chazarroi" and the Arabs "al-Khazar." And he gives "Qagan" but the Greeks give "Chaganos." In the letter we are discussing, the Russians are referred to as "Russo" (l. 73) and the Turks as "Turco." He says (ll. 91–92): "Behold, there are at war with us Asia and Bāb al-abwāb and Zebos and Turco and Lozanio." He mentions also the land of "Turchia" (ll. 51, 57). Only an Italian-speaking Jew could write thus. That the translator of the letter was either an Italian Jew or one quite familiar with that language can be deduced from the form of the name of Prince Oleg in the Hebrew text: "Helgo" (ll. 64, 74). It is certain that in this context the name should be pronounced with a *ḥōlam*.[73]

Based on linguistic evidence alone, the name "Turchia" cannot provide any proof. But this is a geopolitical concept that took root after the Seldjūk conquests in the second half of the eleventh century and was current among the Italians for hundreds of years. If we come upon this name in a text whose content does not indicate that it was written after 949, it undoubtedly proves that we are confronted with a translation. One of the great scholars who struggled with the question of the authenticity of this precious document also solved the problem this way. This scholar pointed to the stylistic influence of *The Book of Yōssīpōn,* which in his view is evident in our letter, and we know that this book was written at this very time in another country.[74] However, since it is indubitably clear that we are dealing not with an original document but with a late translation, it goes without saying that this is not a refutation of the genuineness of the letter .The language of the translator also testifies that he lived in Constantinople or in some other place where Greek was spoken. This is implied by an expression such as *hashmāda* (1. 62), which is characteristic of the Hebrew employed by Byzantine Jews of that era. So we find that the author of *The Vision of Daniel* uses the term *hagrāsha* (instead of *gērūsh*).[75]

The mention of this letter by Y'hūda al-Barcelōnī is proof that the Jews of Spain regarded it as an important treatise, from which they drew highly meaningful information about that Jewish kingdom in southern Russia. Therefore they copied it and preserved it after its translation into Hebrew. However, Ḥasdai Ibn Shaprūṭ was not satisfied merely to receive information about the Khazars; he wanted actual contact. After his hope of sending an envoy to the court of the Khazar kingdom by way of the sea was thwarted, he sought other ways. At first contact with the Khazars by way of eastern Europe seemed to him a remote possibility. Then, since he provided aid for the Jews of Palestine and maintained contact with them, he inquired of them whether they could assist him in this matter. They replied affirmatively. They proposed that he send his missive to the Khazars through Mesopotamia to Armenia and then, by way of the city of Bardha'ah, to Khazaria.[76]

Bardha'ah, in the land of Arran (or, as it was called by the Christians, Albania), which is in the region of the Caucasus, was indeed in those days a large and important city. It was a Christian Armenian city, but during all the days of the Omayyad and Abbasid caliphate, Moslem governors, who ruled Arran and Armenia, dwelt there. In the Russian invasion of 943 they reached this city and wreaked havoc upon it.[77] From Bardha'ah the road led to Darband, the border city between the caliphate and Khazaria.

While Ḥasdai weighed the practical value of this proposal, a new means of implementing his undertaking, one which he found preferable, opened up for him. This new proposal came from a direction that he could not have anticipated. When the two Jews, Saul and Joseph, arrived with the ambassador of the king of Germany, Otto I, they met with Ḥasdai and learned of his overpowering desire to contact the Khazar king and of the failure of his first envoy. They promptly suggested that they transport his letter to the remote Jewish kingdom. They had had no direct contacts with the Khazars but had heard much about them. Among other things, they told Ḥasdai that six years earlier a Jew had come to them from Khazaria. The Jew was blind, but he was a scholar and was experienced in the ways of life. His name was Mar 'Amram, and, as he told it, he had once been a favorite of the Khazar king.

Saul and Joseph told Ḥasdai that they would ask their king to send the letter, by means of his messengers, to the Jews in Hungary, whence it would be transmitted to the Russians and from them to the Bulgars, who would, in turn, pass it on to their neighbors, the Khazars.[78] These Jews, who were well versed in the relationships between nations in eastern Europe, did not, then, propose to Ḥasdai that his letter be transmitted from the Russians directly to their neighbors, the Khazars, but indirectly, by the Bulgars on the Volga, the northern neighbors of the Khazars.[79] They no doubt were aware of the enmity between the Russians, who were the rulers of Kiev, and the Khazars.

Ḥasdai accepted the proposal of Saul and Joseph and directed his secretary to compose a letter to Joseph, king of the Khazars. He also decided to send some of his subordinates to search for this Mar 'Amram who had been in Khazaria and to bring him to him. They sought him in the land of the Franks, but in vain. After some months they returned without having found 'Amram, and so once again Ḥasdai came to grief in his efforts to establish contact with the Khazars. In the summer of 954 Saul and Joseph revealed their desire to bide no longer in Cordova waiting for Johannes of Gorze to reach an understanding with the court of the caliphate. Ḥasdai therefore gave them his letter and sent them on their way.

This missive is also written in beautiful Hebrew and begins with a hymn of praise to the king. Ḥasdai first reports about the Omayyad-Spanish kingdom, its geographic situation and its economic affairs, and about the caliph. He goes on to tell the Khazar king what function he fulfills in the court of the caliph. He speaks of his activity as head of the Customs Department and relates that it is also his function to receive envoys of kings who come to the caliph. It is his practice to inquire of them about the condition of the Jews in their country and whether they have heard of Jews who are free from the yoke of the gentiles. Merchants from Khurāsān have told him about the Khazar kingdom, and when envoys of the Byzantine ruler came they confirmed this report and gave him additional information. They have told him that the name of the Khazar king is Joseph and said that Khazar vessels came to their land bringing fish and hides; they have also reported that relations exist between their ruler and the Khazar king.

Ḥasdai goes on to tell about his attempt to send Isaac bar Nathan to the king of the Khazars and the failure of his mission; he also mentions the proposal of the Jews from Palestine to transmit his letter to Khazaria. Finally, he relates how the two Jews reached him with the mission of the German king and promised that they would transmit his letter to its destination.

After relating how he came to write to the Khazar king, Ḥasdai makes his request. He asks the king to give him information about his kingdom: its size, its cities, the order of succession, its army, and the states that are its tributaries; in particular, he asks whether the Khazar king has a fixed capital city. He asks the king to inform him how many kings ruled before him and what their names were; he wants to know what language the Khazars speak. He also requests to be told the order of their worship and whether war sets aside the laws regulating the Sabbath. In addition, he wonders whether there are Jews in the neighboring countries of the Khazars and what cities are nearby in Khurāsān and the lands of the Caucasus.

When he speaks of the splendor of the Jewish kingdom he cannot restrain himself and lays bare the secret feelings locked up in his heart, saying: "If I knew that the thing is surely so [namely, the account regarding the kingdom], I would reject my honor, leave my high office and forsake my family, and I would go over hill and mountain, on the sea and over dry land to reach the place where my lord, the king, dwells, to behold his greatness and the glory of his majesty, the abode of his servants and the attendance of his ministers, and the repose of the survivors of Israel." But this is not enough. He also puts to the king the question which obsesses the Jew throughout all the ages: are the Khazars involved with the reckoning of the end of days (when the Messiah would appear)?[80]

Ḥasdai's letter illustrates well the circumstances under which he made contact with the Khazars. His observation that he had no initial knowledge of the existence of the Khazar kingdom is only rhetoric, since he himself mentions what he had heard from his forebears, namely, the tradition concerning the Khazars current among the Jews of Spain, as well as Eldad the Danite's report about them. He also mentions the information concerning them that he got from the merchants of Khurāsān, and we do know that there existed strong mercantile ties between Khazaria and Khurāsān and Khwārizm, since industrial products were sent to the Khazars from there. Moreover, Moslem coins found in Russia and in other countries of eastern and northern Europe prove that in the tenth century mercantile ties between these countries and the Abbasid caliphate reached their zenith.[81]

The information about Khazar trade and commerce revealed by Ḥasdai is decidedly correct. It matches what is reported in Arabic sources.[82] This shows, of course, that Ḥasdai had thoroughly investigated the Khazar circumstances. But although it is apparent from what he says that he made extensive inquiries from the merchants and envoys who came to Cordova, the influence of the tales of Eldad the Danite are also discernible in his letter. Ḥasdai inquires whether what Eldad related is indeed correct, and he phrases his question in substance in the actual language of Eldad. Here, as a case in point, is what Eldad relates: "The tribe of Simeon and the half-tribe of Manasseh are in the land of the Khazars . . . and they take tribute from twenty-five kingdoms and some of the Ishmaelite nations pay tribute, etc."; and Ḥasdai's query is as follows: "Let my lord inform me as to the number of governments over which he holds sway and the amount of tribute they render unto him and whether they pay him a tithe." Eldad relates: "And when they so desire, they travel and encamp with their tents from border to border, etc." And Ḥasdai asks: "Does my lord always camp within a certain city in the kingdom or does he move in a circle throughout the entire border of his dominion?" Eldad narrates: "They have a judge and a prince." And this is what Ḥasdai asks: "Does he judge his people or does he raise up judges for them?" As to their wars, Eldad states: "They make war with seven kingdoms, etc." And thus Ḥasdai: "With what nation does he make war and with whom does he battle?" At a later point Eldad observes: "They carry on their fighting on horses and do not dismount all week, but on the eve of the Sabbath they alight wherever they may be, etc." Ḥasdai asks: "Is the Sabbath suspended by battle?" Concerning the language of the Khazars, Eldad observes: "They speak the holy tongue [Hebrew], the language of Ḳedar [Ishmael], and Persian." Ḥasdai inquires: "What language do you speak?"[83]

As for the Khazars originating from the tribe of Simeon, this was related not only by Eldad, but was a view commonly held by the Jews of those times. First Chronicles 4:42, in referring to the exile of the tribe of Simeon, states: "And some of them, even of the sons of Simeon, . . . went to mount Seir." The land of Seir was, of course, said to be located in Babylonia, and all of Babylonia was referred to by the prophets by the name of the river K'bhar (cf. Ezekiel 1:1, 3; 3:15, et al.). In one version of Eldad's tales we do indeed find that the tribe of Simeon dwells in Chaldea, whereas in another version it is located in the land of the Khazars. From this derives the description in Ḥasdai's letter: "Our forefathers told us that in the beginning of your settlement the place was called Mount Seir, but my lord knows that Mount Seir is far from the place where he lives. Our elders say that it was called Mount Seir, but edicts multiplied, and they went from calamity to calamity, till they got possession of the land where they now dwell."[84]

After this segment Ḥasdai mentions what he heard concerning the hiding of the sacred books in a cave, which was the result of those persecutions that caused the tribe of Simeon to migrate to Khazaria. This detail he, of course, got from the letter of the anonymous Khazar Jew, which served him as an important source for his information about the Khazars. Perhaps it was that letter's confusing description of the processes of government that led him to his numerous questions on these matters. The question as to whether there were Jews in the countries bordering on the land of the Khazars also had its source in this letter (l. 53): "Some there were who observed the law of the Jews, namely, the rulers." The narrative about the wars of the Khazars and in particular their triumphs over the Byzantines, which we find in the treatise of the Khazar Jew, is reflected in the opening hymn of Ḥasdai's letter. This hymn hints at the inequality of the forces: the Khazar armies on one side and the combined hosts of the Russians and Byzantines on the other. The hymn also alludes to the warring horsemen and the conquest of Byzantine cities:

Subjugating the remnant among the mighty,
They attack and destroy a city and the fullness thereof.
The mighty arm of the Most High, their strength and their help, was their salvation.
This is the work of the Almighty, the measure of His recompense to the sinful kingdom.

The author of the poem, Ḥasdai's secretary, refers to Byzantium with the epithet current among the Jews: "the sinful kingdom." The yearnings for the messianic era that find expression in Ḥasdai's letter are characteristic of his time. To be sure, the tenth century did not witness the birth of any powerful messianic movements among Jewish masses, but Jewish scholars in every land believed that the time of the Messiah was about to come, and they were very much preoccupied with eschatological speculation. Saadya Gaon devoted a chapter in his great work, *Beliefs and Opinions,* to the subject of redemption, in which he dealt with the chain of events regarding the Messiah the son of Joseph; Armilus, who would slay the Messiah; the son of David, who would slay Armilus; the wars of Gog and Magog, and the ultimate salvation. He collected the tales about the coming of the Messiah and combined into one group. Saadya Gaon, who also was known as one indulging in eschatological reckonings, fixed the year 4768 (according to the Jewish calendar), which was 1008 C.E., as the dawn of the redemption.[85]

Karaite writers, who carried on a polemic with Saadya, were involved no less than he with eschatological reckonings. Salmōn b. Y'rūḥam reached the conclusion that salvation would come in 968.[86] The hope that salvation was close at hand was strong among all the communities of the Diaspora—in Babylonia and North Africa, in Byzantium and western Europe. In 960 the Jews of the Rhineland directed a question to the Jews of Palestine regarding "a report they had heard about the advent of the Messiah."[87]

The style of the letter which Ḥasdai Ibn Shaprūṭ sent to the king of the Khazars is characteristic of his Hebrew secretary, who is known to us from his literary work. Here and there we find the strange term *ḥāḳaḳ* for *kātav* (wrote), the unique use of *ōdōt* in the sense of *'inyān* (subject), *nāfal* (literally, fell) in the sense of *shākhan* (dwelt), the use of the word *ḳoshṭ* for *emet* (both mean truth), *īyīm* (islands) for "lands near the sea."[88] The initial letters of the verses in the poem with which the letter begins form an acrostic of the name of Ḥasdai and his secretary.[89]

Did Ḥasdai ultimately succeed in getting a reply from King Joseph? We are unable to answer this question. Back in the eleventh century a letter was being circulated that was attributed to the Khazar king. But while the text of Ḥasdai's letter stands up under investigation (although it is apparently distorted here and there),[90] the letter of King Joseph, in the form in which it has reached us, is highly suspect.

The king informs Ḥasdai that his letter has reached him by means of a Jew called Isaac b. Eli'ezer from the land of Nemeṣ (the name by which Germany was called by the Slavs, Hungarians, and Arabs), and then he answers Ḥasdai's queries. According to their genealogical records, the Khazars are descended from Togarmah. Togarmah had ten sons, the seventh being Khazar. Their forefathers conquered their land from the Wanantar people, the Bulgars, who were as numerous as the sands of the sea.

After many generations a God-fearing king named Būlan arose among the Khazars. An angel of the Lord twice appeared to this king in a dream, and when the angel was asked to appear to one of the nobles to make Būlan's story credible, he fulfilled this request. Thereafter Būlan assembled all his nobles and his entire people and converted them. This had occurred 340 years earlier. The angel reappeared to Būlan and commanded him to build a sanctuary, and he did as he was told. With his forces he went up to fight against the Moslems penetrating to Ardebil, and from the spoils he took there he built the sanctuary and made therein an ark, a candelabrum, a table, and altars.

When his conversion became known to the kings of Edom and Ishmael, they sent their emissaries to the Khazars to attract them to their respective faiths. Būlan thereupon commanded that a disputation be arranged between the representatives of the three faiths. When he questioned the Christian spokesman, he replied that he preferred the Jewish faith over that of Islam, and when he queried the Moslem representative, he too replied that Judaism is superior to Christianity. Thus it was that the Khazars became convinced that the Jewish faith was the true faith. The king and all his people became circumcised and invited to their country scholars who taught them the precepts of the Torah.

Since then the Khazars had won many victories over their

neighbors, who became tributaries to them. One of Būlan's grandsons, Obadiah, was distinguished for his piety; he ordered the construction of many synagogues and religious schools and brought many Jewish scholars to Khazaria. Later the letter lists the kings who ruled after Obadiah, observing that it was the practice to place upon the throne of the kingdom the son of the deceased king. The letter contains more information about the geographical situation of the land of the Khazars, their capital, and their mode of life.[91]

In this letter, which has been preserved in a long and a short version, it is worth noting the date of the disputation between the representatives of the three faiths and the conversion, which, according to the letter, had occurred 340 years earlier. Surely at that time the religion of Islam was not yet in existence. The description of the conversion in the course of the disputation and the arguments voiced by the representatives of the faiths all bear the stamp of a theological-polemic tract. The geographic description of the land of the Khazars deals mostly with the southern area, with which the Arabs and other Moslems were more familiar, while it neglects its northern and eastern regions.[92] The language of the letter also arouses suspicion, for it contains many Arabisms, such as *dīn* for *dat* (religion), Nazarene for Christian, *ay* as an expression of address which is merely the Arabic word *yā*.[93]

VII

Just as Ḥasdai Ibn Shaprūṭ was the advocate of the Jews in the Spanish-Moslem kingdom and in other countries, and initiated various actions to lighten the pressure of hostile governments, so too the very substance of his status and closeness to the Omayyad caliph had a great influence on the most important phenomenon in the history of Spanish Jews in the tenth century, namely, the migrations which flowed in from other lands, near and far, resulting in the considerable growth of its communities. Great importance inhered in the essential fact that at the royal court there was a Jewish courtier, a man of influence, who could bring to naught any evil designs, a man who had to be reckoned with by the Moslem nobles. In the despotic regimes that prevailed throughout all Islamic countries, the existence of such a courtier had great weight. Everywhere in Spain men told how Ḥasdai recommended the appointment of Jews to posts in the service of the caliph and the nobles, and aided others in getting promotion in rank. Even outside Spain his grandeur and his fine relations with his coreligionists were well known, and these things served as an added factor in drawing Jews to the plains of Andalusia.

It was an added factor, but not the only factor, to be sure. As in earlier eras, the migration of the Jews to Moslem Spain in the tenth century was paralleled by the stream of non-Jewish migration that flowed into that country. This migration was first and foremost the outcome of ʿAbdarraḥmān III's rule. The order and security that the Spanish caliph brought to his kingdom promoted a thriving economy. For decades the Andalusian provinces did not have to endure the raids of foreign armies or any rebellions, and the inhabitants of the cities and villages could devote themselves to the development of the natural resources of their country and various branches of the economy. Military campaigns against the Christians provided them with a large source of cheap labor: the prisoners brought to Andalusia by the caliph's armies.

In the middle of the tenth century the industries of Andalusia, such as the production of fine linens, developed to an extent that they could compete with the industries of Irak and other oriental countries. This flourishing economy resulted in the enrichment of the upper and middle classes. That the entire state became wealthy is attested to by the fact that in the reign of ʿAbdarraḥmān III gold coins were minted for the first time by the Moslem authorities in Spain. Prior to his reign there had been a marked diminution in the minting of silver coins, but during his time a great number of dirhams were minted. The report of Moslem Spain's thriving economy spread throughout all the countries and prompted many to take up the wanderer's staff to migrate to this fortunate state.

Yet another important motive for this migration was the numerical increase of the Slavs in the service of the caliph. These bondsmen, whether castrated or not, served in the caliph's palace, and from among them regiments were assembled to serve in the army and in particular one to guard the caliph himself. The Arabic writers report on the Slavs in the service of the caliph, but the nobles also acquired them as bondsmen. At all events, their numbers steadily increased, reaching many thousands. After carrying out their duties to the satisfaction of their masters, they would be emancipated, even receiving estates and much wealth. Certainly these Slavs, who migrated under compulsion, also attracted to Spain migrants who came of their own free will—some being relatives who came as protégés of kinsmen who had attained power and wealth; and others, men of daring and initiative who hoped to achieve success in the flourishing state of the Spanish caliph.

As we learn from various sources, many Jews also migrated to Moslem Spain in the days of 'Abdarraḥmān. These Jews came no doubt from many lands. But first and foremost the Jews of Morocco were bestirred to emigrate to Spain. This country was involved in the terrors of constant warfare among the princes, who divided among them the rule of its provinces. The military campaigns of the Fatimids and the depredations of the Berber tribes with all their terrors induced an atmosphere of disquiet and insecurity. It is no wonder that many persons crossed the straits to settle in tranquil and affluent Andalusia. The data concerning intellectuals in early Jewish sources testify to the great extent of the migration from North

Africa to Spain that started in that era. Of one we hear that his father came from North Africa to Spain, and of another that he grew up in Morocco and later crossed over to the kingdom of the Omayyad caliph.[94] Particular mention is made of the city of Fez as the place of origin, a city which in the tenth century harbored a large Jewish community.[95]

But many had migrated from Moroccan towns and townlets to Spain after its conquest by the Moslems and after the Omayyad dynasty had been established there. Hence there was nothing new in the migration of Moroccan Jews to Spain in the days of 'Abdarraḥmān III. It was the third wave in that stream of migration which endured a long time, sometimes waxing and sometimes waning. But there also reached Spain in those days a considerable number of immigrants from Jewish communities in the Near East.

While a strong and stable kingdom was established in Moslem Spain and the vigor of its economy developed and flourished, living conditions in that period worsened in countries where a large portion of the Jewish people had been concentrated for hundreds of years. After the death of Caliph al-Muḳtafī in 908 the Abbasid caliphate quickly disintegrated. Not only did the faraway provinces become independent, but also order and security weakened in Irak and its capital, Bagdad. Time and again the troops revolted and ran riot in the streets of the cities; violence and arson were a common occurrence.

In 945 the Būyids gained dominion over Irak and the western provinces of Persia, but before long these princes, who had been powerful, went from bad to worse. Friction between Shī'ites and Sunnīs erupted with an excess of bitterness, causing rioting. The army reverted to its evil ways, bringing havoc to the cities of Irak. In these circumstances the peaceful inhabitants suffered greatly, for no one was secure in his possessions and the fruits of his labor. The canals, without which

Babylonian agriculture could not exist, were damaged or destroyed, and its industries were impoverished. The power of the bedouins waxed throughout all the provinces of Irak, and their onslaughts upon the villages and cities continued unremittingly.

An even greater danger lurked for Irak and the other oriental countries from the Ḳarmaṭians. This movement, which had sprung up in the lands of the Abbasid caliphate at the end of the ninth century, was a social-revolutionary one that strove to change the social structure and bring about social justice. Broad strata of peasants, laborers, and artisans in Irak and Persia, in Syria and the Arabian peninsula, were attracted to it. In all these lands secret groups were established, but in the province of al-Aḥsā, which was in the eastern section of the Arabian peninsula, the Ḳarmaṭians set up an independent state. In 900 their leaders called on the masses everywhere to revolt and laid siege to Damascus. The Ḳarmaṭians' revolt in Syria was suppressed in a sea of blood, but their state in al-Aḥsā continued to exist, and from time to time they made raids from there upon the nearby provinces, especially in southern Irak, where they wrought havoc.

The rulers of Egypt struggled with the Abbasid caliph over the rule of Syria, and for a long time no stable government existed there. Then Saif ad-daula, chief of the Ḥamdānī clan, became the ruler in Aleppo in 945 and spread his dominance over all of northern Syria and Mesopotamia, waging war vigorously against the Byzantines, who were waxing more powerful at that time. The Byzantines aimed at the conquest of Syria and Palestine as a first step in the regeneration of their empire in the lands of the East. In 962 they took Aleppo, perpetrating there a terrible slaughter.

The Byzantine invasions of northern Syria and Mesopotamia were repeated in 964–966, and after the death of Saif ad-daula there was no power in Syria that could withstand them. In 968 the Byzantine emperor Nikephoros Phokas and his army made a raid upon Syria, taking Ḥamā, Ḥimṣ, and many other cities; all of them were plundered. The Byzantines returned from this campaign with 100,000 captives. In 969 Antioch was taken by the Byzantines and was held by them until 1084. John Zimiskes, who succeeded Nikephoros Phokas, penetrated to Mesopotamia in 974 and reached the city of Naṣībīn, which the inhabitants had vacated. Even the faraway city of Mosul paid tribute to the Byzantines. The following year the Byzantine emperor mounted a campaign against southern Syria and Palestine, advancing to Tiberias and Beth-Shean. According to the reports of Byzantine historians, he appointed governors over the cities he conquered, which indicates his intent to establish a new Byzantine dominion over Syria. But in actuality he contented himself with receiving heavy tribute, and in a general way the Byzantine invasions were essentially huge predatory ventures that brought upon the populations of Syria and Mesopotamia unimaginable suffering.

Of course, anyone who was able to leave these unfortunate countries for more secure areas did not hesitate. Men of varying social circles and members of various faiths sold their possessions and emigrated from their homeland. Many among these migrants turned westward. From Irak, which had suffered more than other oriental countries because of the weakening of authority and the raids of the Ḳarmaṭians, they wandered on to Syria and Palestine, which remained in relative tranquillity until the Byzantine incursions. A considerable number continued on their way and settled in Egypt.

Among the Jews this migratory movement reached sizable dimensions. A substantial number of Jews from all class levels went to Syria and Egypt. In the big cities of Syria and Palestine distinct communities of Babylonian Jews were established in those days. Such Babylonian communities existed in Damascus, Tiberias, and Ramleh.[96] The number of Babylonians in

Damascus was quite high. On one page in the journal of the court at Damascus four deeds of betrothal are entered for the months of Adar I and II of the year 4693 (933 C.E.), and all the couples are Babylonian.[97] Because they were numerous they founded perhaps two synagogues. In the fragment with which we are dealing there is mention of "the small synagogue" of the Babylonians, from which we may infer that they also had a big synagogue.[98]

In Egypt communities of immigrants from Irak were established, alongside which Jewish communities from Palestine and Syria gathered; these were called Jerusalemites, or in Arabic *Shāmīyūn*. Such communities existed in Alexandria[99] and Fostat, where they had their own courts and other institutions. Jews wandered into Egypt from all the provinces in the Eastern caliphate. A document from the eleventh century containing lists of Fostat Jews who took part in a fund-raising campaign mentions men from Bagdad, 'Ukbarā, Damascus, Acre, and Gischala,[100] and a similar list mentions people from the cities of Aleppo, Tyre, and Acre.[101] In a list of this kind from Fostat, not yet published, appear many Jews from Aleppo, Damascus, and Tyre, and side by side with them are *ar-Ramlīyūn*—immigrants from Ramleh—as a group, without mention of their names.[102] Jews from various cities of Irak and Upper Mesopotamia who settled at that time in Egypt are also mentioned in many other species of documents. A Jew from Naṣībīn who had sojourned in Damietta is mentioned in a document from the year 989.[103] A document from the first half of the eleventh century mentions a Jew from the city of ar-Raḳḳa, who resided in Fostat.[104]

The flood of emigration from Palestine, which was becoming impoverished, did not cease throughout this time. Many persons migrated to Egypt in hopes of finding a livelihood there. A circular letter of the Palestinian academy of that era addresses itself "to all the Jewish communities in Palestine in its fortified places, its cities, and villages," and also "to all of God's nation, its large and its small ones who have remained in Palestine and those in Egypt who originate from Palestine." The reference is plainly to the Palestinian Jews who had established distinct communities in Egypt and erected synagogues for themselves—the "Jerusalemites."[105]

But while living conditions in Egypt were easier than those in Irak and Syria, circumstances in Egypt itself were not at all happy. The weakening of order, which was the lot of all the oriental countries that had formerly belonged to the empire of the caliphs, had not passed Egypt by. After the death of the *ikhshīd*, the powerful ruler of Egypt, in 946, the foundations of government were utterly shaken. In his stead a black eunuch named Kāfūr became the ruler, but he was unable to pay the soldiers, and they broke out in revolt. Throughout Egypt anarchy prevailed, and pillage was a daily occurrence. In 962 the waters of the Nile, which fructify the land, did not overflow their banks, initiating a period of drought lasting nine years. In the wake of the drought famine and pestilence followed.

Now, at just this time there arose west of Egypt the great kingdom of the Fatimid caliphs, who labored diligently to develop the economic resources of their lands. In those days Kairawan was a large city where industry and commerce flourished and so was also al-Mahdīya, founded in 912 by the first Fatimid caliph. The difference in the political and economic regimes of Egypt and the Fatimid caliphate was great, giving the new kingdom an obvious power to attract.

Many of the Jews who reached Egypt from Irak, Syria, and the other oriental countries moved on to the provinces of North Africa—to Ifrīḳīya, now called Tunisia, to the Central Maghreb, now known as Algeria, and to Maghreb al-aḳṣā, which is now Morocco; from there individuals and groups crossed over to Moslem Spain. Thus began a great migratory movement in the tenth century that brought a large number of Jews from the Near East to the Maghreb—to the provinces of North Africa and to Spain. The ancient communities of Irak and Upper Mesopotamia were depleted, and in their stead a new center for the Jews arose in the West. Information concerning the wanderings of the Jews of Irak to the Moslem West has been preserved in various documents. From this information we learn that a great number of Babylonian Jews settled in Kairawan in the tenth century.[106] From Egypt and Kairawan they crossed over to Sicily. In a letter of the "Sicilian community" (no doubt the Jews of Palermo) to the community of Kairawan, written in the 1030s, favorable mention is made of ʿAmmār b. Joshua "from Aleppo."[107]

The roads traveled by these migrants and the places where they tarried in their long journey from Irak to Spain are mentioned in the many letters discovered in the Geniza archives in Cairo. A man from Irak named Naḥūm al-Baradānī, who had been a renowned cantor, wandered westward, apparently residing in Kairawan, where he dealt in trade. He was called Naḥūm al-Ḥazzān al-Baradānī after the village of Baradān, in the vicinity of Bagdad.[108] This man bought merchandise in Kairawan and sent it to Egypt to be sold. After his death and the death of his son Yannai, his business representative refused to pay his grandsons, Joseph and Naḥūm, the price of the merchandise, and they brought suit against him before the court at Ramleh, where he had settled.[109] There is no doubt that this is the same Naḥūm ben Joseph who wrote a letter in 999 to his teacher and the then *gaon*, Samuel b. Ḥofnī, from Kairawan. The author of the letter, who had left his family in Irak, was in Spain, but many unpleasant occurrences (he does not explain what they were) had befallen him there. After this he tarried in al-Mahdīya and wrote the *gaon* from there. While in Kairawan he received a letter from the *gaon*, and when he had learned from him the state of affairs in the city of his birth (most likely Bagdad), he burst into bitter weeping and transmitted the information found in the letter to all his acquaintances (that is, the Babylonian Jews of Kairawan). He justifies his not returning to Irak by stating that in light of the calamitous information he cannot do so.[110]

We may be certain that merchants wrote more letters than did artisans; it would therefore be wrong to conclude that most of the emigrants actually were merchants. There were certainly many artisans among them. These letters demonstrate how the emigrants maintained ties with their homeland. What is related in trustworthy sources concerning the biography of a leading spokesman regarding the cultural life of the Jews of Spain in the generation of Ḥasdai Ibn Shaprūṭ is typical of the character of the migration and the life of the emigrants. The man was born in Fez and studied in Irak; afterward he returned to Morocco and ultimately, in the middle of the tenth century, he reached Cordova.[111] Moslem writers also relate that many Spanish Jews were of Eastern origin. An anonymous Arabic writer, in speaking of the Jews in Spain, states that they were an amalgam of the descendants of Jews who had dwelt in the Iberian peninsula from days of old and migrant Jews who came to Spain from North Africa and from west Asian countries.[112]

This large migratory movement had important consequences for the development of the Jewish people, and not solely with respect to the numerical increase of Jewish settlements in North Africa and Spain. The dispersal of the Jews throughout many lands, where they lived under a variety of circumstances and under differing regimes, was bound to cause disunity and the disintegration of Jewish groups in their respective areas. The influence of alien religions and cultures was apt to result in the establishing of sects, in spite of the hedges erected by the talmudic scholars in order to set up a dividing wall between the Jews and the non-Jews. Yet this powerful migration created a living tie among remote communities and prevented the development of alien feelings between Jewish groups in different lands. Indeed, it renewed the unity of the nation throughout the Diaspora.

6

THE EFFLORESCENCE OF JEWISH CULTURE

I

In the middle of the tenth century the influence of Ḥasdai Ibn Shaprūṭ was felt throughout all spheres of Jewish life in the Iberian peninsula, but of special importance was his effect on their cultural life. After the manner of enlightened Moslem nobles, he acted with great generosity in behalf of intellectuals in the fields of literature and science. Indeed, he esteemed it an honor to have concern for their livelihood, to allocate fixed grants to them, to send them gifts, and to award them prizes for what they wrote. In giving assistance, Ḥasdai did not limit himself to one class of intellectual, but gave encouragement to all of them in various ways. The great importance with which he regarded the effort toward the development of Jewish culture on Spanish soil was recognized in his own time and in later generations. The Hebrew authors of the Middle Ages unanimously affirm that the efflorescence of Judeo-Spanish culture originates with Ḥasdai Ibn Shaprūṭ.

Naturally, his efforts first and foremost were in behalf of the study of Torah. As the leaders of the communities of Spain who preceded him had done, he gave of his wealth to acquire sacred texts, in particular volumes of the Gemara edited in Babylonia. A poet of that era wrote in his honor:

For the Torah's sages
He provided light and aid
His wealth went to Sura
Whence came the tomes
To teach them the laws
As sweet as honey
And righteous statutes
Clear and just.[1]

It is certain that the poet did not intend to say that Ḥasdai ordered books to be sent from the Academy of Sura alone, but mentioned that city as representing the whole of Babylonia. The subordinates of the Jewish noble of Cordova roamed throughout the towns of the Near East, which were then in the throes of a crisis because of the disintegration of the caliphate, and in every place they endeavored to rescue books so that they could be used in their faraway land in the West. In this Ḥasdai also followed the path of the Moslem nobles in Spain, its kings and princes, who desired to transform their land into a center of Arabic culture. They, too, sent envoys to the oriental countries to acquire from famous authors holographic manuscripts of their works. At times this led to the result that an Arabic book written in Irak or Syria became known in Spain before becoming public in the author's own country.

Ḥasdai acted in like manner. When his functionary, Samuel, who performed various missions for him, tarried in Italy, at Ḥasdai's behest he had a copy made of a book that was large in scope. In the letters wherein the Jews of southern Italy portray to Ḥasdai the oppressions of the Byzantine authorities, there is mention that over a period of several months the aforementioned Samuel had made a transcript of *The Book of Joseph ben Gorion*. Later, robbers deprived him of certain valuables, among them this transcript.[2] The writers of the letter are not explicit as to whether they meant *The Book of*

Antiquities by Josephus or a draft of *The Book of Yōsīphōn,* which its author completed some months after Samuel's visit to southern Italy.[3] Thus it can be seen that Ḥasdai's influence reached out even beyond Spain. His envoys roamed throughout the East and West acquiring texts for study and research by the Jews of Spain.

But they did not limit their search to texts alone; they also looked for scholars with a knowledge of the Torah who could serve as teachers and were prepared to come to Spain. Ḥasdai's agents promised them all manner of rewards, suitable remuneration and great honors, if they would only agree to come to Andalusia. This effort was highly successful. A Judeo-Spanish poet relates of Ḥasdai that "he strengthened the pillars of wisdom and gathered unto him men of knowledge from Palestine to Babylonia."[4] This author goes on to say that Ḥasdai's support encouraged the intellectuals among the Spanish Jews. He states that the "men of undersanding of his day avidly desired to promulgate the wisdom that God had implanted in their hearts and the knowledge with which he had endowed them. They wrote books of distinction, gathering within them marvelous subjects of interest."[5]

While Spain was becoming a center for Jewish culture, the religio-spiritual center in Babylonia had to struggle mightily for its very existence, losing its erstwhile hegemony throughout the communities of the Diaspora. During the tenth century preeminent men who had acquired lasting fame headed the renowned Academies of Sura and Pumbedita. But the solid foundation on which this spiritual center was established was already being undermined. The battles among the several warlords who sought to dominate the various parts of the sinking caliphate, the regimes of exploitation adopted by the new rulers, and the impoverishment of the Babylonian Jews, together with their migration to other lands—all these naturally brought on the decline of the academies. Their sources of revenue steadily diminished, their landed property was stolen from them, and communities that had hitherto sent them gifts regularly discontinued doing so. Centers of Torah that developed gradually in other lands began simultaneously to stand on their own feet, and since the Jews of various countries outside Irak no longer needed the constant guidance of the Babylonian academies, they ceased to give them the regular support they formerly provided.

Even the ties between Spanish and Babylonian Jewry, once so firm, grew ever weaker. The communities of Andalusia had stopped sending queries to the Academy of Sura in the ninth century, and in truth this academy waned grievously. Upon the death of Ṣemaḥ bar Ḥayyīm, Malka was chosen to succeed him, but when he ascended to the gaonate a plague broke out, and he and most of the scholars of the academy perished. Nevertheless, the academy continued to exist; however, the *g'ōnīm* who headed it at that time were poor in achievement, and the number of scholars and students continued to decline.

When the *gaon* Jacob b. Naṭrōnai died in 923, no scholar worthy of the distinguished office could be found, and a man was chosen who was not numbered among the scholars of the academy and was not outstanding for his knowledge. His name was Yōm Ṭōbh Kahana, and he was a weaver. For four years he headed the academy that had once been a beacon to the whole Jewish people, and after his death many expressed the view that it was better to close the academy than to have an undeserving man called *gaon* and *abh-bēt-dīn* of this venerable institution.

At the Academy of Pumbedita, which had moved to Bagdad at the end of the ninth century, there could still be found many students and a considerable number of scholars; and it was headed by *g'ōnīm,* scholars of distinction and energetic men who struggled hard for the welfare of the academy. But quarrels broke out in the academy, which undermined its foundations, and its *g'ōnīm* became involved in disputes with the exilarchs, disputes that occupied them over many years.

In any event, the Jews of Spain maintained contact with this academy at the outset of this period. In a document emanating from the academy in the middle of the tenth century it is reported that these ties were renewed in the beginning of the tenth century, after a temporary interruption. It seems that during the chaotic times prevailing in Moslem Spain at the end of the tenth century, in the days of Emir 'Abdallāh, the Jews of Andalusia discontinued sending questions even to the *g'ōnīm* of Pumbedita. In those troubled times they were preoccupied with needs of the moment. Besides, the roads were cluttered with bands of soldiers.

But when the situation improved after 'Abdarraḥmān ascended the throne in Cordova, the Jews of Andalusia again sent their queries to Babylonia. In the aforementioned document it is related that questions from Spain came to Judah b. Samuel, who headed the Academy of Pumbedita from 906 to 917.[6] Judah carried on a dispute with the exilarch, 'Uḳba, who wanted to take away from the academy the "Province of Khurāsān," namely, the right to appoint judges and collect taxes throughout all the communities in that country. Ultimately 'Uḳba's foes succeeded in having the Moslem government exile him, and no other exilarch was appointed for several years.

Meanwhile, Judah died, and the members of the academy chose as his successor M'bhassēr. Shortly thereafter a new exilarch was also chosen, David b. Zakkai, who, on becoming convinced that he was not recognized by M'bhassēr and his partisans, appointed another head of the academy, Kōhēn-Ṣedeḳ b. Joseph. The Academy of Pumbedita became riven by factions, some persons giving their support to M'bhassēr and some to Kōhēn-Ṣedeḳ, a situation that continued for a number of years. In 922 peace was effected between the exilarch and M'bhassēr, but shortly thereafter the *gaon* died, and thenceforth

Kōhēn-Ṣedeḳ alone headed the academy until his death in 936.[7] The Jews of Spain corresponded with this *gaon*, too, and addressed queries to him.[8]

At this time also ties between the Jews of Spain and the Academy of Sura were reestablished for a brief time. After the heads of the Jewish community in Babylonia had wrestled with the problem of whether to close the Academy of Sura altogether, and the decision to maintain its existence had prevailed, the exilarch decided to place at its head Saadya Gaon, although he was not a student at the academy and was not even a Babylonian. He did this not only because Saadya ranked head and shoulders above all the scholars of all the academies, but also because he depended upon Saadya's ability to establish contact with the Diaspora everywhere—an ability that he had already demonstrated in the years preceding his appointment. With some justice the exilarch hoped that this special talent would stand him in good stead in his administration of the academy.

Saadya did indeed cultivate ties with Jewish communities in various lands, and among others he sent a circular letter to the Jewish communities of Spain, since it had been the practice of *g'ōnīm* to send such letters to the communities in various countries.[9] But in a short while a severe quarrel broke out between Saadya and the exilarch. Saadya was deposed from his office for a period of several years, and the ties he had established were broken.

After Saadya Gaon's death the Academy of Sura became thoroughly impoverished, and the Academy of Pumbedita did not enjoy prosperity either. In 943 Aaron ha-Kōhēn b. Joseph (who was known by his Arabic name, Khalaf b. Sardjadū) was placed at the head of the academy. He was a man who possessed much knowledge and even dallied with authorship; but in point of fact he was chosen because he was very wealthy and powerful. He had many enemies, and even among the scholars of the academy he had his opponents, who set up against him a rival *gaon,* Nehemiah, the son of the *gaon* Kōhēn-Ṣedeḳ. During that interval the Jews of Spain stopped sending queries to the Academy of Pumbedita, although they did continue to send contributions.[10]

In the 950s a powerful trend developed in the religio-spiritual life of the Jewish communities in Spain. The severance of ties with the Babylonian academies did not result from this trend, but occurred simultaneously with it. There is no doubt that even if this trend had not occurred, the Andalusian communities would not have continued to seek guidance from the Babylonian academies, for they were aware of the academies' decline. In any event, what happened in Spain itself gave impetus and direction to this development.

The occurrence was the arrival of a brilliant scholar who came to Spain against his will and settled there. This scholar was Moses b. Ḥanōkh, who was born and raised in southern Italy. The communities in the southern part of Italy in those days were notable for their erudition and the observance of venerable religious tradition. This was the tradition that stemmed from Palestine, for the Jews of Italy drew their inspiration from Palestinian Jewry, since both were for many generations within the same political entity: the Roman Empire; whereas the Jewish center in Babylonia was part of a government hostile to the Roman Empire: the kingdom of Persia. For this reason the communities of Otranto and Bari, Taranto and Oria, fostered not only the Midrash and *piyyūṭ* (liturgical poetry) that came from Palestine, but they also observed Palestinian manners of worship and studied the Jerusalem (Palestinian) Talmud. To be sure, they had an awareness of the Babylonian Talmud, and in time contacts were established between the Jews of southern Italy and the academies of Babylonia, but the characteristic bent in their religious and cultural life remained one of following Palestinian tradition. For many years Moses b. Ḥanōkh studied in one of the colleges that flourished in the communities of southern Italy, becoming a distinguished scholar and absorbing the particular tradition of these Jewish communities. At the time of his arrival in Spain he was already middle-aged and experienced in teaching and rendering judicial decisions.

His migration to Spain constituted one of the most significant events in his life, one of those occurrences that a person does not anticipate but that nevertheless determine the course of his life. Moses b. Ḥanōkh never intended to migrate to Spain but a ship in which he was sailing on the Mediterranean Sea was suddenly attacked by a Spanish galleon, which overpowered the crew without difficulty, taking all the passengers captive. In the 950s such acts took place frequently in the part of the Mediterranean Sea that lies between the western coast of Italy and Sicily and the coast of North Africa.

Caliph ʻAbdarraḥmān had given much attention to his war fleet from the outset of his reign. In 914 he came to Algeciras to be able to observe at close hand matters concerning the fleet; he made it his concern to build new ships and to monitor the coast of Spain constantly, doing all this to prevent surprise attacks by the Normans and to interrupt all contacts between undesirable elements in his kingdom and Fatimid agents.

For many years the commanders of the Mediterranean fleet were the admirals Aḥmad b. Yaʻlā and ʻAbdarraḥmān b. Muḥammad Ibn ar-Rumāḥis, who was also the governor of the province of Pechina-Almería.[11] These admirals labored indefatigably to impose Omayyad rule over the western basin of the Mediterranean. The expeditions and assaults by the ships of the Spanish fleet became more frequent, especially after an incident in 955. In that year a Spanish ship met a ship coming from Sicily that carried an emissary from the ruler of the island under Fatimid suzerainty; this emissary was bringing documents with various items of intelligence to their caliph. When the Spaniards seized the vessel and captured the emissary, the Fatimid caliph reacted with an attack on the port of Almería, the most important military port in eastern and southeastern Spain. The Spanish fleet carried out retaliatory action, making raids in 956–958 on the coast of the African provinces that gave allegiance to the Fatimid ruler. We learn about these activities from the Arabic chroniclers.[12]

But these were not the only activities of the Omayyad fleet. Units of this fleet reconnoitered the expanses of the Mediterranean over a long period of time, seeking out vessels that came from the Fatimid kingdom or were sailing to it; and it is certain that they did not refrain from seizing any Christian vessel. During one of these naval actions the ship in which Moses b. Ḥanōkh and his family were sailing was taken, and he and the other captives were brought to Spain.[13]

Moses b. Ḥanōkh was ransomed by the Jews of Spain and went to Cordova. There his vast erudition was soon noted by the scholars of the city, who decided to appoint him their rabbi and place him at the head of the local academy. The incumbent rabbi of Cordova at that time, Nathan, himself recognized that the Italian scholar was immeasurably his superior and was willing to yield up his post.

The matter was naturally brought to the attention of Ḥasdai Ibn Shaprūṭ, who supported the appointment of Moses b. Ḥanōkh wholeheartedly. To be sure, the self-sufficiency of Spanish Jewry had progressed considerably by now, and for many years the Jews of Andalusia had not found it necessary to turn for help to the academies of Babylonia, but Ḥasdai justifiably hoped that as a result of the activities of a scholar of such stature, Andalusian Jewry would be completely independent of the Babylonian center. This fell in with the diplomacy of the Omayyad caliph whom the Jewish dignitary served, and no doubt it was uppermost in his thoughts.[14]

Rabbi Moses b. Ḥanōkh did not disappoint the hopes placed

in him. He began with extensive activity, and success favored him. He was first and foremost a teacher of halakha, and after his fame had spread throughout all the provinces of Spain, students from all the communities flocked to him to acquire knowledge of Jewish law from him. His school in Cordova became a center of Torah in the highest degree. He also headed the Jewish court in the capital of the Omayyad kingdom and responded in writing to questions directed to him by other communities. These questions and the responses dealt largely with practical matters: legal disputes such as marriage documents and problems of inheritance, pledges, promissory notes, and the like.[15] Moses b. Ḥanōkh remained loyal to the traditions of Italian Jewry; he followed their custom in prayer and endeavored to spread it throughout Spain too.[16] To be sure, he did this gradually and in general was popular and behaved modestly. This was even evident in the style of his responsa. He never employed the strong language of the Babylonian *g'ōnīm,* but expressed his views in an unassuming manner.

The way in which he conducted himself with all people impressed the Jews of Spain as much as his learning did, and for this reason he was accepted as a religious leader whose position was beyond dispute. The sympathetic attitude that he won for himself from Spanish Jewry with the passage of time helped him carry out his mission: to establish in Spain a center of Judaism totally independent of the Babylonian academies.

Thus it came to pass that in the days of Ḥasdai Ibn Shaprūṭ the cultural ties between Spanish and Babylonian Jewry, which for many generations had been the very foundation of their religious and spiritual life, were broken. As the religious center at the western edge of the Mediterranean basin rose to ever greater eminence, the old center in Babylonia faded away. Its condition at that time was at the nadir. At the Academy of Pumbedita the bitter quarrel between the *gaon* Aaron b. Joseph and Nehemiah b. Kōhēn-Ṣedeḳ endured for a long time.

The two factions acquired supporters outside the academy and wrangled over the sources of income—meanwhile neglecting the study and teaching as a result. The Academy of Sura was completely impoverished after the death of Saadya Gaon and was on the verge of closing.

The political situation in Irak also seriously worsened. The caliph's government was powerless, and each man did as he pleased. In consequence, the income of the academies shrank more and more, compelling them to write many letters to the Jewish communities in various lands pleading for donations. The style of these letters is ample testimony to the sad plight of the academies. They contain entreaties and are composed in language bespeaking utter obsequiousness. How great a difference there was from the resolute authority of the *g'ōnīm* of the eighth and ninth centuries and the tone of the letters of the heads of the academies in the tenth century!

One of the letters sent in that era from a Babylonian academy to the Jews of Spain relates at length how the scholars of the academy continue studying and teaching even though they find themselves in very distressing circumstances. The writer of the letter speaks of the debts that press upon the academies and the great suffering—the pangs of hunger endured by the scholars and their families. He therefore addresses himself to the heads of the Jewish community in Spain, who are distinguished scholars, with an urgent plea to raise their contribution in behalf of his academy and to send it by the hand of Saul b. Joseph, an officer of the academy in the city of Kairawan.[17]

A letter couched in a similar style was issued from the Academy of Pumbedita in 953, as its close indicates. The beginning of the letter is missing and thus there is no way of knowing who the author was, but beyond all doubt the letter was directed to Ḥasdai Ibn Shaprūṭ. This is evident from the flowery language with which the author of the letter addresses the person to whom it is directed: phrases such as "Fortunate is the generation whose leader you are, for you know the scholars and are aware of the means by which they sustain themselves," and so on; this is particularly indicated by the phrases that refer to his position of authority in the government. The author of the letter extols the distinguished character of Ḥasdai, who generously supports scholars, providing for all their needs.

He complains bitterly at the change in attitude that occurred in the Jews of Spain toward the academies of Babylonia. Earlier they had supported the academies regularly, but now —so he reports—they have dropped this custom and no longer continue the tradition of their forebears. It is true that two years before the writing of this letter, in 951, they did send a sum of money, but a large part of it was stolen and only a small amount was salvaged by the exilarch, Solomon (that is, Solomon b. Josiah, the brother of David b. Zakkai).[18] On that occasion Ḥasdai had sent his own special contribution, and he had done likewise a short time before the letter was written. The author of the letter relates that someone wanted to steal this money also—and he apparently has in mind not some unknown embezzlers but members of a faction in the academy that opposed his supporters.

The situation of the academy was very perilous—so reported the letter. The quarrels among the scholars consumed it, and its income was almost nil. The letter writer complains that the scholars of the academy had to sell their furniture to buy food, retaining only their books. Thus it is not surprising that he implores Ḥasdai most urgently to do all in his power in behalf of the academy and not to forget to send his own contribution.[19] He also requests that the Jews of Spain once again send questions to the academy, as was their wont in past generations. The author of the letter pleads that the questions and contributions be sent through Aaron b. Abraham b. Aaron, an important merchant in Bagdad, who, with his brother Moses, labored mightily in behalf of the academy.[20]

This letter still speaks of "the academies," but shortly thereafter the Academy of Sura shut down entirely. To such a state had matters come in Babylonia. The poverty was too great, the members of the academies and the young rabbis sought those livelihoods with substance, and the academies became empty. The cries for help that were sent to other countries were not properly heeded. However, Ḥasdai Ibn Shaprūṭ did not turn a deaf ear and, upon receipt of the letter, once again made his contribution to the Academy of Pumbedita. The scholars of the academy appreciated his attitude and wanted moreover to spur him on to further activity; therefore they decided to give him an honorary title they held in especial esteem, one not ordinarily granted to a person outside the academy except on rare occasions and only for special merit. They appointed him *resh kalla* at the Academy of Pumbedita. The letter informing him of the award did not refrain from mentioning the crushing debts of the academy and pleaded for him to take action in its behalf. Among other things, the scholars stressed that support of the academies is a sacred obligation incumbent on all Jews, replacing the sacrifices offered in the Temple, and that the practice was instituted by Ezra the Scribe, Daniel, and the prophets of their era.[21]

In 960 Aaron b. Joseph died, and in his place Nehemiah b. Kōhēn-Ṣedeḳ, who had been his competitor, was appointed. But Sh'rīra, who had served as president of the court of the academy during the incumbency of Aaron, refused to recognize Nehemiah, left the academy, and set up his own, albeit he did not receive the appellation *gaon* till the death of Nehemiah.

Each of these men appealed to the communities in various lands to address questions to them and give them financial support. In a circular letter that Sh'rīra wrote to "the Jewish communities residing in Andalusia and Spain and all the lands of the West and the land of Ifrīḳīya"—that is, the Jews of Moslem and Christian Spain and Morocco and Tunisia—he pleads with them to send him contributions. Nehemiah, on the other hand, addresses communities and individuals, complaining bitterly that they have discontinued support of the academy and do not even answer the letters written to them by the academy each year. How much the relations between the Jewish communities outside of Babylonia and the Babylonian academies had changed can be learned from an observation by the *gaon* Nehemiah, who asks whether the level of knowledge of the members of the academy and that of himself is in doubt.[22] These old letters, which were discovered in the Geniza of Cairo, add up to one picture: they describe for us how the hegemony among the Jewish people passed from the Jews of Irak to the Jews of Spain.

II

The role played by Ḥasdai Ibn Shaprūṭ in the development of the study of Jewish law in Spain was very important. But even in earlier generations, academies having a long tradition behind them already existed in Andalusia, and hence there was nothing novel in the appointment of Moses b. Ḥanōkh or in his activity.

But until that period the Jews of Spain had practically never dealt in any of the other branches of learning and literature. From a cultural aspect they were, over many generations, held within the confines of their community, having no cooperative activity whatsoever with their Moslem neighbors. However, a decisive change in this regard occurred in the middle of the tenth century. The Jews of Moslem Spain emerged from their cultural seclusion; they ceased being one-sided in their cultural interests and began to take part energetically in the flourishing culture of the Omayyad kingdom in Spain.

This new trend suited the overall aims of the government and its inhabitants of whatever degree; for it was a main principle in the policy of the enlightened Caliph ʿAbdarraḥmān III to bring together the various religious and ethnic groups within the borders of his kingdom, destroy the walls that separated them, and bring about a resulting collaboration. The Jews of Andalusia gladly pursued this new course, and indeed before long this collaboration between them and the other inhabitants of Spain bore fruit within the framework of both the Jewish and the general culture.

In respect to this new development in the cultural life of the communities in Spain, the Jewish courtier Ḥasdai Ibn Shaprūṭ played a part of the highest importance. His efforts to promote the development of the more general branches of culture and literature had even greater weight than his support of the theological studies. Given the conditions of life prevailing in Moslem Spain in the tenth century, the latent creative cultural powers of the Jewish populace no doubt would have been aroused of their own accord sooner or later. But there are times when the factors that direct historical development become embodied in one man, who forges ahead to meet them and is marked by his strength and the inclination to direct others. Such a man becomes a leader, marching in the van and imposing his will on the masses. One such personality who achieved prodigious marvels was Ḥasdai Ibn Shaprūṭ, and his guiding hand can be discerned in almost all the cultural aspects of the life of the Jews of Spain of his day.

Ḥasdai Ibn Shaprūṭ was an Andalusian courtier in every fiber of his being. With all his energies he strove to serve his king and his goals; whether in foreign diplomacy or in internal government, he was a guiding light. He also adopted the manners of the Arab nobles and modeled his way of life on theirs. These nobles played an important part not only in the affairs of the government but also in the cultural sphere, inasmuch as they gave assistance to writers, especially poets. The majority among them were of Arabic stock, and throughout the ages poetry was held in very high esteem among the Arabs. A hymn of praise would eternally embellish the name of a tribe or of a noble, and conversely an opprobrious ode could heap derision upon a group of tribes or one man, condemning him to everlasting disgrace. Nobles and rulers paid large sums to poets who sang their praise, knowing full well that these poems would have wide circulation and win for them fame and glory. Ḥasdai Ibn Shaprūṭ, who rose to eminence in the Andalusian court circles, acted in like manner, becoming a Maecenas to writers.

Among the Arabs there was a strong link between the cultivation of the poetic muse and the study of the Arabic language, and many were both poets and Arabic linguists. From early times the Arabs had taken pride in their rich and developed tongue, and at receptions held in the nobles' houses long discussions were held on the meaning of uncommon words and the significance of various grammatical forms. The Jews who lived in Spain among the Arabs were influenced by this state of mind, and several of them began to delve deeply into the study of the Hebrew language. Ḥasdai's home became a gathering place for the first writers among the Jews of Spain. He supported them materially and encouraged them to persist in their work. One of the Spanish Jewish poets of the later Middle Ages relates how Ḥasdai concentrated Hebrew poets about him:

That prince restored to life those who were dying of folly with the dew of his grace
Attracting the hearts of the dispersed nation with the cords of his generosity
And making a proclamation: Whosoever is for the Lord, let him come to me
And I will provide for all his needs
And every gaon and rabbi were gathered unto him

From the lands of Edom [Rome] and Arabia, from the
East and from the West. . . .
Grumblers have since learned
And princes have welcomed men of song
For his kindness has made the tongues of the dumb to
break out in song
Opening hearts grown obdurate
So that they gathered about him with sweet songs
Bright as the stars on high.[23]

After the fashion of the Moslem nobles, Ḥasdai would arrange receptions at his home where writers would read their creative efforts: poems and other works. These gatherings, which the Arabs termed *madjlis* and the Hebrew poets *mōshābh,* would come together at fixed times, and their participants would witness keyed-up, and at times really glowing, literary discussions.

For a number of years the most respected man in this circle was M'naḥem b. Jacob, a member of the Ben Sārūḳ family, who was a poet and a Hebrew philologist. M'naḥem Ben Sārūḳ was born in one of the cities of northeastern Spain and acquired his knowledge of Judaism under difficult circumstances. From earliest youth he studied diligently, and his greatest interest was in Hebrew philology and Bible commentaries. But here lay the seat of his difficulty: in a Spanish provincial town it was hard to find books written in other countries which he knew of by hearsay alone. He also endured material hardships, inasmuch as his father had died, leaving a number of orphaned children.

M'naḥem decided to go to Cordova, where, according to reports, all paths lay open to a youth hungry for knowledge and diligent in the pursuit of learning. He had even heard about the libraries in the schools in Cordova and in the homes of individuals, and he had also heard much about the virtuousness of the wealthy, who gave generous assistance to men of the spirit. His hopes were not disappointed. Upon reaching Cordova, he found favor in the eyes of a wealthy man, who made it possible for him to devote himself to his studies. This rich person was a brother of Ḥasdai Ibn Shaprūṭ. The young scholar became closely bound to him and remained grateful to him all his life. As was the custom in Andalusia in those days, M'naḥem Ben Sārūḳ, functioned as poet laureate of the family and on appropriate occasions would compose a special poem. When the lordly Isaac Ibn Shaprūṭ built a synagogue, M'naḥem formulated the poetical inscription engraved on the ark of the Torah whereon the praises of the man who had established the synagogue are sung.

M'naḥem sojourned for a long time in Cordova, delving deeply into the writings of Judah Ibn Ḳuraish and the philological studies of Saadya Gaon; and he himself began to write down his own explanations of words, guarding these notes very zealously. Eventually, he decided to return to the city of his birth and did so, staying in his city for a short time and engaging in commerce, from which he derived a dignified livelihood for himself and his family.

In the meantime, Ḥasdai Ibn Shaprūṭ had risen in eminence at the court of 'Abdarraḥmān III and had also become the *nāsī* of Andalusian Jewry. His role required that he correspond with various communities within the borders of the Omayyad kingdom, and at this time he also came into contact with Jewish communities in other lands; he therefore needed a secretary who was well versed in the entire treasure-house of the Hebrew language and could write letters in good taste. He recalled the youth his brother had assisted, who spent his days in diligent study of the Hebrew language. Ḥasdai therefore urgently requested that M'naḥem Ben Sārūḳ return to Cordova, promising him ample rewards if he would become his Hebrew secretary.

The request of the Jewish courtier perplexed M'naḥem. On one hand, he had attained success in his business affairs and had come to enjoy the pleasant taste of economic independence; but on the other, the notion to start writing an important work in the field of Hebrew philology had begun to unfold, and for this project he needed books available only in Cordova. The urge to publish the fruits of their studies is imbedded in the heart of scholars, and in this instance it was stronger than any other impulse. M'naḥem accepted Ḥasdai's invitation and went to Cordova.

Naturally, the Jewish noble did not require his services in the writing of Hebrew letters every single day, and he was pleased when his secretary occupied himself with literary efforts and encouraged him in this enterprise. The book on which M'naḥem had set his heart was a dictionary of the Hebrew language, and from the time he returned to Cordova he worked on his project with much diligence; at the same time many students came to him for instruction. He also continued composing Hebrew poems in which he lauded the noble traits of Ḥasdai; these poems were circulated among all the communities of Spain.

When Ḥasdai's father died, M'naḥem Ben Sārūḳ composed a cycle of laments to be recited in the synagogues during the time of mourning. When his mother died, an incident occurred that engraved itself deeply in M'naḥem's memory. At midnight the noble went to his erudite secretary to request that he immediately compose an elegy, and to his great surprise found him already engaged in doing this. Ḥasdai was greatly moved by M'naḥem's devotion and swore that he would never forget it and would reward him generously for his services. But in actuality his attitude to M'naḥem was one of coolness. He needed his services but he never liked him. Nor did he fulfill properly his promises regarding M'naḥem's livelihood, but merely allowed him a pitiful remuneration that did not at all meet his needs, so that for a long time Ḥasdai's brother had to provide for M'naḥem as he had during his student days.

However, M'naḥem was a man gentle in nature, modest and tolerant, who endured his burden with submission to his lot and found satisfaction in his literary work. No matter how much he was humiliated, no matter how great his distress, when he sat in his modest dwelling occupied with his sacred task—his research into the Hebrew language and the writing of his book—at such moments none could compare with him. The satisfaction he derived from his work gave him strength to endure his burden over many years.

As their style testifies, it was M'naḥem who composed Ḥasdai's letters to the Byzantine king and his wife in 948, and also the letter to the Khazar king written six years later, in 954.[24] The poem that has M'naḥem's name at the start of the letter to the king of the Khazars does not show the influence of any Arabic poetry. It is written in the style peculiar to the liturgical poets of the Jews in oriental countries and shows the yearning for redemption, the longing for the Messiah so characteristic of the religious life of the Diaspora communities in the tenth century and of the Jews of Spain generally.

About that time M'naḥem completed his lexicon, which he had labored over many years, and he gave it a title that was then in vogue for philological treatises: *Sefer ha-piṭrōnīm* (The Book of Interpretations).[25] In this lexicon the words are arranged according to roots, and next to each, verses and fragments of verses that exemplify their various meanings are cited. Under each letter of the alphabet the author lists first those roots which, in his opinion, consist of one letter; next two-lettered roots, three-lettered roots, and so on.[26] M'naḥem Ben Sārūḳ thus based his system on the assumption that the roots of Hebrew words consist of one, two, three, four, or five letters. He regarded as roots only those letters that are never eliminated. Hence in his view the root of the verb נגע (*nāga'*) is גע (*gā'*), and the root of the verb נתן (*nātan*) is, according to him, ת (*th*).

M'naḥem saw it as his main objective to distinguish between root letters and the formative letters. He wrote on this problem in an introduction to Hebrew grammar with which he prefaced the lexicon and in several excurses in the body of the work. In this regard M'naḥem was actually basing his thinking on that of Saadya Gaon, except that he was more consistent and more systematic. But he differed from Saadya Gaon and from Judah Ibn Ḳuraish in his opposition to any support from a comparison of the Hebrew and Arabic languages. He and many other Spanish Jews of that generation held it to be a profanation of the name of God to make any attempt at explaining the sacred tongue by means of Arabic words or by the principles of Arabic grammarians.

M'naḥem endeavored to explain the words of infrequent occurrence, especially the *hapax legomena*—those words appearing only once in the Scriptures—by viewing them in context; he also argued that we have difficulty understanding them because the entire store of Hebrew vocabulary has not come down to us. If we had not forgotten the meaning of a large part of the vocabulary, as a result of the destructions and devastations ensuing from the dispersion, we would surely have no difficulty in understanding even these words—this was his opinion. His precursors among the Hebrew grammarians had accepted many expressions from the specialized terminology of Arabic grammar, but M'naḥem opposed even this, although at times he would employ one of them without being aware of it or because he had not found a better one.

In general, M'naḥem labored strenuously to coin grammatical expressions in Hebrew. In endeavoring to explain biblical words by means of the Hebrew language he also found not a little difficulty. There is no doubt that M'naḥem used not only the philological treatises of Saadya Gaon, but also the writing of the Karaites, who had considerable influence upon him. Thus he explains the matter of *tōṭāfōt* (Deuteronomy 6:8), not as the rabbis do, but in accordance with the Karaites, who do not derive from it the commandment concerning *t'fillīn* (phylacteries).

M'naḥem was not the first to compose a Hebrew lexicon, but he was the pioneer of Hebrew philology in Spain, and by means of his treatise he brought to the Jews in his country the philological concepts of oriental Jews. In his work he demonstrated a well-developed instinct for philology and an independence from grammarians who preceded him. Where he found it necessary to engage in a polemic with these writers, he did it in a dignified manner and in unassuming language. The use of his lexicon was rendered somewhat difficult because M'naḥem began his work in his youth, when his style was not yet as polished as it became in his mature years. Nevertheless, his book greatly impressed his generation, and even later generations of Jewish scholars used it extensively, particularly in the countries of Christian Europe, where the grammars and lexicons that were written later in Arabic did not encroach upon his.[27]

After the *Sefer ha-piṭrōnīm* had become famous and M'naḥem's reputation among the scholars had increased, he imagined that after many years of poverty and degradation he would find gratification, and that even Ḥasdai would have a change of heart in his favor. But before much time had elapsed M'naḥem became convinced that his hopes were in vain. Even as modest and retiring a person as M'naḥem had enemies, and in the atmosphere of intrigue prevalent in the court of an Arabic kingdom, such as that of the Omayyads at Cordova, it was not at all hard to attack anyone with a falsely libelous accusation. Enemies abounded who went to the Jewish noble with evil reports concerning M'naḥem.

Ḥasdai Ibn Shaprūṭ, who was experienced in connivance and

was always apprehensive of enemies, lent a willing ear to the denunciatory remarks and became very angry at his erudite secretary. He had never had any affection for him and therefore did not hesitate even a moment to act with severity against him. Without having M'naḥem brought before him to hear what he could say to justify himself, Ḥasdai ordered him punished without delay, so that everyone might take proper notice. The noble's armed men, themselves Jews, went on the Sabbath to the house where M'naḥem lived, beat him severely, tore his clothes from his back, plucked out the hair from his head, and drove him out of the city. This attack fell upon him unexpectedly, and he had to leave behind in Cordova his most valuable possessions: his books, among them the original manuscript of *Sefer ha-piṭrōnīm*.

M'naḥem returned to the city of his birth, but without delay sent the dignitary a letter demanding satisfaction for the wrong he had suffered. He asked why he had received such treatment and why he had not been given the opportunity to purge himself of the charges laid against him. Among other things he requested that the manuscript of his lexicon be restored to him. This letter did not make the impression on the Jewish courtier that M'naḥem had hoped for. He received a cynical reply: "If you have sinned, I have made it possible for you to receive punishment. If you have not sinned, I have made it possible for you to attain life in the world to come." Nevertheless, he granted his erstwhile secretary's request for the return of the manuscript of *Sefer ha-piṭrōnīm*, perhaps out of contempt. His subordinates searched for it, and when it was found it was delivered to one of M'naḥem's friends, who took it upon himself to have it delivered to its owner.

However, M'naḥem's enemies were not idle; they continued to speak ill of him to Ḥasdai, and once again he gave orders that his unfortunate secretary be punished. No doubt they did not fail to bring to his attention interpretations that were tinged with Karaite significance, and even though everyone knew that he was not a Karaite at all, it was decided to punish him in a manner that would show that they did not consider him a true Jew anymore. On this occasion also the order was not executed on a weekday, but on a holiday, when all the Jews would be found in their own quarters. During the Passover festival M'naḥem Ben Sārūḳ was attacked in the city of his birth; he was ejected from the house he had inherited from his father and put into prison, and the house itself was razed to its very foundation. Thus the festival was turned into a disaster for him.

M'naḥem quickly tok up his pen to protest to Ḥasdai against his actions; he wrote him a long letter in which words of appeasement and protest alternate. As he makes his mordant reckoning with the haughty courtier, he voices the smoldering anger that had become stored up in him over many years. He is no longer the modest and submissive youth, making his peace with the social system and being resigned to his judgment, but rather a man aware of his abilities and demanding his due. He flings defiance at the noble, observing that all mortals are equal—coming from the dust and to dust returning. He chides Ḥasdai for his scheming, unfolds before him the entire chapter of their relationship, reminds him of the promises made to induce him to come to Cordova, and asks how he was rewarded for his services. He tells how he was maltreated and asks whether he was fairly judged. In a sort of postscript to his letter, M'naḥem thanks Ḥasdai for the return of the manuscript of his book.[28]

III

M'naḥem Ben Sārūḳ did not know into whose hand this manuscript had fallen, nor did he hear that meanwhile someone had collected together every copy of the *Sefer ha-piṭrōnīm* that he could obtain in Cordova. The man who occupied himself thus was—like him—a student of the Hebrew language and a poet, and he had assembled the copies of M'naḥem's lexicon because he planned to write strictures against it.

His name was Dūnash b. Labraṭ ha-levi, and he too was not a native of Cordova, but had recently arrived at the capital of Andalusia. He was a member of a family from Bagdad that had migrated to Morocco. He himself was born in Fez around 920, and he spent his youth in that city. His name (or more precisely the two names) are Berber and were common among Jews who inhabited Morocco.[29] His parents gave him an excellent education. He was reared in intimate knowledge of Hebrew and devoted himself day and night to the acquisition of a knowledge of both the written and the oral Jewish law.

Since the youth displayed many talents and won praise and encouragement from his teachers, his parents sent him to Irak to continue his studies there. In those days the fame of Saadya Gaon had spread throughout the Diaspora, in both the East and the West, and he was the spiritual leader of the entire Jewish nation. Dūnash, who had gone to Irak to study under him, was only one of many young men who streamed to the distinguished teacher.[30] After the *gaon*'s death, Dūnash b. Labraṭ returned to his birthplace and stayed there several years.

In the 990s the fame of Ḥasdai Ibn Shaprūṭ became widespread, and his eminence at the court of the Omayyad caliph and his beneficent acts in behalf of communities and individuals—and especially of intellectuals, scholars, and writers—became well known. Dūnash decided to make his way to Cordova, which had become a great Jewish center. In his new place of residence he maintained himself as a cantor,[31] winning the favor of the public—for in those days cantors were sought to compose liturgical hymns and chant them in the synagogue during the service, particularly on festivals and festive family occasions. Who could do this more proficiently than Dūnash, whose desire since he had reached maturity was to be a poet? At the same time he became prominent in Cordova as a student of the Hebrew language. Interest in the Hebrew language was not foreign to the scholars in Moroccan communities, and some had begun to investigate its rules and its vocabulary. Dūnash was influenced by them. Before long Dūnash brought together in Cordova a circle of disciples who held him in honor and esteem.[32]

But Dūnash b. Labraṭ's high status in the field of Hebrew literature and his great fame came to him because of his poetry. His achievements as a poet were various. He composed liturgical poems similar to those of the hymnologists of the oriental countries, both in form and content. One of his typical compositions in this genre was a group of hymns for the Day of Atonement based on a verse in Nehemiah (1:6).[33] No doubt he must have composed many others like it, but in the course of time they were lost. The underlying note in the sacred poetry of Dūnash, in terms of its content, was the yearning for Israel's redemption, the longing for the coming of the Messiah, which was felt strongly in the hearts of Jews everywhere. Dūnash poured out his bitter complaint over the servitude which the gentiles imposed upon the Jews, and from his words it can be inferred that in his view the Christians had been more culpable, in that they oppressed the Jews more severely than the Moslems did.

But Dūnash's poems that were based on those of earlier hymnologists were not typical of his verse. His name is engraved in golden letters in the annals of Hebrew poetry because of a major innovation: he introduced Arabic meter into Hebrew poetry. While he was still in Irak, sitting at the feet of Saadya Gaon, he began to write Hebrew verse in metered form. He showed them to his great teacher, who was greatly excited over them and meted out to him the praise that his innovation warranted.[34] The introduction of Arabic meter to Hebrew verse was indeed of the utmost importance, since it led to a complete reorientation in its development. Insofar as form was concerned, Hebrew verse was utterly transformed. It became smoother and more polished. In those days poetry was frequently quoted and declaimed orally, and the meter rendered it easier to remember, resulting in the greater circulation of the poems. But Dūnash learned from the Arabs not only meter but also verse structure, such as the use of an introduction, a transition, and rhetorical flourishes.

Dūnash employed the new form in every kind of verse and even began to compose sacred verse in meter. But the change that began with the introduction of Arabic meter found expression mainly in secular verse. In these poems Dūnash imitated not only the form of Arabic verse but also its content. He introduced to Hebrew poetry the subjects and motifs of the Arabic poets. One of the subjects that Arabic poets were especially fond of was the praise of wisdom, and Dūnash also wrote verse on this theme. He composed many verses in praise of patrons, in keeping with the best Arabic tradition. In these poems he lauds the wisdom and generosity of the "lord," who scatters his gifts abroad as the dew from heaven or as the clouds that pour rain profusely upon the earth. The subject of this praise is faithful to his friend and for his part severely punishes his foes. But above all, the patron's importance in the king's service, in which he holds a high post, is described.

Dūnash also acclaims his own verse in these poems, for this was the way of the Arabic poets. Defamatory verse is also one of the important and characteristic species of Arabic verse, and Dūnash imitated this too. Moreover, he wrote drinking songs that include all the well-known aspects of this genre to be found in Arabic literature: the description of the beverage, the garden setting, the chirping birds, the youth who serves the wine, and the song and the music accompanying the banquet.[35] However, because this theme was altogether new to Hebrew literature and likely to provoke sharp opposition and much anger, Dūnash would at times give it a negative aspect —which was only simulated. Thus he wrote of a wine feast as though warning against it, although the pleasure with which he describes it is more than transparent. An imaginary friend invites him:

We shall drink among the flower beds hedged with roses
And put sorrow to flight with all manner of gaiety
Partaking of sweets and drinking from goblets;
And then disport ourselves like giants, imbibing from basins.

And he replies:

I chided him unto silence: How can you prefer these vanities
When the holy Temple, God's footstool, is in the hands of the gentiles!
You utter folly and choose sloth,
And speak vanity like scorners and fools.

To be sure, Dūnash b. Labraṭ's ability as a poet was not very great. He was distinguished neither by a rich imagination nor by elegant or delicate phraseology. Moreover, he had to struggle with the Hebrew language itself in order to adapt it to the new form of poetry.[36] However, these shortcomings must be discounted in consideration of his great contribution to Hebrew poetry: the credit he earned as the innovator of meter. Of course, like all innovators Dūnash knew how to evaluate properly his own merit. He was noted for his courage and was always prepared for an encounter against other writers. He was not shy but rather haughty and sharp of tongue. For the majority of scholars of the Maghreb and Spain he had only indifference and contempt, especially since he viewed only those who had studied in the Babylonian academies worthy of his good opinion.

When he reached Cordova it seemed to him that he was entitled to first place at the position of honor among the Hebrew writers, and when he saw how much they esteemed M'naḥem Ben Sārūḳ, regarding him as a great poet and grammarian, he was not a little vexed. At first he bore his resentment in silence. But when M'naḥem published his lexicon, he held that the time had come to reveal to all who indeed was a student of the Hebrew language worthy of the name. Dūnash decided to write a critical treatise on M'naḥem's lexicon, thereby making him a figure of public ridicule. He began collecting as many copies of the lexicon as he could, to prevent M'naḥem's disputing his arguments by claiming that Dūnash had chanced upon a copy having scribal errors.

Now, at that very time M'naḥem lost favor with Ḥasdai Ibn Shaprūṭ, and after he was driven out of Cordova without taking his books, the original manuscript of the lexicon fell into Dūnash's hands. One can imagine that his joy at this find was boundless.[37] With great celerity Dūnash went over the *Sefer ha-piṭrōnīm* several times, noting every phrase he intended to comment on; as a result, his treatise *T'shūbhōt* (Answers) has no formal arrangement or orderly presentation of subjects, but is simply a collection of animadversions.

Dūnash prefaced his book *T'shūbhōt*,[38] which he published in 959, with two long poems. The first is a hymn of praise to Ḥasdai Ibn Shaprūṭ in which he dedicates the book to him, extolling his great deeds and dwelling in particular on his success in his negotiations with Toda, the queen of Navarre whom he had brought to Cordova. In the second poem he launches a diatribe against M'naḥem. These poems are followed by an introduction in which Dūnash discusses those problems that a Hebrew philologist should endeavor to solve. Here, too, there is no systematic discourse on the author's views, but it is easy to grasp their essentials. Whereas M'naḥem Ben Sārūḳ rejects the comparison of the Hebrew language with Arabic as a working methodology for Hebrew lexicography, Dūnash b. Labraṭ holds it to be valid; thus he is in harmony with the methods of the North African philologists who occupied themselves in those days with the study of the Hebrew language. He indicates 167 words whose form and meaning are identical in both languages.

The influence of Saadya Gaon is manifest in Dūnash's discourse, and like his master, whom he defends against M'naḥem's strictures, he divides Hebrew words into three species: verbs, nouns, and particles. But on the question that we would view as crucial, he is in agreement with M'naḥem. Like him, he holds that verbs consist of one letter, two, three, and even more letters. In his opinion verbs whose third consonant is a he or whose middle letter is a waw are biliteral. Dūnash therefore is in dispute with M'naḥem only over details; for example, where M'naḥem holds that the root of a certain word consists of one letter or two, Dūnash will argue that the root is biliteral or triliteral. In the poems with which his book begins Dūnash declares it to be his intention to bring forward two hundred disputed points against M'naḥem, but in fact he never reaches this figure in his book.[39]

Many of Dūnash's strictures deal with the fixing of the root, others relate to the meaning of words, but Dūnash directs most of his barbs against M'naḥem for having brought together verses or fragments of verses for the purpose of clarification, out of context. Inasmuch as Dūnash was endowed with a penetrating grasp and a fine sense of distinction, he succeeded in pointing out the vulnerable points in M'naḥem's lexicon and was justified in most of his strictures.[40] Thus there was a measure of progress for Hebrew philology in Dūnash's volume of criticism, but the manner in which Dūnash presented his views flaws his work. He is very sharp and arrogant and treats M'naḥem as a master would his disciple. Even more, Dūnash does not merely attack his views as they pertain to grammar, but also heaps opprobrium on M'naḥem's religious views, claiming that he surreptitiously introduces into his lexicon heretical opinions—for example, in the matter of free will—and interprets verses in accordance with the Karaite view.[41] Thus there was a pronounced Spanish note in this literary polemic.

IV

The stinging criticism that Dūnash b. Labraṭ leveled at M'naḥem's lexicon really shocked the Jewish intellectual circles of Cordova and other Jewish communities of Spain. Here was a man who was esteemed as a distinguished scholar and one well versed in the arcana of the Hebrew language; yet he was presented as being devoid of worth. Dūnash's style did not please them at all, especially since it carried a note of contempt toward natives of Spain. In consequence, M'naḥem's adherents soon bestirred themselves and paid back blow for blow.

M'naḥem himself did not reply to Dūnash's slanderous remarks. It is true that the Jewish nobles of Cordova no longer caused him any distress, but he was broken in body and spirit and had no heart for polemics or disputes. No doubt he was apprehensive lest he bring upon himself fresh calamities, knowing what ties Dūnash had established in Cordova; and he was also hurt by the stinging sarcasm of his remarks, inasmuch as he regarded Dūnash with contempt and revulsion. But some of M'naḥem's disciples and adherents decided to deliver a retort in place of their teacher and master. True, when Ḥasdai had first dismissed M'naḥem Ben Sārūḳ, they shunned him and were careful not to raise their voices. However, when the dignitary's heated passion had abated, they did not hesitate to become identified with M'naḥem. They decided to compose collectively a rejoinder against the strictures of Dūnash and to distribute them publicly as much as was feasible, in order to protect the honor of their master.

The most venerable of the group was Isaac Ibn Djiḳaṭilla, who in time became an important grammarian. But he was less active in the preparation of the polemic treatise being put forth by the disciples of M'naḥem than were two other scholars. One was Isaac Ibn Ḳaprōn, a resident of Cordova. He was a scion of an old and honorable Spanish family, whose name indicates that they were of Roman origin. Isaac himself was a poet who composed both secular and sacred verse.[42] The third who participated in preparing the treatise was Judah b. David, a young scholar who had come to Andalusia from a Christian country.[43]

The disciples of M'naḥem also dedicated their polemic work to Ḥasdai Ibn Shaprūṭ. Isaac Ibn Ḳaprōn prefaced their answer with a laudatory poem to Ḥasdai, in which he extols the diplomatic successes that Ḥasdai had achieved in 958 in his negotiations with the kings of Christian Spain. This laudatory poem was written in meter and rhyme identical to those employed in the poems that open the *T'shūbhōt* of Dūnash.[44] A defamatory poem against Dūnash follows it.

In their polemic, M'naḥem's disciples defend the honor of the Spanish scholars and reject the major innovation that Dūnash had introduced, namely, verse employing Arabic meter. At great length M'naḥem's disciples indicate the defects that would occur in metered verse based on Arabic meters. In their opinion, poets would have to violate the rules governing the Hebrew language, particularly vocalization. They would have to alter the accents (such as changing penultimates to ultimates), replace the *pātaḥ* with the long *kāmeṣ*, drop the *ḥaṭaf* from the guttural letters, replacing it with a *sh'va*, and the like.[45] The fact that they themselves prefaced their polemic with a poem in meter form was, they claimed, merely to demonstrate that it was not something beyond their capability.

The grammatical concepts of M'naḥem's disciples were identical with those of their master. By way of an example, M'naḥem was of the opinion that the root of *hōga'atem* (Malachi 2:17) and *tīga'* (Proverbs 23:4) is *ga'*,[46] whereas Dūnash held[47] that the root is *yaga'* with the waw replacing the yod. M'naḥem's disciples[48] defend the opinion of their master and retort sharply that Dūnash himself does not regard all verbs whose first letter is a yod as verbs whose root is triliteral. Such are the arguments of M'naḥem's disciples in most of the fifty-five sections of their treatise; but they also present explanations of grammatical problems: verb forms and the like.

However, this treatise in defense of the lexicon of M'naḥem Ben Sārūḳ did not bring an end to the controversy being waged over the methodology of Hebrew grammar among the intellectuals of Andalusia. Dūnash himself considered it beneath his dignity to reply to the arguments put forth by M'naḥem's disciples; this was done by one of his followers, Y'hūdī b. Shēshet. Following his master, he too opened his treatise with a poem, and in the body of the text he defended the employment of Arabic meters, as well as the philological explanations made by Dūnash. In the pungency of his style, Y'hūdī b. Shēshet greatly surpasses both Dūnash and M'naḥem's disciples. His polemical treatise is replete with personal attacks and has an abundance of insulting references.[49]

Thus the literary dispute continued and aroused emotions in Jewish intellectual circles in Spain. Some took one side and some the other; and as each side searched for arguments and evidence to contradict its opponents, the field of knowledge was broadened.

The prominence of M'naḥem Ben Sārūḳ, whose lexicon had

brought on the dispute, waned after he was driven from Cordova. This scholar was a luckless person. Almost all his lifetime he suffered poverty and privation; when success did smile upon him briefly, troubles befell him that led to his being quickly forgotten and overshadowed. His fate was typical of scholars and writers who devote their lives to their studies, men who have no share in the goods of this world.

Dūnash b. Labraṭ emerged triumphant from this literary dispute. Unlike M'naḥem, Dūnash did not take insults in silence, and in consequence he won esteem and happiness in his lifetime, and fame and glory for all generations. During middle age he did not wander from one country to another, but remained in Cordova, becoming the poet laureate of his generation. He lived long and wrote many verses. His poem "To a teacher whose wisdom is as great as the sea"[50] was composed in honor of Sh'marya b. Elḥānān, the rabbi of the Jewish community of Fostat at the end of the tenth century. In addition he composed nuptial songs and sacred poems, such as admonitory verse.

People of that era saw no contradiction in the composition of gay, secular verse and the writing of sacred poetry condemning mundane vanities. The selfsame person who wrote drinking songs and love poetry that were thoroughly materialistic could also compose lofty religious verse. For his part, he was not contradicting himself, and there was no need to explain it by saying that he wrote these apparently contrasting types of poetry at different times in his life. People living in those days were schizoid in spirit. Unable to comprehend the marvels of nature or surmount its afflictions, they inclined to profound piety—yet they were avid of mundane pleasures as long as they could enjoy them. These two tendencies that struggled within them derived from one source. The very same people who drank themselves into a stupor and who committed adultery without any hesitation would pray to excess and would fast, even rising in the middle of the night to recite prayers. Both Christians and Moslems did this, and Spanish Jews too saw no contradiction between overt secularity and deep piety.

Naturally, this position was not adopted by all Jewish communities in the Middle Ages. The Jews of Germany were far removed from it; that is, their intellectual and spiritual leaders did not consciously include these two aspirations in their approach to life. But the Jews of Spain of the tenth century were meshed with Spanish society; in the view of the Jewish upper class, Judaism was restricted to the confines of religion and national aspirations, and in areas outside the religious boundaries they shared with their neighbors their mode of life and their approach to important problems. Members of this class were steeped in the political intrigues devised on the soil of Spain and enjoyed life's transient moments after the fashion of their Moslem (and later their Christian) neighbors. But they were not like the Moslems only in their lifestyle; like them, the Jews engaged in the secular sciences without any restraints being put upon them by their religious consciousness.

The satisfaction of both aspirations in the hearts of the Jews, in which they found no contradiction, and their harmonious dovetailing offered a solution to a difficult problem with which Jews struggled, especially in the Diaspora, a problem that perplexes them to this very day. It is the age-old problem of how to fit Judaism into general secular society. Spanish Jewry found a solution—naturally, a medieval one. They joined in the secular life of their Moslem neighbors with all their hearts and souls, taking part in their cultural life also. But aside from their enjoyment of transient pleasures and being occupied in the general sciences, they searched for an answer to the important questions pertaining to eternal life in their ancestral faith; likewise, they found a broad field for expressing their literary talents in their national heritage.

This approach finds expression for the first time in the poems of Dūnash b. Labraṭ. Even though he was born and educated outside Spain and did not reach Spain till he was mature, he became well acclimatized. As a poet he expressed what the Jews felt in their hearts and personified their yearnings. He thus stands at the cradle of Hebrew poetry in Spain, as the first in a line of poets who wrote a glorious page in the annals of our literature. He was the first to elevate their feelings and desires to the point where they became the subjects of Hebrew poetry, and he was the first to array it in its fixed garb; for the Arab meters that he introduced into Hebrew poetry proved congenial to the poets and took root there.

7

EARNING A LIVELIHOOD

During the many generations our forefathers dwelt in Diaspora lands and in the special circumstances that attended them there, most of them, or at least a large portion of them, were confined to a limited number of occupations—such as commerce and banking—from which to earn a living. These were functions that the non-Jewish society in whose midst they lived required, and constituted the condition under which they were permitted to reside in the country. Christian society and governments forced Jews into a narrow area of economic activity, and since they were prevented from engaging in other occupations, they suffered from the hostility that their occupation—e.g., that of moneylenders—provoked. This development began at the start of the Middle Ages, simultaneously with the crystallization of the hegemony of the church.

Now, just as the Jews of Spain were different from the rest of the Diaspora communities in other respects, they were also distinguished by their sound and diversified socioeconomic structure. They never became stratified as bankers or merchants, but rather drew their livelihood in every period from a variety of diversified occupations. Over the generations, of course, there were many alterations in their economic status.

With the changes that befell the Arabic-Andalusian society and government, the socioeconomic status of Spanish Jewry also changed. Just before the Moslem conquest their economic position had been very grave; the Visigothic kings forbade them to engage in a number of occupations, such as international commerce. The sources for the history of the tenth century, however, emphasize the strong economic position the Jews of Andalusia had attained in various branches of the economy. Moreover, the information adduced by these sources demonstrates that in some branches Jews constituted the majority, and these occupations were not commercial enterprises. Furthermore, there was evident a process of becoming rooted in the economy that was a complete reversal of the economic trend in many Diaspora communities, where the Jews moved or were moved further away from the primary source of productivity, concentrating instead on economic areas that were remote from it. The Jews of Andalusia established themselves in every sector of the economy, so that by the tenth century they constituted one of the ethnic groups on the Iberian peninsula that were deeply rooted economically, exactly like the Arabs, Berbers, and Mozarabs.

I

This development is especially discernible in their connection with agriculture. Changes in agriculture between the beginning of the Arabic conquest and the end of the tenth century were conditioned by the general evolution in agrarian relations within the Hispano-Arab kingdom.

The distribution of lands in Moslem Spain was very difficult. The Moslem conquerors had seized vast territories, so that when other Arabs arrived later there were no more estates at the disposal of the government, and enmity and strife arose between the different groups. The rulers were compelled to distribute the "fifth" (of the booty; in that case, the land reserve) which, according to Moslem law, had to be kept for the poor and needy. Later, in 741, the Syrian Arabs were settled as military colonists who were paid from the poll tax.

In organizing the distribution of various lands after the conquest, estates were given to the soldiers as feudal benefices, for the usufructuary rights alone. But in time they acquired full possession, and the government lacked the power to regain control over them. The fact that the first Omayyad ruler, 'Abdarraḥmān I, had to confiscate formerly Visigothic crown lands that were being held by the Christian prince Ardabast testifies to the acuteness of the problem. Here was the ruler of Moslem Spain himself facing the problem of a lack of land. In the course of time much land was set aside as endowment for the maintenance of mosques and for other religious purposes, and these holdings certainly could not be transferred to a new ownership.

In other words, during the first and second generations of Arab rule in Spain there was very little land that Jews could have acquired. The conquerors were very avid of holding land, and they certainly had greater power than did the Jews. The Jews of Spain were engaged in agriculture from early times. They possessed estates and themselves cultivated their fields. Jews were also administrators of the estates of the Visigothic nobles. But it is almost certain that as a result of the persecutions in the final period of Visigothic rule, their status in agriculture was shaken and their landed property restricted. At the time of the conquest they too no doubt wanted to acquire a portion of the huge amount of spoils, and we may assume that here and there they contrived to acquire ownership of lands that had originally belonged to the nobles who had fled, the very estates which they had managed. In sum, however, the time was not ripe for their acquisition of much landed property.

This condition changed in the second half of the ninth century. When chaos prevailed in the Hispano-Arab kingdom and nobles and officers raised the standard of rebellion in every district, a decisive change took place in agrarian relationships. The rebels gained control over the remnants of the "fifth"[1] and thereby caused the impoverishment of many Arab latifundistas, the owners of great landed estates. The uprising of the *muwalladūn* and the forays by bands of rebels resulted in rich landholders' losing their possessions and starting to sell their lands. This was especially true in southern Andalusia. But in addition, the natural process whereby estates were divided among inheritors also had its effect in the course of time. Smaller estates came into existence,[2] and it became possible for Jews to acquire land. Simultaneously, an unending stream of immigrants flowed into Spain from North Africa, poor Berbers for the most part, who constituted a cheap agrarian labor force.

Under these new circumstances the Jews increased their landed property and developed their estates. Many of the Jewish immigrants who came to Spain from North African countries and were accustomed to agricultural work tied their destiny to the cultivation of the soil. Thus was created a body of Jewish peasantry, whose life is reflected in the responsa of the Spanish rabbis of the tenth century.

From the questions submitted to these rabbis it is apparent that the Jews of that era owned a substantial amount of land, and fields and vineyards in abundance. They deal with the purchase and sale of land,[3] especially vineyards.[4] These simple Jews who addressed their questions to the rabbis of Cordova inherited and bequeathed lands,[5] houses, and farms.[6] Land was given to women as a dowry and in fulfillment of a marriage contract, or as a gift.[7]

The deliberations over problems connected with such marriage contracts constitute the subject matter for relatively many responsa.[8] In one of the queries addressed to Ḥanōkh b. Moses it is reported that "Jacob married Leah, who bore him daughters, and later he married Rachel, who bore him sons. As a dowry Rachel had conveyed to him real estate without any estimation of its value, and later he sold that land and in its place made over to her real estate located elsewhere . . . and wrote for her a deed certifying to these changes. . . . Thereafter Jacob gave his daughters, born to him from Leah, in marriage to husbands, giving them the land that was the property of Rachel as a consequence of the aforementioned interchange; and he had land of his own elsewhere, and his wife Leah had land as part of her dowry, and he did not give his son Benjamin land from either of these sources but from the property of Rachel."[9]

When a man could not pay his debt he would give the lender his vineyard,[10] and it was customary to mortgage land until the produce thereof repaid the debt.[11] Men would barter fields and vineyards to consolidate landholdings,[12] and it is certain that these Jewish farmers would vigorously employ the law relating to an abutter to prevent a non-Jew from driving a wedge between their holdings.[13]

Many of these farmers had no other form of property to bequeath to their children, and they particularly lacked ready cash; thus they were compelled to divide among themselves their own lands, and as a consequence disputes broke out concerning the nature of the soil that fell to their children as an inheritance. After all, there were both choice and barren lands, and the farmers, understandably, defended their rights most stubbornly.[14] The majority of these questions were addressed to the rabbis of Cordova by the Jews of Andalusia, but the Jews also possessed much land in the other provinces of Spain.[15]

The conditions determining the development of the branches of agriculture differ greatly in the many provinces of Spain.

A large part of the peninsula is poorly supplied with water, whereas in other sections methods of irrigation have been employed from the earliest times, rendering intensive farming quite possible. In the arid regions, grain and various beans were raised, and especially was there a cultivation of vineyards. But the Spanish grain crops did not suffice for the needs of the population, and during the entire period of Arab dominion it was necessary to import it from North African countries. On the other hand, Andalusia produced fruit trees in profusion, especially in olive groves, which yielded a harvest abundant in quantity and excellent in quality. Flax, cotton, and mulberry trees were grown in Andalusia as well, providing the raw materials for the manufacture of cloth. The methods of irrigation practiced in Spain in those areas rich in water were further developed by the Arabs, who supplemented the experience they had acquired in the oriental countries, thus reaching a high technical level. Areas with year-round irrigation produced crops three times a year.

There were pronounced differences between the arid and the irrigated areas in the pattern of the settlements. The maintenance of irrigation required that the farmer be on the land throughout the year; as a result, the settlements in such areas were small and scattered over the open country. The farmers lived in small villages. But the farmers in the arid districts lived in large settlements, urban in character, sustaining themselves from agriculture. The largest part of Andalusia, where the Jewish settlement was densest, was considered one of the arid sectors of Spain, and in consequence many Jews could derive a living from agriculture and at the same time live in sizable communities, making it possible for them to fulfill their religious duties.

The responsa of the tenth century enable us to know the way of life prevalent in those villages and the branches of agriculture with which the Jews of Andalusia were occupied. The questions in these responsa show clearly that a large segment of those asking the questions actually tilled their lands.[16] The questions deal very often with fields of grain[17] and groves of fruit trees.[18] In the vineyards the Jews had to do the work themselves for religious reasons—but this was merely an added reason, since they did this in any event. One question involves a Jew who had borrowed money and, not being able to pay it back, discharged his debt by working in the lender's vineyard.[19] There is a detailed discussion concerning the cultivation of vineyards in a query addressed by the Jews of Andalusia in the middle of the ninth century to the *gaon* Naṭrōnai bar Hilai: "And as for your inquiry regarding your vineyards, their pruning and plowing occur at the beginning of Nīsān and at times the rains come, lasting till Passover, and if they are not treated and pruned in their proper season they will become impure and a heavy loss will result. There are times when the vineyards are pruned before the Passover and the rains prevent their being plowed, and they become impure and are cut down within five days; and when they are again plowed, the buds drop off or fall because of the plow and the vineyard is destroyed, resulting in heavy losses." Those who make the inquiry add an explanation that "such losses could be avoided by pruning and plowing during the *intermediate days* of Passover, whether by a Jew or a non-Jew," and they therefore ask "whether this is permissible so that the Jews not suffer a financial loss"; and they go on to explain "that most of the people in the area have no other financial resources save for these vineyards." The *gaon* replies that it is indeed permissible for them to do the work during the intermediate days.[20]

These questions and answers speak plainly. They give abundant testimony that a large number of Spanish Jews in those days earned their living from agriculture. Particularly edifying is the proportion of questions addressed to the Cordovan rabbis concerning land matters as against questions dealing with commerce and trade. The questions concerning matters of trade are few, their number insignificant compared to the many questions dealing with land.[21] The economic amalgam of Spanish Jewry was different not only from the community structure of Gallic Jewry, most of whom earned their living from trade and commerce even in those days, but also from the Jews of North Africa and Irak, where the majority of them had long since become artisans and traders.[22] There can be only one reason for this: in Spain the outside pressures that drove Jews in other countries to occupy themselves with trade, and other branches of the economy far removed from productive activity and toil, did not operate. As long as they were not compelled to transfer to these occupations, the Jews never, any time or any place, showed a tendency to earn their bread as nonlaborers—a charge leveled against them by their enemies; nor did they fill any specific economic functions that, as it were, justified their existence.

II

Moslem Spain needed to import grain, but its handicrafts and industry were well developed and their products were sold to many countries. Characteristic of the economy of Moslem Spain was the division of its crafts and industry into very many branches and subbranches, whose boundaries were well defined. The majority of the craftsmen were petty manufacturers who were assisted by a laborer and an apprentice. Anyone strolling through the marketplaces of Cordova or Seville would see entire streets consisting only of long rows of small shops—really niches—where workers diligently plied their craft and displayed their products for sale; and the artisans in all these shops would be engaged in the same type of work. The shops were so tiny that the purchaser was unable to enter. Their floors were raised above street level, and the only daylight to penetrate them came by way of the doorway, which served as both entrance and display window. But these workers, sitting in the dark stalls from dawn to dusk, with bent backs and legs spread out, produced articles wondrously beautiful.

Spanish leather was excellent and renowned throughout other countries. The leather and products made from it—shoes, boots, saddles, wallets, and bags—were sent in large quantities to the countries of North Africa and to the Christian kingdoms of the north. When a Merovingian king, Chilperic II, gave a writ of privilege to the monastery of Corbie in 716, allotting the monks various quantities of precious wares to be obtained annually from the stores of the treasury, he also included a quantity of "Cordovan leather,"[23] The term *cordonnier*, "one who works on Cordovan leather," to this day designates a shoemaker in French.

Great value was also attached, in the economy of Spain, to the production of textiles: linsey-woolsey, cotton, and flax. Ibn Ḥauḳal, writing in the second half of the tenth century, tells of the export of Spanish textiles to Egypt and Persia. Clothes made in Pechina were sold—according to him—to Egypt, Hedjaz, and Yemen.[24] Also al-Muḳaddasī, writing at the end of the tenth century, reports about the export of textiles from Spain.[25] Andalusia was especially renowned, during the resplendent era of Omayyad rule, for the manufacture of silk, which was concentrated mainly in Cordova. Silk textiles were exported from Spain to many countries.[26]

In general it can be said that from the time of 'Abdarraḥmān II the manufacture of luxury products developed in Moslem Spain, and in manufacturing Andalusia began to compete with the Byzantine Empire and Irak. The jewelry and other gold objects manufactured in Cordova and Seville—rings, bracelets, goblets, and other table articles—all acquired a reputation in the neighboring countries. Much of this merchandise was sold in the Christian principalities in northern

Spain, whose nobles and wealthy men sought to emulate the mode of life of the Cordovan nobles. The Arabic names that these products bear in Spanish even today commemorate the superiority in manufacture that Arabic Andalusia held in those days.

In the Hispano-Moslem cities all branches of work were under the supervision of the "officer in charge of markets," who filled those functions that in the Moslem lands of the East were under the authority of the *muḥtasib*; indeed, in a later period the person holding this position in Spain was given the same title. His first and chief concern was that craftsmen should not deceive their customers; he also tested their weights and measures. Before he appeared on the scene, this responsibility was carried out by representatives of the various branches of handicrafts, who were organized into professional associations. Their function was simply to control working arrangements, and they had no religious character whatsoever.[27] Thus it was possible for Jewish artisans to ply their craft without encountering hostile organizations. They had equal rights with the Moslem craftsmen.

As in all Moslem lands, many Spanish Jews also engaged in certain occupations that were at first despised by the Arabs, because such workers would become very dirty and repulsive—occupations like dyeing and tanning, for example. In some of the Moslem countries the Jews had a virtual monopoly over these occupations, as is indicated by the names of streets and squares in the old Jewish neighborhoods of cities in Spain. In the Jewish quarter of Seville, there are to this day two squares that are known as "Place of the Tanners": Plaza de los Curtidores and Plaza de los Zuradores.[28] It is worth noting that these two squares are located near where the city wall used to stand, as was the custom in all Moslem cities during the Middle Ages. Of course, it was the intention of the authorities to locate workshops that were very filthy far from the heart of the city. One of the streets in the former Jewish quarter of Seville is even today called Calle de los Tintes—"Street of the Dyers."[29]

The names of the streets in the Jewish quarter of Saragossa and other data of the later Middle Ages demonstrate that even in this large community there were a substantial number of dyers and tanners.[30] In Saragossa the production of leather and all branches of work connected with it were highly developed, and it would seem that from an early period there were many shoemakers among the Jews in that city.[31] But Jews in other cities also drew their living from this occupation. Among the names of Jews of León at the beginning of the eleventh century there appears the family name Ashkhafa, which is Arabic for "cobbler"; we thus have an instance of a Jew from the Arabic sphere of dominion on the peninsula who earned his living by this trade and who migrated to the Christian kingdom in northern Spain.[32]

Among the smiths—goldsmiths and silversmiths—there were a large number of Jews.[33] This was an occupation in which Jews took a leading part in all the Moslem countries, but the Jewish smiths in Spain, who came there from the oriental countries, were the only ones who knew how to work in accordance with Arabic taste. They developed this profession in Spain until in the tenth century it reached a standard that brought its products great fame in lands near and far. The Jews also played an important part in the manufacture of silk. In Cordova and Mérida and in other cities they had workshops whose products received much praise.[34]

Thus, among the Jewish communities in Spain there was, along with the agricultural workers, a body of artisans deeply rooted in the economy of the country. Among these artisans were families that had been living in Spain from ancient days, long before the Arab conquest—families in which occupations descended from father to son over many generations; and there also were among them immigrants who had only recently arrived from lands of the Near East and from North African countries.

III

Commercial activity in Moslem Spain was very much astir. A large group of merchants were occupied with the exchange of goods among the various provinces of the peninsula, and at the same time a great number of men earned their living from them as transporters of the goods. Convoys, heavily laden with merchandise, moved incessantly between Toledo and Cordova and between Cordova and Seville, from the south to the north and from the north to the south. Arabic sources have preserved copies of agreements that the merchants drew up with the transport services, and in them are set down precisely all the terms. The high level of business relationships is evident in all the arrangements pertaining to the exchange of goods.

The economy of Moslem Spain was one of highly developed finances. As was the case in the Abbasid caliphate in the East, it was the practice of the Moslem-Spanish merchants to settle their accounts by means of money orders called *suftadja*.[35] The branches of retail trade, like the various sectors of labor, were under the supervision of the "officer in charge of markets," and the shops were concentrated in special streets according to type. But for certain wares, especially those of high value, specific locations were designated. Every city had its market hall called *alcaicería*, generally near the chief mosque, where precious objects and silk fabrics were sold.

There were also shops in the residential sections, especially near the gates of the city walls in those areas. Naturally, the shops in the Jewish quarter belonged to the people of the neighborhood. Foods were sold in these stores, some being of the kind that they would not buy from gentiles. The other

Jewish merchants who were occupied with various branches of trade opened shops in the general markets. The Jews of Spain dealt in all forms of commerce but had special ties with trade in silk textiles and silk garments. The names of streets and squares in the Jewish quarters of a number of cities that have been preserved from the Middle Ages are proof of this.[36] These names show that, contrary to accepted notions, the silk markets were established in the Jewish quarter, even though it was a residential area. Veronica Place, in the Jewish quarter of Saragossa, was once known as *alcaicería* (*al-Ḳaisarīya* in Arabic—a covered market hall) *de los judios*.[37] In the city of Velez-Málaga also the *alcaicería* was within the Jewish quarter.[38]

The trade relations of the Omayyad kingdom of Spain with other countries were very close. By its annexation to the caliphate empire, Spain became one province in a giant economic domain stretching from the mouth of the Indus to the Atlantic Ocean, and from the steppes in the heart of Asia to Mozambique on the coast of East Africa. After the disintegration of the caliphate, all these countries remained an economic sphere whose various segments continued to exchange wares. Spanish merchants derived the fullest measure of advantage from these opportunities. Spain exported its manufactured goods; it bought not only grain but also other agricultural products from the countries of North Africa. From the oriental countries, mainly India, Spain bought spices and gems. The Arabic writer al-Muḳaddasī stresses the fact that the Spaniards were noted for their tendency to organize expeditions to other countries for the purpose of trade.[39] The Spanish traders were indeed briskly mobile, roaming throughout all countries. In a biographical compilation of the Arabs, we read of Cordovan traders journeying to Irak, Hedjaz, and Aden in connection with their business in the ninth and tenth centuries.[40]

Spanish Jews took an active part in this flourishing trade.

But the difficulties with which the Jewish merchants wrestled and the dangers that lurked for them were many. Customs officers would often scheme against them, and their exaggerated demands would have to be met. The Jews also had to placate with hard cash mere scoundrels, who sought, for motives of religious animosity, to build themselves up.[41] In the course of their travels at that time the merchants endeavored to the best of their ability to fulfill all the Jewish laws, particularly the observance of the Sabbath, as they made their way overland by caravan and on the sea by ship. But despite all these hardships, they did not refrain from going to all countries to establish commercial ties with a number of nations.

The Arabic historian Ibn Ḥayyān gives an account about a Jewish merchant, testifying to his initiative and courage. This happened in the middle of the ninth century. In 857 the Normans once again appeared on Spanish shores and carried out raids against the cities on its western coast. One of their captives was a man who had filled an important role in the revolt of the *muwalladūn* in the region of Mérida which erupted in the eighth decade of that century. His name was Sa'dūn b. Fatuḥ as-Surunbāḳī, and he became a faithful ally of Ibn Marwān. When he fell into the hands of the Normans—so runs the account of Ibn Ḥayyān—a Jewish merchant ventured forth and ransomed him. The leader of the *muwalladūn* took it upon himself to repay the ransom money with interest. For a while he remained with the Jew in the assurance that his friends would meantime get the money; but in the end he fled and organized a band of robbers that carried on its activity in the no-man's-land between Coimbra and Santarem. The Jew, however, received nothing and lost his money.[42]

In the responsa of the Cordovan rabbis in the tenth century there is also mention of the problems that resulted from the participation by the Spanish Jews in the country's foreign trade. The rabbis were called upon to deal particularly with marital questions arising from the protracted absence of the merchants from their homes; at times they were away for years on end. Since they would leave for countries where danger awaited them, their wives were apprehensive of becoming abandoned, and they therefore sought to obtain a divorce in the event that the husband did not return by a certain time.[43]

Because of their close commercial ties with Morocco and other countries of North Africa, the Jewish merchants of Andalusia often went there to establish relations with merchants in the port cities. An inquiry directed from Kairawan to a Babylonian *gaon* in the middle of the tenth century speaks, among other matters, about men from Andalusia who were visiting North Africa,[44] and a question directed to a Babylonian *gaon* at the end of the tenth century reports on two partners, one in Kairawan and one in Spain.[45] The Jewish merchants also often visited the Christian countries north of the kingdom of the Spanish Omayyads.[46] In an inquiry brought to one of the Spanish rabbis in the tenth century there is an account concerning a merchant who went to a Christian country, tarrying there over six years.[47] The export of luxury goods from Andalusia to the Christian kingdoms of northern Spain apparently was mainly in the hands of Mozarab and Jewish merchants. They took there textiles and magnificent and expensive clothes, as well as precious gems from the lands of the Abbasid caliphate and the Byzantine Empire.[48]

IV

The scope of business dealings of Spanish Jewish merchants with the Frankish kingdom north of the Pyrenees was by no means insignificant. Moreover, during the period of Omayyad dominance in Cordova a very special condition developed in international trade relations whereby the Jewish merchants of Arab Spain and Frankish Gaul were able to fulfill a highly important function in the exchange of goods between all the Moslem and Christian lands.

During the era of the Merovingian dynasty, trade between Gaul and its neighbors and between the countries along the southern and eastern coasts of the Mediterranean Sea continued along the lines of its development in the days of the Roman emperors. From the lands of the Near East, Greek, Syrian, and Jewish merchants brought spices, papyrus, textiles, oils, and wines, all these wares being found for sale in great abundance throughout all the cities in Gaul. Marseille was the focal point for this trade, since it was through that port that most of the wares from the East came to Gaul. But the foreign merchants, the majority of whom were Syrians, would also visit cities in the interior, and they similarly had business dealings with Italian cities and the other countries of western Europe.

The establishment of the caliphal empire caused a decided change in these trade relations. To be sure, the Moslems did not drive the Christian merchants away from their ports, nor did they hinder the Syrians from exporting merchandise to Christian lands; nonetheless, the increase in Moslem power throughout all the regions of the Mediterranean Sea resulted in the cessation of trade between the Near East and Western Europe in the form in which it had previously been conducted. In 652 the Moslems made a raid upon Sicily, and their attacks upon the island continued until they conquered it entirely in the ninth century. From the time of the completion of the conquest of North Africa, particularly after Spain fell to the Moslems, their power waxed greater in the Tyrrhenian Sea. In the selfsame year in which they conquered Spain, the Arabs attacked the island of Sardinia and immediately thereafter began their incursions into Provence, whose southern portion they conquered and annexed to Spain. Southern Italy and the western coast of the peninsula became, for a long period, an arena for recurring raids.

The zenith of Moslem hostility was reached with an attack on Rome, mounted in 846, but the attacks continued into the second half of the ninth century. On the other hand, the Byzantine naval forces did not accomplish anything of consequence in the regions west of Sicily; and inasmuch as the Franks did not have a war fleet of any importance, the sea-lanes between Sicily and Spain and between Provence and Tunisia were completely at the mercy of the Moslem war fleets and pirates. In 828 a group of Spanish Moslems brought the island of Crete under their dominion, and their raids inspired dread over the entire eastern basin of the Mediterranean Sea.

Thus the sea-lanes between western Europe and the Moslem and Byzantine East were disrupted and the ties of maritime commerce between Gaul and the western coast of Italy and the Near Eastern countries declined. The Syrians disappeared from the cities of Gaul, as did many of their wares, which they had formerly brought from the East. To be sure, this was also in some measure a consequence of the economic policy followed by the Byzantine Empire and the caliphate, which were each immersed in an intense economic war, imposing export taxes on important products in which the Syrians and their associates dealt, such as papyrus.

At all events, the cessation of trade by the Syrians resulted in far-reaching consequences for the economy of Christian western Europe. All commerce shrank, and the cities became impoverished. At this very time Charlemagne expanded the Frankish kingdom, establishing a great empire embracing all the countries of western and central Europe and a large part of Italy. Thus a mighty Christian empire and a Moslem empire, two hostile and isolated worlds, confronted each other.

However, all the commercial ties between the Frankish Empire and the Moslem countries were not broken; but there was a great change in international trade. It is true that Moslem traders were apprehensive about going to Christian countries;

but Christian traders were allowed to enter Moslem lands and availed themselves of the permission granted them. From a Christian source we know, for example, that in 848 merchants from Gaul sojourned in Saragossa.[49] On the other hand, Mozarabs from Spain visited Christian countries for purposes of trade. In the course of their travels in connection with their commercial ventures, two brothers of Eulogius, the leader of the fanatical Christians of Cordova, reached the city of Mainz (Mayence) in Germany.[50]

But it was the Jews who worked wonders in this regard. With the Mediterranean Sea closed to Christian merchants, the hour of importance for Jewish traders arrived. They moved easily between the two hostile empires, for, not belonging to either side, they became the natural go-betweens. The small amounts of spices and other Eastern wares still obtainable in Gaul were made available through Jewish merchants who brought them overland from Moslem Spain.[51] Among the nobles, especially those in the royal court of the Franks, there was naturally great interest in these luxury wares; therefore they gave encouragement to the Jewish traders.

As an outgrowth of this situation the attitude toward the Jews in the kingdom of the Franks changed entirely. The kings of the Merovingian dynasty had turned a receptive ear to the slanders of the fanatical clergy and treated the Jews with great severity. In 582 King Chilperic I had ordered that all Jews in his kingdom be forced to become Christians, and in 629 King Dagobert I had commanded all Jews who would not convert to Christianity to leave the land of the Franks. This was not the way the Carolingians conducted themselves. They extended their protection to the Jews, granted them writs of privilege that allowed them to be occupied freely with trade and commerce, and exempted them from paying tolls; they also appointed special officials to protect the interests of the Jews (*magister Judaeorum*). The stability of the kingdom of the Franks and the safety of the roads enabled Jewish merchants to broaden their business affairs, and, as we are able to discern from various sources, they were very successful.

The international trade in which important Jewish merchants dealt in those days and in which the Jewish merchants of Spain had a significant share is described in detail in a geographic treatise, *The Book of Roads and Kingdoms,* written by Abu'l-Ḳāsim 'Abdallāh Ibn Khurdādhbeh, who managed the postal and information service of the caliph in the province of Media. His book, which is based on information he acquired in executing his duties, is the first that has come down to us from the geographic lore of the Arabs. He started his treatise in 846 and thereafter amended it, adding supplements to it over a span of forty years. His portrayal of methods of commerce in his time has the importance of historic evidence of the highest order.

He reports on the "trading practices of the Radhanite Jewish merchants," who spoke Arabic, Persian, Greek, the Frankish tongue, Andalusian, and Slavic. They would journey—so runs his report—from East to West and from West to East by sea and on land. From the West they exported eunuchs, male and female slaves, expensive silk fabrics, all sorts of hides and furs (such as beaver and weasel), and swords. From the land of the Franks they traveled by sea,[52] reaching al-Faramā in Egypt; then they transported their wares overland to al-Ḳulzum, a distance of about one hundred miles. There they again boarded ships and sailed to the cities of al-Djār and Djidda in Hedjaz and on to India and China. From China they brought back musk, camphor, cinnamon, and other commodities. They would return by the same road, some going from Egypt to Constantinople and some going to the king of the Franks.

At times they would travel by sea to a place near Antioch, transfer their merchandise overland to the Euphrates, sail on that river to the vicinity of Bagdad, continue from there on the Tigris to the city of al-Ubulla, and from there would sail by sea to Oman, India, and China.

At times they would travel on land. Departing from Spain or the land of the Franks for Morocco, they would then travel in caravans to Tunisia, and thence to Egypt, to Ramleh in Palestine, and then to Damascus and Irak, from there they traveled by way of the southern provinces of Persia to India and China. A fourth approach to the Far East was to cross over the country of the Slavs to Khamlīj, a Khazar city, sail the Caspian Sea, and then go to Khurāsān and the lands of the Turks.[53]

We also have an account of this trade by the geographer Abū Bakr Aḥmad b. Muḥammad Ibn al-Faḳīh, who wrote his treatise *The Book concerning the Countries* in 903.[54] His work is based on that of another Arab geographer, Ibn Khurdādhbeh, but contains some variations worth noting.

Whereas Ibn Khurdādhbeh writes of Radhanites, Ibn al-Faḳīh refers to these important traders as Rahdanites, and the term no doubt is a Persian name meaning "one who knows the way."[55] The Arabic writers describe the Radhanites as merchants whose origin and permanent seat was in western Europe; we therefore need not think that they were familiar with all the Eastern languages which are mentioned. Surely they do not mean to say that all Radhanite merchants were wont to arrange prolonged journeys as enumerated by them; their intention was rather to set before the reader the manner in which world trade was at that time conducted, it having become, in considerable part, trade operated by Jews.[56] There is no doubt that only a few traveled by sea from the land of the Franks by the route first mentioned by Ibn Khurdādhbeh; nor did many use the route described as the fourth one.[57]

The majority of Radhanite merchants who made available to the Frankish nobles the spices of the East went to Moslem Spain, from where they sailed in ships that were considered to be Moslem—and thus secure against the fleets roaming the seas; or they made their way overland by way of the countries of North Africa. Because of the prolonged journey involved in bringing their wares to Europe, prices naturally increased, but so too did profits. This, then, was a venture that yielded great profits, even though the quantity of merchandise was not large. The Arabic writers do not provide us with details concerning the organization of this trade; they do not inform us whether they are discussing a more or less permanent association or casual partnerships. One thing is clear, however: only men of substance—whose number was not large—could engage in such ventures. The Radhanites constituted a small group in comparison with the large traders.

Ibn Khurdādhbeh does not stress the role of Moslem Spain as a principal transfer point between the Moslem world and Christian western Europe, even though the fact in its essence cannot be held in doubt.[58] The Arabic geographers mention Spain alone as a point of egress in the third of the four paths followed by the Radhanites, and they also list among the languages they knew that of *al-Andalus,* which is Romance, the dialect that developed on Spanish soil from the late Latin and over the generations evolved into modern Castilian. But their words hold an added hint as to the importance of Moslem Spain to the activities of the Radhanite traders. The most important items of trade exported by the Radhanites from Europe to the East were slaves, who originated in different lands. The pelts mentioned by Ibn Khurdādhbeh as merchandise brought by the Radhanites from Europe no doubt came for the most part from northern Europe, yet the Arabic geographer al-Muḳaddasī mentions the skins of weasels as merchandise found in northern Spain.[59] However, silk fabrics could be brought from Spain alone, and silk as well as other fabrics were listed among their most important wares. The name *Radhanites* does indeed also appear in a variant version

—*Rahādina*—whose meaning, according to al-Muḳaddasī, is "one who sells flaxen and cotton fabrics."[60]

While it is true that Ibn Khurdādhbeh does not tell where the costly silk fabrics, which were exported from the West, came from, Ibn al-Faḳīh says that they got them from the land of the Franks. This is no doubt an error on the part of the Arabic writer, for it is well known that the silk fabrics of Andalusia were famous in those days and that other Arabic geographers accord them extravagant praise and tell of their being exported to the Moslem countries in the East.[61]

The mention of this merchandise is thus definitive proof that Moslem Spain was a main depot for the wares of the Radhanities.[62] One of the secrets of their success was probably the collaboration between them and the Jewish merchants in all the countries touched by their trade routes. In all these countries they were aided by Jews who provided them with important information and removed many obstacles in their way. It is clear that Moslem Spain was not merely a way station in their long journeys, but that a group of native Jewish traders took part in their activities and even filled a leading role in them. One of these was no doubt Abraham of Saragossa, who for a time maintained trade relations with the land of the Franks and, on ultimately deciding to settle there, received a rescript giving him that privilege from Emperor Louis the Pious.[63]

The traffic in slaves, some of whom the Jews obtained from Slavic countries and then transported by way of the kingdom of the Franks in order to sell them to the Moslems, was the cause of a conflict between the Jews and Agobard, the archbishop of Lyons, in the 830s. The zealous cleric wanted to convert those slaves who were in Jewish hands to Christianity and then to manumit them. When the Jews opposed this, a long drawn-out dispute erupted, involving the local authorities and the royal court. In 822 Agobard addressed himself to Louis the Pious's chancellor, to the abbot of the monastery of Corbie, and to his brother, asking that they intercede with the emperor in the matter of the slaves held by the Jews, to the end that no obstacles should be placed in the way of his effort to convert them to Christianity. Among other things, he claimed that he did not want to deprive them of their slaves by force, but wanted to return to the Jews the money they had paid for them.[64] In 826 he sent a letter to the archchaplain and abbot of Corbie in which he complained about the official in charge of Jewish affairs, who was preventing him from converting to Christianity the slaves of the Jews.[65]

Meanwhile, the Jews had complained to the royal court about Agobard, and emissaries were sent to Lyons to deal with the matter. Agobard fled the city and then addressed himself in writing directly to the emperor, claiming, among other things, that all this was happening because he preached to the Christians that they should not sell Christian slaves to the Jews or allow the Jews to sell Christians to Spain.[66] He went on to relate that while he was drafting this letter, a man came from Spain and reported that some twenty-four years previously, when he was only a youth, he had been stolen by Jews from Lyons and sold as a slave to Moslems. The man had gone on to say that he was a slave in Cordova for many years and had just escaped with another Christian, who had originally been from Arles and had also been sold as a slave to Spain six years earlier.

Agobard continues, stating that he inquired into the matter regarding the man from Lyons and that he did indeed find people who knew him. Then he goes on to say that he was told that the Jew who sold this man stole other Christian children, and also bought others and then sold them; he relates that this was the practice of other Jews. Toward the end Agobard intimates that they would castrate the youths to be able to sell them as eunuchs.[67]

Whether all that Agobard reports in this letter is true or is merely propaganda, his testimony as to the destination of the slaves stands. In any event, Agobard himself testifies that he did not benefit by his preachment or his letters. Among other things, he states that at the request of the Jews, the Frankish officials fixed the market day in some places on Sunday instead of Saturday.[68] Apparently the Franks showed kindness to the Jews because they did not want to relinquish the spices the Jews brought them from Spain.

The ninth century was the golden era for this Jewish trade. But toward the close of that century and throughout the tenth century events took place that proved detrimental to it. As long as the Tang dynasty ruled in China, foreign merchants could visit its ports and trade freely. This dynasty welcomed foreigners warmly and encouraged trade relations with other lands. But in 878 a revolt erupted in south China that resulted in the slaughter of thousands of foreign merchants. In 907 the Tang dynasty reached its end and China sank into chaos, which lasted several decades. Generally speaking, foreign merchants refrained from visiting it.

In the 960s the trade routes in the great plains north of the Black Sea also became disrupted. Although the Radhanite merchants themselves did not visit the Khazar kingdom very often, the government there nevertheless established security on the roads and this country supplied them with various commodities. But in 965 the Russians took the capital city of the Khazars, who thereafter grew ever weaker, until only a shred of their kingdom remained in the lower Volga region.

However, the chief reason that the trade of the Radhanites diminished was the rise of Venice. In the tenth century the city of the lagoon became an important mercantile power that did all it could to supplant its trading rivals in the Mediterranean Sea basin. This was a competitor whom the Radhanites could not withstand.

However, the Jews were not entirely removed from international commerce. To be sure, the Venetians dealt in all branches of trade; they brought spices from the East and did not refrain from selling Christian slaves to the Moslems. But the Jews continued to take part in this trade, which at that time brought in especially large profits. In the oriental countries there was a big demand for white slaves, especially since the supply continually decreased. The caliphs of Cordova were also concerned to increase the number of Slavs, the white slaves on whom their dominance depended more and more. Arabic geographers of the tenth century report that these slaves originated in Calabria and Lombardy, in northern Spain and the land of the Franks as well as in the countries on the coast of the Black Sea.[69] White female slaves were equally in demand. In Spain they were taught singing and instrument playing and were also given the necessary education to equip them to be successful in offering proper divertisement to their masters. The countries of the Moslem East especially sought after eunuchs, of whom there was always a lack.

But the Frankish authorities, while permitting slaves acquired in eastern Europe to be transported through their country, were adamant in forbidding the sale of any of their countrymen into slavery to the Moslems. Even more, as the Christianization of the peoples of Europe progressed, it became harder for slave-traders to acquire their "merchandise." The clerical and secular authorities forbade slave-traders to sell Christians to devotees of other faiths; and the church stood for the principle that a slave of a Jew who became a Christian should go free and that most certainly it was forbidden to sell a Christian to a Jew. Because of all this, slave-traders had to buy prisoners or adopt highly contemptible devices such as the purchase of children and the like. They naturally had to circumvent the authorities by various means.

Occasionally the responsa of that epoch deal with slave-trading. In one of the responsa of the ninth century we read about "Jews who entered a city or a port, with them being slaves and small eunuchs, and an officer came and took them away, whereupon they placated him with a bribe and he restored some of the [slaves] to them."[70] Another responsum tells about Jewish merchants whose ship foundered; they were tossed up naked upon an island. Men who had never seen a Jew came and wanted to slay them, but a miracle occurred and they were saved. Afterwards—the responsum continues—one of them went and bought a certain kind of goods that involved danger, inasmuch as the king had proclaimed that whoever bought such goods would have his head chopped off. All the Jews who were there adjured the merchant against dealing in these goods, but nevertheless he purchased them, making a big profit for himself.[71] It is not necessary to state expressly what goods are being discussed here. The picture of the difficulties and perils involved in this trade, as portrayed in this responsum, fits the information supplied in all the other sources.

In the tenth century one of the chief markets in which traders purchased slaves was the city of Prague; from there they transported them to the West by way of southern Germany. The Bavarian tariff rate that was fixed in 906 speaks of slave-traders among the Jews and others.[72] In no country were the Jews the only ones to deal in this branch of commerce. In Gaul the city of Verdun was renowned for its slave mart and as a site where castrations were performed. The traders of Verdun were not Jewish. Liutprand, an Italian author and diplomat of that epoch, relates that the Verdun traders sold the eunuchs to Spain,[73] but there is not even a hint in his words that these traders were Jews. The same applies to other sources.[74]

A late Arabic source states that Jews in the land of the Franks and in the region of Spain abutting upon their land dealt in castration, as did also Moslems in that region who had acquired that skill.[75] But the Jewish merchants of Moslem Spain did engage with regularity in this base practice. Ibn Ḥauḳal relates that among the important items of trade exported from Spain to the Moslem East were male and female slaves taken captive from among the populace of Galicia and the Franks, as well as Slavs who were emasculated. He goes on to say that all the Slav eunuchs in the world came from Moslem Spain, where Jewish traders castrated them.[76] The geographer al-Muḳaddasī gives the same report,[77] and he also relates that this operation was performed on their persons in a city behind Pechina whose inhabitants were Jews. It is quite certain that he, or more accurately the person who gave him this information, referred to the city of Lucena.[78] There is no reason to doubt the veracity of the accounts since in that era people of all nations and creeds were engaged in this business.

8

THE COMMUNITIES OF SPAIN DURING THE ERA OF THE OMAYYADS

I

Even the most superficial observer who saw the many stores laden with wares and the beautiful clothes of the inhabitants of *Cordova* in that epoch would be convinced that here was a rich and prosperous city, growing larger day by day. The Kordubé that is mentioned in Greek and Latin sources beginning with the Second Punic War, which was merely a small and unimportant town, had changed under Arab rule, becoming the capital city of the whole of Spain and a blooming metropolis.

Its geographic location destined it for this. Cordova lies in the very heart of fertile Andalusia, and the region south of the city particularly is a very prosperous agricultural sector. North of Cordova stretches a chain of lofty mountains suitable for cattle-raising, and the city, which is on the banks of the Guadalquivir, is a natural market for products of all branches of agriculture. In Cordova itself flourishing industries existed producing, for example, all kinds of leather goods and silk fabrics; but they were especially noted for the elegant and expensive garments made there, which were renowned throughout the entire world.

It stands to reason that this opulent metropolis attracted

residents from everywhere. During the ninth century large suburbs were built west of the city, containing markets and mosques. Outside the city the rich built for themselves magnificent villas, on both banks along the length of the river. Arabic writers who visited Cordova during the age of splendor of Moslem dominance could not find words to express their admiration for this great city. The geographer Ibn Ḥauḳal, who visited Spain in the middle of the tenth century, states that neither in Syria nor in Egypt nor in all the countries of North Africa could a city to compare with Cordova be found.

However, almost a thousand years have passed since Cordova was the metropolis of the West, and the tourist coming from afar to visit this old city, which has become a quiet provincial town, will look in vain for remains of magnificent mansions, palaces, and splendid columns. But one who can trace the past skillfully and walk the streets of the capital of the caliphs will sense that the soul of the city remains unchanged. As you thread your way through those crooked and winding streets, so narrow that two walking abreast can traverse them only with difficulty, and when you look at the sealed alleys and the subdued plazas with their small gardens and acacias and date palms, over which stretches the blue vault of southern skies, you will imagine yourself to be strolling in Damascus, the selfsame city from which the Omayyads were driven and whose essence they wished to impart to their new capital far off in the West. Many streets like these have remained unchanged over the centuries. The walls of the houses, which have latticed windows or sometimes no windows at all, seem to hide unfathomable secrets and arouse longings for a time that has gone, never to return.

During the era of splendor of the Omayyad kingdom in Spain, Cordova, the capital, had an important Jewish community. The Jewish community of Cordova was a very old one; at the time of the city's conquest by the Moslems, Jews already

CORDOVA
Jewish Quarter

1. Calle de los Judíos
2. Calle Ibn Rushd
3. Calle Salazar
4. Plaza de la Judería
5. Calle Tomas Conde
6. Calle Abulcasis
7. Calle Manriques

a. Chapel San Bartolomé
b. Synagogue

lived there. But in the seventh and eighth centuries the community of Cordova was not large. One of the Babylonian *g'ōnīm*, who was in very close contact with the Jews of Spain, writes that in this city "the Arabs are numerous and the Jews—few."[1] Apparently over a long period of time, the Omayyad authorities were concerned that Moslems should enjoy decisive superiority in their capital and thus secure themselves against any plots by their subjects of other faiths. Therefore, while they did not send away the Christians and Jews already living there, they placed obstacles in the way of any new settlers.

The topographical data relating to the Jewish quarter of Cordova support in its entirety the information contained in the remarks of the aforementioned *gaon*. To this day the southwest sector of Cordova is known as the Jewish quarter. In the west this sector borders on the city wall, and in the south, on the site where the palace of the Omayyads was located, as well as other buildings attached to it, such as the servants' quarters and those of the guards (presently the location of the bishop's palace and other church establishments).[2]

Actually, we possess no proof that in the period of Omayyad rule Jews really dwelt in that quarter, but it is logical to assume this. Generally speaking, Jewish sectors in Moslem Spain were located near the walls of the city. The Jewish quarter in the old city of Cordova was also near the palace of the Omayyads. Its location thus met their security needs and fits nicely the information regarding the Moslem conquest of the city and the inclusion of Jews in the garrison, as reported in the writings of Arabic historians. From yet another aspect the location of the Jewish sector within Cordova was altogether characteristic with respect to relations between the Jews and the ruling Arabs. While the Moslem authorities allowed the Jews to remain within that part of the city between the walls after the conquest, they expelled the Mozarabs from there. From the end of the eighth century on, no church was to be found within the city walls. The Christians resided in sectors outside the walls of the city, especially in areas on the eastern side, and they had their churches there. At the time of the conquest and later the Moslems kept the Christians away from the heart of the city in other places also, but allowed the Jews to remain there.

Naturally, many changes befell the old Jewish quarter in Cordova itself. The houses now standing there were all built after the fifteenth century, when almost all the houses then standing were razed. But although new houses were erected the old network of streets remained, and this is why even today all the streets in that quarter are very narrow.

The street that runs along the north side of the courtyard of the Great Mosque is now named after Cardenal Herrero, but an extension of it on the western side is called Judería (the Jewish sector). At one time it contained the gate of the Jewish district (Puerta de la Judería).[3] From there one comes to a street running from the southwest to the northeast; its southern section is called Manriques (the name of an old Cordovan family) and its northern section is known as Deanes. At its southern end Manriques Street reaches Tomas Conde Street, which runs north and south and was once called Calle de las Pavas (so named for the peacocks over the gate of the palace at the southern end, on the western side of the street).[4] As one goes along Tomas Conde Street to the northern side, one comes to a street that branches off from it eastward, linking it with Manriques Street. This street is called Abulcasis.[5] Opposite Abulcasis Street winding away from Tomas Conde Street is an alley named Calle de Cevallos (so called for the house at its edge, which once belonged to Tomas Conde de Cevallos).

Tomas Conde Street itself reaches a square once called Plaza de la Judería[6] but now known as Plaza de las Bulas. Apparently this was once the marketplace of the Jewish quarter where various food products were sold. From this plaza a street turns northward that is now named for the Rambam (Calle Maimonides) and was formerly called Jews' Street (Calle de los Judíos). This was the main street of the quarter. It is long—160 meters—but very narrow. It is two to three meters wide. North of the plaza, on the west, stands the old synagogue, which was built in the fourteenth century, perhaps on the site of the synagogue from the days of Moslem rule.[7] Behind it, to the east, there branches off Ibn Rushd Street, which brings one to a small street before the Chapel San Bartolomé that gives the street its name.[8] This street connects Ibn Rushd Street with Cardenal Salazar Street, which emerges from the Plaza de las Bulas eastward to Romero Street.

Calle Maimonides itself extends north to the Almodovar Gate (Puerta Almodovar). This is one of the seven early gates of Cordova and in the era of Moslem rule was called Bāb al-Djauz or Bāb Baṭalyaus (the Gate of Badajoz) or Bāb Coria and later, after its conquest by the Christians, Puerta de Nogel.[9] The gate itself measures about eight meters in height, and from its sides stretch other portions of the city's wall, which is about seven meters high.

This Jewish quarter was truly limited in area and demonstrates that the information in the Babylonian *gaon*'s responsum at the end of the ninth century regarding the smallness of the Jewish settlement in Cordova was indeed correct. This quarter was much smaller than the Jewish sectors in the other large cities of Moslem Spain. Moreover, the eastern boundary of the quarter is very strange. With the quarter reaching on one side to the northwestern corner of the Great Mosque and on the other to the Puerta Almodovar, it would be natural to draw the boundary by way of Romero Street, with its extension going to the northwest side known today as al-Manṣūr Street; and indeed there are to be found in this street the remains of a strong wall, which was perhaps the inner wall of the Jewish quarter, that is, the wall dividing it from the other sections of the city.[10]

In the middle of this street is located the hospital that Cardenal Salazar built at the beginning of the eighteenth century and opposite it, south of the street named for him, the monastery of San Pedro Alcantara. The rear or western part of the hospital building—that is, the wing facing the Jewish quarter—contains the Chapel San Bartolomé. Concerning this house of worship, which its architecture shows to have been erected in the second half of the sixteenth century,[11] various traditions abound. According to one tradition, at the end of the tenth century this building was a part of the palace of the viceroy whose name was given to the street west of the hospital, and it is said that the edifice served as his private mosque.[12] According to another tradition, which the scholar Vazquez Venegas discovered in the eighteenth century among documents in the archives of the church in Cordova, this was an old Christian church, which the Moslem conquerors allowed to remain in Christian hands. But originally—so this investigator learned from the records spread before him—this was a synagogue.[13]

The arrangement of the edifice proves that it was in truth originally a Jewish or Christian house of worship, inasmuch as it faces from the west to the east, in contrast to Spanish mosques, in which the *miḥrāb* is located on the southeastern side. But the known historical facts, culled from the writings of Arab chroniclers, refute the account that this was a church in which the Mozarabs were permitted to conduct their worship after the conquest of Cordova by the Moslems. The Arabs at first left the Christians only half the cathedral, which they later took away from them at the end of the eighth century. But as always there is a grain of historical truth in this garbled tradition. The popular tradition can be trusted in that a Jewish house of worship was located here, and it may be surmised that it served this purpose at the outset of Arab dominance, when the number of Moslems in the conquered city was small. At a later period in the Middle Ages, after the recapture of Cordova by the Christians, this site was already beyond the boundaries of the Jewish quarter, and it is even possible that during the era of splendor of Arab dominion, the area of the quarter was reduced—that is, that the western streets of the sector were taken from the Jews. At the western entrance to Cardenal Salazar Street there is an old arch (recently restored), and another arch can be found on the second side of the lane in front of the chapel; according to the townsfolk, an arch once existed opposite the Almodovar Gate. It may be that these arches are the remains of gates for the Jewish quarter that were erected after its area was reduced.

With the expansion of the entire city in the tenth century, the Cordovan community increased steadily. As the era of anarchy in Moslem Spain drew to an end with the ascent of ʻAbdarraḥmān III to the throne, and as Cordova became the capital of a strong government, people streamed into it from all the cities and towns of Andalusia, because they hoped to earn their living more easily and take advantage of the opportunities to rise in the social scale. Among the new residents were many Jews, and it is quite certain that the small quarter in the southwest part of the city became too confined to hold all the Cordovan Jews, the old as well as the new residents. It is possible that the Jews were then given a new section in the northern part of the city. And there may perhaps be a connection between the contraction of the quarter in the southwest and the flourishing of the new quarter in the north. At all events, Arabic historians of the Middle Ages called the northern gate of Cordova Bāb al-Yahūd (the Gate of the Jews).[14] This gate has several other names. There were some who changed the letters in its name, calling it Bāb al-Hudā (the Gate of Upright Guidance);[15] some called it Bāb Talavera and some, Bāb León, because of the roads that led from it to northern Spain. This is, then, the gate at the end of the Calle del Osario, which the Christians called the Puerta de Osario; it stood on this site until 1903.[16] Near this gate was a sector that Arab writers named Rabaḍ Bāb al-Yahūd (the suburb of the Gate of the Jews).[17]

In the second half of the tenth century the Cordovan community was the largest and most important in all Spain, both in number of people and social and cultural level. Many of Cordova's Jews dealt in industry and commerce on a large scale, or became wealthy as purveyors to the highest royal circles. Within this large community there were many respected families who played a most important part in the life of the group. One of these was the Falyadj family, which was very influential. One of the girls in that family was married to Ḥanōkh, the son of the chief rabbi of Cordova, and his daughter married one of the Falyadj men.[18] In a collection of poems by a Hebrew poet of the close of this epoch, we find a poem he sent to Joseph Falga, who may have been a member of that family.[19] One of the notables of Cordova in the tenth century was a man named Fardjōn. He and his nephews were wealthy and occupied themselves with the needs of the community.[20] Among these distinguished families was the wealthy Ibn Ḳaprōn family, one of whose members was Abū Sulaimān Dā'ūd Ibn Ḳaprōn, who lived at the end of the tenth century.[21]

Many of the Jewish intellectuals in Spain were concentrated in Cordova because they could benefit from the patronage of the very wealthy. Some are mentioned by name in our literary sources. One author states that among the writers living in Cordova at that time were Abū 'Umar Ibn Yaḳwā and Hakōhēn Ben al-Mudarram.[22] Apparently both wrote poetry and engaged in Hebrew philology. The group of writers in these fields also included Abū Zakariyā Y'hūdā b. Ḥanīdjā, who lived at the end of the tenth century.[23] There were, of course, other intellectuals within the large and flourishing

Cordovan community at that time who were concerned with other branches of knowledge. One of these was the judge Ḥasan b. Mar Ḥasan or, according to another source, 'Alī b. Mar Ḥasan,[24] who wrote three treaties on the Jewish calendar. He, too, lived in the second half of the tenth century, since he employs the date Ṭebhet 4732 to demonstrate his method of calculation. He was well versed in the writings of the Arabic astronomers and depended upon the method of al-Battānī.[25] His writings, of which three were known to Abraham Ibn 'Ezrā, are lost.[26]

The Andalusian city next in rank was *Seville.* Throughout the entire period of Moslem dominance this city had a large population and was very affluent. The city's surrounding area was extremely fertile. The broad plain in which Seville is located yields a bumper crop of grapes, olives, and especially wheat. The inhabitants of Seville marketed the region's agricultural products widely. The city's commerce was particularly thriving, inasmuch as the Guadalquivir River, which ran along its western side, was wide enough so that ocean-going vessels could reach the city proper.

After the Moslem conquest many Arabs took up residence in Seville, and after a short period they became the dominant factor in the city and supplanted the Christians. It appears that in the days of the Omayyad dynasty, the Mozarabs were concentrated in the suburb of Triana, west of the Guadalquivir; they nevertheless retained, even within the city itself, churches and whole neighborhoods. Moslem and Christian neighborhoods were intermingled, and the Jews too had a number of districts within this large city. It was not the practice of the Spanish Moslems to isolate Christians and Jews everywhere in specific quarters—that is, all Christians in one quarter and all Jews in another—as was the common practice generally in the oriental countries. On the other hand, neither the Christians nor the Jews felt a need to shut themselves off. The lack of absolute isolation of the non-Mos-

SEVILLE
Jewish
Quarter

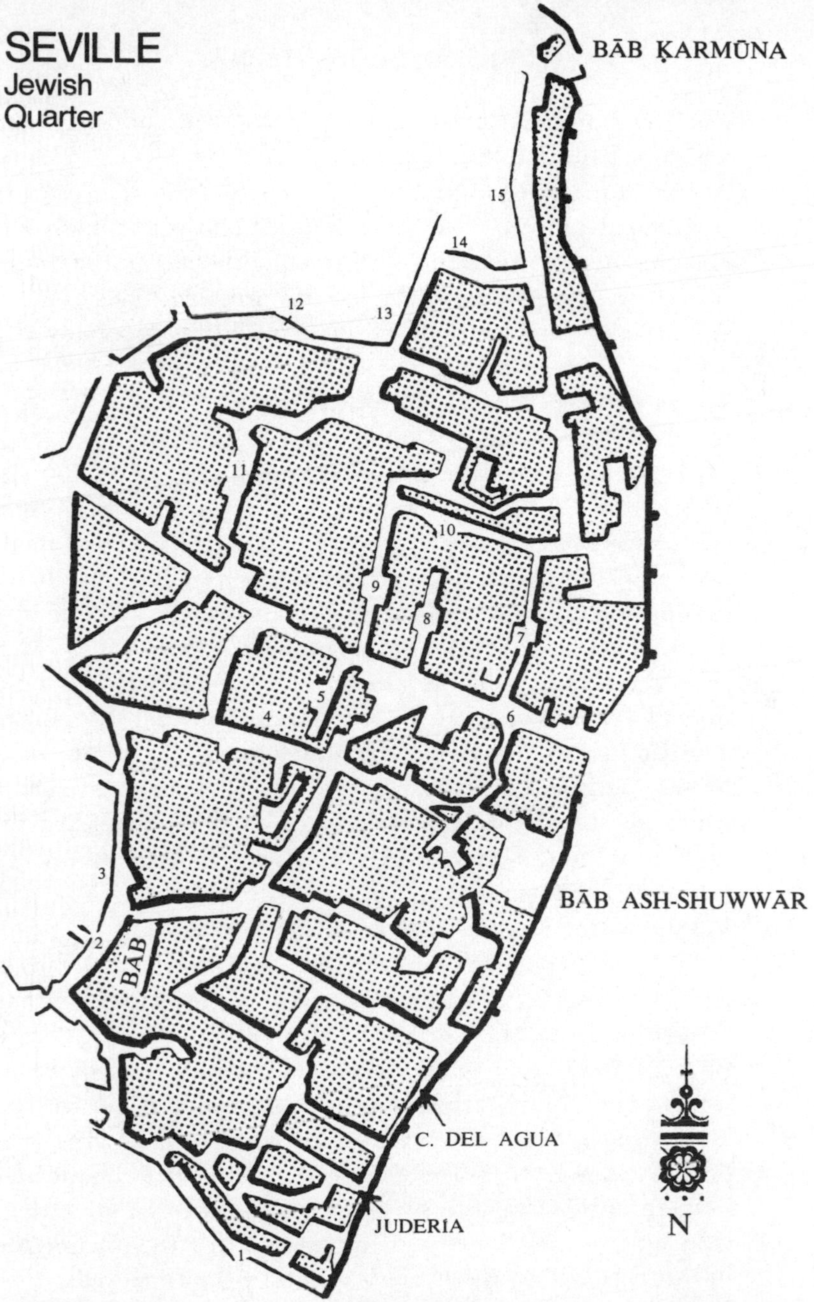

1. Calle de la Vida
2. Calle Borciguenería
3. Calle de los Menores
4. Calle Fablola
5. Calle Farnesio
6. Calle San José
7. Calle Arquéros
8. Calle Dos Hermanas
9. Calle Cespedes
10. Calle Verde
11. Calle Levíes
12. Calle Toquéros
13. Calle Vidrio
14. Calle Armenta
15. Calle de los Tintes

lem communities fits the pattern of Moslem rule in Spain, which was quite tolerant.

The Moslems occupied the neighborhoods in the heart of Seville and converted the Church of San Salvador into their chief mosque. South of the chief mosque the mercantile center of the city spread. The streets in this area held long rows of stores laden with merchandise of fine quality, especially silk fabrics. The sections north of the mosque were inhabited by Moslems. The Church of San Juan de la Palma is simply a former mosque converted, after the Christian conquest, to a Christian house of worship.[27] The same applies to the Church of San Pedro.[28] But east of these central sectors was an area containing Mozarab neighborhoods. The Church of San Nicolas[29] and the Church of San Ildefonso were Christian houses of worship during the time of Moslem rule.[30] On the site where the Church of San Esteban now stands, there was a church from which the Mozarabs would come forth annually to hold a procession in memory of Saints Justa and Ruppina.[31] The Church of San Roman is also located on the site of a former Christian house of worship named for San Miguel.[32] Although the Mozarab sector was quite large, the principal church of the Christians was not located there. The role of cathedral was filled in Omayyad times by the Church of San Vicente, in the western part of the city.[33]

As the old names of the streets demonstrate, the Jews had a settlement on the west side of the city. In the district of the Church of Santa Magdalena one street still retains the name Calle de Cal[34]—and *cal* is merely the Spanish form of *ḳahal* (community). In a northwest section of the city, in the district of the Church of San Lorenzo, there is a street which even now bears the name Cal Mayor.[35] The conjecture that Jews dwelt in these neighborhoods is supported by the fact that other than the Church of San Vicente there were apparently no churches in this part of the city during the rule of the Omayyads. Jews apparently also dwelt in the vicinity of San Pedro at one time. After Seville was taken by the Christians this neighborhood was allotted to the Moslems and was therefore called Morería, but in the later Middle Ages it was also known as la Judería Vieja (the Old Jewry).[36]

Aside from these sectors in the western and central parts of the city, Jews had dwelt since olden times in the southeastern part of the city, in the neighborhoods allotted them by Fernando, the king of Castile, when he took Seville from the Moslems in 1248. It may be assumed that initially the Christian king assigned to the Jews quarters that were theirs before the Christian conquest, and this assumption has support. One piece of evidence is the absence of Mozarab churches in this area. Houses of worship in these sectors were converted to mosques in the days of the Almohades, to synagogues at the beginning of Christian rule, and churches afterwards, but there exists no tradition whatsoever that they were Christian houses of worship in the days of Moslem dominion. Moreover, the site of this quarter within the city fitted the needs of the community, since it was located between the wall and the Mozarab area and was particularly secure.

To this day these sectors differ from the other quarters of the city. Whereas one may walk in other neighborhoods along streets broad and straight, the streets in this section of the city, especially at its southern end, are almost all narrow and crooked and winding, each alongside the other. The scope of the Jewish quarter in the days of Christian rule is well known, and bearing in mind the existence of the Mozarab churches on its western flank, it can be assumed that even in the era of the Omayyads it was no larger.[37] On the east the city wall surrounded the quarter, and on the west was an inner wall, the remains of which were preserved until the past century.[38] The boundary of the Jewish quarter apparently passed through streets now known as Calle de la Vida, Calle Borciguenería, and

Calle de los Menores, until it reached the vicinity of the Church of San Nicolas. From there it turned again eastward by way of Toquéros Street until it came to Vidrio Street. Thereafter it crossed Armenta Street to the Calle de los Tintes[39] and came up near the Carmona Gate. In this vicinity, too, on Toquéros Street, there are still vestiges of the inner wall that separated the Jewish quarter from other sectors of the city.[40]

Within the boundary of this quarter was one of the gates of the city, at that time called Bāb ash-Shuwwār, after the Christian conquest known as Puerta de la Judería, and later named Puerta de la Carne (the Gate of Flesh), after the meat that was brought by way of it from the slaughterhouse to the city.[41] Besides the name Bāb ash-Shuwwār there is mention of the name Bāb Ben Aḥwār or Menḥoar, and according to a report this was the name of a Jew who dwelt nearby.[42] There were two portals within the inner wall encircling the Jewish quarter: one in the Calle Borciguenería at the point where the street called Meson del Moro branches off from it, and the second opposite the Church of San Nicolas.[43]

The main street in this quarter was no doubt the broad thoroughfare beginning at the Puerta de la Carne and bringing one to the Church of San Nicolas. On the north side of this street was the synagogue that was later converted into the Church of Santa Maria la Blanca, which at present gives its name to the stretch of thoroughfare near the site of the gate, formerly the Calle Santa Maria la Blanca, the square in front of it being called Plaza Santa Maria la Blanca. The stretch of road from there to the Church of San Nicolas is presently called Calle San José.[44]

From this street there radiate in a northeasterly direction several streets: Canarios,[45] Arquéros (or Archcro),[46] Dos Hermanas, Cespedes,[47] and at the very end a street known till now as Calle Levíes. This street has this designation because in the house whose address is Number 4 there lived some centuries ago a respected Jewish family that held high position at the royal court of the Castilian kings. But it is quite possible that even in the days of the Omayyad caliphs a wealthy Jewish family lived in this house—a conclusion based on the appearance of certain portions of the building.[48] Running parallel with the Santa Maria la Blanca Street there cut across it from the northeast to the southeast, beyond the site of the former wall, the narrow Verde Street[49] and Alegria Street. On the latter street there formerly stood a synagogue that was later converted into a church named for San Bartolomé.[50] East of this church and parallel to what was once the wall of the city runs the narrow street called San Clemente.[51] Opposite Cespedes Street and emerging southeastward from San José Street is Farnesio Street, which runs to Fabiola Street, which in turn parallels Santa Maria la Blanca Street. South of this street extends the area of the Church of Santa Cruz, which was formerly a synagogue.[52]

The streets in this area are particularly narrow and dark. Although the houses in the neighborhood are no older than the eighteenth century, it is evident that the network of streets is similar to that of an earlier epoch. The names the streets bear, such as de la Vida, del Muerte, del Ataúd, and the like, bring to mind family tragedies during the time of the Inquisition, when certain people appeared before the judges of that tribunal to inform against members of their family.[53] The long street named Jiménez Ensiso[54] brings one to the hospital of the "Venerabiles." Alongside this institution, from northwest toward the southeast, runs Shamardana Street, a name that apparently is a corruption of a Hebrew word.[55] This is the southern end of the old Jewish quarter on whose eastern side a part of the city's walls and towers are still preserved. Del Agua Street,[56] which at its southern tip is called Judería, runs parallel to the wall. Naturally, there were small markets within the neighborhood. One of them was at the end of Arquéros Street.[57] Outside the Puerta de la Carne was the cemetery of the Jews of Seville.[58]

The community of Seville was very old. Yet even in the days of the Visigoths the number of Jews in the city was not inconsequential, since they supplied members of the garrison during the Arab conquest. The first Arabs to settle in the city, which in their tongue was called Ishbīlya, were landowners, and therefore did not come into conflict with the Jews, who could engage to their hearts' desire in every branch of work and industry. The Jews of Seville benefited from all the great possibilities given them in the flourishing city, and many were very successful and became quite wealthy. During this entire period Seville had a large community, and Saadya Gaon numbers it among the important Jewish communities of Spain to whom he addresses himself in his epistle.[59] This community had a number of distinguished families. One of the great Spanish rabbis of the eleventh century relates that after the destruction of the first Temple, descendants of the House of David came to Spain and settled in Seville, among them being the family of Abrabanel.[60] Isaac Abrabanel maintained that this was his family.[61]

In the two metropolises of Andalusia there were large Jewish communities, both as to the number of individuals they included and with respect to their social standard. But besides these large communities there were also small communities in the various towns of this richly endowed province. In the towns and villages of every district of Andalusia dwelt many Jews, some with only a few families or even only one, some with many more. The density of the Jewish population in Andalusia was greater at that time than in other parts of Spain —and for various reasons Andalusia was, and still is, one of the most fertile areas in all of Spain; even one who was not engaged in agriculture could easily make a living in work or trade. For this same reason the Arabs who reached the Iberian peninsula also settled first and foremost in Andalusia.

Other factors entered into there being a great number of Jews in this part of Spain. No doubt the number of Jews in Andalusia was especially large because in migrating from North Africa to Spain many stayed on in the region to which they first came. Andalusia was also far removed from the boundary between the Moslem and Christian kingdoms, along which the fighting continued for centuries. The cities of Andalusia did not, in those days, expect invasions by Christian armies, and each man dwelt securely "under his vine and under his fig tree."

Information about a community in a small city, no longer existent, can be found in the circular letter sent by Saadya Gaon to the Jews of Andalusia. In this letter, wherein he addresses himself to the chief communities of southern Spain, he also includes the community of *Calsena*.[62] This city was situated south of Seville by the estuary of the Majacete River as it flows into the Guadalete River near the city of Arcos de la Frontera. In the ninth century Calsena was the capital of the province of Sidonia. This was one of the most opulent regions of Andalusia. It was outstanding because of the fertility of its soil, and its inhabitants also benefited greatly from their nearness to the sea and the availability of fishing. Calsena itself was well known for its production of textiles.

At the end of the ninth century a revolt against the Omayyad government broke out in this region, and the heads of the Ibn as-Salīm family who led this movement made the ancient city of Sidonia (which thereafter was known by their name as the Madīnat Ibn as-Salīm) the chief city of the province of Sidonia. Because of this, the two names were combined, and the city is called, even today, Medina-Sidonia.[63] Yet despite this Calsena did not lose its important status right away, for we learn that Caliph 'Abdarraḥmān III built a large mosque there.[64]

Apparently there were a large number of Jews and organized

communities, especially in the plain stretching southward from Cordova. This plain, which alternates here and there with a region of hills, is rich in water, inasmuch as rivers cut across it and its climate is especially hot. From ancient times this piece of land was famous for its fertility and was always densely settled. Here there were many cities and towns, some very old, founded by the Iberians, the first inhabitants of the land. In most of these cities Jews dwelt from the beginning of Moslem rule till the close of the Middle Ages. But in nearly all cases any trace of these small communities belongs to the limbo of a forgotten past; no knowledge about them has come down to us, particularly from the earliest period of Moslem rule.

Most important among these communities was the old city of *Lucena,* which the Arabs had corrupted into Alyusāna. Until the tenth century the community of Lucena served as a spiritual center for the Jews throughout Andalusia. In the tenth century Cordova filled this role, but even at that time Lucena had scholars of great repute. Lucena is situated in a very fertile agricultural region, especially rich in vineyards and olive groves. The city itself serves as a processing and marketing center for the area's agricultural products. For many generations the Jews constituted the majority in this city.

In the second half of the ninth century one of the *g'ōnīm* of Babylonia wrote to the Jews of Lucena: "And as for your question relative to the fact that since Alyusāna is a Jewish city having a large Jewish population . . . without a single non-Jew among you. . . ."[65] There was no exaggeration in the words of the *gaon,* and evidence from other sources proves that the condition described by him did not change over a long period of time. An Arabic geographer of the twelfth century reports that Lucena was a Jewish city with only a few Moslems residing there. The Jews—says that geographer—lived inside the fortified city and the Moslems in the unwalled suburbs.

He speaks elsewhere in high praise of Lucena's excellent fortifications. A very strong wall and a deep moat full of water ran round the city. If his word is to be trusted, the Jews did not permit the Moslems to enter the city. Even in the suburbs the Moslems constituted only a part of the populace, for Jews dwelt there too.[66] Other Arabic writers also portray Lucena as a Jewish city.[67] It is no wonder that the legend was circulated that Jews had founded the city.[68]

The occupations of the city's Jews were highly diversified. In this Jewish city people were engaged in all branches of industry and commerce. The merchants of Lucena sold the agricultural products of the region to the other Spanish provinces, and the big ones made connections, by way of the nearby port of Pechina, with other countries ringing the Mediterranean Sea, growing wealthy through their trade.[69] Some of the wealthy families also took pride in their lineage. One of these was the family of Ibn Dā'ūd, which traced its descent from the House of David. Members of this family held that their forebears came to Spain after the destruction of the first Temple.[70]

Hundreds of years have passed since Lucena was a distinguished Jewish city. Today it is merely a small village with almost no traces of its Jewish past.[71] But our literature does preserve memories of the scholars who dwelt in Lucena and taught there, as well as the authors who produced their literary work in that city. In the second half of the ninth century a scholar named Joseph lived there. He corresponded with the heads of the Babylonian academies, and it was to him that the 'Amram Gaon sent his prescribed list of one hundred benedictions and a number of responsa.[72] In the first half of the tenth century the community of Lucena maintained a contact with Saadya Gaon, for he addresses himself to it in a circular letter to the Jews of Spain.[73]

At the close of that century the study of the Hebrew language and Hebrew poetry were especially cultivated. In those days a group of philologists and poets greatly renowned throughout the entire Diaspora were settled in that city. One of the great Spanish writers of a later day refers to Lucena of a former time as the "city of song";[74] and it also is well known that young men of talent would come to Lucena from all the cities of Spain to study under its teachers and rabbis. Among these scholars one of the most esteemed was Abu'l-Walīd Ibn Ḥasdai, whose Hebrew name appears to have been Jonah b. Ḥasdai Halevi.[75] Abū Ibrāhīm Ibn Barūn, who also was engaged in the study of philology, was apparently a member of a distinguished family which produced several men of importance.[76] This group also included Abū Sulaimān Ibn Rāshela, whose Hebrew name was David. He was one of the notable men of that city.[77]

II

In the eastern provinces of Andalusia Jewish settlements were less dense, but there were several important communities in that section too; among these the community of *Granada* held first place.

Southeast of Granada a chain of mountains rises to a height of 3,480 meters. The Arabs called these mountains Djabal Shulair or Shulair ath-thaldj (the Mountain of Snow), since the snows never melt on the mountaintops. This name has continued to this day, but is translated into Spanish: Sierra Nevada. Paralleling these mountains on the northwest is a chain of mountains that are volcanic, which causes their slopes to be arid. But between the two chains spreads a very fertile valley, called Vega in Spanish (this being essentially a corruption of the word *baḳ'a,* meaning valley). Groves of fruit trees and orchards crisscrossed by canals of limpid water for irrigation and all manner of pleasant villas—these make up the environs of the city.

In the thousands of years of Granada's existence, the rulers

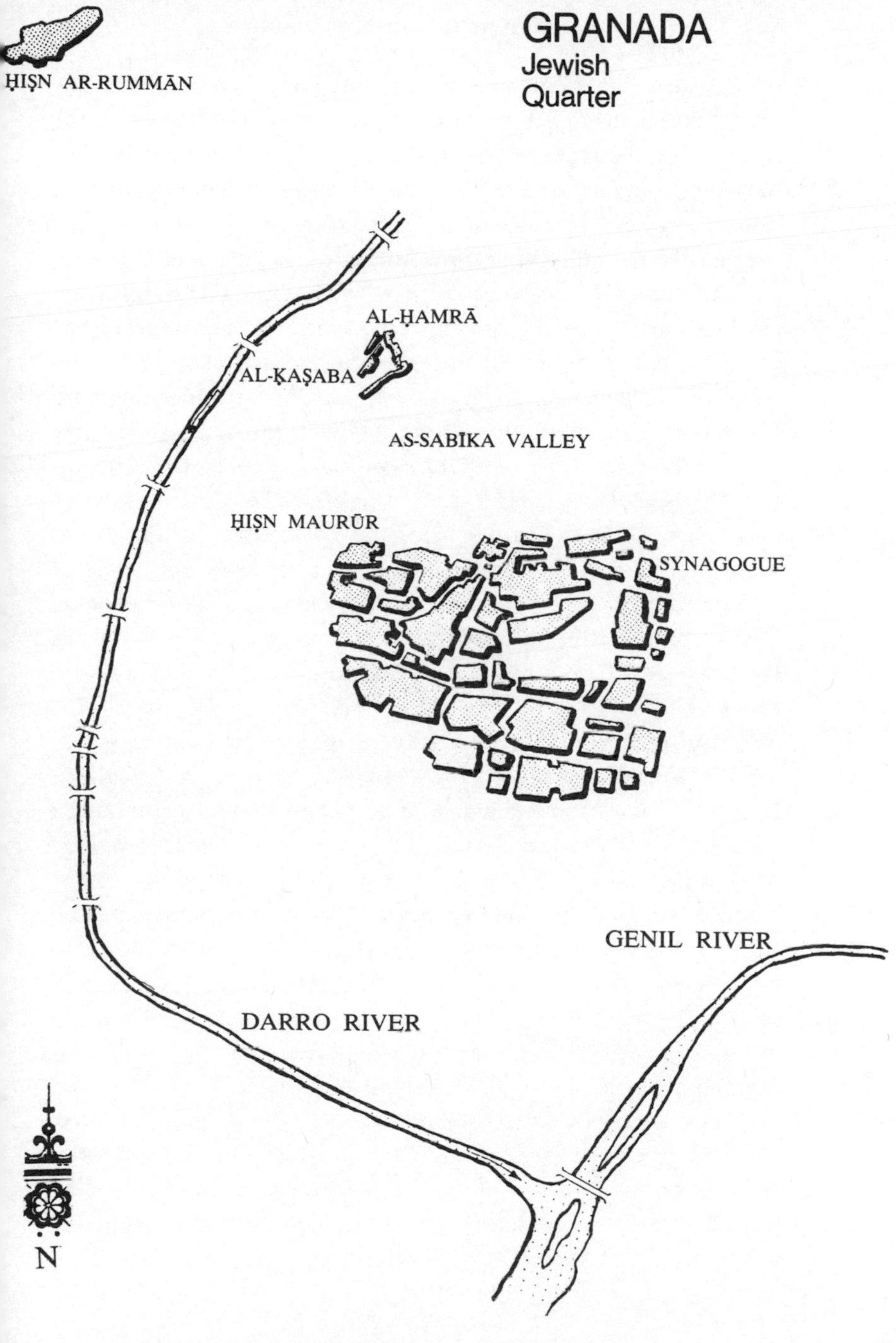
GRANADA
Jewish
Quarter
ḤIṢN AR-RUMMĀN
AL-ḤAMRĀ
AL-ḲAṢABA
AS-SABĪKA VALLEY
ḤIṢN MAURŪR
SYNAGOGUE
GENIL RIVER
DARRO RIVER
N

of the various nations and faiths that have dominated it one after another have generally put forth great effort to erase the memory of their predecessors. But they never succeeded. The dark and narrow streets that traverse the crowded masses of houses and the marble domes glistening in the light of the southern sun against high mountains whose peaks are covered with clouds—all bear silent witness to the splendor of a former time, when the cry of the muezzin could be heard from the towers of the mosques. But as great as the splendor of the city by daylight, it is ever so much greater when the sun sets and the moon illuminates the streets with a lambent glow, projecting long shadows. Anyone who has spent some time in Granada can never forget those nights. The air is saturated with fragrant odors wafted from the flower beds in the courtyards and gardens of the houses, from a distance the tones of a stringed instrument are heard, and when one sees the lights among the trees of the orchards and lifts his eyes to gaze at the star-strewn heavens, then the lips murmur a prayer of thanks to the Creator of heaven and earth who made this beautiful world and this magnificent spot in the land of Spain.

This, then, is Granada, the chief city of eastern Andalusia for many generations. It is true that when the Arabs conquered the Iberian peninsula, the capital of its southeastern province was Illiberi. This was an ancient Iberian city that, under Roman rule, became *Municipium Florentium Illiberitanum.* In Gothic times it played an important part in the life of the government. It was a political and religious center, inasmuch as coins were minted there and it was the residence of a bishop. The city became renowned particularly as the site of the first council of the Spanish church.

Illiberi was located at the foot of a chain of mountains to which it gives its name to this day: Sierra Elvira, near a settlement presently known as Atarfe, some ten kilometers northwest of Granada, on the banks of the Cubilas River. Remains from the Roman and Gothic period have been found there: remnants of houses and coins, a cemetery, and various Christian symbols. Granada was one of the suburbs of this city. As the ancient name of Granada attests, it too was an Iberian city.[78] During the Roman and Gothic rule it was connected with Illiberi from an administrative aspect, and inscriptions have been discovered in Granada bearing the words *Municipium Florentinum Illiberitanum.*[79] From these inscriptions we learn that in Granada, too, many churches were built during the rule of the Goths.

But even from early days the Jews were the strongest element in this city. Apparently they were later removed from Illiberi or stayed away from it of their own free will. Yet in ancient days a legend spread throughout Spain that Jews had founded Granada. According to the tale, an army officer named Pirus reached the Iberian peninsula after the destruction of the first Temple, bringing with him from Judea many captives; they founded Granada and Toledo.

The esteemed tenth-century Arabic historian Aḥmad ar-Rāzī maintains this view and states that this is the oldest city in the region; elsewhere he says that the city is called "Granada of the Jews."[80] From his words we learn that in the days of the Spanish caliphs the Jews were in the majority among the inhabitants of Granada, and everything related in Arabic sources pertaining to the history of the city in that epoch confirms what he reports. Ar-Rāzī speaks of the "fortress of Granada," but he never refers to the part of Granada where the Jews dwelt. He goes on to state that Granada bisects the river once called Calom, which empties into the Genil.[81]

This river is the Darro, called by the Arabs Hadaro. It bisects the city from the north to the southwest. In the city as it is today constituted it then turns southward, emptying into the Genil. Nowadays its waters are used for irrigation, and during the summer its bed is almost always dry. At present a large portion of the bed is not visible at all, for it has been covered, and the Plaza Nueva and the street called Calle de los Reyes Católicos, a busy thoroughfare of modern Granada, have been constructed over it. But in former times there were mills along the Darro and waterwheels with which river water was brought to the orchards and bathhouses.

During the rule of the Omayyads the area north of the Darro was sparsely populated, although it contained remnants of buildings and fortifications from an older era. In the small street that today is named for the Church of San Nicolas stood the remains of an old fortress called by the Arabs the "Pomegranate Fortress" (Ḥiṣn ar-rummān). Apparently they inquired as to the meaning of the name Granada, and when the inhabitants of the city, who had already forgotten its Iberian derivation, said that it means "pomegranate," the Arabs translated the ancient name of the fortress into their own tongue, designating it by the name of Ḥiṣn ar-rummān. The Jews also accepted this explanation and called the entire city Rimmōn S'fārad (Pomegranate of Spain).

The Jews occupied quarters south of the Darro River. On the southern bank of the river, opposite the ancient fortress a row of hills rises, upon which were built, in a later era, the magnificent palaces of the kings of Granada, known by their early name: *al-ḥamrā*. But in the first generations of Moslem rule only the remains of a Christian settlement from Roman and Gothic times were visible. South of these hills rises a lower hill, formerly called Maurūr (now known as Caidero). On the western end of this hill stood the remnants of an ancient fortress called Ḥiṣn Maurūr. These fortifications, which were restored in various periods and are presently known as Torres Bermejas,[82] served as a fortress and sanctuary for the inhabitants of the place from ancient times.

The Jewish neighborhoods lay to the west and south at the foot of the hill upon which this old fortress had been built.

On the west they dwelt in that narrow area between the slope of the hill and the Darro, where the Cuesta de Gomeres now ascends to the Puerta de las Granadas. To the south of the hills their residential area spread to the plain now called Campo del Príncipe, formerly (during Arab rule) Faḥṣ Albunest.[83] North of this plain the Christians, after the reconquest, built the Church of San Cecilio, and according to an old tradition among the inhabitants of the area, a synagogue was once located there.[84] The areas of Jewish residence were thus quite extensive. Between the Maurūr hill and the hill farther north the magnificent forest called Alameda de la Alhambra now stretches. But in those faraway days this was an open field called as-Sabīka; more than once it served as a battlefield for the various factions struggling for hegemony in Moslem Spain.

After the conquest of Spain, the Arabs made the city of Illiberi, which in their tongue was changed to Ilbīra, the seat of provincial government in the southeast region of the peninsula; until the end of the tenth century the city remained the seat of the *wālī*, the ruler of the province.[85] The province was named after this city; Kūrat Ilbīra, and the city proper was called Madīnat Ilbīra or Ḥādirat Ilbīra, that is, the chief city of the region of Ilbīra. For the Arabs, Granada served as a rallying point near the province's chief city, from which it was possible to take various kinds of military action against the inhabitants of Ilbīra or against the governor who resided there. The inhabitants of Ilbīra were for the most part Christians, or *muwalladūn*, whereas the residents of tiny Granada were mostly Jews who were loyal to the Arabs. Thus Granada is referred to in the sources of that time as the "Fortress of Ilbīra."

In 889 Sawwār b. Ḥamdūn entrenched himself in Granada after he had risen up against the governor of the province and had defeated him. At the western edge of the Alhambra hills he settled down in the old castles remaining there from generations past, whose ruined portions outnumbered the sound, and he repaired them. The Arabic writers explain that Sawwār's men worked on the erection of the fortifications at night by lantern light, so that the walls appeared to be red; because of this the fortress was given the name Alhambra—the Red (Building). Thus was built al-Ḳaṣaba, the citadel of the Alhambra, which stands on the site to this day.

The *muwalladūn* did not sit idly by, but besieged the Arabs entrenched there. Eventually Sawwār issued forth from his fortress, smiting the *muwalladūn* down and pursuing them as far as the Gate of Ilbīra north of Granada. In this battle, which took place in the middle of Jewish Granada and was called "Yaum al-madīna" (the Battle of the City), twelve thousand men were slain, according to reports by Arabic writers. The *muwalladūn* had their revenge; they murdered Sawwār, and, aided by some of the troops of 'Umar b. Ḥafṣūn, they gained control of the province.

When 'Umar b. Ḥafṣūn was defeated in 891 by the army of Emir 'Abdallāh, the province of Elvira was restored to Omayyad rule. But after a brief interval civil war erupted anew in the troubled region. After Sawwār, the Arabs were led by his companion, Sa'īd ibn Djūdī, the prototype of the Arabs of that age: valiant, poetry-writing courageous, fickle. He was murdered while dallying with a Jewess in her house.[86] When the *muwalladūn* once again had the upper hand, they defeated the Arabs, and a governor acting in behalf of 'Umar b. Ḥafṣūn took over the government of the province, until an Omayyad army succeeded in subduing the rebels in 893. So war raged in Granada, "the Jewish city," and in its environs.

The Jews apparently did not take an active part in this struggle. Insofar as they could, they remained aloof. From neither faction disputing over the governance of the area—the Arabs rebelling against the Omayyad government or the *muwalladūn* who inclined toward 'Umar b. Ḥafṣūn—could they expect to benefit. They rejoiced at the return of the province to the authority of the Omayyad government. During the reign of 'Abdarraḥmān III the inhabitants of Granada experienced happiness in their lives. Thanks to the security and calm which prevailed there, and thanks to their own diligence, their economic situation improved. The Jews were the special beneficiaries of the bettered conditions. During the days of the Omayyad kingdom the community of Granada was one of the most important in all of Spain. Saadya Gaon addresses himself, in a letter he sent to the Jews of Spain, to the Jews of Elvira among others, and it is certain that he had in mind the Jews of Granada and the entire province.[87] Among the inhabitants of this city were distinguished families who prided themselves on their origins from Judean nobility and traced their lineage to the House of David.[88]

During the tenth century a large Jewish community was located near the bay on which the city of Almería was founded. The site on which Almería was later built was desolate till the end of the ninth century. Only a watchtower (called *al-mariya* in Arabic, whence the name of the city is derived) stood there. Some ten kilometers to the north, on the left bank of the small Rio Andarax, lived Yemenite settlers who had taken it upon themselves to guard the seashore from Norman attacks. The Yemenite settlement was called Badjāna. This was a mere village, for the Yemenites dwelt in scattered farms, distant one from the other. In 876 Spanish seafarers appeared on the bay near the watchtower; they were engaged in the transport of goods between their country and the ports of North Africa and had settled in that location. They made the settlement on the bay their home port, but built houses in Badjāna to live in between voyages and for their families in their absence.

At first they were given a friendly welcome by the Arabs, and even the Omayyad government placed no obstacles in their way. These seafarers encircled Badjāna with a wall and transformed the place into a city. In a short time they established their authority over the entire area. Thus a maritime commonwealth was founded. Its leaders were able to bring security to their region at a time when nearly all of Spain was sunk in a dreadful chaos—with the result that merchants and various other people came to settle in Badjāna. The new city became a place of flourishing commerce and wealth. Besides the maritime trade, the city expanded because of the industry that developed within it. The peasants around Badjāna raised silkworms, and in the city proper silk cloth of outstanding quality was manufactured.

Badjāna continued to flourish in the first half of the tenth century. But in the middle of that century the city of Almería developed right on the seashore, near the watchtower, and in 955 it was made the seat of the district governor. This marked the beginning of Badjāna's decline, and by the eleventh century it had become a village as before. It has remained one to this day and only its Spanish name, Pechina, brings to mind its distinguished past.

During the three generations in which Badjāna was a city of importance, it was inhabited by many Jews, since opportunities for a livelihood abounded within the city. Merchants and craftsmen of all sorts earned a respectable living in this maritime city. When Saadya Gaon addressed himself to the important communities of southern Spain he numbered among them the community of Badjāna.[89] Even at the end of the tenth century, when the city was already in a state of decline, it still had an important community. Its leader, apparently, was Samuel ha-Kōhēn b. Josiah, who originated in Fez, Morocco. He was a man well versed in Jewish law and he corresponded with Sh'rīra Gaon.[90] Samuel was a member of the last generation of the city of Badjāna and of its community. In the following generation the name Badjāna was already missing from among the cities of Spain, and the Jewish community had disappeared. No doubt the majority of the Jews of that city moved over to nearby Almería.

Over the entire period of Moslem rule, the ancient city of Aurgi, called by the Arabs Djayyān and (in accordance with Spanish pronunciation) now called *Jaén*, was the chief city of an extensive district in eastern Andalusia. It is situated on the slopes of a mountain till now called Djabal Kuz and is west of the Guadalbullon River, which fertilizes the district east and north of the city, where all kinds of grain are grown, especially wheat. The Arabic geographer of the tenth century al-Muḳaddasī states that Jaén was the granary for Cordova, and he also praises its fruits.[91] Another Arabic writer reports that the silkworm was cultivated in this region, and he also extols its fruitfulness.[92] The city itself was protected by the fortress on top of the hill west of the city, and its walls were connected with the fortifications. A tourist coming to Jaén nowadays is impressed by its narrow and crooked streets, which are so typical of Moslem cities, and by the houses crowding one another without an empty space between them. But the Arabic writers of the Middle Ages commend the gardens within the courtyards of the houses, which were watered by the many fountains within the city. Here, too, a Jewish community existed, for it was Jaén that the father of Ḥasdai Ibn Shaprūṭ came from.[93] Though it was not an overly large community, it existed till the end of Moslem rule in Spain.

III

The number of Arabs who dwelt in *Toledo* was small, most of the Moslems residing there being of Spanish extraction. On the other hand, the Christians and Jews in the city were very numerous. In Toledo, too, the residences of people of various faiths were intermingled. We learn this from the fact that the Moslems left six churches for the Mozarabs, located in various sections of the city. But the majority of Christians dwelt in the central and southern sections of the city. In the center of the city the Moslems left them the Church of San Marco, in the south, the Church of San Torcuato, and in the southeast corner, the Church of San Lucas.

As for the Jews, almost all of them lived in the western section of the city. Over the many generations that the large community in Toledo existed, the range of the Jewish quarter on Toledo's west side underwent change; after Toledo was restored to Christian authority, its area diminished greatly.

On its western flank the Jewish quarter had a natural boundary: the steep slope on the side of the Tagus. In the south the Jewish quarter reached the hill now called San Cristóbal but formerly known as Montichel. According to a report, on this hill, on the site where the Church of San Cristóbal was later erected, there was a palace in which Governor 'Amrūs executed a large number of the city's notables in 807.[94] From there the boundary went northward the length of the plaza now known as the Plaza del Conde to a small street, the Travesia del Conde, on whose right stands the Church of San Tomé, which was formerly a mosque and was rebuilt in the fourteenth century.

Some of the names of streets in this neighborhood are reminders of its past. From Travesia del Conde, San Juan de Dios Street makes a westerly descent, and at the street's end Samuel Halevi Street turns to the southeast and in a northwesterly direction the Travesia de la Judería runs. Opposite the Church of San Tomé a small street, narrow and dark, climbs upward; it is called Calle de los Bodegones. It extends to the Plaza de Valdecaleros. It is most likely that the boundary of the Jewish quarter passed through there. Thus the eastern boundary of the quarter ascended from the plaza now called Paseo del Transito, one of the lowest places in the city, to one of its highest hills. The plaza now named Valdecaleros also rises from south to north. From it, running northward, emerges the Calle de San Clemente, which got its name from the nearby monastery of San Clemente; it extends to the Church of San Román, which stands where a mosque used to be during Moslem rule.[95]

A document from the year 1131 points to the fact that Jews lived in this neighborhood until the end of Moslem rule and were removed from there after the reconquest by the Christians. In this document King Alfonso VII transfers to the monastery of San Clemente the ownership of a bathhouse that had formerly belonged to the Jews.[96] It is certain that this bathhouse was located in the vicinity of the monastery.

The end of the Calle de San Clemente is the highest point in the western part of the city, and indeed the northeast segment of the Jewish quarter, which was nearby, was called the "high quarter."[97] From this spot the boundary turned northward, from the slope on the other side of the city's wall. We have no means of fixing precisely or guessing at the extent of the Jewish quarter at its northeast end, but it must be remembered that when the Moslems took Toledo, many Christians left the city and numerous houses became vacant.[98] No doubt it was then that the area of the Jewish quarter was broadened. In any event, it appears that the boundary of the Jewish quarter did not extend to the mosque that stood on the site of the Church of San Román but descended in a northwesterly direction on the other side of the Puerta del Cambrón (Cambrón Gate), by way of the street now named after a girls' school, Covertizo del Colegio de Doncellas, in its upper section and the Calle Colegio de Doncellas in its lower part. It is quite likely that the boundary of the Jewish quarter ran along this line, because north of these streets that descend to the Cambrón Gate, and near the Calle de San Clemente, was located the Church of Santa Eulalia, one of the churches the Moslems had allowed the Christians to retain,[99] presumably because many Mozarabs dwelt there.

TOLEDO
Jewish Quarter

1. Calle Samuel Halevi
2. Calle San Juan de los Reyes
3. Calle del Angel
4. Calle San Tomé
5. Calle de los Bodegones
6. Plaza de Valdecaleros
7. Calle de San Clemente
8. Calle de Santa Anita

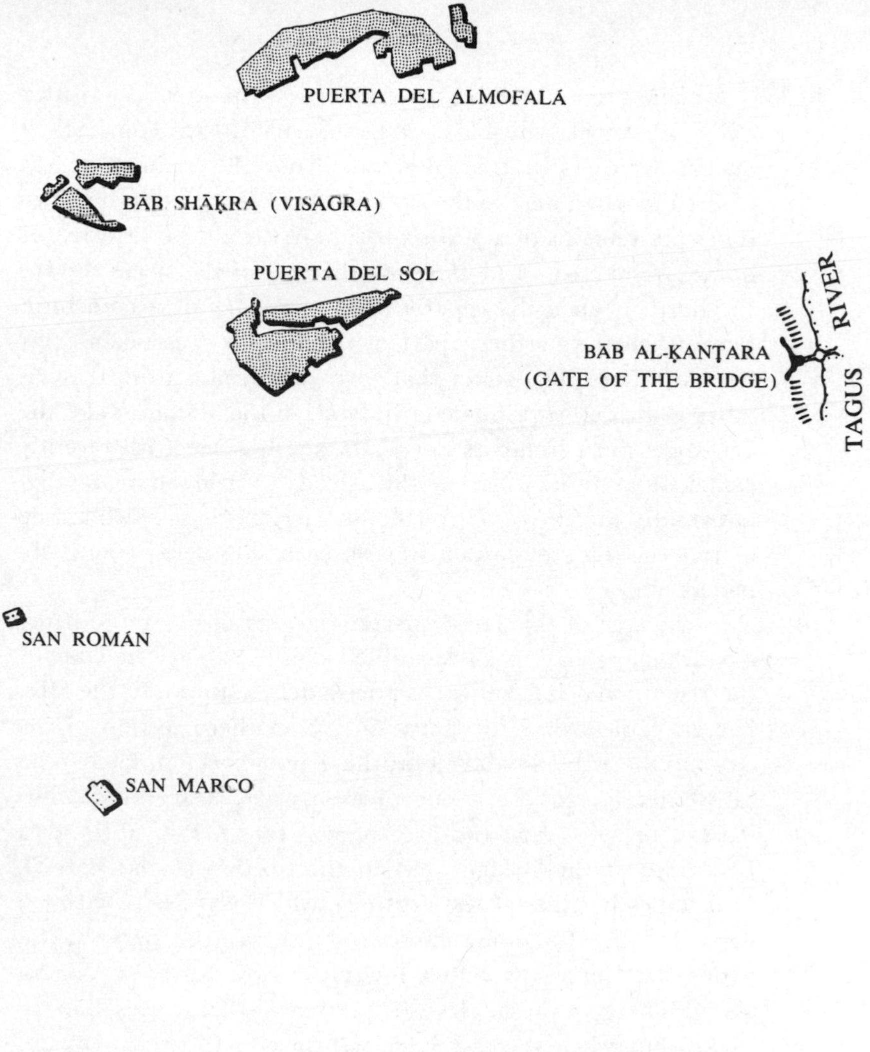

9. Calle Colegio de Doncellas
10. Calle de Arquillo de la Judería
11. Calle de la Judería

A main artery of the Jewish quarter was the street now called Calle del Angel, which is a continuation of San Tomé Street on the west. This street descends from the vicinity of the Church of San Tomé to the slope of the Tagus. Up to our own times the remains of a Jewish bathhouse could be seen in the houses numbered 13 to 15.[100] At the end of the street toward the north is an arch, apparently the remains of a gate built there when the northern part of the quarter was taken away from the Jews. The street that turns northward from there is called Calle del Arquillo de la Judería. At the midpoint of Calle del Angel there branches out to the south a street till recently called Calle de la Judería, which leads to a broad plaza that apparently was the center of the quarter and is called Plaza de la Judería. This plaza is a square, each side being twenty-six meters long.

In the area of this large quarter was one of the gates of the city, which in that epoch was called Bāb al-Yahūd (the Gate of the Jews); today it is known as Puerta del Cambrón. In the Moslem era Toledo had five gates. In the southern section of the city was the Bāb ad-dabbāghīn (the Tanners' Gate), later to be called del Fierro. At its northeast corner, near the famous Roman bridge, stood the gate named for it. Bāb al-Ḳanṭara (the Gate of the Bridge) and to the north was the Bāb al-Muḥādda (the Gate of the Fortress), which was destroyed by a flood in 1151. The most important gate was the Bāb Shaḳra, which the Christians called Puerta Visagra (the old Visagra Gate). The gate of the Jewish quarter was known as Bāb al-Maḳra but when the city later returned to Christian control the gate was renamed Puerta del Cambrón because of a thorn-bush seen in the gate's turret. Naturally, like the other gates, this one was repaired and replaced several times. The gate now standing, Puerta del Cambrón, was erected on ancient foundations in 1102.

Opposite this gate, outside the city, formerly stood an old

church that had been erected in the fourth century and named for the maiden Leocadia, who suffered martyrdom for her faith and was buried there. The Moslems destroyed the church, leaving only its foundations.[101] After the reconquest by the Christians it was rebuilt and is now known as Cristo de la Vega.

The Gate of the Jews was an important one since by means of it ties with the city and its vicinity to the northwest and the west were maintained. The Gate of San Martin has not yet been erected at that time.[102] Of course, besides the Gate of the Jews there was an additional link between the areas surrounding the city and the spacious sectors between the Gate of the Jews and the Tanners' Gate. North of the San Martin Bridge, which was erected at the beginning of the twelfth century, there was then a pontoon bridge, which was frequently demolished. A vestige of it is apparently the tower called Baño de la Cava, for according to a legend, King Roderick saw the daughter of Julian, the governor of Ceuta, bathing in the waters of the Tagus and fell in love with her.[103] Near this link was a fortress built by Governor 'Amrūs and later repaired in 836.[104] In any case, the Jewish quarter also included the entire northwest corner of the city, the area now known as Barrio de San Martin.[105]

The Jewish quarter in the west of the city was surrounded by a wall, which separated it from the other quarters of the city. This wall was constructed in 820 when Toledo's inhabitants raised the banner of revolt against the Omayyad emir. An Arabic source relates that the wall was built by order of the leader of the revolt, Muhādjir ibn al-Kaṭīl.[106] It had some entrances through which one passed from the Jewish to other quarters.[107] Within the Jewish quarter there was also a fortress for defense against sudden attacks. Mozarab documents of the twelfth and thirteenth centuries mention the fortress of the Jews on the Tagus River, it can thus be assumed that it actually stood on the river's bank, and that the Jewish quarter was narrowest at its southern edge. From there danger from the city itself lurked, since it looked out upon the hill of Montichel. From this it can be concluded that the fortress was in a corner of the Jewish quarter.[108]

For many generations the Jews of Toledo had in their western quarter a central synagogue called Bēt ha-k'nēset ha-gādōl. This synagogue, which went up in flames in 1250, was later rebuilt and existed until the Expulsion. But its site is unknown. In a Hebrew source from the Middle Ages there is mention of an old synagogue (the source refers to it as the ancient temple), but its location is also unknown.[109] However, two of the synagogues built in the Jewish quarter and later converted into churches still stand on their original sites. One of these is the synagogue between the Calle del Angel and the square of the Jewish quarter, which later became a church called Santa Maria la Blanca. At all times writers who were engaged in a study of the chronicles of the city expressed the view that before the construction of the present building, a synagogue stood in its place.[110] The new house of worship, in the view of some investigators, was built around 1200.[111] An inscription on a wooden tablet was discovered in Toledo, upon which is the following: "Its ruins were raised up in the year 4940 [1180 C.E.]." There are grounds to believe that the tablet originates from this house of worship; if this is indeed so, it is evidence that on this place a synagogue once stood during the period of Moslem rule. The expression "ruin" testifies to a destruction by violence, not by a natural phenomenon.[112].

The entire Jewish quarter was not one of trade. The Jewish merchants had shops in the center of the city, north of the Great Mosque, between which and the northern wall of the city was its commercial center. Mozarab documents of the twelfth and thirteenth centuries have much to say about the Jewish market called Alcaná, which was spread out in that area until the end of the fourteenth century, when the archbishop, Pedro Tenorio, removed the shops near the church (which had meantime become a cathedral), gave the Jews shops farther away from it, and built there the cloister and chapel of San Blas. The Alcaná was located between the Great Mosque and the market of the perfume merchants, and in the Moslem era its stores belonged to the *waḳf,* a foundation created by an endowed trust fund. The narrow street Calle del Hombre Palo, which runs from the cathedral northeastward, is an outstanding commercial street even today. From this street rise, in a northwesterly direction, side streets that link it with the Calle de Granada and the Plaza de San Jines. The first among these streets to the south is presently called Calle de la Sinagoga, so that its name reminds every passerby that this is a former Jewish neighborhood. This trade area, which had not merely shops but also some Jewish residences, was also fortified to some extent.[113]

Jewish merchants had many shops in other areas within the city. Near the large Jewish quarter in the west of the city, on its eastern flank, they had a special market, and it too was called the Alcaná.[114]

Even if no credence is given to legends, there is no doubt that Jews had lived in this ancient city of kings since early times. Both Christian writers and Jewish scholars were of the opinion that Jews had come to Toledo after the destruction of the first Temple.[115] Certainly during the Omayyad dynasty they made progress, advancing in the economic, social, and cultural scale. The extensive area of the Jewish quarter in the western region of the city testifies to the large size of the community. The livelihood of its people was indeed based on both labor and commerce. Yet there is no doubt that throughout the generations there were in the city many intellectuals who engaged in all branches of knowledge and devoted time to Jewish learning. In this large community there were wide circles of persons concerned with innovations by the grammarians, and especially with Hebrew verse, which flourished anew on Spanish soil.[116]

From among the various communities of Castile and Aragon there has come down to us authenticated information about two large communities in this era.

Greek and Roman writers mention the city of Bilbilis, southwest of Saragossa, as one of the important cities in Spain. After the country was conquered by the Romans, this city, which was surrounded on three sides by the Jalón River, became a support point for their army, since it was located along a military road that traversed Spain from the south and the west to the other side of the Ebro Valley in the northeast. The Arabs abandoned the city and built, some distance away to the west, a new city called Ḳal'at Ayyūb. This name has remained to the present day, except that the Spaniards changed its pronunciation into *Calatayud*. For the Arabs, too, this was an important support point on the road from the south to the Ebro Valley. The Arabs developed agriculture within the area, taught its inhabitants how to raise flax, and also raised grain in the city's environs, besides planting many vineyards.

However, Ḳal'at Ayyūb was not an important city until the end of the ninth century. In the last quarter of that century, the struggle between the Omayyads of Cordova and the rebels whose uprising threatened to break up the Moslem kingdom in Spain, members of the Banū Ḳasī were among the strongest local authorities, governors of Saragossa and Tudela. The Omayyad emir Muḥammad I, in opposition to them, gave his support to the Tudjībs, an Arab family that since the days of the Arab conquest had inhabited the region of the Jiloca River, which empties into the Jalón at Calatayud. The emir handed over to 'Abdarraḥmān b. 'Abdal'azīz, who was the head of that family, the governance of the entire region.

One of the first steps taken by this feudal chieftain was to

CALATAYUD
Jewish Quarter

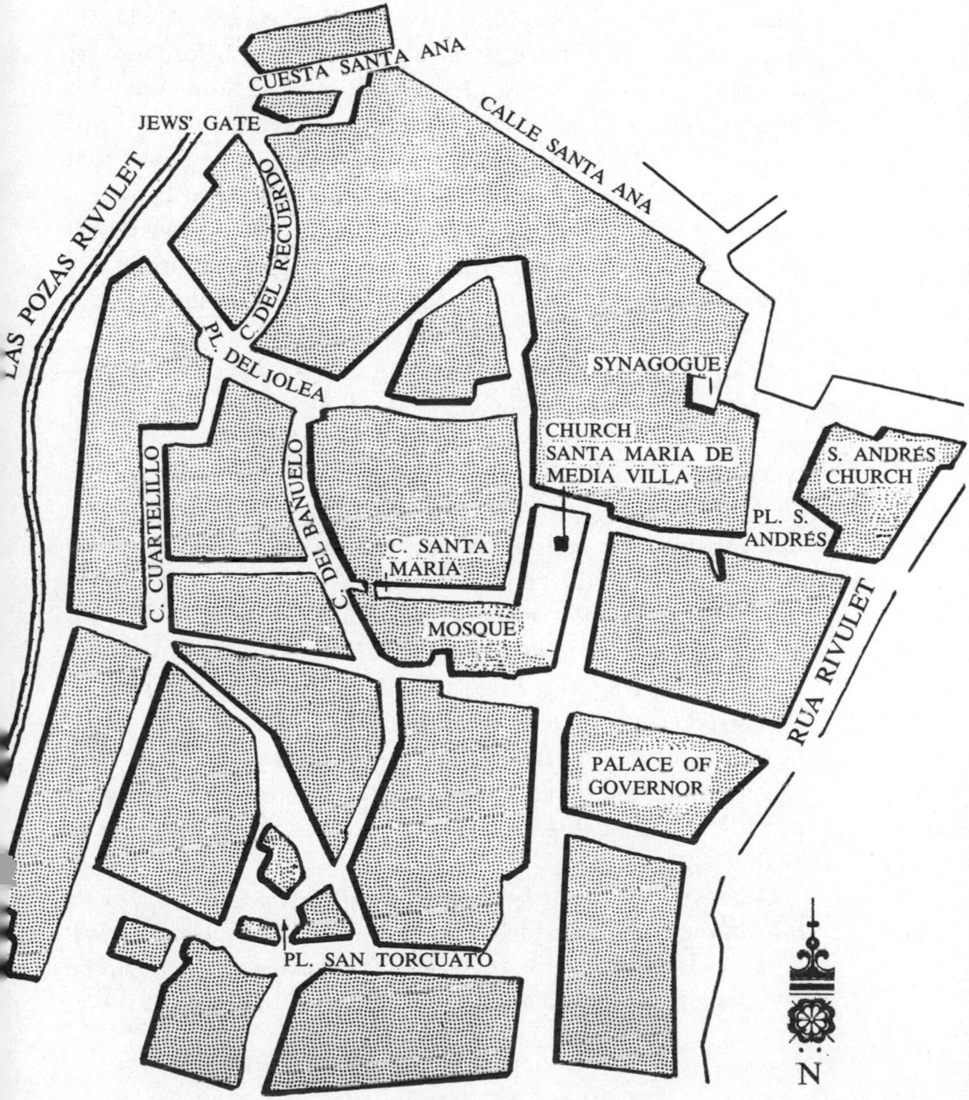

repair the fortifications of Calatayud, thereby turning it into a strong fortress. From then on the city began to flourish. A son of ʿAbdarraḥmān named Muḥammad al-Anḳar became the governor of Saragossa and another son, al-Mundhir, inherited from his father the cities of Calatayud and Daroca. Sulaimān, the son of al-Mundhir, rebelled against ʿAbdarraḥmān III; as a result the caliph, in 934, appeared before the city at the head of an army, defeated him, and appointed his brother Ḥakam as governor. The sons of Ḥakam also governed Calatayud and its environs,[117] and there can be no doubt that they were much concerned about the city, which had become a "family heirloom" over the generations. Arab writers report that among other things an industry developed within the city whose products were sold throughout all the Spanish provinces —products such as plates and other gilded tableware.

During the Omayyad dynasty many Jews resided in this city, and in time it had one of the most important communities in all of Spain. In 1882 a monument for a Jew named Samuel b. Solomon was found near Calatayud; he had died on the eleventh of Marḥeshvan in the year "280." The laborer who had engraved the inscription omitted the millennial year and even abbreviated the centuries. But there is almost no doubt that the date should read in its complete form: 4680. It follows then that this man, Samuel b. Solomon, died on October 9, 919.[118] During the long period of Jewish settlement in Calatayud many changes of government occurred, and at the beginning of the twelfth century the city fell to the Christians. But in spite of all these changes the Jews maintained their area of residence from the time of the caliphs to the end of the Middle Ages.

Calatayud was built between the Jalón River and a row of hills in the north on which a number of fortresses were erected. The most important of these was the fortress for which the city was named—Ḳalʿat Ayyūb, currently known as Plaza de Armas. This fortress was at the very center of the fortifications. On a hill west of the city stood a fortress in which the Christians, after conquering Calatayud, erected the Church de la Peña. East of this fortress, near the city wall, was the tower afterwards to be called Torre Mocha, while northeast of the city was a citadel which the Spaniards named Reloj Tonto. All these fortresses were linked together by protecting walls.

On the east and west the beds of two streams formed the natural boundaries of ancient Calatayud and near them stood the city's walls. The stream east of the city was called Rua and the stream on the west, Pozas. Near the eastern wall stood the chief mosque (today the Church of Santa Maria de Media Villa or Santa Maria la Colegiata) and near it, on the southeast, the governor's palace, which became the bishop's residence after the Christian reconquest.

The Mozarabs were removed by the Moslems from the midst of the city that lay between the walls and were resettled in neighborhoods east of the city, which were named for the churches of San Benito and Santo Sepulcro. These neighborhoods extended to the gate now known as the Saragossa Gate.[119]

The Jewish neighborhood was apparently always located in the city's northern section, which is its highest area. They dwelt in streets northwest of the chief mosque.[120] In this direction, extending from the Church of Santa Maria, runs the street now called Calle del Bañuelo, which ascends in a slight degree northward and becomes very narrow on its northern end.[121] On this street stood the house of the renowned Jewish family named Santangel, who converted to Christianity and played an important part in the political life of Spain at the end of the Middle Ages.[122] West of this street runs Calle Quartelillo, a street that runs parallel to the city wall. These two streets, which are connected by Para Street rising eastward, reach the Plaza Jolea, from which the Calle del Recuerdo, where the gate of the Jewish quarter was located, runs in a westerly line.[123]

To the northeast rises the steep slope Cuesta de Santa Ana, which leads to the Calle Santa Ana, which in turn crosses in a southeasterly direction from the top of a high hill, finally descending to the plaza before the Church of San Andrés. According to one tradition, Jews also resided on this street, at whose eastern end was the gate of the quarter and near it a synagogue. In a house on the western side of this street one can see, in a big hall, five arches, and it appears that at one time they extended into what is now a courtyard.[124] If the tradition that Jews also dwelt on the Calle Santa Ana atop the hill is indeed true, it must be concluded that the number of Jews in this city was quite large.

At all events, the area occupied by the Jews in the era of Moslem rule and in the first days of Christian dominance did not vary greatly, and the number of persons was always large. Testimony on this point can be found in the large number of families among those who left Spain who bear the name of Alcalay.[125] Within this large community were also many wealthy people and intellectuals.

In the Ebro Valley and in the entire region nearby there was for many generations the Jewish community within *Saragossa,* a community of the utmost importance.

The old Roman Caesarea Augusta became, under the Arabs, Saraḳusṭa, the chief town of the upper frontier. In the ninth century it was the capital of the Banū Ḳasī and later, from 890 onward, the family of the Banū Tudjīb succeeded there as virtually independent rulers.

But throughout this period the appearance of the city and its environs remained as fixed by the Romans. After the fashion of Roman cities, Saragossa was built in the shape of a rectangle whose two long sides were the Ebro River—which traverses nearby from northwest to southeast—and the wall paralleling it on the south. Within the walls were four chief gates: near the bridge spanning the river was the gate named for it; in the

SARAGOSSA
Jewish Quarter

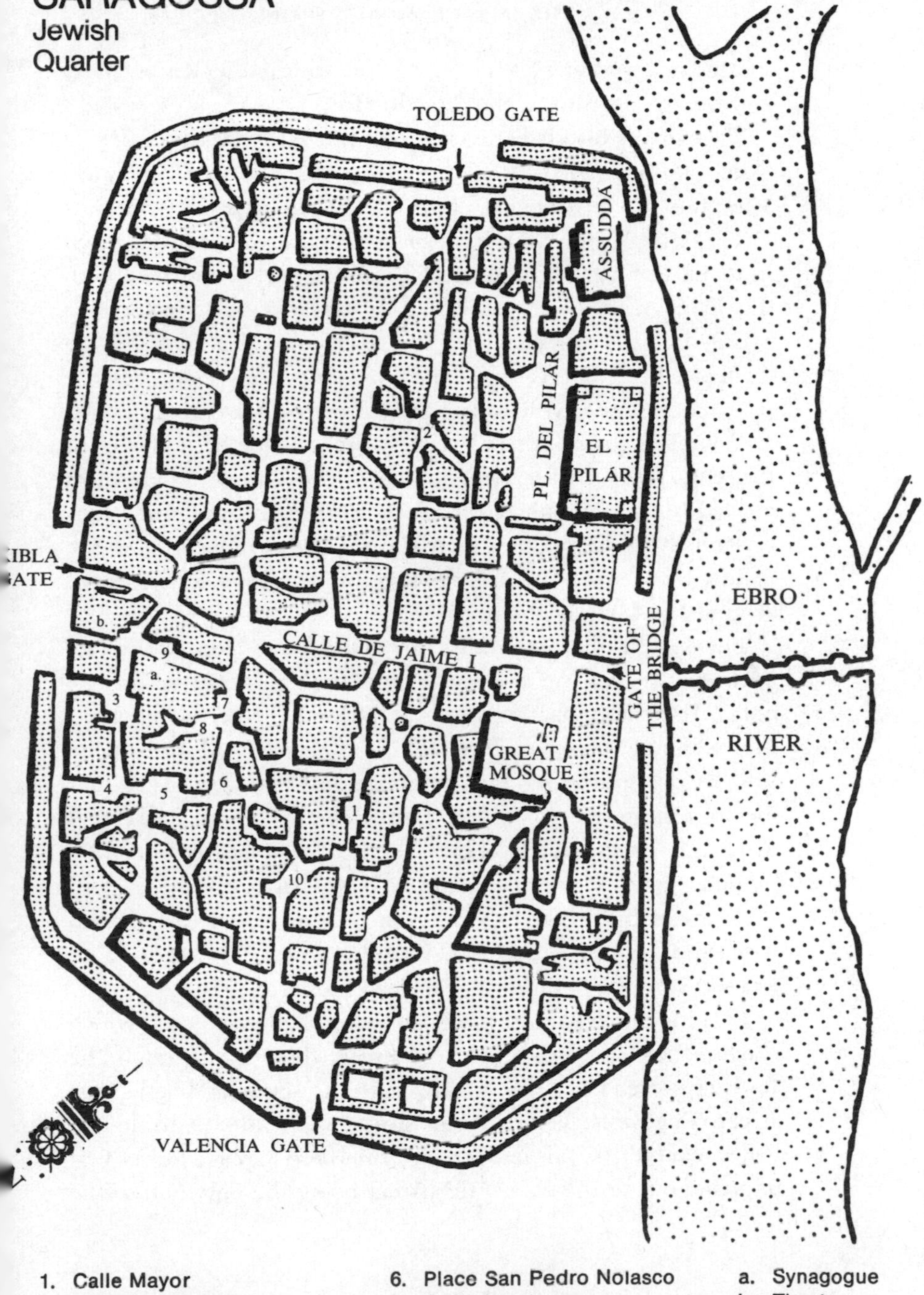

1. Calle Mayor
2. Calle Manifestación
3. Calle Veronica
4. Place Veronica
5. Calle San Pedro Nolasco
6. Place San Pedro Nolasco
7. Calle San Jorge
8. Calle Saporta
9. Calle San Andrés
10. Calle San Lorenzo

a. Synagogue
b. Theater

southeast, the Valencia Gate; to the south, the Ḳibla Gate; and on the northwest, the Toledo Gate.

Two streets bisected the city: one started from the Valencia Gate and extended to the Toledo Gate—the Decumanus Maximus of the Romans. This street still exists and is now called Calle Mayor in its eastern part and Calle Manifestación in its western part. The Gate of the Bridge was connected with the Ḳibla Gate by a street that is also extant today and is called Jaime I Street. This is the Cardo Maximus of the Romans. East of this street, not far from the river, was the principal mosque, which was later converted to a church named La Seo. The governor's palace stood in the northern corner of the city. This palace, which the Arabs called Sudda, was erected in the first half of the tenth century on the foundations of Roman buildings. Between the principal mosque and the Sudda was the quarter of the Mozarabs, who were concentrated around the Church of Pilár.[126]

The Jewish quarter was in the southeast section of the city between the wall on the south and the Calle Mayor on the north. Its border on the west was Jaime I Street. Three main thoroughfares traversed the Jewish quarter from the northwest to the southeast. The southernmost was the street that for four hundred years has been called Veronica Street.[127] From this street, which begins north of the theater currently located there, Romero (formerly San Cristóbal) Street and Peral Street branch out to the south, while on its eastern end it reaches a plaza which also bears the name Veronica. This was the site of the market of the Jewish quarter.[128]

Turning north from there is San Pedro Nolasco Street, which reaches the second of the three streets that run through the Jewish quarter from the northwest to the southeast: San Jorge Street. The western part of this street, once called Alto de San Pedro, extends to Jaime I Street. From here Saporta Street first branches out to the south, this street being the only one in the quarter bearing a Jewish name. This is in fact a common Spanish Jewish family name, and the street is named for a wealthy man of Jewish origin who had loaned a large sum of money to Emperor Charles V, for which he was honored with a title of nobility.[129] Behind it, in a more westerly direction, San Andrés Street turns southward; in derived its name from the church formerly located at the site, where later the house bearing the number 4 was erected.[130]

North of San Jorge, between Saporta and San Pedro Nolasco Streets, now stretches out the plaza, also called San Pedro Nolasco.[131] From it, going northward, runs Los Argensola Street (formerly Señales), linking it with the Calle Mayor. It appears that the Jewish quarter extended to Los Argensola Street;[132] however, the streets and houses between it and Jaime I Street did not belong to it. In this corner of the quarter stood a church called, in a document dated 1155, San Juan el Viejo, indicating that it already existed during the period of Moslem rule.[133]

The third of those streets which cut through the Jewish quarter was the one now named San Lorenzo. This was the last street in the north of the quarter, since the Calle Mayor was beyond its boundary. At its eastern end, this street extended to the walls of the city.

Between the Jewish quarter and the other districts of Saragossa there was, as in other Spanish cities, an inner wall penetrated by gates to permit communication between the various districts. It can be surmised that at the time of Moslem rule, as in later periods, there were passageways such as these at the western end of Veronica Street[134] and in the vicinity of the eastern end of San Lorenzo Street. The fixing of the passage ways at these points not only enabled the Jews to reach the Moslem neighborhood, but also linked their quarter with the city's gates.

In the southern corner of the Jewish quarter a fortress stood.

Sources dating from the end of the Middle Ages provide a detailed description of it. The account given there reports that the fortress had seven turrets, one of them being atop the main entrance.[135] During riots the fortress served as a refuge for the inhabitants of the quarter, and when tranquil times prevailed, it was used as a storehouse.[136] Near the fortress, on the western side, was a gate within the wall called the Gate of the Jewish Quarter. Its site was on a street later called Hiedra, which, following changes in the array of nearby structures, has now disappeared.[137] Over the gate were inscriptions in Hebrew.[138]

Northeast of the fortress stood, from early times, the principal synagogue of the Jews of Saragossa. It was situated where later a seminary for priests was erected, which is still there. The house of worship was thus located, as in other cities, near the city's wall, at that place in the Jewish quarter farthest away from Moslem neighborhoods.[139] No doubt there were other synagogues in Saragossa during Moslem rule. One of these was at the western end of the Jewish quarter, the structure later to become the Church of San Andrés.[140] The southern corner of the quarter served as its center of the various activities for the entire sector. There the meat markets were located, and before being slaughtered the animals were kept in the fortress.[141]

The Jewish quarter was quite literally a quarter, for in area it was approximately one-fourth of the city of Saragossa located between the ancient walls. From this, conclusions can be drawn as to the number of Jews then residing in the city. It no doubt reached several thousand. The Christian-Latin literature of those days provides us with testimony concerning the importance of the Jewish community of Saragossa at the outset of the Moslem epoch. During the time of the governors appointed by the caliphs at Damascus (the *wālīs*), namely, in the first half of the eighth century, there lived in Toledo a Mozarab priest called Evanzio. This priest had written an epistle against "the wicked Christians" in the province of Saragossa who had come under Jewish influence and believed that the blood of animals was forbidden.[142] The writing of this epistle proves how great the influence of the Jews was over their neighbors.

In the large Jewish community of Saragossa there were, of course, people who earned their livelihood from many varied occupations. Saragossa was an important industrial city, and the manufacture of textiles and other branches of industry connected with tanning flourished. Many made their living from these industries, and their products—shoes, boots, saddles of all kinds, purses, and the like—were highly regarded. In these occupations, and particularly in shoe manufacture, the Jews of Saragossa were no doubt engaged throughout the generations.[143] There were many Saragossa Jews who were artisans, and many who engaged in commerce. The Jewish merchants came into contact with other countries and were successful in their ventures.

IV

In the cities and towns of northeastern Spain were to be found, from earliest times, many Jewish settlements. Except for Andalusia, this was the region of densest Jewish settlement. In the Roman age there were many of cities here whose livelihood depended on industry and trade with other countries. Jewish communities, which had gathered into these cities in the days of the Roman Empire, continued their existence in the Visigothic epoch; but the conquest of the country by the Arabs brought a new prosperity to the Jewish settlements. Even when the Christians succeeded in regaining control of some of the provinces, the Jews were not expelled from them. This unbroken Jewish settlement, which was unusual even in Spain, can only be explained by the fact that the various rulers needed the Jews, especially because they maintained close economic and even political ties with the inhabitants of the southern provinces of Gaul.

Barcelona was always one of the important cities in this region. This was an ancient Iberian city that later became a Roman support point; but in Visigothic times it twice became, for a short period, the capital of the whole of Spain. Arab dominion over Barcelona, which they called Barshelūna, lasted only for three generations, a period that was not a happy one for the city. Because of the proximity of the Frankish kingdom, it was open to incursions; moreover, the distance between it and the center of the Moslem government in Andalusia caused the local governors to aspire to independence and even to enter into negotiations with the Frankish kings, proclaiming themselves to be their vassals.

In 801 Barcelona was taken by Louis the Pious, who was then king of southern Gaul, thereby ending the era of Arab dominion over the city and its environs. According to an old tradition, the Jews helped the Arabs to take the city;[144] but since there is no trustworthy evidence to support such a report, we must treat it with much skepticism. Inasmuch as it was known that Jews did give the Arab conquerors aid in a number of places, there was a tendency in other places to charge them with bringing about Moslem control over former Christian regions. But perhaps we can conclude from this tradition that at the time of the Arab conquest Jews did dwell in Barcelona.

However, another consideration also obliges us to accept the existence of a Jewish community in Barcelona during Moslem rule in the eighth century. As is apparent from the exchange of letters, both questions and answers, between the Jews of Spain and the *g'ōnīm* of Babylonia, during the ninth century the community of Barcelona was a religio-spiritual center for the other communities in this part of Spain. We cannot assume that the conquering Franks brought Jews to the places they captured and that in a short interval a large community was thus assembled. But the Jews who dwelt in Barcelona at the beginning of the ninth century no doubt were, for the most part, already residents of the city whom the Franks did not disturb, since they did not want to empty it of inhabitants.

Barcelona, today a bustling metropolis with a population of two million, was in those days a small city. The shape of the city was roughly a hexagon whose southeastern side extended the length of the seashore. The city was encompassed by a wall the Romans had built, remnants of which are still visible today. Anyone emerging from the Plaza de Cataluña, the noisy hub of traffic in modern Barcelona, who turns toward the southeast in the direction of the cathedral, will see, to the right of the splendid church, two strong towers, atop which dwellings for priests were built. Here formerly stood one of the four Roman city gates—the northwestern gate.

The street that starts at this spot leads to the Plaza San Jaime, which serves as the center of a block of dark and narrow streets, fortified palaces, and small squares. This is the old Barcelona. From the Plaza San Jaime runs, in a southwesterly direction, the Calle del Cal (Community Street). In the later Middle Ages this was the main thoroughfare of the Jewish neighborhood and was therefore named Cal Mayor. This street winds along until it reaches the New Baths Street (Calle de los Baños Nuevos), which issues from the Fernando VII Street and turns northward. In the era of Christian dominance, the Jewish neighborhood spread out between the Calle de los Baños Nuevos and the street called San Honorato, which runs parallel to it on the east. Near to this street and parallel to it there is a street whose name is currently Santo Domingo del Cal, but in the Middle Ages was known as Calle de la Sinagoga Mayor, since the Great Synagogue stood on it.[145]

But when the Arabs still ruled over the city—and the ancient church upon whose site the cathedral was later erected served as a mosque—the Jewish residential area was not confined to these few streets. Then the Jewish quarter apparently extended to the western city wall. Even in the ninth century, when the number of Christian inhabitants was still small, the Jews were not compelled to move from the vicinity of the wall.[146] The Jewish cemetery was south of the city, on the slopes of the mountain that is still called the Jewish Mountain (Montjuich). There many monuments bearing inscriptions from the later Middle Ages could be found. Other monuments were removed from the mountain after the Jews were expelled from the city and were used as stones in the construction of buildings.

But among the Jewish monuments that were found in Barcelona there is one with an inscription whose ancient letters, in the view of the experts, point to its having been engraved in the eighth century, after the Arab conquest. This monument, which was apparently brought to the city from Montjuich, had already been used for such a purpose even before the Hebrew inscription was engraved upon it, for the remains of a Latin inscription were discovered on it.[147] This discovery constitutes an additional proof that a Jewish community existed in Barcelona during the period of Arab dominion in the eighth century.

Tarragona, south of Barcelona, changed hands several times. The town was taken by Louis the Pious in 808 and soon evacuated. Tarragona was a border town located in a region where dominion constantly changed hands. Sometimes it was abandoned by its Moslem inhabitants. In about 950 the town came into the possession of the Christians,[148] a report confirmed by Johannes of Gorze.[149] Even Ibn Ḥauḳal, who visited Spain in the middle of the tenth century, says that Tortosa was the last town the Moslems held on the eastern coast of Spain.[150] But some years later Tarragona once again fell to the Moslems.

Thus many changes and vicissitudes befell the city and, together with the city itself, its Jewish inhabitants. The Jewish settlement in Tarragona was very old. Apparently a large Jewish community was established in the city in Roman times, continuing its existence during the Visigothic epoch. Jews also resided in the towns and villages in the vicinity in those days. Jewish inscriptions discovered in Tarragona and its vicinity are evidence of this, some being in Latin and some in three languages: Hebrew, Latin, and Greek.[151]

When the city was captured by the Arabs many of its inhabitants were slain, and thereafter the Christian element in the city grew weaker; but on the other hand, it appears that not many of the Arabs settled in Tarragona.[152] However, the number of Jews continued to grow steadily during the period of Arab dominance. It grew both actually and relatively. It is possible that many of the Jews who had helped the Moslems take Barcelona in the 850s later feared the vengeance of the Christians and fled to the sphere of Moslem rule, settling in nearby Tarragona.[153]

No doubt many of the Jews of Tarragona earned their living from trade, mainly from marketing the argicultural products of the area, which was noted for its fertility. They also had trade contacts with the inhabitants of Barcelona and Christian cities in the north. In any event, in the later periods of Moslem dominion over Tarragona it was considered a Jewish city. Arabic geographers maintain that at that time the Jews constituted the majority in Tarragona, but that only a small number of Christians dwelt there.[154] But since life in that city was so hard, each man being preoccupied with his daily problems, the members of the community did not take an active part in the life of the large Jewish community in Spain, and there were not to be found among them men of literary repute—with the result that there is no mention of their community in literary sources until the end of the caliphal era.

In the days when the Jews constituted the most important element in the populace of Tarragona, they dwelt in most of the streets of the upper city, which was encircled by a wall, northeast of the area that is currently built up (but not on the hill where the governor's fortress and the mosque stood and where the archbishop's palace and the cathedral now stand). As time went by, the area occupied by the Jews steadily became smaller as they were crowded more and more into the southern edge of the city. The area of their residence in this part of Tarragona is well known from many documents.

The chief entrance into the city from the east was the gate today known as San Antonio. Emerging from it and running in a southwesterly direction the length of the wall is En Granada Street, and, paralleling it, En Talavera Street, Santa Ana Street, and Nazareth Street traversed the city. All these streets extend to the Plaza del Rey in the west.

In the later Middle Ages, when the number of the Jews of Tarragona had diminished, they occupied only the southern part of En Granada Street, (which in those days was called Judería or Jews' Street), the street that paralleled it, En Talavera, and some of the back streets in this area. At the beginning of the Jews' Street, at its northern end, there was a small gate in the city wall, and in the middle of En Talavera Street was a plaza known as the Plaza of the Jewish Neighborhood.[155] On the slope outside the southern wall, above a strip of the coast named Playa del Milagro (the Miracle Coast) (or, more exactly, near the road called Camino de los Fortins), was the location, over many generations, of the cemetery of the Jews of Tarragona. There one could find tombstones bearing Hebrew inscriptions dating from the Middle Ages.[156]

Tortosa, south of Tarragona, was in that period a rich and populous town. It was a commercial town whose inhabitants traded with all provinces of Spain and with the Christian countries in the north.

Jews had dwelt in this city, too, long before the Arabs conquered it. The gravestone of a Jewish woman was discovered bearing an inscription in three languages: Hebrew, Latin, and Greek; it was apparently engraved in the sixth century C.E.[157] Perhaps the Jews dwelt, even in the days of the Roman Empire, in the northern part of the city, which was their neighborhood during the Moslem era. In the eastern part of the city there was a fortress (at present the fortress of San Juan stands there), and north of it was the neighborhood still called by its ancient name: Remolins. Farther north, northeast of the Remolins quarter, lay the Jewish neighborhood, and to this day the names of some of the streets in that district bring to mind their earlier inhabitants. Here is to be found a street called Jerusalen, as well as a lane and a passageway known by this name.[158] East of the city wall was the Jewish cemetery.[159]

The number of Jews in Tortosa was considerable, inasmuch as the city provided many opportunities for earning a livelihood. Some Tortosan Jews engaged in the large-scale commerce that was concentrated within the city, and derived from it a fine living. But just as many Arab intellectuals who were preoccupied with all the branches of their culture dwelt in this opulent city, so too there were Torah scholars and all manner of intellectuals among the Jews of Tortosa. The majority of the Jews of Tortosa were very pious and heedful of both positive and negative precepts in Jewish law.

Characteristic of the Tortosan Jews' way of life during that period is the question they directed to a revered rabbi, referred to with brevity in the source we have before us as "Rabbi Mōshē Gaon," who is probably Moses b. Ḥanōkh.[160] An inhabitant of Tortosa named David had reached the city on the Sabbath in a boat that had traveled upon the Ebro River. The sailors brought it near the shore, but when David's friends came to greet him, they were apprehensive of going aboard. Finally—so it is related in the question on which the rabbi was asked to pronounce judgment—David held that it was permissible for them to enter the boat because it was very close to shore (so that one could stand near it in the water without having to swim). The rabbi speaks with much respect about this David, and tries to explain David's view, which the Tortosan Jews found satisfactory, so that it would harmonize with the law forbidding entrance to a boat on the Sabbath, unless it has been drawn up out of the deep waters and placed on dry land and thus for practical purposes is not floating on the water. He held that the sailors had no doubt done this and that it merely seemed to David's friends that the boat was afloat.

Both question and answer testify not only about the strict observance by the Jews of Tortosa but also as to how well versed they were in the laws of the Gemara. It was from this community that emerged the first grammarian among the Jews of Spain whose literary work has come down to us. M'naḥem Ben Sārūḳ was a Tortosan, and when he lost favor with Ḥasdai Ibn Shaprūṭ, he returned to his native city; it was there that that lord found him when he determined to punish him.[161]

Besides the scholars devoted to the study of Jewish law, there were, among the Jews of Tortosa, intellectuals who had a strong desire for secular learning. In the generation of M'naḥem Ben Sārūḳ, such a Jewish scholar lived in Tortosa who is known to us through the writings of Arabic geographers. His name was Ibrāhīm b. Ya'ḳūb, but the Arabic writers added the surname al-Isrā'īlī or aṭ-Ṭurṭūshī, or both.[162] Ibrāhīm received an excellent education and was especially diligent in his study of the natural sciences. After the manner of intellectuals of those days, he did not devote himself to one field, but constantly read many books on various branches of science, finding something of interest in all of them. It is true that two areas especially attracted him: medicine, which was the profession of such intellectuals at that time, and even more than medicine, the study of geography.

After the inhabitants of the caliphal empire became acquainted with Greek science and learned to arrange their knowledge systematically, the intellectuals were prompted to collect historical, ethnographic, and geographical information concerning the colossal Islamic Empire. Arab scholars, particularly geographers, did not rely on information transmitted to them by others, but undertook long journeys by sea and on land to become acquainted at first hand with many countries. Contemporary with Ibrāhīm b. Ya'ḳūb were al-Mas'ūdī, who made a circuit of all the countries of western Asia, also visiting India and East Africa; al-Muḳaddasī, from Jerusalem, who toured almost all the Islamic countries; and Ibn Ḥauḳal, who combined his investigative travels with geographical research.

Naturally, the geographers' thirst for knowledge was whetted by unknown regions in non-Moslem countries, and during the tenth century Arab scholars went forth on travels to various non-Moslem lands and wrote special treatises about them. In 921 Caliph al-Muḳtadir sent a mission to the Bulgar king on the banks of the Volga. One of the members of this mission was Aḥmad b. Faḍlān, who, on his return, wrote a comprehensive description of the countries through which he had traveled. Twenty years later the ruler of Bukhara added an Arabic writer and poet, Abū Dulaf, to an Uiguric mission which was about to return to its homeland, and he too described his travels in a very important treatise.

In that period a caliph who was absorbed in matters of science and literature ascended the throne at Cordova, al-Ḥakam II. This cultural ruler supported intellectuals and encouraged scholars to write books, a particular aim of his being to enlarge his library and enrich it with precious manuscripts. Ibrāhīm b. Ya'ḳūb, the Jewish scholar of Tortosa, went to Cordova, the capital of the Omayyad kingdom in Spain. Aided by the recommendations of right-minded advocates, he found the palace gate open to him and was received by the caliph. His knowledge impressed the ruler, and he joined a group of scholars that found itself at home in the royal court. When he told al-Ḥakam of his interest in geography and said that he had already traveled through the Christian kingdoms in the northern part of the Iberian peninsula, the idea occurred to the king to send a scholarly mission to the unknown countries of Europe, with Ibrāhīm b. Ya'ḳūb at its head. Al-Ḥakam was of the opinion that since other kings sent scholars to the countries of the infidels so that they could describe them, it was unseemly for a ruler as interested in the sciences as he was not to follow the same course. For was not his kingdom located at the very end of the Moslem world, with a long border and many ties with the Christian kingdoms?

From the days of his youth al-Ḥakam had been interested in the history and geography of the lands north of the Pyrenees. Al-Mas'ūdī states that when he was in Egypt in 948, he found a book about the history of the Franks written by a Frankish bishop for al-Ḥakam in 940.[163] Thus it is not surprising that he wanted to take advantage of the abilities and knowledge of the Jew of Tortosa. Little time passed before the thought was translated into action. Ibrāhīm b. Ya'ḳūb got letters from the caliph that were designated for various rulers of western Europe, one in particular being intended for the German emperor Otto I. In these letters al-Ḥakam explained the scientific goals of the journey and requested that all possible aid be extended to his emissary. The caliph also provided Ibrāhīm with an escort and servants to attend to his needs during the journey.

Ibrāhīm first went to France, reaching the coast of the channel that lies between France and England. We learn this from an Arabic geographer who recounts what Ibrāhīm b. Ya'ḳūb saw in Rouen.[164] The chief goal of Ibrāhīm was to describe central Europe, concerning which the Arabs knew little.

Therefore he traveled continuously eastward and reached Germany. After a long journey, he arrived in 966[165] at the royal court of Emperor Otto I and was received by him with honor. The Saxon emperor welcomed the Jewish scholar graciously, showed interest in his mission, and held long conversations with him. Ibrāhīm b. Ya'ḳūb recounts a tale he heard from the emperor concerning a women's state in the vicinity of Prussia. These women would go forth to battle—so went the account of Otto the Great—and become pregnant by the male captives they took; but they would slay the male children they bore.

Ibrāhīm also reports that the emperor expressed the wish to send an emissary to the caliph in Cordova in order to put a request to him. He had heard—so he told the Jew—that near the city of Lorca, in southeast Spain, the bones of a saint were hidden in a church and near them stood an olive tree that gave fruit the day after it blossomed. The emperor told him that he strongly desired to receive the bones of that saint, which worked miracles, and would deem it a great privilege if the caliph were to prompt the clergy of that church to give them to him.[166] As a final gesture, the emperor gave Ibrāhīm permission to tour his land to his heart's desire and go wherever he chose; he gave him written documents so that the authorities would not place obstacles in his way.

Ibrāhīm made use of the permission granted him, touring the length and breadth of Germany; everywhere he was aided by both secular and clerical authorities to an even greater degree than heretofore. He visited the cities of Mainz and Fulda[167] and also the province of Schleswig, far to the north.[168] Thereafter[109] he went to Bohemia, reaching as far as Prague. In those days this city was an important meeting place for merchants of eastern and western Europe. Here merchants from Slavic countries and Hungary and merchants from western Germany came together, particularly since Prague served as a major market for the slave trade.

Ibrāhīm reports on the industries in the city and its great

commerce and enumerates the members of various nations who met there. His account gives the impression that he did not continue his travels toward the East. What he relates about Poland (the land of Duke Mieszko) does not indicate a personal impression of that kingdom, but he was, at all events, the first travel writer to mention this Slavic country.[170] As for his account concerning the Bulgars (on the Danube), he himself notes that he never was in their country but merely heard about them from emissaries of their king whom he saw in Magdeburg.[171] It can be safely presumed also that his account of the Serbo-Croatians is not based on a visit to their country, but came to him indirectly.

At all events, this was a very long journey for a man from Moslem Spain, a real journey of discovery. Throughout his wanderings Ibrāhīm kept notes, which he then joined into a complete and comprehensive description of his travels. After his return to Spain, he presented this work to the Omayyad caliph at Cordova.[172] From the fragments of his travel account that have come down to us, it is evident that Ibrāhīm b. Ya'ḳūb was endowed with a fine gift for observation and a nice critical sense. Whereas men of those days were inclined to write all sorts of fantastic tales (the Arabs called these stories *'adjā' īb*), especially when they told about faraway, unknown lands, Ibrāhīm was very circumspect in his account. The only tale of this sort that he included in his travel descriptions (as far as we know) is his account of the Amazonian state—but he included a qualifying note that he was reporting this story because he had heard it from the emperor himself.

What is particularly exceptional in the descriptions by Ibrāhīm is the characteristic scope of his interest. After the manner of the Arabic geographers, he gives the distance between cities and gathers information pertaining to the natural phenomena of the countries of eastern and central Europe; nor does he omit a description of living phenomena. He describes the inhabitants of those countries from their anthropological aspect, telling about their customs and manner of livelihood. His concern with economic problems is very great. He gives an account of the yield of fields and gardens, of coins, of prices of merchandise, and of methods of trading. He also gives information about the religious life of the peoples of central Europe. This Tortosan Jew describes in detail a large church in the city of Fulda[173] and discusses the Slavic translation of the New Testament. But his interest was particularly evident in respect to the diet of the various peoples and their systems of therapy for illnesses—a valid testimony to his profession: medicine.

In his long journeys Ibrāhīm also met Jews. How great was the joy of this Spanish Jew, who crossed over high mountain ridges and arid plains and wore his feet out pounding rough roads for weeks and months among people whose language he did not know and whose religion was alien to his spirit, when he suddenly came upon his own people, who worshiped God exactly as he did. No doubt they reminded him of his own beloved kin at home in Spain, and his joy was very great. He reports on Jews who came to Prague and mentions a Jewish family near the German city of Nineburg on the Saale.[174]

But the non-Jewish writers who cited him were, understandably, not interested in such details, and it may also be doubted whether he himself found it appropriate to mention every such contact in a report destined for a Moslem ruler. On the other hand, the description of his travels provided for the Arabic geographers a never-failing source of information about the countries of central Europe, and they quoted him—at times mentioning his name and at others making no mention of it whatsoever.[175] They also depended upon him for a description of Christian Spain.[176]

The community of Tortosa, from which M'naḥem Ben Sārūḳ and Ibrāhīm b. Ya'ḳūb emerged, as early as the tenth century produced that type of Jew, familiar in the later centuries of the Middle Ages, who was loyal to his faith and his people, yet at the same time at home in the general culture and permeated with the scientific spirit. It is surely no accident that the first Hebrew grammarian among the Jews of Spain and the traveling geographer came from this community situated on the border between the Moslem and the Christian kingdoms.

V

The number of Jews in the west of the Iberian peninsula was much smaller than in the south and in the region of the Ebro, even as the entire settlement there was much less dense. The number of Arabs who went to settle in those regions was not large either, because a considerable part of the area was arid and because in those days these regions were far from the routes of important trade. Nevertheless, there were many communities in these provinces, some of them large. But because they were remote from centers of the group life of Spanish Jewry, these communities were rather isolated. Yet they adhered to the tradition and also fostered sacred study insofar as they could.

The most important community of all the western provinces of the peninsula was that of the city of *Mérida.* Nowadays it is a small and forsaken city, with few inhabitants and no vitality. But at one time Mérida was a big city with a large population. The city, which lies on the right bank of the Guadiana River, was founded in 23 B.C.E. by the Roman emperor Augustus as a colony for soldiers who had completed their term of service (*emeriti*); hence it was called Emerita Augusta. The colony became a large city and the capital of the entire western part of the peninsula—or, as it was then called, Lusitania.

The remains of the splendid edifices erected by the Romans

in Mérida excited the enthusiasm of the Arabs even in the later Middle Ages—so much so that they used the beautiful marble columns they found there to embellish the palaces they built in other cities, particularly Cordova. The walls with which the Romans encircled the city were very strong, and it is no coincidence that this city defended itself against the Arab conquerors for many months. The Arabs made Mérida the chief city of the "lower border region"; that is to say, they located the headquarters of the western provinces within the city. But the stream of Arab immigration to Mérida was a weak one. Many Berbers took up residence in the vicinity of the city; in the city proper a strong Christian community remained.[177]

However, most of the inhabitants were *muwalladūn*: those Christians who became Moslems and regarded themselves discriminated against by the arrogant Arabs, who boasted of their family lineage. Hence Mérida became a focal point of rebellion. In the first half of the ninth century the inhabitants of Mérida were involved in successive uprisings, so that the emirs of Cordova were compelled to march west at the head of their troops from time to time and besiege the rebellious city. On orders from 'Abdarraḥmān II, one of those fortresses known in Spain as al-Ḳaṣaba was erected in 835 to serve as barracks for the garrison. This fortress, which stood on the banks of the river near the magnificent Roman bridge, was noted for its thick walls, and the Omayyad government was of the opinion that thenceforth it would not have to fear any new rebellions by the inhabitants of the city. But in the days of Emir Muḥammad I the people of Mérida once again raised the standard of rebellion, and when they were reduced to submission, the emir ordered the destruction of the city's fortifications, except for the fortress. This marked the start of the decline of the city. Many inhabitants refused to dwell in an unwalled city and moved elsewhere—particularly since at this very time a new city was developing a short distance from Mérida, which became the center for the entire region: Badajoz.[178]

The Jews had dwelt in Mérida from ancient times; according to legend they had arrived there immediately after the destruction of the second Temple. A Spanish-Jewish historian of the twelfth century reports that when "Titus conquered Jerusalem, his commander who was in charge of Spain appealed to him to send him some of the nobles of Jerusalem, and he sent some, among them being a man named Baruch who knew how to make curtains and was skilled in silkcraft. They stayed on in Mérida, begot children there, and became a large community in Mérida."[179] From this folkloristic tradition it may be concluded that from days of old there were many artisans in Mérida who were engaged in the manufacture of silk. It is certain that a Jewish community existed in the city in the days of the Visigoths,[180] and when Mérida was taken by the Arabs, this community continued to develop. Many gravestones have been discovered in Mérida bearing Latin inscriptions, and among them are the gravestones of Jews. One of these inscriptions was engraved—judging from certain indications—in the eighth century, that is, at the beginning of the Arabic era.[181]

In the second half of that century and in the first half of the ninth, Mérida had a large Jewish community, which was the chief community of all the provinces in the western part of the peninsula. The leaders of the Mérida community had supreme juridical authority over all these communities.[182] Within the community there was an especially prominent family, Ibn Bālia, that traced its descent from the aforementioned curtain-weaver, Baruch, who came first to Mérida.[183] When Saadya Gaon addressed a circular letter to the Jews of southern Spain, he mentioned, among others, the community of Mérida.[184] But by that time Mérida's importance had waned, and many members of the Jewish community had left the city and gone elsewhere.

The report of a Jewish historian of the twelfth century runs thus: because of war Mérida was destroyed, and the forefathers of Isaac, namely, Ibn Bālia, went into exile to take up residence in Cordova. Other sources mention more individuals and families who did likewise.[185] Although the city waned and the exodus was evident, however, the Mérida community did not fall apart, but continued its existence for several more centuries—until the Expulsion toward the end of the fifteenth century.[186]

Over the many generations that a Jewish community existed in this city, it had its own quarter, near the Church of Santa Catalina. This house of worship was once a synagogue but became a church after the Expulsion.[187] North of the city the Jews had a cemetery above the Panicaliente Mill, not far from the Albarregas River. Some time later this site was called Cortinal del Osario.[188]

From time immemorial Jews dwelt also in the cities and villages of those westernmost provinces of the peninsula, which were later to constitute the kingdom of Portugal. One of the oldest communities in these regions was that of *Béja*. This is one of the oldest cities on the Iberian peninsula, and the Arabic geographers are of the opinion that this was the first city to be built in Andalusia.[189] Béja was indeed an important city in Roman times, and even today it is encircled by the remains of the Roman wall. After the spread of Christianity on the peninsula, it became an ecclesiastical center and the seat of the bishop; during Moslem rule it was also the chief city of the province.

A Jewish settlement existed in the city over many generations. In his book concerning the conquest of Spain by the Arabs, Rodrigo Jimenez de Rada, the archbishop of Toledo, states that Mūsā b. Nuṣair, on conquering Seville, populated it with Jews and Arabs and thereafter attacked Béja, where he employed the same method.[190] Even though it is not true that Mūsā was the conqueror of Béja, there is no reason to doubt the information concerning the assigning of Jews to guard duty or about their being found in Béja. The Jewish community, no doubt, continued its existence throughout the time of the region's domination by the Arabs, who named it al-Gharb: the West (its southern portion even now is called Algarve).

When the region was restored to Christian authority and the kingdom of Portugal established, Béja was one of the first cities to receive from King Alfonso I writs of privilege in which the statutes applicable to the Jews were set down.[191] What the Christian chronicler reports about the settlement of Arabs in the city also agrees with the established facts, for Béja and its environs were one of the districts in which many Arabs settled.[192]

9

TOWARD THE END OF THE TENTH CENTURY

I

All the Jewish communities in Spain regarded Moses b. Ḥanōkh as their cultural and religious leader, heeded his every utterance, and conducted themselves in accordance with his judgments. It therefore struck them like a thunderbolt out of a clear sky to learn that this great rabbi had died. This occurred in approximately 970 C.E., after he had served for many years as chief judge and head of the Talmud school at Cordova. In every community the rabbi was eulogized with aching hearts and a pall of gloom, and he was mourned for many days. All the Jews of Spain felt that they had suffered an irreplaceable loss, because the deceased rabbi was a man of authority who contributed stability to the Jewish community in Spain and enhanced its honor throughout all Jewry.

The days of lamentation passed and it was necessary to fill the place of the departed rabbi. Before long this matter became a subject of great contention, arousing strong emotions. Moses b. Ḥanōkh had produced many disciples, but among them were only two scholars really deserving of the distinguished post, who also had supporters and a following.

One of them was Ḥanōkh b. Moses, the son of the deceased rabbi. Ḥanōkh, who was still a boy when brought to Spain, studied at his father's Talmud school, becoming one of his outstanding disciples. He dedicated all his time to the study of the oral law, becoming familiar with its lore; he was also present when disputes were put to his father, thus learning from him to render judgment by a practical application of the law. It is true that his education was one-sided, inasmuch as he confined himself all his days to the limited field of halakha, without any deviation therefrom. In character he was like his eminent father. He was a man of noble traits, modest and unassuming, a person who did not aspire to greatness, who was likable and hard to provoke. For these reasons he was well liked by the public, and when the problem of appointing a new rabbi in place of his father arose, it was natural for many people to incline toward Ḥanōkh. In those days it was customary for a man to inherit his father's post, and if it turned out that the deceased rabbi had a deserving son, he would, of course, be the first candidate for his office.

The second candidate was a person of an altogether different stamp, both as to his origin and his education and character. This was Joseph b. Isaac Ibn Abītūr. He was the scion of a family that had dwelt in Spain for generations and was greatly revered by the populace. As Joseph himself relates it, in the ninth century a member of his family stood at the head of the Jewish community in Moslem Spain and assumed authority. For a long time this family dwelt in Mérida, Joseph himself being born there and referring to himself as a "man from Mérida."[1] Inasmuch as his family was an old one in Spain and intermingled with Arabs, it also received an Arabic surname, for Abītūr = Ibn Abī Thaur (father of the ox). Besides the Arabic name, the family also bore another name, which was apparently given them by the Mozarabs who spoke Romance: Santas, which the Jews altered to Satanas.[2]

Joseph was endowed with ability and had received an excellent education. He was taught various branches of learning by eminent teachers and later went to Cordova, where he studied with Moses b. Ḥanōkh, becoming famous as one of his outstanding disciples. Joseph Ibn Abītūr acquired a reputation for great learning and expert knowledge in talmudic lore and g'onic responsa, and many depended on his judgments. Collections of early responsa have preserved many of his decisions, which indicate that Spanish Jews were wont to address themselves to him in matters of religion and law.[3] In content and spirit his responsa resemble those of Moses b. Ḥanōkh and other rabbis of that generation, from whose decisions it is apparent that the Andalusian rabbis were guided by those of the Babylonian *g'ōnīm*. Whatever was "sent to them from the academy," that is, the Babylonian academies, was determining and binding.

Some of the responsa of Joseph Ibn Abītūr are brief and some are well reasoned, based on proofs from the Gemara and g'onic responsa. All are stamped with a personal style marked by use of definite rhetorical devices, such as "The response to this question—if the situation is as set down therein . . . ," "So it would seem to me, in my humble opinion . . ."; he also shows a special affection for Aramaic locutions. A consideration of the responsa of Joseph Ibn Abītūr shows how comprehensive and profound his knowledge of halakha was. But this was only one aspect of his intellectual attainment and his activity as a writer.

Renowned as a teacher of halakha, he also achieved fame as an author of religious poetry. In the field of poetry he continued in the tradition that the Jews had received from the oriental countries. He adhered to the content of religious poetry traditional among the Jews of Babylonia and Palestine, dealing with the same concepts. From this aspect his hymns show how great was the influence of the Saadya Gaon, whose religious poetry served as an example for succeeding generations. Joseph was endowed with great poetical ability and could express his feelings with strength and clarity. He was very prolific, composing hundreds of hymns.[4] He composed "sevens" (hymns to be recited when the Seven Benedictions were chanted on the Sabbath and festivals), penitential hymns (*s'līḥōt*), and hosannas (hymns for the New Year and the pilgrimage festivals).

But it was his collection of hymns for the Day of Atonement, a group of poems for all prayers to be recited on that day, that won especial renown. Such a collection was then known as a *ma'amad,* and the poet Judah Alḥarizi stressed the point that Joseph Ibn Abītūr was the first among the Jews of Spain to write such a group of poems.[5] Characteristic of his adherence to the accepted form of hymns is his " 'Abhōda" (a part of the liturgy for the Day of Atonement). He opens with a description of biblical history, beginning with the creation of the world and going through to where the tribe of Levi was chosen for the sacred service; thereafter he describes the service in the Temple on the Day of Atonement. Some of his poetry, such as the penitential verse, expresses the inner feelings of the individual; in these poems he lays his supplication before the Creator. In other liturgical verse the entire congregation of Israel gathers or "is united together as one" in the houses of worship.

Joseph's liturgical verse is permeated with strong nationalist emotions reflecting the agony of exile. The vicissitudes that have befallen the Jews are all alluded to in the Bible, even including the names of the nations who oppress the Jews. Yet he does not write much poetry on the subject of redemption and does not strive for an exalted mood through a description of the messianic era. His spirit is uplifted by observing the marvels of nature, all of whose details stir his unbounded admiration. Being susceptible to the influence of tales and descriptions in the Midrash and Aggada (folkloristic literature), the poet sees in the cosmic harmony the work of the Creator. At the very hour that the Jewish people forgather to voice their supplications on earth, the angels send forth their voices on high. Thus the dwellers on high unite with those who dwell on earth to laud the Creator of heaven and earth. And so the poet proclaimed:

His throne of glory is on the heights of the earth,
The corners of His train fill His temple.
Seraphim stand over Him,
Some to His right and some to His left,
While in various places on earth the people of God
Stand today like a mendicant beggar,
In praise and thanks to the Rock who redeems and saves,
Declaring holy the Sacred One of Jacob and the God of Israel.

In the heavens on high the name of Shaddai is proclaimed
And every heart is aflutter and all flesh stands on end.
Group asks group, "Where is His place of glory?"
And one calls to the other in reply.
And among the terrestrial inhabitants who inherited the law engraved on stone,
The chosen holy ones cleave to His name
And the Lord of hosts is exalted by His mighty hand
And the holy God is sanctified in righteousness.

The poetry of Joseph is especially distinguished for its artistic form. It has acrostics that are varied and lengthy, such as: "I, Joseph, the son of Rabbi Isaac. Be strong!" or "The small Joseph of Mérida." It also has wonderfully colorful versification. One of his poems contains twenty-three stanzas, each having eight lines subdivided into half-lines, in which the first half rhymes with the first half of the next line. The first seven lines of each stanza begin with the same letter, these letters occurring in alphabetical order throughout the poem. The second half of the second line in each stanza is a verse quoted from the Bible.

Generally Joseph tends to compose poems based on prayers

found in the Scriptures—Jonah's prayer, the prayer of Habakkuk, and the like; or he constructs his poems on the basis of combinations of verses out of one or several psalms. Thus he imposes many difficulties upon himself but succeeds in overcoming them. It is true that in the artificial arrangement of his verse he follows the method of the poets of the oriental countries, but Joseph is particularly outstanding in this regard. At times he struggles with the Hebrew language. At times his language is difficult. But generally speaking his mastery over it is quite evident. He not only employs biblical Hebrew but also that of the Talmud and also coins new forms of expression. His poetry won acceptance by the public and was included in the festival prayer books of many communities on the rim of the Mediterranean Sea: Aragon, Catalonia, Tlemcen, Tunisia, Sicily, and others; many more are preserved in manuscript without ever having been printed.[6]

Joseph Ibn Abītūr also tried his hand at biblical exegesis, and wrote a commentary on the Book of Psalms. This commentary has not yet been discovered, but quotations from it have come down to us. They indicate that the commentary was written in Hebrew with an admixture of Aramaic, its style being that of the Midrash.[7] As the scion of an old family in Moslem Spain, Joseph knew Arabic well, and it is apparent that he also acquired a broad knowledge of the secular sciences as these were then cultivated by the Arabs. A Hebrew author who wrote at the end of the Middle Ages, but drew upon primary sources, is able to report that Joseph Ibn Abītūr "was informed in Greek lore and the Arabic language and in their literature."[8] In respect to his knowledge Joseph was thus far superior to Ḥanōkh, who was only a talmudic sage.

In his character he was the very opposite of Ḥanōkh. Joseph was a very haughty person who took pride in his abilities, his knowledge, and especially his family tree. From his forebears he inherited forcefulness. He belittled his opponents, intimidating and threatening them, after the fashion of those who exercise authority. Joseph represented, first and foremost, the epitome of the Spanish Jew who was equally at home both in Jewish and general culture and moved freely among kings and nobles, one who knew his worth and was sure of himself to the point of conceit. It is natural that these traits would be likely to repel many and to acquire for him a number of enemies.

When the problem of appointing a new rabbi came up, opinion in the Jewish community was divided. Some supported the candidacy of Joseph Ibn Abītūr. But in the end no view prevailed, for all looked toward the *nāsī*, Ḥasdai Ibn Shaprūṭ, for a decision. The Jewish dignitary was old and enfeebled by the years, but still held his high standing at the royal court and in the Jewish community. The caliph who succeeded 'Abdarraḥmān III at his death showed favor to Ḥasdai, as had his father, and greatly esteemed him. Because of his own nature, the new ruler felt especially close to people like Ḥasdai.

Al-Ḥakam II, the son and heir of 'Abdarraḥmān III, was forty-seven years old when he became king; he reigned in Cordova for fifteen years (961–976). During the many years he had to wait before ascending the throne, he was able to devote himself to his heart's content to those matters which attracted him, particularly study and reading. Thus al-Ḥakam became the scholar among the Omayyad rulers who reigned in Spain and one of the most learned ones ever to occupy the throne in a Moslem country.

But his father had endeavored to instruct him also in the rules of statesmanship, and governmental matters were not strange to him. When at long last his great moment arrived to be crowned as caliph, he continued the diplomacy of his father, straying neither right nor left from its path. Both in his relations with the Christian kingdoms of northern Spain and with regard to Moroccan affairs, he acted precisely as his father had.

Immediately after al-Ḥakam ascended the royal throne, a

crisis developed in the relations between the Omayyad government and the Christian kingdoms in the north of the peninsula. Sancho I, the king of León whose rule had been made secure thanks to the aid extended him by the Moslems, proved to be an ingrate; he denied any promises he had made and assurances he had given. He entered into a treaty with the rulers of Castile and Barcelona and with the king of Navarre, to the end that they all united against the caliph; in 963 war erupted on several fronts. One column of soldiers led by al-Ḥakam himself went across Castile, taking the city of San Esteban de Gormaz while the governor of Saragossa and his troops simultaneously attacked the kingdom of Navarre, defeating its forces. Hostilities continued in 964, and in 968 the Moslems captured the city of Calahorra from the king of Navarre, placing therein a garrison.

Meantime, however, King Sancho had already died and his sister, who was a nun, reigned in place of his son, who was very young. Then a number of the nobles of León raised the standard of revolt, sending emissaries to the caliph to inform him that they recognized him as their suzerain ruler. In 970 García, the king of Navarre, and Fernán González, the count of Castile, died; their successors likewise sought peace and friendly and good-neighborly agreements with the caliph. When the Castilians and Navarrese resumed the war, they were defeated.

During al-Ḥakam's reign, a fierce pitched battle was fought in Morocco between the tribes of Ṣinhādja, who supported the Fatimids, and the tribes of Zenata, who leaned toward the Omayyads. In this war the Ṣinhādja had the upper hand. But in 972 the Fatimids left Ifrīḳīya (Tunisia) for Egypt, which had been conquered by their forces three years earlier; they turned their attention to the Near East, and therefore the Omayyads lost their fear that Spain might be invaded. Toward the end of his reign, al-Ḥakam II sent to Morocco a Spanish army that fought successfully against the Idrisi princes, remaining there as a conquering army. Al-Ḥakam was, therefore, very successful in his foreign diplomacy and in his wars against the enemies of the Omayyad kingdom.

The strong position of his government enabled the caliph to devote much time to study and reading even after he himself occupied the throne. Al-Ḥakam II engaged in the study of theology, belles lettres, and especially Arabic history and genealogy. In all these fields he amassed much information, and later writers have depended at times on the caliph's annotations, which he set down in the margins of manuscripts. Al-Ḥakam's library was one of the biggest collected by any prince of those days. His agents made the rounds of faraway lands—Egypt, Syria, Babylonia, and Persia—to acquire precious manuscripts for his library, and in Cordova proper, copyists worked to complete the library in systematic fashion. Theologians and writers coming from other countries to Spain were received at the court of the scholarly caliph with open arms. When his gracious regard for men of the pen became known, many of these made their way to the Moslem country on the western end of the Mediterranean Sea so that they too could enjoy his bounty.

Al-Ḥakam II carried on the diplomacy of his father also with respect to non-Moslem groups. He too endeavored to show them favor and foster their attachment to the government, giving those officials who were appointed over them important functions and giving encouragement to non-Moslem scholars.[9] It goes without saying that this enlightened ruler, who was so wrapped up in literature, felt much sympathy for Ḥasdai Ibn Shaprūṭ, a physician and scholar who in his time had engaged in the translation of a Greek work into Arabic. He retained Ḥasdai as physician to the royal court. In Ḥasdai's biography, as it is recorded by some Arabic writers,[10] it is stated that he was al-Ḥakam's physician, having found favor in the caliph's eyes and becoming one of his favorites. From this we could deduce that his principal ties were with al-Ḥakam, rather than with his father, ʻAbdarraḥmān. Such a passage in the Arabic sources testifies, at all events, to the close ties that prevailed between Ḥasdai and Caliph al-Ḥakam II.

While Ḥasdai held his status at the royal court, he continued to be the *nāsī* (patriarch) of the Jews of Moslem Spain. He thus had the final say in the appointment of a new chief rabbi. Ḥasdai, who had previously supported Moses b. Ḥanōkh, regarded his son favorably and made a decision in his favor. The supporters of Joseph Ibn Abītūr did not dare oppose him, and Ḥanōkh was designated as chief rabbi.[11]

II

Not long after the appointment of Ḥanōkh, Ḥasdai Ibn Shaprūṭ died. At that time, about 975, he was nearing seventy. To the end of his life he remained vigilant and great in accomplishment. Throughout the communities eulogies were arranged in an atmosphere of quiet mourning; parents told their children about all the good things he had accomplished for the Jews living in Spain.

Immediately after the death of the *nāsī,* the problem concerning the chief rabbi at Cordova arose anew. Those who had not dared oppose the will of Ḥasdai no longer placed any restraints on their tongues. With redoubled energy the partisans of Joseph Ibn Abītūr resumed stating their views and adducing abundant proof that he and he alone deserved the post of chief rabbi. Joseph had support from those old families among the Jews of Spain who had risen in the social scale and, having grown rich, had established ties with the Moslem rulers. On occasion Joseph even presented himself before the caliph. Al-Ḥakam even requested that he translate the oral law into Arabic, so that no area of learning should be absent from his library. Acting at the ruler's behest, Joseph wrote an Arabic treatise containing a digest of the Talmud.[12]

In any case, Joseph had access to the ministers of the government, and he therefore hoped that after Ḥasdai's death he would win the post he so avidly sought. But Ḥanōkh also had many supporters. He married a woman of the esteemed Falyadj family, and of course this family and its relatives put themselves out to retain the post for him. The members of the middle class in the Cordova community and the other communities leaned, for the most part, toward Ḥanōkh; in consequence he had more supporters than Joseph.

The dispute grew very bitter and since neither side would yield, each turned to the caliph. Large delegations from both factions made their way to Madīnat az-Zahrā, where the caliph stayed near Cordova, in order to bring the matter to his attention and to request that he decide in their favor. The caliph rendered his opinion that the minority must accept the view of the majority: Ḥanōkh should be allowed to retain his post.

Joseph Ibn Abītūr made a desperate attempt to bring the caliph around to his side through a personal appeal. He no doubt thought that the treatise on the Talmud he had written for the caliph would weigh in his favor and that the ruler was already inclined toward him. But he suffered a great disappointment. The caliph rejected his plea, stating that he must yield to the majority and adding that if the Arabs had rejected him as the Jews rejected Joseph, he would flee wherever his feet would carry him.

For their part Ḥanōkh's followers decided to take steps to end the dispute and silence for all time the quarrel-mongers who refused to abide by the will of the majority. They excommunicated Joseph, putting him outside the pale of Jewry. The magnitude of his defeat hurt Joseph to the very depths of his soul; being unable to endure the disgrace, he left Spain, which had been his family's home from time immemorial. On reaching Pechina he made one more weak attempt to change the course of events: he turned to Samuel ha-Kōhēn b. Josiah, the rabbi of the community, with a plea that he dissolve the ban. But the rabbi feared that he himself might fall under the ban and refused to speak to Joseph. Whereupon Joseph sent him a long letter written almost entirely in Aramaic, after the fashion of a talmudic scholar; the rabbi did respond to this letter. But whereas Joseph's letter was full of anger, the rabbi of Pechina couched his reply as is proper for a scholar—in gentle terms.[13]

Joseph wished to journey to Palestine, but when he was making his way through North Africa with his two sons, Mordecai and Isaac, he tarried here and there, thus prolonging the journey. On reaching Egypt, he spent some time in Alexandria, where he met a learned Jew named Khalfa b. Ḥakhmōn; he advised Joseph to go first to Fostat, where a certain important scholar who occupied a place of importance had heard of Joseph and his writings and held him in high esteem. Joseph took this suggestion and wrote a letter in Hebrew informing the man in Fostat of his intention. From what he had to say it is apparent that the recipient of the letter was one of the heads of the Jewish community in Egypt. Among other things, Joseph alluded to the fact that he had no intention of competing with the local masters in halakha.[14] When he reached Fostat he was indeed graciously welcomed, his reputation having preceded him.

Then he went up to Jerusalem, meeting there the head of the Palestinian academy, the *gaon* Samuel ha-Kōhēn b. Joseph, who also treated him with respect, showing no concern about his having been excommunicated in Spain. The two scholars, moreover, entered into bonds of friendship. Nevertheless, Joseph did not remain in the Holy City but went down to Egypt again, settling in its capital. That far removed from his birthplace he thought he would find healing for his hurt and be able to engage in the study of the Law and write books and hymns. Joseph was indeed held in esteem by the Jews of Egypt, and students sought him out to be instructed by him. They also addressed questions to him and sought his opinion; some of his responsa and judgments have come down to us.[15]

During his stay in Egypt's capital, Joseph maintained contacts with Sh'rīra Gaon, the famous head of the Academy of Pumbedita, and also with his son, Hai. He directed many questions to them; for example, he requested an explanation of words and phrases that are found in the tractate 'Erūhīn. Neither the *gaon* nor his son—who was the head of the academy at Bagdad and later succeeded to his father's post—showed any concern over the ban that had been laid upon Joseph, and they responded to his queries.[16]

But the dispute over the post of rabbi of Cordova had created repercussions even in other countries and spread to Egypt. This could only mean that the communities of Spain had already become one of the principal settlements of the whole nation and that whatever occurred there would involve the interest of the entire Diaspora. Spanish Jews were in close contact with the other countries surrounding the Mediterranean Sea; they traveled a good deal and involved even communities in distant lands in their affairs. Eventually in Fostat, too, a Jew began to denounce Joseph Ibn Abītūr. He insulted him in public and had friends and partisans who supported him and encouraged him. They held that Joseph's family name testified to its nature, for in their opinion Satanas was derived from the name Satan; they also heaped scorn on the judgments he had rendered.

In consequence, Joseph and his faction placed this man under a ban and sentenced him to a flogging. Every Sabbath Joseph repeated the proclamation of the ban, but the man refused to submit himself to the execution of the judgment. He pleaded that a substitution for his punishment be made, that he be required to give charity instead. He appealed in the matter to Sh'marya b. Elḥānān, the head of the Talmud school at Fostat, but Sh'marya did not reply to his appeal. Joseph Ibn Abītūr then sent a circular letter to various communities to inform them of the excommunication against the man, so that if he went to another city, he would not escape the ban.

For their part, those who supported the man, that is, the adherents of Ḥanōkh in the Egyptian capital, threatened that if he were compelled to accept the penalty, he would convert to the Moslem faith. In response Joseph addressed a long letter to the head of the Palestinian academy, Samuel ha-Kōhēn b. Joseph, inviting him to become a party to the ban. He also requested that the *gaon* ban those Jews in Fostat who supported the man and encouraged him not to accept the judgment. Joseph reminded the *gaon* of what he had written concerning this man in another instance where he was subject to flogging.

As to his adversaries' arguments regarding his name, Joseph explained that his family received this appellation because one of his forebears was a communal leader and dealt very sternly with wrongdoers; consequently, he was called "*shōṭ enōsh*" (the lash of mankind). Moreover, he requested that Samuel ha-Kōhēn should most definitely refrain from addressing his opponents in writing, since every line he wrote would be interpreted as supporting them. He mentioned that the *gaon* had written a letter to Ḥanōkh, a copy of which was sent from Spain to his opponents in Egypt, where it was exhibited throughout the synagogues, and used it to support their contentions. Joseph further argued—so goes his report—that the *gaon* wrote whatever he wrote to ridicule Ḥanōkh, inasmuch as he knew his nature. A copy of this letter that Joseph Ibn Abītūr sent to the *gaon* in Palestine was found close to the copy of a letter written in 989, from which it can be inferred that it itself was written about the year 990.[17]

From Joseph's letter it is apparent that the head of the Palestinian academy refrained from taking a position in the dispute that had been carried over from Spain to the Near East. Although he and the head of the Talmud school at Fostat had received Joseph with the honor proper to such a great scholar with no concern about his excommunication, they also maintained a correspondence with his rival, Ḥanōkh.

At all events, this entire episode of humiliations and accusations caused Joseph searing pain. He was convinced that his adversaries in Spain were prepared to work against him even in the lands of the Near East, and he speaks of them bitterly in his correspondence. He is particularly scathing in regard to Ḥanōkh himself, referring to his "stupidity and folly." The proud but unfortunate sage could never forget or forgive. Living in a distant land, he addressed to his opponents in Spain a letter in Hebrew studded with verses out of the Scriptures, a letter in which he gives expression to his bitterness. He addresses them with the words of Jephthah: "Did not ye hate me, and drive me out of my father's house?" (Judges 11:7) and protests to them: "You have all gathered as one against me." He prays that God will give them their recompense and judge between him and them, threatening his enemies with the punishment that awaits them.

One of Ḥanōkh's supporters, Ben Ḳalīma, retorted sharply and in his reply enumerated all the transgressions of which Joseph's opponents in Spain accused him. He charges that Joseph slandered his people before the authorities: "You handed over money to the wicked and spread slanderous reports about." He condemns him for having done this for his own benefit and for his transgressions against the sacred Law, saying that he has become like Aḥer (Elisha ben Abuja) in his time.[18] These letters were spread throughout the communities for propaganda effect.

Thus the dispute continued within Spain and abroad for

many years, while the hostile factions hurled slanders at each other. Neither side viewed the matter as ended, each instead waiting for the day when a decisive blow could be struck against the opponent. In view of the circumstances in which the inhabitants of Spain and the Jews in general found themselves, there was indeed some hope for this. In the despotic government, where everything depended on the whim of one man, there were always possibilities for sudden changes. And in truth, before much time had elapsed a new turn of events did occur.

III

After the death of Caliph al-Ḥakam II, the government came into the hands of a man completely different. The new ruler was not a member of the Omayyad family; he was an official who took the reigns of government into his own hands, leaving to the lawful caliph only the title of ruler. He was a master at diplomacy, there being none to compare with him for fomenting intrigues and conspiracies. When he needed someone, he would show him favor—but later he would send murderers to slay him in cold blood. He was the kind of person who regarded every means as proper to attain his ends. He had fixed his own goal while he was a youth, and thereafter he hewed to it consistently and with unusual stubbornness: to attain dominion over Spain. Indeed, he rose with dizzying speed up the hierarchy of the kingdom, until he reached the top of the pyramid.

This man was Abū 'Āmir Muḥammad, the scion of an Arab family that was descended from one of the officers who had accompanied Ṭāriḳ b. Ziyād. The family, called Banū Abī 'Āmir, settled in the vicinity of Algeciras, where it had an estate. Some members of the family were theologians who had received government posts, but they never had reached the uppermost levels in the state. Abū 'Āmir Muḥammad was neither a member of a family of estimable rank within the state, nor was he graced with a pleasing exterior. His face was pleasant and attractive, but he was a hunchback. On the other hand, he was endowed with ability and a strong determination. At a tender age he came to Cordova, where he studied Islamic canon law and Arabic literature with the best teachers.

On the completion of his studies, he became an official in the court of law. But he did not find favor with the chief judge of Cordova, who, in order to be rid of him, recommended to the chief vizier of Caliph al-Ḥakam II that he give him a position at the royal court. This vizier, whose name was Dja'far b. 'Uthmān al-Muṣḥafī, suggested to Ṣubḥ, the caliph's wife, who had borne to him the heir to the throne, that she place Abū 'Āmir in charge of the boy's property and her own. Ṣubḥ accepted the suggestion, and thus the young man entered the service of the court. He knew how to get along with the caliph's wife, ingratiate himself with her, and become her favorite. Less than seven months after he had been given this post, he was appointed to a more important one that brought in large revenue: Abū 'Āmir became the mintmaster at Cordova. A year later he was put in charge of escheatable property, and a short time later became the judge of the regions of Seville and Niebla.

Abū 'Āmir used his revenues with consummate sagacity. He doled out monies on all sides in an attempt to gain friends, and he showered lovely gifts on Ṣubḥ, who was the first of the caliph's wives and took precedence over all the ladies in his harem. Before long every child in Cordova's streets was chirping songs concerning relations between the judge and the queen. When the heir to the throne died and another child, Hishām, whom Ṣubḥ had also borne, came upon the scene, Abū 'Āmir became his representative and took charge of his property, even as he had been in charge of the deceased boy's property. Thus it was that Abū 'Āmir progressed with sureness.

During a military venture in Morocco in 973, he was sent there as a supreme judge, but for practical purposes he was there to supervise the numerous expenditures of money and to keep an eye on the army officers. This was a delicate task that could make him hated by the officers, but with his great ability he knew how to win their friendship. By the last days of the reign of al-Ḥakam II, Abū 'Āmir Muḥammad was, in fact, an important officer, but he had not yet reached the highest ranks in the leadership of the kingdom. The way for this was opened to him with the death of the caliph.

The successor, Hishām II, was twelve years old when his father died, but despite the oath of loyalty given him during the reign of al-Ḥakam II, shortly after the caliph's death a plot to remove his son and make another Omayyad the ruler in his place was uncovered. The scheming courtiers did not ask the Omayyad prince for his opinion and made their plans without giving him any information. The vizier, al-Muṣḥafī, who directed the government when al-Ḥakam died, assembled the high dignitaries to take counsel with them, and Abū 'Āmir accepted the assignment to murder the prince whom the schemers wanted to make caliph. He executed the deed as promised. After the murder of a man innocent of all wrongdoing, Abū 'Āmir compelled the princes and dignitaries, the courtiers and the chief officials, to swear loyalty once again to Hishām II. He himself became a vizier and right-hand man of the *ḥādjib* (prime minister), al-Muṣḥafī.

Overtly he acted as if he was in full agreement with this division of posts, but in fact he began to undermine al-Muṣḥafī by all possible means. This was facilitated for him because of the strained relations existing between the *ḥādjib* and the majority of the high officials and courtiers. Al-Muṣḥafī was a Berber, and the members of the noble Arab families who provided most of the high officeholders regarded him with envy for this reason, since in their view the office of *ḥādjib* should have fallen to one of them. Moreover, al-Muṣḥafī appointed members of his family to high posts, supplanting the haughty Arabs. They complained, in addition, that he did not act toward them with respect, was tightfisted, and was always avid of acquiring money for himself.

Abū 'Āmir did whatever he could to draw the officials to his side and win for himself followers from among them. However, he was well aware that he would not achieve his desired ends unless he had the support of the army. For this reason he went forth with the troops on punitive expeditions against the Leónese and Castilians, who had made forays within the borders of the kingdom, and as was his wont he succeeded in ingratiating himself with the officers and the soldiers. Early in 978 he brought down on al-Muṣḥafī a decisive blow. He obtained from the boy caliph an order calling for the dismissal and arrest of al-Muṣḥafī, and it was natural that Abū 'Āmir himself was appointed *ḥādjib*.

For the next twenty-five years Abū 'Āmir was the all-powerful ruler of Moslem Spain. At first the caliph was still a mere youth, and when he did mature, everything possible was done to keep him from becoming involved in governmental affairs; he was thrust into a pattern wherein he whiled the time away in pleasures of the harem and in prayer. The youth was deliberately kept in a state of stupefaction so that in the end he was like a person without reality in the palace. The powerful minister surrounded the palace with a trench and strong wall, and placed police and spies at the gate to prevent any contact between the caliph and the world outside. When the caliph ventured forth at times to one of his villas outside the city, the roads would be sealed off by rows of soldiers, and the caliph himself would be wrapped in a cloak that covered his face after the manner of Moslem women.

But in spite of his power and heavy hand, the *ḥādjib* was never secure in his position. From time to time plots against him were uncovered. In 979 his police revealed a plot to set on the throne another grandson of 'Abdarraḥmān III who also bore that name. Later on, in 981, the supreme commander of the troops on the borders of Castile rose up against Abū 'Āmir and fought against him with the aid of Christian soldiers—but that general suffered a defeat. After this dangerous adversary had been overcome and he had retaliated against the Christians by forays into their provinces, Abū 'Āmir was given the appellation of al-Manṣūr bi-'llāh (he who triumphs with the help of God), the name by which he won renown throughout all countries.

With his political instincts, which had in them more than one spark of genius, Abū 'Āmir al-Manṣūr was aware that there was no better way to sustain his authority than by dazzling his people with victories over the Christians and exciting the masses with the spectacle of prisoners on parade. Therefore, year by year he planned military ventures against the Christian kingdoms in northern Spain, and generally arranged two expeditions a year, one in the spring and one in the fall. At the head of his cohorts he invaded all the provinces of northern Spain, from Santiago in the west to Barcelona in the east. Everywhere he destroyed the churches and took enormous booty and countless prisoners. Needless to say, devout Moslems were full of enthusiasm and poets eulogized his exploits.

Al-Manṣūr was a cruel tyrant who unmercifully destroyed whoever appeared to him to be dangerous. The person sent to carry out an act of murder at his suggestion was later himself slain by his order, so that all traces would be obliterated. But the Andalusian masses benefited from the security that he brought throughout the state, and they extolled his sense of justice. At every appropriate occasion al-Manṣūr would demonstrate his exaggerated religious orthodoxy. He persecuted anyone suspected of heresy and those who were lenient in religious observance. He purged the library of al-Ḥakam II of philosophical works and any other books tainted with heresy—such as books about astronomy and all the natural sciences—setting them afire with his own hands. He enlarged and embellished the Great Mosque of Cordova. Writers who recount his deeds mention that he himself made copies of the Koran, perused it intensively, and willingly listened to the sermons of the preachers, even when they were overlong.

On the other hand, there is no account of any harm befalling the non-Moslem communities within Andalusia throughout the long period of al-Manṣūr's dominance. Incidents of conversion among the Jews of Spain in those days were, to be sure, not rare.[19] But this is a customary phenomenon among minorities that does not always ensue from the pressure of the authorities. Al-Manṣūr therefore appears on one hand as the hero of Islam, and Arabic chroniclers do not grow weary of telling how many monasteries he laid waste; and yet on the other they tell us that he respected the rights of Christians and Jews in Moslem Spain itself. It is true that he never elevated members of those communities to prominent office in the upper strata of government, but he did refrain from any oppressive acts against them.

The fanaticism which al-Manṣūr displayed toward the Christians and their churches outside his borders, which was far severer than that shown by the Moslem kings in the East who fought the Crusaders in prolonged and bitter battle, and the fine posture of the tyrannical *ḥādjib* toward the non-Moslems in his kingdom are proof that he was acting on a coolly calculated basis. His purpose was to ingratiate himself with the pious masses; yet he was apprehensive of any disorders within the state, for who knew how they might end? Disturbances directed against non-Moslems were likely to affect and confuse

Christian mercenary soldiers, who were to be found in considerable numbers among the troops of al-Manṣūr. Al-Manṣūr wanted to prevent this at all costs. Such considerations explain the apparent contradiction in his actions.

At all events, the fate of religio-ethnic minorities depended upon the attitude of this ruler who had it in his power to move in completely different directions. Such dependence on the whim of the individual was greater than was usual in the Middle Ages, because al-Manṣūr's power was in general so much greater than the power and authority of most kings that he did not have to take into account other factors.

Among other people who found ways of getting close to al-Manṣūr and winning his favor were two brothers who were Jews from Cordova, Jacob and Joseph Ibn Djau. These two brothers were engaged in silk manufacture. They produced silk clothes and became purveyors to the government. As we are informed by an early Spanish Jewish writer: "They made costly garments and very expensive pennants for the tops of the flags of the Arabs."[20] And indeed the Arabic chronicles frequently tell about the costly silken garments that al-Manṣūr awarded to those who distinguished themselves by their deeds, especially to his favorites: officers and soldiers. These silken garments, upon which the ruler's name was woven, were called *ṭirāz*; they were made upon order of the government, and one of the high officers was in charge of the depot in which they were kept. He was known as *ṣāḥib aṭ-ṭirāz*.[21]

The two Ibn Djau brothers presented al-Manṣūr with numerous gifts, and they rose ever higher in esteem. Ultimately al-Manṣūr appointed Jacob Ibn Djau to be the *nāsī* over all the Jewish communities in Moslem Spain and in those provinces of Morocco and Algiers that owed him obedience. He received permission to impose taxes upon them and appoint judges. At a festive assembly the Cordovan community, for its part, approved the appointment, and moreover announced its desire that the post of *nāsī* become hereditary within the Ibn Djau family. Like the Moslem nobles, Jacob Ibn Djau had an entourage of slaves and servants who did his bidding, and he was also provided with eunuchs from the royal court. In all his activities he modeled himself after the highest nobles in the kingdom. With a princely hand he bestowed gifts and maintained many poor men at his table; and he also gave assistance to scholars and poets. Poetasters as well as renowned poets wrote verse in his honor and the honor of his family, praising his character traits and in particular his hospitality.[22]

The new *nāsī,* who had risen to great station because of his ties with the minister who had thrust the caliph aside, tried to do something similar. He was one of the sworn supporters of Joseph Ibn Abītūr and, on being designated *nāsī,* considered that the time had come to return Joseph to Spain and appoint him in place of Ḥanōkh. Jacob Ibn Djau thereupon sent a messenger to Ḥanōkh forbidding him to continue to act as judge. This order was conveyed in discourteous language. Ḥanōkh was told that should he dare to judge between two people, he would be taken to the seacoast and lowered into an oarless boat, this being an allusion to the fact that he and his father had been brought to Spain as captives. Then Jacob Ibn Djau compelled the leaders and notables of the Cordovan community to draft a letter to Joseph Ibn Abītūr, inviting him to return to Spain and become their rabbi. All who had sided with Ḥanōkh and had vigorously opposed Joseph were forced to sign this letter, so great was the power of Jacob Ibn Djau.

Ibn Abītūr's faction waited for his reply several months, but to their great surprise he informed the Jews of Cordova that he would not respond to their call or return to Spain. This did not represent any change in the view he had always held. He was as convinced now as he had been previously that the office of rabbi of the capital of Spain was justly his; but he had had enough humiliations and regarded with contempt those leaders who had changed their mind under the pressure of a noble; moreover, he was apprehensive that the situation could change once again.

Joseph therefore remained in Egypt. From information containing dates it can be proved that he dwelt there in the 990s. One decision penned by him carries the year 303 according to documentary dating, this being 992 C.E.[23] At the end of a manuscript of the Hagiographa arranged after the custom then obtaining in Palestine (that is, with the Book of Chronicles being the first), there is a note by the copyist stating that he copied the collection and vocalized the entire Bible for "Rabbi Joseph the S'fardī [from Spain] ben Rabbi Isaac" and completed this task in the month of Elul [4]754, that is, 994 C.E. From this we infer that Joseph gave to an expert scribe the task of making for him a copy of the Bible with the Palestinian system of vocalization. Over the colophon Joseph inscribed a poem in which he expresses the hope that his prayer will be heard.[24]

Joseph lived to an old age, and over the many years that he lived in Egypt, he continued to compose hymns whenever the poetic muse overcame him. Influenced by his environment he wrote, in the manner of the Palestinian hymnologists, a cycle of *yōṣ'rōt* (hymns usually recited before the Sh'ma') for all the Sabbaths throughout the year.[25]

At the beginning of the eleventh century the Fatimid Caliph al-Ḥakam began to persecute non-Moslem groups within the borders of his kingdom, which included Egypt, Palestine, and Syria. In 1004 he introduced the law requiring non-Moslems to identify themselves with a distinguishing emblem, and in 1008 he ordered the destruction of their houses of worship. Later, in 1012, the decrees were made even more severe, and many more houses of worship were destroyed. Joseph Ibn Abītūr composed a *ḳīna* (elegy) in which he poured out the anguish of his spirit, describing what was perpetrated upon the Jews in Palestine and especially in Jerusalem.[26]

When Joseph rejected the invitation to return to Spain, he very properly evaluated the lack of stability among the Jewish communal leaders, who were dependent upon the graciousness of a despot. He was well aware that this despot could change his mind within a moment; and this did indeed occur. After a year had passed, Jacob Ibn Djau lost favor in the eyes of al-Manṣūr, particularly since the taxes he collected from the Jews did not seem to him to be sufficient. Al-Manṣūr ordered Jacob Ibn Djau to be put into prison, where he was locked up for a year. At this time Ḥanōkh's supporters again waxed powerful among the Jews of Cordova, and they reinstated him in the office of rabbi. Ultimately Jacob Ibn Djau was released from prison and even received once again the post of *nāsī*. Such were the vagaries of the despotic rule of al-Manṣūr.

However, Ḥanōkh retained the post of rabbi even after Jacob Ibn Djau was freed and served in that capacity until his death. As had his father, he headed the academy at Cordova, disseminating knowledge of the Torah and producing many scholars; he also rendered judgments and responded to questions addressed to him. Collections of responsa of that age contain a number of his responsa.[27] Some of these are long, containing basic proofs gleaned from the Talmud, and his conclusions were accepted by authorities of the halakha. Not only in his generation but in later generations too, Ḥanōkh was regarded as one of the great halakhists; and his observations and decisions are cited in the works of the early scholars.[28]

The bitter struggle for his position and the severe tribulations he experienced did not effect any change in his character. He remained gentle in manner as he grew older. He refused to accept remunerations for his activities as rabbi and head of the Talmud school and lived modestly throughout his life. No doubt his qualities and life-style made a deep impression on the members of his community. But Ḥanōkh could stand firmly by his opinions where the matter, in his view, warranted it.

The evident progress in halakhic studies in Spain that began when Moses b. Ḥanōkh arrived there and the status of the Hispano-Jewish community relative to the entire Jewish world by the end of the tenth century found expression in the relationships between the Talmud academies of Spain and Babylonia and between their heads. Ḥanōkh took an independent stand vis-à-vis Sh'rīra Gaon, the head of the academy in Bagdad; he even disparaged him. Sh'rīra sent dispatches to Ḥanōkh a number of times, to which the Cordovan rabbi did not even trouble to reply. Contact between faraway Babylonia and the Spanish communities was maintained in those days, as in previous generations, by the Jews of Kairawan who relayed the correspondence between the two points. In a letter Hai Gaon wrote to the noble Judah bar Joseph in Kairawan he urged him to rebuke Ḥanōkh for failing to reply to the letters that his father, Sh'rīra Gaon, had sent without eliciting a reply.[29]

Ḥanōkh died in 1014 as the result of an accident. On the festival of Simḥat Torah it was a custom in the Cordovan community for the rabbi to go up to the reader's desk to complete the reading of the Torah, accompanied by three notables of the congregation. When he went up to the Torah on Sh'mīnī 'Aṣeret in the year 4775, the rotted platform gave way beneath his feet; he fractured his spine, and some days later he breathed his last.[30]

The dominance of al-Manṣūr, the security which Moslem Spain enjoyed, and the flourishing economy that resulted therefrom all contributed to the increase in strength of the Jewish community within the state. In that generation the number of Jews in Andalusia continually waxed greater, thanks to a wave of immigrants from across the sea. In the time of al-Manṣūr, too, Jewish immigration into Spain was a concomitant phenomenon of the strong wave of Moslem immigration. The authority of al-Manṣūr rested mainly on regiments of Berber soldiers who were devoted to him with all their souls. He encouraged the Berbers' immigration to Spain and lured them with good pay and gifts; indeed, those Berber tribesmen who came to Spain and enlisted in his army had no cause for regret. They came singly or in groups—even complete tribes of fighting men immigrated.[31] Al-Manṣūr treated the Berber soldiers with especial kindness and showed favor to their officers.[32] Thus the number of Berbers in the Spanish army grew constantly, and these new immigrants became an important element in the population, particularly in Cordova. Arabic chroniclers report that Cordova's suburbs were too confined to hold all the Berbers serving in the army of al-Manṣūr.[33]

Many Jews followed in the Berbers' footsteps. They migrated to Spain, attracted not by the opportunity to serve in the army but mainly by the good economic situation. The data relating to the history of the Jewish intellectuals in Spain at that time testify to the great extent of Jewish migration from North Africa to Spain that occurred just then. Most of these migrants came from those regions in North Africa that today belong to Morocco and Algeria, while the migratory movement from the more easterly regions grew discernibly weaker and almost ceased altogether from the Near East.

After the Fatimids succeeded in conquering Egypt and establishing the center of their empire there, a new epoch in the history of this land began, an epoch marked by security and economic growth. The first caliphs of this dynasty who ruled over Egypt, al-Mu'izz and al-'Azīz, were excellent rulers who established their empire on a firm foundation and were outstanding for their organizing abilities. The inhabitants of the land of the Nile always prospered as long as the government there was strong and had proper concern for the country's needs. For this reason Egypt began to attract Jewish immigrants not only from the East—from Irak and Syria—but also from the West. The Geniza of Cairo has eleventh-century documents that mention the large numbers of Jews then dwelling in Egypt who originated in Western lands: Tunisia, Algeria, and Morocco. But until the beginning of the eleventh century, as long as the political situation of Moslem Spain was stable and its economy flourishing, its power of attraction did not wane. In Morocco itself there was no change in circumstances. In the days of al-Manṣūr's rule, the wars between the supporters of the Omayyad government at Cordova and the Fatimid armies continued, and from time to time expeditionary forces were sent from Spain to crush rebellions in the Spanish spheres of influence. Naturally, the unstable conditions in Morocco, the constant wars and the disturbance of trade relations resulting from them, on one hand, and the stability and economic growth in Andalusia, on the other, prompted many Jews to cross over from Morocco to the Iberian peninsula.

IV

The security and economic growth from which the Spanish Jews benefited in the second half of the tenth century also set their mark upon their intellectual life. The affluent among them followed in the footsteps of their Moslem neighbors, supporting writers and scholars and especially poets who sang their praises. The climate among the upper strata of Andalusian society was highly cultural. The important men of the kingdom and the nobles imitated al-Ḥakam II, establishing big libraries for themselves and gathering circles of intellectuals into their palaces. True, their intellectual interests did not encompass a wide area. Even religious questions did not greatly occupy the social groups that came together in their drawing rooms. After the death of al-Ḥakam II, books dealing with philosophy were not at all in evidence.

Among those branches of learning that did interest the

Arabs from earliest times, philology held first place. In the Middle Ages, when a group of scholars in one of the countries of Christian Europe would come together, they would debate theological problems, whereas in a gathering of Arabs at Cordova or Seville the discussion would concern linguistics. During the second half of the tenth century a number of important Arab philologers taught in the capital of Moslem Spain. Ismā'īl b. al-Ḳāsim al-Kālī, who came from Irak to Spain in 942 and was active as a language teacher at Cordova until his death in 967, is regarded as the founder of Arabic philology in Spain. Abū Bakr Muḥammad b. 'Umar Ibn al-Ḳūṭīya (died 977) was a distinguished historian and philologist. One who acquired great renown as a student of the Arabic language was Muḥammad b. al-Ḥasan as-Zubaidī who was, for a time, the tutor of Caliph Hishām II and later a judge in Seville (where he died in 989). These teachers concentrated around them many disciples, whom they infused with pride for their language and enthusiasm for the subject of their studies.

The Jews who dwelt on the Iberian peninsula among the Arabs adapted themselves to their areas of interest, but being loyal members of their own people, they regarded Hebrew as their national tongue, even though they were immersed in Arabic culture. They loved the language of the Bible and esteemed it as a precious treasure. Jewish scholars knew of no more interesting subject than innovations in language study, and when a number of friends who had gathered together were informed that a writer had coined a new word, all the company would hearken attentively. Thanks to this alert interest, the study of Hebrew philology progressed in a marked degree. The disciples of M'naḥem Ben Sārūḳ probed deeply into the problems of philology and surpassed their master in their knowledge.

Side by side with study of the Hebrew language went study of the Bible, in which many engaged. Language teachers interpreted the Scriptures in their own way, gathering their interpretations and comments into special collections. These teachers became famous even outside Spain, and young men thirsting for knowledge of the Bible and Jewish law came from nearby lands to study with them. The teachers of Cordova and Lucena imparted their lore to students from the communities of Morocco and southern France.

But the literary aspirations of the Jews of Spain found their chief expression in Hebrew poetry in its various categories, and in this area, too, it was natural for them to go in the path of the Arabs. The great innovation by Dūnash b. Labraṭ, his introduction of meter into Hebrew poetry, held everyone enthralled. Hebrew poets sent metered verses to their friends, who responded in verse of similar meter and rhyme. In communities large and small there were clubs in which people met for the recitation of verse—or more precisely to listen to poetry, it being their custom to hear it from people who declaimed poetry, who were called in Arabic *ruwāt*.[34] Competitions were also arranged, with judges deciding who had been outstanding, and declaring him to be the winner. In these competitive meets one of the poets would begin a poem with a certain meter and rhyme, and his fellow poets were required to respond then and there with a poem of like meter and rhyme. At times one poet would compose the opening line of a stanza, and another would be called upon to write the closing line. Sometimes poets would personify: the one, summer and the other, winter. One would sing about gold and one about iron.

Such was the fashion of both Arabs and Jews. A knowledge of poetry was a road to advancement and office. Whoever knew Arabic well, and Arabic verse in particular, could get a good post in the service of the nobles; on this same pattern Jewish nobles would employ scholars who could compose letters in polished Hebrew. This was the practice in Spain for many generations, which led a later Spanish Jewish writer to state that "poetry is the path which leads to the acquisition of office and the favor of kings, and such a person has no cause for concern."[35]

Creativity in poetry is an expression of the desire for outstanding form and beauty. But whereas the Arabs could satisfy these ambitions in highly ramified artistic creativity, such as the erection of magnificent structures and in contemplation of them, the Jews had to limit themselves to purely cultural areas. From this it followed that the fostering of poetry became the preoccupation of almost the whole intellectual community. Since the Jewish poets, adopting the manner of the Arabs, wrote laudatory verse in honor of the nobles and the wealthy in the Jewish communities—doing so in order to be rewarded—from its earliest days secular Hebrew poetry acquired a sheen that was definitely aristocratic and courtly. This becomes more and more pronounced with the blossoming of Spanish Jewish poetry in the generations following Dūnash b. Labraṭ. Spanish Hebrew poetry was designed for noblemen's drawing rooms, and its whole purpose was to impart pleasure to them and their friends. Even as the poet never wearies of extolling the distinguished qualities of the "benevolent" noble, so he was enchanted by the flower beds and furrows and beautiful gardens of their lovely houses. The patron was not merely a source of support for poets and writers, but served as a focal point for their circle and stimulated them to creative expression.

Even the style evidenced in the language of this courtly aristocratic poetry reflects its social background. Compared with the constant flow of hymnology by the early hymnists, the language of these poets is biblical, with meticulous attention paid to the strict rules of biblical grammar; this is a mark of the aristocratic character, which fosters the form and beauty of restraint.[36]

The bitter outcry against the cruelty of the wealthy to which the poet at times gave utterance was no more than protest by an individual who felt humiliated because he was not properly appreciated. The poet considered himself as one belonging to the social stratum of the affluent because they needed his service. The other social strata have no place in the cultural community. Among the Spanish communities of that epoch, the men of culture have left us religious hymns and poems of various types. These compositions were not influenced in a perceptible manner by Arabic poetry and thought, at least not with respect to its content. The hymnologists continued to write hymns as before, showing the influence in particular of Saadya Gaon, the great teacher of all the Jewish communities throughout Arabic lands. The external form of the hymns remained practically unchanged; for the greatest part, they did not compose hymns in metered verse.[37]

V

In view of the great interest in philology and the degree of importance ascribed to its cultivation, Jewish intellectuals were very much vexed that throughout the Jewish communities they could not find grammarians with sufficient stature to establish the study of the Hebrew language as a complete and solid edifice, after the pattern of the comprehensive investigations being carried out on Arabic. Some of these intellectuals put themselves to the test of writing such treatises without giving the matter any publicity; but others read their works before circles of their friends, so that they could make their comments and thereby fructify their thinking.

Among these intellectuals whose hearts throbbed with a strong love for the Hebrew language was Abū Zakariyā Yaḥyā b. Dā'ūd, whose Hebrew name was Y'hūda b. David. Among his friends he was of course called by his Arabic name, but he was especially known by his surname: Ḥayyūdj. This name has not been fully explained. Some claim that it is a diminutive of Yaḥyā, supplemented by the Spanish suffix *udj*; others hold that it is a Berber name[38] that Abū Zakariyā brought with him from his birthplace. He was indeed born in Fez, Morocco, in about 970, and went from there to Spain. His place of residence in his second homeland was in the capital city, Cordova,[39] where he found all that his heart desired: circles of scholars with whom he could discuss matters in which he was vitally interested and large libraries where he could find numerous manuscripts.

All of Abū Zakariyā's desires were linked to the study of Hebrew philology, and his ideal in life was to write a basic grammar of the holy tongue. He delved into the works on grammar written by the Arabs, endeavoring to apply the methods and principles they had discovered to the Hebrew language, the sister tongue of Arabic. Gradually the problems inherent in the Hebrew language became clear to him, and he reached definite conclusions, all without the guidance of a prominent teacher. He earned his livelihood by teaching,[40] devoting all his free time to investigation. Abū Zakariyā was a one-sided person; after the fashion of experts, he was completely preoccupied within the limits of his narrow field of inquiry. In this labor he found satisfaction. When he felt that he had succeeded in explaining the core problems of Hebrew philology that had perplexed the earlier investigators, he began putting his thoughts into written form.

By the time Ḥayyūdj began writing his treatise, two generations had gone by since Jewish scholars had started their inquiries into the rules of the Hebrew language. But Ḥayyūdj's forerunners in this field had not succeeded in clarifying the basic principles of Hebrew phonetics, the interchangeability and assimilation of the weak letters alef, he, waw, and yod. They therefore were unable to explain the conjugation of verbs, and all their investigations proved to be in vain. Whereas the Arabic philologists had shown as early as the eighth century that every verb is triliteral, the Hebrew grammarians who preceded Ḥayyūdj held that verbs may be based on one, two, three, or four letters. Because they did not properly recognize roots containing weak letters, they erred egregiously in their understanding of words, and poets coined incorrect forms in great number. Abū Zakariyā Ḥayyūdj was noted for his analytical mind and critical thought, and in following in the footsteps of the Arabic grammarians he demonstrated that Hebrew verbs also are triliteral. This was a most important revelation. With one sweep Ḥayyūdj illuminated the problems that had defied the grammarians until his time, thus opening up a new epoch in Hebrew philology.

But this is not Ḥayyūdj's sole merit. He was necessarily dependent upon the methods of the Arabic grammarians, but thanks to his philological instincts he knew to what extent it was permissible to carry these methods over to another language. He clarifies various language phenomena by means of the natural impulse to simplify pronunciation—which is, after all, a principle of Arabic philology. To be sure, there were times when he erred, as when he spoke of an alef being elided in the third person of the *ḳal* conjugation of a regular verb (thus, for example, between the shīn and the mem of the verb *shamar* an alef is elided). But generally speaking his ability stood him in good stead, and he blazed new trails for the Hebrew grammarians.

However, he did even more. Until his time Hebrew grammarians had no fixed terminology, but in his treatises on the Hebrew language (which were all written in Arabic), Ḥayyūdj adapted for his purposes terms that the Arabic philologists had coined in their studies. These expressions carried over by Ḥayyūdj to Hebrew philology have become accepted and are in use to this very day, but they have been translated into Hebrew.

Ḥayyūdj wrote two books on the conjugation of verbs, employing in them the principles he had discovered. Of course, he chose as the first subject those types of verbs concerning which the grammarians had, until his time, been most confused. One treatise was devoted to verbs having one of the weak consonants: alef, he, waw, yod. This treatise is called *Kitāb al-Af'āl dhawāt ḥurūf al-līn* or, more briefly, *Kitāb ḥurūf al-līn*, which the Hebrew translators called *The Book of the Weak Letters.*[41]

In the introduction to the book Ḥayyūdj deals with the elements of Hebrew phonetics. He discusses the mobile *sh'va* and the quiescent *sh'va*, clarifies the matter of the letters bet, gimel, dalet, kaf, pe, and tav and the *dagesh*, and he particularly explains the nature of the weak consonants from their phonetic and morphological aspects. He holds that they are called secret letters and letters of prolongation, because at times they are part of the root of a word and sometimes they are annexed to it. He then gives a list, in the next three chapters, of verbs containing a weak consonant. The first chapter has a list of verbs whose first letter is weak; the second chapter deals with verbs whose second letter is weak; and the last chapter, with those in which the third letter of their root is weak. Like the Arabic grammarians, he speaks of verbs whose pe, 'ayin, or lamed is weak, and this nomenclature for the root letters was incorporated into our literature.

In his second treatise Ḥayyūdj deals with verbs whose second and third root letters are identical, such as *ḥābhabh, ḥāgag*. The treatise is called in the Arabic original *Kitāb al-Af'āl dhawāt al-mithlain* and in the Hebrew translation *Sefer po'olē ha-kefel.* Also in this treatise Ḥayyūdj has a preface dealing with the principles of conjugation of such verbs. Then he adds an alphabetical list of verbs, and next to each verb he cites some instances of these forms as they occur in the Bible.

In both treatises the author employs a concise style without recourse to any rhetorical language. He does not engage in polemics with any writers or cite them, but he does express his own views with sureness. Whoever peruses the books of Ḥayyūdj is astonished at the absence of parallels between the Hebrew and Arabic languages, the kind of parallels that run like a scarlet thread throughout the treatises of the Hebrew grammarians of the Middle Ages. This is especially conspicuous since Ḥayyūdj's method is exactly that of the Arabic grammarians. It is possible that Ḥayyūdj was apprehensive of opposition from certain circles if he imitated the methods of Arabic grammarians; it is also possible that he took for granted the similarity of the linguistic formations of Hebrew and Arabic.

These two books, which became the basic works for Hebrew grammar, became identified with the name of their author and were called *The Book of Ḥayyūdj.* They were translated into Hebrew three times and were also paraphrased a number of times.[42] A third treatise that came from the pen of Ḥayyūdj deals with the rules of vocalization; in it he discussed the vocalization of words in the absolute and construct state, words to which terminal letters are added, and the like. This work, whose designation in the Arabic original is *Kitāb at-Tanḳīṭ* and in Hebrew is *Sefer ha-niḳḳūd,* is of small compass and intended to meet the needs of the student.[43]

Besides from these works, a fourth treatise has come down to us from Ḥayyūdj. It is called *Kitāb an-Nutaf* (The Book of Selections). This is a commentary on the Prophets and consists of eight sections. The first part is a commentary on the Book of Joshua and the last a commentary on the twelve minor prophets. It consists mainly of philological comments. In the preface Ḥayyūdj states that he has no wish to speak of matters that everyone knows about, but actually he explains grammatical forms of the simplest kind and repeats what he had already clarified in detail in his two treatises on verbs. This work is incomplete, since in the only preserved manuscript we find verses that the author jotted down without making any comment upon them. Compared with his two books dealing with verbs, books that were a turning point in Hebrew philology, there is really no great significance to the *Kitāb an-Nutaf*.[44]

This commentary was not the only work Ḥayyūdj did not manage to complete; still other treatises were at various stages of processing. One of the great Hebrew grammarians observes that if Ḥayyūdj had not died at an early age, he would have completed his books on the verbs and not left any behind unfinished.[45] Ḥayyūdj himself mentions a treatise on guttural letters[46] and states that he had intended writing a work on common nouns having the definite article.[47] In books of later writers and in various manuscripts, quotations from the works of Ḥayyūdj have also been found, from which it can be deduced that he was gathering material for commentaries on the Pentateuch and the Hagiographa. A manuscript of a commentary on the Pentateuch by Abraham Ibn 'Ezrā contains such quotations,[48] and Ibn 'Ezrā himself cites Ḥayyūdj on Exodus 21:2, as well as in his commentary on Psalms 102:27.[49] In manuscripts containing exegetical comments on the Hagiographa by various Spanish writers, Ḥayyūdj's commentaries are also cited;[50] but the treatises from which these quotations are cited have not come down to us, indicating that they were inchoate material that was far from being completed. Abū Zakariyā Ḥayyūdj died in the prime of life, before he could finish them. He passed away in the first decade of the eleventh century.[51]

But although he did not succeed in completing his books, Ḥayyūdj worked wonders; all scholars and writers in later generations have appreciated his achievements properly and decided unanimously that he was the father of Hebrew grammar.[52]

Just as not all of Ḥayyūdj's works have come down to us, many books written at that time by other writers and scholars also have been lost. What was preserved constitutes the choicest of literary production—those books that became very famous and of which many copies were made. But in addition to the authors of books of distinction, mediocre scholars were also active. They too tried their hand at writing books of various kinds: textbooks for students, commentaries on noted treatises, and strictures upon them. Many began writing books but did not complete them, and there can be no doubt that the manuscripts of such books were thrown away after the death of their authors. It goes without saying that precisely works of this sort were characteristic of the cultural way of life of Spanish Jewry in those days.

By chance, there has come down to us an incomplete book containing critical comment on the translation of the Bible by Saadya Gaon.[53] From internal evidence, it is apparently the work of two writers. One part of the book is written in a difficult but restrained style, with terse critical comment; the other part is marked by fluent language and a pungent style, with rhymes, for the most part, accompanying the critical comment. The author of the part written with restraint may have taken into consideration the fact that the *gaon*'s disciples were still alive. The writer, no doubt a teacher of grammar, was not yet aware of the rule concerning triliteral roots. Apparently he wrote his comments in Arabic, which were then translated into Hebrew by a student who was not well versed in this langauge. The name of this writer was Adōnīyah, for as a mnemonic for the formative letters he gives אדניה שלו כתם טב (Adōnīyah of the fine gold). From what he says it is evident that he lived in Spain.[54]

Some two or three generations later the manuscript fell into the hands of a scholar who was well versed in the writings of the grammarians of the eleventh century. He adapted the comments, endeavoring to arrange them alphabetically. He is mainly to be distinguished from Adōnīyah, who first set down the critical comments on Saadya Gaon, by his unrestrained aggressiveness in speaking about the *gaon*. This anonymous writer, too, died before he succeeded in finishing his work.[55] Such was the fate of the work of a mediocre scholar who wanted to write a book and emulate renowned cultural leaders.

VI

One of the most renowned scholars in the communities of Spain was Isaac Ibn Djiḳaṭilla, who in his youth was a disciple of M'naḥem Ben Sārūḳ and participated in writing the statement in defense of his teacher and master. Isaac Ibn Djiḳaṭilla continued to devote himself to the study and teaching of the Bible, and by the end of the tenth century was one of the most renowned among the Jewish scholars and writers of Andalusia. His name is testimony that he was a scion of an old Spanish family. This name, which was widespread among Spanish Jews, derived from the Spanish word *chico*, small; since the Arabs have no *ch* in their alphabet, they spelled the name with a *dj*, and the Jews did likewise.

When Isaac Ibn Djiḳaṭilla took part in writing the polemic against Dūnash b. Labraṭ, he was already an adult, which means that he was born around the year 930.[56] He enjoyed longevity, living, apparently, until the end of the first decade of the eleventh century. His fixed place of residence was in the city of Lucena.[57] He applied himself diligently to the subject he had studied with M'naḥem Ben Sārūḳ, becoming a grammarian of renown. He also delved into Arabic philology and was greatly influenced by it. For many years he taught Hebrew grammar and biblical exegesis at Lucena, as young men thirsty for culture came to study with him. Among the students who sat at his feet was a young man destined to become a famous grammarian, who included quotations from him in his books and designated him with the title "our master."[58] It is certain that he prompted his disciples to follow in his footsteps and acquire a basic knowledge in Arabic philology and literature to facilitate their understanding of the Scriptures and Hebrew grammar.

Like many of the scholars whose greatest desire was the knowledge and fostering of the Hebrew language, Isaac Ibn Djiḳaṭilla engaged in writing, and traces of his work have come down to us. From the time that Shim'ōn Kayyara, in *Halākhḥōt g'dōlōt,* had set down a list of the 613 precepts in the ninth century, a new kind of religious poetry had developed. This list did not meet the needs of the synagogue, and the poets therefore set it down in poetic form. These poems, which were designated for the festival of Sh'bhū'ōt, the festival celebrating the giving of the Torah, were termed *azhārōt* and enumerated the precepts in the language of the codifiers. For the greatest part, they were preceded by a *R'shūt* as an introduction.

At the end of the ninth and the first half of the tenth century many *azhārōt* were composed, and among these the most famous were the poems written by Saadya Gaon. His *azhārōt* had a decisive influence on the poets who followed him and composed such poems. Isaac Ibn Djiḳaṭilla too composed *azhārōt,* in which the influence of Saadya Gaon was clearly perceptible. Like the *azhārōt* of the *gaon,* each of his verses begin with the concluding word of the preceding stanza, and in like manner each stanza ends with a verse from the Scriptures. To be sure, he uses freedom in quoting the verses to make them match his own words.

The influence of the *gaon* on the language of Isaac Ibn Djiḳaṭilla was also very great, and he tends to follow the *gaon* in the enumeration of the precepts, which varies from that in the *Halākhḥōt g'dōlōt.* The *azhārōt* of Isaac Ibn Djiḳaṭilla are arranged in stanzas of three lines and one verse, and all the lines in a given verse start with the same letter. In the first stanza all lines begin with the letter alef and the last with the letter tav. Generally, each letter of the alphabet is assigned to two stanzas, but at times the poet deviates from this rule.[59] Such were the devices used by our poets in the Middle Ages in order to set down their poems in artistic form.

At that time there lived in Lucena yet another man who had won renown as an important philologist and poet—Isaac b. Levi Ben Mar Saul.[60] He was born, apparently, in the middle of the tenth century and was still living at the start of the eleventh century. He, too, was a teacher, giving instruction in the Hebrew language and explaining the Scriptures to his disciples.[61] From what can be deduced from quotations cited from his works, he was considered in his time to be one of the great philologists and one who was well versed in the Bible.[62] Many eminent philologists in the communities of Spain wrote commentaries on the Scriptures, and Isaac Ben Mar Saul was one of them; but none of his commentaries have come down to us.[63]

He also was endowed with outstanding ability as a poet and composed both religious and secular poetry. His poems do not exhibit any new ideas, but they are distinguished by a talent for expression. His language is beautiful and clear, and he knew well all those ingredients of the art of poetry that in the fullness of time became the hallmark of Hebrew poetry in Spain. In the hymn "Mī kā-mōkhā" (Who Is Like unto Thee) each stanza ends with a verse from the Scriptures whose last word is the name of God. Among his religious hymns one of the most successful was the supplication "My God, judge me not according to my guilt," which was designated for the New Year service. This hymn, written in metered verse, was included in the festival prayer book of several rites.

Thus his poems emphasize the progress that occurred in the religious poetry of Spanish Jewry in the generation after Dūnash—although it actually progressed less than secular poetry. The fertilization by Arabic poetry and the powerful influence to which it was amenable—which found its first expression in the acceptance of Arabic meter forms—can be most plainly seen in the secular poetry of Isaac Ben Mar Saul himself. He would compose poems on various occasions and send them to men of distinction and to his friends in the cities of Spain.[64] In these poems appear ideas and imagery familiar in Arabic poetry: "*sōd ha-ahābha*" (the secret of love), "*ha-s'rēfa*" (the conflagration) that erupted within the lover, and the yearnings for the companionship of friends. Isaac Ben Mar Saul also poetized on the beauty of young men, a subject completely new to Hebrew poetry. To be sure, this had been a familiar theme in Arabic poetry for a long time, and in the generations following Isaac Ben Mar Saul it became familiar also in Hebrew poetry.[65] This poet was thus a trail-blazer. His contemporaries were aware of this, and he acquired much fame as a poet.[66]

The number of Jewish intellectuals in Spain who wrote poetry grew apace by the end of the tenth century. It is true that most of them were mere poetasters devoid of true poetical skill. A later poet observes that in that era there were many poets who "make noises like bears."[67] Not even the names of most of these have come down to us. Nearly all of them sought to imitate the work of the Arabs. One of these whose real name was Ibn Abī Yaḳwā was known by the appellation al-Mutanabbī,[68] a name he borrowed from the great Arab poet who, as is well known, laid claim to prophecy. Aside from the scholars who poetized for the pleasure of it and from a desire to express themselves in the holy tongue, there were poets and versifiers who wrote for monetary gain. They would write paeans of praise and present themselves to men of wealth, reading their verse before an invited gathering; or alternatively, sending them to men in other cities in the hope of being rewarded.

Particularly representative of this class of poets was Abū Ibrāhīm Isaac Ibn Khalfōn,[69] who was, however, a poet of distinction. He was neither a scholar nor a teacher, but a poet who wrote only secular verse; and it is not for naught that a later writer referred to him as "the poet par excellence." Isaac Ibn Khalfōn was a writer of Maghrebin origin. During the time of the great efflorescence of the Omayyad kingdom, his father had come to Spain from Morocco and remained in Andalusia. Isaac himself, who was born around 970,[70] sojourned at Cordova in his youth. At an early age he had a marked ability for composing verse, which opened for him the doors to the homes of the wealthy who gave assistance to such as he; among others he frequented the home of Jacob Ibn Djau.[71] During his stay in Cordova he married into a distinguished family, that of Ibn Ḳaprōn.[72]

But his stay in the capital of Andalusia did not last long. As was the case with many Arabic poets, Ibn Khalfōn's livelihood depended solely upon poetry. He composed poems for affluent men in order to be remunerated, and he therefore began a circuit of Spanish cities in order to visit these benefactors and to declaim before them his laudatory poems.[73] As can be learned from the names of the men for whom he composed his verse and also from its content, he tarried awhile in Kairawan. He wrote poems in honor of Abraham ben Nathan ben 'Aṭā, who was the head of the Jewish community of Kairawan, and in honor of Judah b. Joseph, who was also one of the leaders of the community in that city.[74] He also sent verse to Joseph b. Jacob Ibn 'Aukal in Fostat and to the Jewish official Menasseh b. Abraham al-Ḳazzāz in Damascus.[75]

In his laudatory verse he extols the noble traits of the benefactors and at times he makes very transparent allusions to the assistance he hopes to receive from the benefactor. Among Ibn Khalfōn's verse that has been preserved we find poems composed for various occasions, such as family festivities, and elegies for those who have died. There are love poems and poems of friendship written after the manner of the Arabic poets. One of the themes that recur frequently in his verse is the anguish at parting from friends. In these verses Ibn Khalfōn especially excels. One of his poems runs:

With troubled heart and bitter mourning I lament
And sigh and weep bitterly.
I will give utterance, like the ostrich, to my sorrow
And will stir up my wailing and sobbing;
For time pursues me to destruction,
Seeking, like a foe, to bring upon me every evil
And on the day of parting, as though in a drawer,
My soul, life's breath, will be laid away.
To whom shall I go, on whom shall I look, and to whom
Shall I turn, and in whose name give voice to my song?[76]

Because he earned his living by his verse, Ibn Khalfōn had to compose numerous poems, but no more than fifty that are his of a certainty have been preserved. From one manuscript it appears that his diwan (collection of poems), or one of the diwans, contained elegies for the deceased in the first section and in the second, laudatory verse.[77] Because of their large number, the value of his poems varies greatly, but in the greatest number the true poetical ability and power to express the emotions of the poet are discernible.

Isaac Ibn Khalfōn filled an important role in the development of Hebrew poetry in Spain. After Dūnash b. Labraṭ had introduced meter into Hebrew poetry and made the form of Hebrew poetry similar to that of Arabic verse, the poets of the end of the tenth century also adopted the content of their verse for our literature; and of course they continued to adapt for their purposes the artistic forms of Arabic verse. Isaac Ibn Khalfōn, who composed much metered verse, accomplished a great feat in this respect, and his verse became an example and a model for Hebrew poets who followed in his footsteps. A remnant of his love songs has come down to us in which it is related how the poet goes to his beloved and encounters members of her family, who are guarding her. This is a variant on the well-known motif in ancient Arabic poetry wherein there appears a guard, called in their tongue *raḳīb*. (This motif was indeed already to be found in the work of the Latin poet Ovid.)

But particularly characteristic of the creations of Ibn Khalfōn are the laudatory verses he sent to his patrons. In Arabic poetry there is a fixed formula for the laudatory poems composed in honor of tribes and individuals. The poet first describes the site of the encampment of a bedouin tribe that has uprooted itself from its location, leaving practically no traces behind. The poet next brings to mind the hours he spent in the camp with his beloved, who has forsaken him. He sings about the camels, without which life would be impossible for the bedouins and upon which he pursued his beloved. Finally he moves on to his real theme: an encomium of the tribe or patron. The Arabic poets maintained this formula for a long time, and after some had rebelled against this conservatism, they returned to it at the end of the ninth century; in the tenth century the tendency to classicism grew ever stronger.

The *ḳaṣīdas* written in those days contain, as they formerly did, a poem that speaks of the beloved who has gone away (in Arabic this segment of the poem is called *nasīb*); then the poet mentions his wanderings—either to search for his beloved or because of despair; and at the end he recites the praise of the patron. Like the Arabs, Ibn Khalfōn also begins a poem he wrote in honor of a patron with a description of his forlorn beloved and the sufferings she endures; thereafter he moves on to his theme: praise for his patron (as for the wanderings, they are concentrated into one line). But the love of which the poet sings is—his love for a handsome youth, referred to in the rhetoric of the poets of that age as a "gazelle."

Alas for my heart and its multitude of sorrows
Its woes and its pains and its anguish—

With eyes of perfect beauty, graceful and charming
Who wounds, albeit painlessly, with his eyes,
My beloved who prolongs the night of his victims
While he slumbers at rest in his dwelling.[78]

The praises which the poet bestows in abundance upon the patrons are, Arab-fashion, somewhat commonplace. They are all exemplary for their modesty and their uprightness; they protect the poor and the wretched and carry on a struggle against the wicked, while the doors of their houses remain open to the impoverished who receive their benefactions.

For the greatest part Ibn Khalfōn directs his pleas to his patrons for financial assistance, whether he employs explicit language or through veiled hints. But after the fashion of roving minstrels among the Arabs, he also requests that he be given wine, "which causes sorrowful souls to dance," so that he may rejoice and be merry with his friends. And, like the Arabs, he writes boastfully about his talents and qualities. At this time he needed help and assistance and asked his friends to intercede with the wealthy in his behalf. Throughout his poetry there runs, like a thread of scarlet, his complaint against the rich, who, having promised him assistance, either did not fulfill their promises at all or were tardy in giving him succor. Then the poet would pour forth his wrath against the world, which did not appreciate him properly and belittled his talents.

But his embittering experiences with the patrons who had deceived him did not alter Isaac Ibn Khalfōn's way of life. He remained the wandering poet, moving from place to place, seeking supporters who appreciated the beauty of his verse. Meanwhile, he had reached middle age and his hair had whitened. But he held his ground. In those days he sojourned for a time at Granada and won much success in his appearances at the homes of the wealthy.

One evening, at the beginning of the summer, he was invited

to go immediately to the house of a rich Jew, who had been appointed to a high post in the royal service and had that very day gathered his friends to celebrate his appointment. Just as this man had not known that before nightfall he would have occasion to arrange the soiree, Isaac Ibn Khalfōn had not known that he would be invited to attend. He scored a triumph that evening that became engraved in his memory.

By a narrow door he entered a long and dark corridor that led to a spacious quadrangular courtyard enclosed on three sides by wings of the new dignitary's house. In the middle of the courtyard were grassy plots surrounded by flower beds giving forth a powerful fragrance. In the center was a pool fed by the waters of a fountain that flowed unceasingly. Around the two long sides of the courtyard sat about twenty-five men, their feet outstretched before them, on rugs that were spread on the floor of the courtyard, which was paved with marble. All were garbed in white, and both the broad white *zihāra* and the trousers encasing their legs were of glistening white silk. On their heads they wore small caps.

A girl was playing on a harp and singing in Arabic those tender folk songs that end with a stanza in Romance, which repeats itself as a refrain—songs that were so popular with the Andalusians. Next, another girl played on a flute, accompanied by a youth beating a drum. The guests partook of fruits placed in big heaps on low tables, while from time to time servants would bring wine, offering it in small glasses.

At last the host gestured to the poet to declaim his verse, and Ibn Khalfōn recited a florid poem in which he proclaimed all the qualities of the new officeholder, his deeds in behalf of his coreligionists, the alms he gave to the poor, and the merits of his forefathers, who were nobles in Israel. Not all those present understood the beautiful biblical Hebrew, but all listened intently; not a sound was heard. When the poet had finished he bowed to the host, who drew forth from the folds of his coat a purse full of gold pieces and handed it to Ibn Khalfōn. All his friends voiced cries of enthusiasm over the beauty of the poem and the generosity of the noble lord. A few arose from their places to stroll in the corners of the courtyard, where tall trees stood; others remained seated and engaged in spiritual but friendly conversation.

It was a warm and pleasant summer night, the skies were strewn with innumerable stars, and the moon shone with a brilliant light. From a distance could be heard a monotonous voice, yet pleasant to the ear: "There is no God but Allah, and Mohammed is the prophet of Allah. Life to those who pray to Him, life to those who serve Him." Again and again the voice repeated its cry saturated with yearnings. This was the muezzin calling the Moslem to prayer, for this was the month of Ramadan, when the call to prayer is sounded before dawn. East and West had met under Andalusian skies.

ABBREVIATIONS

BAC *Boletin de la Academia de Ciencias, Bellas Letras y Nobles Artes de Córdoba*

BAH *Boletin de la Academia de la historia* (Madrid)

BJPES *Bulletin of the Jewish Palestine Exploration Society*

CB Catalogus librorum Hebraeorum in Bibliotheca Bodleiana . . . digessit M. Steinschneider

CHE *Cuadernos de historia de España*

HB Hebraeische Bibliographie

HUCA *Hebrew Union College Annual*

JQR *Jewish Quarterly Review*

MAH Memorias de la Academia de historia

MGWJ *Monatsschrift für Geschichte und Wissenschaft des Judentums*

PAAJR *Proceedings of the American Academy for Jewish Research*

RABM *Revista de archivos, bibliotecas y museos* (Madrid)

REJ *Revue des Études Juives*

ZDMG *Zeitschrift der Deutschen morgenländischen Gesellschaft*

SOURCES

Short form used in Notes is given in parentheses

1. IN HEBREW

Abraham b. Dā'ūd. *The Book of Tradition* [Sefer *ha-ḳabbāla*], ed. G. D. Cohen. Philadelphia, 1967 (Abraham b. Dā'ūd).

'Amram Gaon. *Seder Rabh 'Amram*. Warsaw, 1865 (*Seder Rabh 'Amram*).

Cantera, F. and Millás, J. M. *Las inscripciones hebraicas de España*. Madrid, 1956 (Cantera-Millás).

Ibn 'Ezrā, Moses. *Sefer Shīrat Yisrāēl*, ed. B.-Z. Halper. Leipzig, 1924 (*Shīrat Yisrāēl*).

Isaac Abba Mari. *Sefer ha-'iṭṭūr*. Venice, 1608 (*Sefer ha-'iṭṭūr*).

Ginzberg, L. *Geonica*, vols. 1 and 2. New York, 1909 (*Geonica*).

Al-Ḥarīzī, Y'hūda. *Taḥk'mōnī*, ed. Kaminka. Warsaw, 1899 (*Taḥ-k'mōnī*).

Kokowzow, P. K.
Leningrad, 1932 (Kokowzow).

Müller, J. *Die Responsen der spanischen Lehrer des 10. Jahrhunderts*. Berlin, 1889 (Müller).

Sha'arē Ṣedeḳ. Salonica, 1792 (*Sha'arē Ṣedeḳ*).

T'shūbhōt g'ōnē mizraḥ u-ma'arabh, ed. J. Müller. Berlin, 1888 (*T'shūbhōt GMUM*).

2. IN ARABIC

Akhbār madjmū'a fī fatḥ al-Andalus, ed. E. Lafuente y Alcantara. Madrid, 1867 (*Akhbār madjmū'a*).

Fatḥo-l-Andaluçi: Historia de la conquista de España. Algiers, 1899 (*Fatḥo-l-Andaluçi*).

Gayangos, Pascual de, ed. *Memoria sobre la autenticidad de la cronica denominada del Moro Rasis.* Madrid, 1850 (ar-Rāzī.)

Ibn 'Abdalmun'im al-Ḥimyarī. *Kitāb ar-Raud al-mi'ṭār,* ed. Lévi-Provençal, French translation *La péninsule ibérique au moyen âge.* Cairo-Leiden, 1837-38 (*ar-Raud al-mi'ṭār*).

Ibn Abī Uṣaibi'a. *'Uyūn al-anbā.* Cairo, 1882 (Ibn Abī Uṣaibi'a).

Ibn al-Athīr. *Al-Kāmil fi 't-ta'rīkh,* ed. Tornberg, vols. 1-14. Leiden, 1851-76 (Ibn al-Athīr); French (partial) translation: *Annales du Maghreb et de l'Espagne traduites et annotées par E. Fagnan.* Algiers, 1898 (Fagnan).

Ibn 'Idhārī. *Al-Bayān al-mughrib,* vol. 2, ed. G.S. Colin–E. Lévi-Provençal. Leiden, 1951 (Ibn 'Idhārī).

Ibn Khaldūn. *Kitāb al-'ibar,* vols. 1-7. Būlāk, 1284 (Ibn Khaldūn).

Ibn Khurdādhbeh. *Kitāb al-Masālik wa'l-mamālik.* Leiden, 1889 (Ibn Khurdādhbeh).

Al-Idrīsī. *Description de l'Afrique et de l'Espagne . . . publiée avec une traduction par R. Dozy et M.J. de Goeje.* Leiden, 1866 (al-Idrīsī).

Al-Maḳḳarī. *Analectes . . . publ. par Dozy, Dugat, Krehl et Wright,* vols. 1 and 2. Leiden, 1855-61 (al-Maḳḳarī).

Al-Muḳaddasī. *Kitāb aḥsan at-taḳāsīm,* 2d ed. Leiden, 1906 (al-Muḳaddasī).

An-Nuwairī. *Historia de los musulmanes de España y Africa.* Granada, 1917 (an-Nuwairī).

3. OTHER

Baer, (F.) Y. *A History of the Jews in Christian Spain,* vols. 1 and 2. Philadelphia, 1961-66 (Baer).

Kirjath Sepher, a bibliographical quarterly.

Zion, a quarterly for research in Jewish history.

NOTES

See Sources for full references

CHAPTER ONE

1. *Akhbār madjmū'a*, p. 14; al-Maķķarī, 1, p. 166. The compiler of *Akhbār madjmū'a*, who is identical with the author of the chapter on the conquest, was apparently a Cordovan, and his account of the capture of the city reflects an old and trustworthy tradition. Al-Maķķarī copied a great deal from the Arabic historian Ibn Ḥayyān, and what is related in *Akhbār madjmū'a* apparently reached him in this fashion. Cf. Cl. Sánchez-Albornoz, *El Ajbār maymū'a*, pp. 47, 76, 260 ff.
2. *Akhbār madjmū'a*, p. 12.
3. Al-Maķķarī, 1, p. 166.
4. *Akhbār madjmū'a*, p. 12; al-Maķķarī, p. 166. Cf. Cl. Sánchez-Albornoz, "Itinerario de la conquista de España por los Musulmanes," *CHE* 10 (1948):34.
5. The first source is the monk Lucas de Tuy (d. 1249). See *Chronicon mundi, Hispania illustrata*, 4, pp. 70-71. His words are repeated by Gil de Zamora, who some fifty years later wrote his *Liber de preconiis civitatis Numantine*. See Fidel Fita, "Dos libros (inéditos) de Gil Zamora," *BAH* 5:138. Other Christian authors added many details. The account of the Christian procession and the handing over of the city by the Jews has already definitely been refuted by E. Saavedra, *Estudio sobre la invasión de los Arabes en España*, p. 79, mainly because the Christian writers relate that this was on the Sunday before Easter, and we would therefore have to assume that the capture of the city was preceded by a protracted siege, which does not correspond to the historical facts as they are reported in trustworthy Arabic sources. See the sources cited in the following note, and see note 7: see also the account of Ibn Abi 'l-Fayyāḍ in M. Casiri, *Bibliotheca Arabico-Hispana Escurialensis* (Madrid, 1760-70), 2, p. 320. From Ibn al-Athīr, 4, p. 446, it can be concluded that the conquest of Toledo occurred during year 92 after the *hidjra*, the last day of

which was October 18, 711. (In the treatises of later Christian authors there is great confusion as to the year in which the city was captured. But this is not as important as the date within the year.) At all events, the Arabs took the city without the need of a siege. Apparently the Christians knew that the gate opposite the Church of Santa Leocadia was called, since early times, "the Jews' Gate"; therefore they held that the Jews opened this gate, and it appears that they opened precisely that gate through which the inhabitants of Toledo passed in procession, that is, they acted treacherously before their very eyes.

An important proof against these Christian writers can also be advanced from the absence of the account of the treachery of the Jews in the book of Rodrigo Jimenez, who was archbishop of Toledo and a responsible historian (see note 10 below). It must be assumed that the aforementioned writers, for whom the loss of Toledo symbolized the loss of all of Spain, wanted to create a link between the fall of the capital city and the activity of the Jews after the conquest of Spain, and the date is characteristic of the symbolism of the entire story. The Christian writers add that this occurred on the day when the Jews had "sentenced Jesus to die"! And indeed, as against the story about the treachery of the Jews, Spanish authors (and at times these selfsame ones) stress that the city was handed over by means of a treaty of submission, and they even know the paragraphs it contains. See A. Martín Gamero, *Historia de la ciudad de Toledo* (Toledo, 1862), pp. 531-32; Pedro de Alcocer, *Hystoria o descripcion de la imperial ciudad de Toledo* (Toledo, 1554), p. 39a.

6. Ar-Rāzī ed. Gayangos, p. 72; Ibn 'Idhārī, p. 12; Ibn al-Athīr, 4, p. 446 (Fagnan, p. 46); al-Maḳḳarī, 1, p. 167.
7. In the Arabic sources the exact date of the capture of Toledo was not indicated, but it may be assumed that it happened in the beginning of October. After the capture of Ecija. Ṭāriḳ did not meet any substantial opposition, and since his success resulted primarily from the speed of his march, it is fairly certain that he arrived at Toledo within five weeks.
8. *Akhbār madjmū'a*, p. 16; Ibn al-Athīr, 4, p. 447; al-Maḳḳarī, 1, p. 170. Some sources state that Mūsā besieged the city for several months, but this is incorrect.
9. Ar-Rāzī in Casiri, 2, p. 105; see also M. Gomez Moreno, "De Illiberi a Granada," *BAH* 46:49; cf. Sánchez-Albornoz, "Itinerario," pp. 53 ff.
10. Rodrigo Jimenez, *Rerum in Hispania gestarum chronicum,* book 3, (Granada, 1545), p. 29a.
11. R. Amador de los Rios, *Historia social, politica y religiosa de los judios de España y Portugal* (Madrid, 1875-6), 1, p. 107; A. Ballesteros y Beretta, *Historia de España y su influencia en la historia universal* (Barcelona, 1918-36), 2, p. 107.
12. Baer, 1, p. 23 (more emphatically in the Hebrew edition, p. 14); cf. Lévi-Provençal *Histoire de l'Espagne musulmane* (Paris, 1950-53), 1, p. 80.
13. See *Fatḥo-l-Andaluçi*, p. 8; Ibn 'Idhārī, 2, p. 229; al-Maḳḳarī, 1, p. 368.
14. See sources indicated in notes 2 and 3. The word *ḳaṣaba,* which appears

in these texts, means both the chief city of a region and a citadel.

15. According to Saavedra, *Estudio,* p. 96, the policy of the conquerors changed after the siege against Mérida. According to him, that is when the cooperation between the Moslems and the inhabitants of Spain who had first sided with them came to an end; but the Spanish scholar's words are without proof (see below).
16. See R. Dozy, *Histoire des musulmans d'Espagne* (Leiden, 1932) 1, p. 141.
17. Ibn 'Abdalḥakam, *Futūḥ Miṣr,* ed. Torrey (*The History of the Conquest of Egypt, North Africa and Spain,* New Haven, 1922), p. 82.
18. An anonymous chronicle in Latin from Cordova, *España Sagrada,* 8, p. 302.
19. Ibid., p. 306.
20. Ibid., p. 307.
21. Ibid.
22. Ibid., p. 312.
23. Ibid., pp. 312-13.
24. Ibid., p. 321.
25. A. C. Vega, "Una herejía judaizante de principios del siglo VIII en España," *Ciudad de Dios* 153 (1941):57 ff.; idem, *Bulletin de théologie ancienne et médievale* 7 (1954):63.
26. *Sha'are Ṣedeḳ,* part 3, section 5, no. 7, 10. The Byzantine-Christian sources in H. Graetz, *Geschichte der Juden,* 4th ed. (Leipzig, 1888 ff.) note 14. Concerning events in Spain, the anonymous writer from Cordova gives an account, *España Sagrada,* pp. 306–7. (His words must be accepted with reservation, especially since the text is corrupt; compare what Graetz wrote.) Regarding the false Messiah, see Brüll, *Jahrbücher für jüd. Geschichte u. Literatur* 9 (1889): 119; I. Friedlaender, "Jewish-Arabic Studies," *JQR,* n. s. 1:210–11; S. Krauss, *Studien zur byzantisch-jüdischen Geschichte* (Vienna, 1914), pp. 38 ff. See also S. Poznanski, "M'yasdei kitot b'Yisrael," *R'hsumot* 1:209. However, Syrian sources published by J. B. Chabot invalidate all these conjectures and leave no room for doubt that the man's name was Severa-Severus. See J. Starr, "Le mouvement méssianique au début du VIIIe siècle," *REJ* 102:81 ff.

    The *gaon's* response, which no doubt relates to this movement, decisively refutes the supposition that this was a Christian who wanted to deride the Jews, but instead, as stated, points to a movement rooted in the stream of Jewish thought. Brüll, Friedlaender, Poznanski, and especially Ginsberg, *Geonica,* 1, pp. 50-51, dispute the identification of the responding *gaon* as Naṭrōnai bar Nehemiah, the *gaon* of Pumbedita at the time of the Severus movement, with whom Graetz identified him, and the prove that he was Naṭrōnai bar Hilai, the *gaon* of Sura. If that is so, we must assume that those who supported Severa maintained their view for 130 years, and indeed one of the aforementioned responsa does speak of "members" of these sectarian groups.

    Starr is of the opinion that a copyist who found information on an incident that occurred in the Orient introduced it into the text of the anonymous chronicle and wrote, in place of the name of the Syrian ruler, that of the Spanish ruler, who was better known to his readers. However, the chronicle is replete with the names of Arab rulers in Eastern lands; why should he change precisely this name? The text hints clearly at preparations by Jews to return to Palestine. The supposition that the passage was introduced by a later writer does not render its trustworthiness invalid. The knowledge of the spread of the movement in various countries—in this instance Spain—is in line with the fact embodied in the question addressed to the *gaon*: that this heresy existed 130 years. Thus, this was a movement that embraced wide circles and possessed a considerable measure of inner strength. Cf. S. W. Baron, *A Social and Religious History of the Jews*, 2nd ed. (New York, 1952 ff.), 5, p. 381.

CHAPTER TWO

1. *Akhbār madjmū'a*, pp. 54-55; Ibn 'Idhārī, p. 41; al-Maḳḳarī, 2, pp. 18–19; cf. Dozy, 1, pp. 193–94. This account bears the stamp of originality, for it is apparently taken from ar-Rāzī, who transmits the account of 'Abdarraḥmān's companion.
2. Cf. I. Cagigas, *Los Mozarabes* (Madrid, 1947-48), 1, p. 112.
3. See al Maḳḳarī, 1, p. 215.
4. Ibn 'Idhārī, p. 229; al-Maḳḳarī, 1, p. 368. Doubt was cast on this account by H. Terasse, *L'art hispano-mauresque des origines au XIII siècle* (Paris, 1932), p. 59, and K.A.C. Creswell, *Early Muslim Architecture* (Oxford, 1932–40), 2, p. 139, because in their opinion it was copied from an account dating from the later Middle Ages concerning the partition of the large church in Damascus, and was then included in the chronicle of ar-Rāzī, on which Ibn 'Idhārī and al-Maḳḳarī base their accounts; whereas ar-Rāzī relies on Muḥammad b. 'Īsā, who was a young contemporary of 'Abdarraḥmān I; see Cl. Sánchez-Albornoz, *En torno a los origenes del feudalismo* (Mendoza, 1942), 2, p. 45 ff. Moreover, in the Arabic account it is stated that the Moslems first "built" a mosque in a part of the church that they had taken for themselves. From this it can be concluded that they built a mosque for themselves in the large courtyard, near the church. And the scholar who made a meticulous examination of the account of the partition of the mosque in Damascus himself came to the conclusion that the Moslems did indeed build for themselves a mosque in the capital of Syria near the large church. H. Lammens, *Etudes sur le siècle des Omayyades* (Beirut, 1930), pp. 281-82; and Creswell (1, p. 131) also reached the same conclusion.
5. The information concerning the persecution of Christians and the destruction of churches in the days of 'Abderrahmān I is more than questionable. See E. Saavedra, "Abderrahmen I," *RABM* 3a, series 3 t. 23, pp. 37-38; Sánchez-Albornoz, *En torno*, 3, p. 211.
6. J. Migne, PL 98, p. 385.
7. See below, p. 66.
8. Ibn al-Ḳūṭīya, *Ta'rīkh iftitāḥ al-Andalus* (Madrid, 1868), pp. 53-54;

al-Marrākushī, *Al-Mudjib fī talkhīs akhbār al-Maghrib* (Cairo, 1324), p. 13; an-Nuwairī, p. 39; al-Maḳḳarī, 1, p. 900.

9. See above, p. 45.

10. See *Sefer Sha'arē T'shūvōt* by Maharam of Rothenburg (ed. Mēḳīzē Nirdāmīm), p. 193.

11. The Arabic source that relates in detail the founding of the city of Fez, from which conclusions may be drawn regarding the settlement of the Jews in the new city immediately after it was founded, is the book *Al-Anīs al-muṭrib*, by Ibn Abī Zar'; in the passage that depicts the stream of settlers who came to Fez immediately after its founding (ed. Tornberg, p. 24), there is, to be sure, no mention of Jews. In Beaumier's translation this is his own addendum. See A. Beaumier, *Roudh el-kartas, Histoire des souverains du Maghrib* (Paris, 1880), p. 55; on p. 573 Beaumier, in connection with this passage, clarifies that the Jews came from Spain; this too is his own addendum. It is true that Ibn Abī Zar' speaks of Spaniards settling in Fez; see the above citation and ed. Tornberg, p. 29 (in Beaumier's translation, p. 65). He also mentions the huge amount of taxes imposed on the Jews shortly after the city's founding. On this matter see Lévi-Provençal, "La fondation de Fès," *Annales de l'Institut d'Etudes Orientales de l'Université d'Alger* 4 (1938): 49.

12. See J. Aronius, *Regesten zur Geschichte der Juden im fränkischen u. deutschen Reiche bis zum Jahre 1273* (Berlin, 1902), no. 83; cf. G. Caro, *Sozial-u. Wirtschaftsgeschichte der Juden in Mittelalte und der Neuzeit,* (Frankfurt-Leipzig, 1924), 1, pp. 133-34.

13. Al-Maḳḳarī, 2, p. 85; E. Lévi-Provençal, *Histoire de l'Espagne musulmane* (Paris, 1950-53), 1, p. 269.

14. According to one chronicle Bodo converted to Judaism in 839. See *España Sagrada*, 10, pp. 601-2; but in the other sources the date indicated is 838. These sources are cited in a study by M. Kayserling, "Eleasar und Alvaro," *MGWJ* 9 (1860): 241-51; see especially p. 244, note 9, and see also Aronius, no. 103. Kayserling, following in the footsteps of Florez, *España Sagrada*, 11, pp. 20-21, secks to harmonize the two traditions, stating Bodo became a convert in 838 and reached Spain in 839. He also expressed the view that Bodo became a convert in southern France, but this conjecture has nothing to support it. H. Vogelstein and P. Rieger, *Geschichte der Juden in Rom* (Berlin, 1896) 1, p. 135, conjecture that Bodo became converted in Rome, but this conjecture too has nothing to support it. For the reasons for Bodo's conversion, see A. Cabaniss, "Bodo-Eleazar, A Famous Jewish Convert," *JQR,* n. s. 43: 313-28; he does not take into consideration the influence of the Jews. Concerning this, B. Blumenkranz commented in "Au nouveau sur Bodo-Eleazar?" *REJ* 112: 35-42.

15. "Epistola sive liber contra Judaeos ad Carolum regem," Migne, 116, col. 171.

16. He is thus called ibid., and this is an appropriate name for a proselyte, having been the name of Abraham's servant. But most sources give Eleazar, and perhaps the name was pronounced like Eleazar.

17. Blumenkranz, "Au nouveau," holds that it must not be inferred from the account that he wore a *cingulum militare*. In his view this is a *zunnār,* a mark of identification, a mark of ignominy, which the Moslems imposed upon non-Moslems. But as against this, the Christian writer would under no circumstance have referred to a *zunnār* as a "military belt" because it did not resemble it. The report in the Christian source that from the time of his conversion Bodo had the "exterior appearance [*habitus*] of a Jew" refers, no doubt, to his beard!
18. On these heretical movements see F. J. Simonet, *Historia de los mozárabes de España* (Madrid, 1903), pp. 261 ff.; M. Menendez-Pelayo, *Historia de los heterodoxos españoles* (Madrid, 1956), 1, pp. 352 ff. Note there that the influence of the Jews upon these movements did not escape the notice of the church authorities.
19. Alvaro says of himself (in addressing Bodo): "Who is more deserving of the name Israel [Jew]: you, who are not of Jewish stock but only of its religion, or I, who am a Jew by race and religion albeit I am not called a Jew, for I received a new name [in the spirit of Isaiah 51:2]? Is not my father Abraham?" See *España Sagrada,* 11, p. 196. He states, moreover: "*Majores mei . . . expectantes enim Messiam venturum et recipientes venientem*" (ibid.). From this it can be concluded that his forebears became Christian converts in the days when the Visigoths ruled. It is unreasonable to assume, as does Flores, *España Sagrada,* 2, p. 11, that his forebears accepted Christianity in its earliest days. Flores seizes upon the present tense of the last-mentioned passage, but it is unthinkable that a Christian family remembered its Jewish origin over a period of eight hundred years and took pride in it, while on the other hand it is well known that a time much closer to the life of Alvaro thousands of Jews in Spain itself had been forced to become Christians. His ancestors, of course, did marry into Visigothic families, and therefore Alvaro boasts of his Gothic blood. On this matter see J. Madoz, "Alvaro de Cordoba," *BAC* 20: 21-22.
20. This date, of course, confirms that the conversion occurred in 838; otherwise how could he manage to delve into the writings of the sages and become renowned as one seeking to win converts to the Jewish religion?
21. These letters were printed in *España Sagrada,* 11, pp. 171-218 and in J. Madoz, *Epistolario de Alvaro de Cordoba* (Madrid, 1947), pp. 211-81; see, too, the introduction, pp. 56-57, for the sources on which Alvaro depends. There is also an analysis of the letters in B. Blumenkranz, "Auteurs latins du Moyen Âge sur les juifs," *REJ* 119: 37. Blumenkranz also attempted a restoration of Bodo's words, but he, too, restored them as if there were only one document (and not an exchange of letters); see "Un pamphlet juif médio-latin de prolémique antichrétienne," *Revue d'histoire et de philosophie religieuse* 34 (1954): 401-13.
22. "Numerabis tibi septem hebdomadas annorum," *España Sagrada,* 11, p. 176.
23. "Epistola sive liber contra Judaeos ad Carolum regem," Migne, 116, col. 171.

24. Printed in Annales Bertiniani contained in *España Sagrada,* 10, pp. 602-3.

CHAPTER THREE

1. According to Eulogius's account, Muḥammad I dismissed all the Christian officials on the day he mounted the royal throne; but his account is incorrect, as is demonstrated by the information concerning the official Gomez b. Antonian. See the sources cited in Dozy, 1, p. 353. He nevertheless follows the view of Eulogius.
2. The monastery of Pinamelaria, for example, existed in 858. See *España Sagrada,* 10, pp. 396-97. It had been founded somewhat earlier. See ibid., p. 415.
3. *España Sagrada,* 11, p. 384; Amador de los Rios, *Historia,* 1, p. 132.
4 It was printed in *España Sagrada,* 11, pp. 325-561.
5. Ibn al-Athīr, 7, p. 38; cf. Lévi-Provençal, 1, p. 212.
6. Ibn al-Athīr 7, pp. 53-54; Ibn 'Idhārī, pp. 95-96.
7. Ibn al-Athīr, p. 71; an-Nuwairī, p. 54.
8. Lévi-Provençal is of the opinion that the chronicler has reference to the military campaign of 856. See his first volume, 313-14.
9. Annales Bertiniani in *España Sagrada,* 10, p. 603.
10. Ibn Ḥayyān, ed. Antuna, p. 93. Cf. Dozy, 2, p. 67. Lévi-Provençal, 1, p. 372, erroneously states that the city was captured by 'Umar b. Ḥafṣūn. But cf. Simonet, "Biografia de Omar Eben Hafsun," appended to *Descripción del reino de Granāda bajo la dominación de los Naseritas* (Madrid, 1868), see p. 154.
11. Kokowzow, p. 10.
12. Ibn Djuldjul, *Ṭabaḳāt al-aṭibbā wa 'l-ḥukamā* (Cairo, 1955), p. 85; and from it Ibn Abī Uṣaibi'a, 2, p. 36. Basing himself on Leo Africanus, Wolf, in *Bibliotheca Hebraea,* 1, p. 686, refers to Isḥāḳ b. 'Imrān as a Jew, and E. Carmoly also states that Isḥāḳ b. 'Imrān was a Jew, while the physician from Spain was a Christian. Moreover, since Carmoly found, in Leo Africanus, that Isḥāḳ died in the year 183 A.H. (799 C.E.), he determined that there were two people called Isḥāḳ b. 'Imrān, a man who lived at the end of the eighth century and his grandson, who bore the same name and lived at the beginning of the tenth century; see *Histoire des médecins juifs* (Brussels, 1844), pp. 19, 25. However, even prior to Carmoly, F. Wüstenfeld had observed that the statement of Leo Africanus (in his treatise *De viris illustribus*) was refutable. See *Geschichte der arabischen Aerzte* (Göttingen, 1840), pp. 32-33; *Magazin f. d. Wiss. des Judentums* 7 (1880): 103; and the article by N. Slouschz: "Isaac b. Imran the Physician," *The Jewish Physician* 18 (1945), no. 2: 66-67. Slouschz refers to both physicians as Jews.
13. Ed. Klar, p. 14.
14. *España Sagrada,* 2, p. 318; M. Gomez-Moreno, *Iglesias Mozárabes* (Madrid, 1919) pp. 106 ff.; Cagigas, 1, pp. 268 ff.
15. Chronicle of Alfonso III in Gomez Moreno, "Las primeras crónicas de la reconquista," *BAH* 100: 619-20.
16. Ibn 'Idhārī, p. 124.

17. See Sánchez-Albornoz, *CHE,* number 3: 44. J. Eloy Díaz-Jiménez, "Immigración mozarabe en el reino de León," *BAH* 20: 123 ff.
18. Amador de los Rios, *Historia,* 1, pp. 166-67.
19. Y. Baer, *Tōl'dōth ha-y'hūdīm bi-s'fārād ha-noṣrith* (Tel Aviv, 5719/1959), 1, pp. 42, 45.
20. Gomez-Moreno, *Iglesias Mozárabes,* p. 115; Eloy Díaz-Jiménez, "Immigración," p. 140; C. Sánchez-Albornoz, "Serie de documentos ineditos del reino de Asturias," *CHE* 1-2, no. 14: 346-47. There are also those who read it as Nabaz (Arabic for "one who sells wine"); however, the name Habaz also appears as a Jewish family name in other documents from León.
21. J. Rodríguez, "Judería de León," *Archivos Leoneses* 2, no. 2 (1948): 7, 29; no. 7 (1950): 31. In the first article, p. 51: Totadomna (in 985), that is Sayyidat al-kull. In the second article in the same document in which Yūsuf appears also (in 998) Crescente, that is perhaps Zaid.
22. F. Baer, *Die Juden im christl. Spanien* (Berlin, 1929-36), 2, no. 1.
23. J. Rodríguez, "Judería de Sahagun," *Archivos Leoneses,* no. 14 (1953): 37.
24. Amador de los Rios, *Historia,* 1, p. 173.
25. Ibid. The Jews of León are also mentioned in Jewish literary sources of that time. See *Sefer ha-riḳma,* ed. Wilensky, p. 338.
26. See F. Fita, "Paleografia hebrea," *BAH* 4: 206, concerning a Jew named Yaḥyā.

CHAPTER FOUR

1. R. Moses b. Naḥman (Ramban), *Milḥamōt adonai,* on P'sāḥīm, p. 30 (marginalia in *Hilkhōt ha-Rīf* [Isaac Alfasi] [Vilna, 1912], p. 7b), on Baba Kama, p. 85b (op. cit., p. 31b); *Ḥiddūshī R. Sh'lomo b. Adret* (Rashba) on P'sāḥīm, pp. 26a, 30a, 41a, 55b, 54a.
2. In the Hebrew sources his father is called both Ḥanīnae and Ḥakhīnae. The correct version is Ḥabībae; see below.
3. *Sefer ha-pardes* (Constantinople, 1802), p. 28, col. a; A. Harkavy, *Ha-Ṣōfē,* suppl. to *Ha-Maggīd* 15 (1871): 246; *Or zarū'a* (Zitomir, 5622), part 1, 57, col. b.
4. The letter of Sh'rīra Gaon (ed. Lewin), p. 104; *Sefer ha-'ittīm* by Judah bar Barzilai of Barcelona (Cracow, 5663), f. 267; cf. pp. 255-56. See also *Geonica,* 2, pp. 16-17; J. Mann, Responsa," *JQR,* n. s. 7: 486 (on the date) and also A.D. Goode, "The Exilarchate in the Eastern Caliphate, 637-1258," *JQR,* n. s. 31: 157.
5. See the words of the Nagid in *Sefer ha-'ittīm,* f. 267, and the beginning of the letter published by H. Cowley, "Bodleian Geniza Fragments," *JQR* 18: 401.
6. Abraham b. Dā'ūd, p. 47 (translation p. 65).
7. See *Sefer ha-'ittīm,* f. 267.
8. So stated in the aforementioned letter published by Cowley, loc. cit.
9. The nature of the taxes has not yet been fully clarified. For a summary of various opinions, see S. Assaf, *T'ḳūfat ha-g'ōnīm v'sifrūtah* (Jerusalem, 5715), pp. 68-69.

10. *Ḥemdah G'nūza* (Jerusalem, 5623), no. 15, *Geonica,* 2, p. 30; cf. A. Büchler, *REJ* 50: 159; Mann, *JQR,* n. s. 7: 482; Assaf, *Kirjath Sepher,* 18, p. 320.
11. *JQR* 18: 401.
12. *Seder Rabh 'Amram,* p. 41a; cf. *Halākhōt G'dōlōt* (ed. Hildesheimer), p. 144, and S. Assaf, *Ha-Shilōah* 35: 405. To be sure, it is not known whether this responsum was sent to the Jews of Moslem or Christian Spain (to Barcelona), and this applies to other responsa.
13. *Sha'arē Ṣedeḳ,* part 3, section 5, no. 4; cf. *Seder Rabh 'Amram,* f. 52b and *Halākhōt G'dōlūt,* p. 106; *Seder Rabh 'Amram,* 40a.
14. *T'shūbhōt GMUM,* no. 26; cf. *Hilkhōt R. Isaac Giyyāt* (*Sha'arē Simḥa,* Fürth, 5621-5622) part 2, p. 20; "Thus did Naṭrōnai respond to our ancestors, etc."
15. (a) *Geonica,* 2, pp. 318-25; see Epstein in his introduction to the commentary to *Seder Ṭohorōt,* p. 85, which states that the commentaries were sent to Spain; (b) S. Assaf, *Gaonic Responsa from Geniza MSS.* (Jerusalem, 1928), pp. 147-48. The commentaries published by Ginzberg and Assaf were sent to various questioners; those published by Assaf were written first, inasmuch as Naṭrōnai is alluded to three times in the commentaries published by Ginzberg.
16. Besides the responsa mentioned in the two preceding notes, reference should be made to the following responsa, which, according to various indications, were sent to Spain: *T'shūbhōt GMUM,* no. 24-26, 28; *Geonica,* 2, pp. 114-17; *Hilkhōt R. Isaac Giyyāt,* part 2, p. 44; *Sha'arē Ṣedeḳ,* part 3, section 4, no. 12; *Ḳ'bhūṣat ḥakhāmīm* (Vienna, 1861), pp. 110-11; *T'shūbhōt ha-g'ōnīm,* ed. Mussafia (Lik, 5624), no. 87; *Halākhōt p'sūḳōt min ha-g'ōnīm* (Cracow, 5653), no. 130; *Seder Rabh 'Amram,* 24b, 25a, 26b, 37b f., 41b, 42a, 43b; *Sefer ha-manhīg,* 63b.
17. See E. Ashkenazi, *Ṭa'am z'ḳēnīm* (Frankfurt on Oder, 5615), pp. 55a, 56a; Commentary on *Sefer ha-y'sīra* by Judah bar Barzilai of Barcelona (Berlin, 5645), pp. 103-4. The sources from the Middle Ages tell of two Naṭrōnais who came from Babylonia to Spain, and some scholars held them to be a single identical person. See Schorr in introduction to *Sefer ha-'itlim,* p. xi, and S. Poznanski in *Sefer ha-zikkārōn l'Harkavy,* p. 219, and also Ginzberg, *Geonica,* 1, p. 17. But the truth is that both persons filled an important role in the dissemination of the Talmud in Spain. However, even as nothing prevents one's belief in the old tradition that the deposed exilarch, Naṭrōnai b. Ḥabībae came to Spain, it is also clear that the account of the journey of Naṭrōnai Gaon is merely a legend stemming from the historical fact of his close ties with the Jews of Spain.
18. See *T'shūbhōt ha-g'ōnīm* (ed. Mussafia), no. 56-58; *Geonica,* 2, pp. 326-45; Assaf, *T'shūbhōt ha-g'ōnīm,* pp. 61-75.
19. See the letter that Cowley published in *JQR* 18: 401. It is difficult to reach sure conclusions as to the chronology of the *g'ōnīm* of Sura because of the deficiencies in the chief source, *Iggeret* (the Letter) of Sh'rīra Gaon, and because of the limited number of responsa bearing dates. For this reason, scholars have struggled very much with this problem. See especially H. Graetz, "Die Chronologie der gaonäischen

Epoche," *MGWJ* 6 (1857): 336 ff., 381 ff.; idem, *History of the Jews* (Philadelphia, 1891-98), 5, p. 522.

20. On his ties with the Jews of Spain, see Cowley, op. cit.
21. See ibid.; see also *T'shūbhōt GMUM,* no. 19, and a corrected text in S. Assaf, *Geonica* (Jerusalem, 1933), pp. 103-4. This is a responsum that was sent to Spain.
22. See Cowley, op. cit.
23. See J. Mann, *Texts and Studies in Jewish History and Literature* (Cincinnati and Philadelphia, 1931-35), 1, p. 561.
24. *Geonica,* 2, pp. 118-19.
25. See *Ginzē Schechter,* 2, pp. 62-65.
26. Published in *Geonica,* 2, pp. 114-17.
27. See A. Harkavy, "L'tōl'dōt R. Samuel ha-Nagid" in Rabinowitz, *M'asse* (Saint Petersburg, 1902), 1, pp. 6, 39; Mann, "Responsa," *JQR,* n.s. 7:468; Assaf, *Ha-Shilōaḥ* 35: 403-4.
28. See sources in note 18 above.
29. *JQR* 19: 105; *Hebrew Union College Jubilee Volume,* p. 249.
30. Abraham b. Dā'ūd, p. 46.
31. *Hebrew Union College Jubilee Volume,* p. 249.
32. See *T'shūbhōt GMUM,* no. 26.
33. *Geonica,* 2, p. 121; cf. Eppenstein, *MGWJ* 56: 87.
34. *Sha'arē Ṣedeḳ,* part 3, section 6, no. 15, 23, 36; see also Müller, *Responsa,* p. 19. Also cf. Fürst, *Litbl. des Orients,* col. 197-98.
35. *Sefer ha-'iṭṭūr,* f. 16, col. 4, *Halakhōt pesuḳōt min ha-geōnīm,* p. 130: "We have already clarified the response to this question in the responsa to the questions [of] Mar El'āzār."
36. *Sha'arē Ṣedeḳ,* part 3, section 6, no. 15, 17; line 2; see also *Saadyana,* no. 36, 36a; ibid., p. 76, his father's name is given.
37. Samuel ibn Djama', "Sefer ha-agur," article Abbas, published by Buber in the *Graetz Jubelschrift,* Hebrew section, p. 17. Cf. Mann, *Texts,* 1, pp. 64-65.
38. This can be concluded from the transfer of the money to this academy and also from the responsum published by Harkavy in his collection *T'shūbhōt ha-g'ōnīm,* no. 386.
39. See Harkavy, loc. cit.
40. *Sefer ha-eshkōl* (published by Albeck), 1, p. 118.
41. Samuel ibn Djama', "Hilkhōt sh'khīṭa," M. Steinschneider, HB, 4, p. 107. According to Albeck in the preface to *Sefer ha-eshkōl,* p. 71, he is also the one referred to in Harkavy's *T'shūbhōt ha-g'ōnīm,* no. 47 (p. 23).
42. In a responsum to an inquiry directed from Spain he was not referred to as *resh kalla.* See *Sefer ha-'iṭṭūr,* loc. cit., and *Saadyana,* loc. cit.; however, in all the responsa in *Sha'arē Ṣedeḳ* the copyist added the appellative *Allūf,* even as he added *zekher ṣaddīḳ l'bh'rākha* (blessed by the memory of the righteous). But nothing should be concluded from this.
43. *Seder Rabh 'Amram,* 38a.
44. Assaf, *T'ḳūfat ha-g'ōnīm v'sifrūtah,* pp. 168-69.
45. This edition was published in Venice, 5308.

46. Published by Hildesheimer, Berlin 5648.
47. See A. Epstein, article about Sefer *Halākhōt G'dōlōt in ha-Gōren* 3:71-72; S. Poznanski, "Anshē Kairawān," *Festschrift, A. Harkavy* (Hebrew section), p. 177, note 2; Assaf, *T'ḳūfat ha-g'ōnīm*, p. 170.
48. *T'shūbhōt talmīdē M'naḥem*, ed. S. G. Stern (Vienna, 1870), pp. 67-68; (*Liber Responsionum*).
49. *Sefer ha-riḳma* (Vilna edition), p. 253, note 6; but at its end it is necessary to correct the item אזור [to gird], instead of עזור [to help]. See also the addenda, pp. 338, 539.
50. I. Z. Idelsohn, "Ha-Habhāra ha-'ibhrīt," *Ha-Shilōaḥ* 28: 132. Cf. Assaf, ibid. 35: 516*n*.
51. A. Z. Eshkoli, "Ha-Halakha v'-ha-minhag bēn y'hūdē ḥabash," *Tarbiz* 3: 37, 53, 54, 55-56, 129; and A. Epstein, *Eldad ha-Dani* (Pressburg, 1891), p. 171.
52. Metz, "Zur Geschichte der Falaschas," *MGWJ* 27: 392 ff.
53. Of all the scholars who wrote about Eldad, the only one who perceived his real intentions was Epstein, *Eldad ha-Dani*, p. xx.
54. See in A. Jellinek, *Bēt ha-midrash*, 2, p. 112; G'dalya b. Yaḥyā, *Shalshelet ha-ḳabāla* (Venice, 1587), p. 37b. It must be borne in mind that in these sources it is not stated that Eldad was seen outside of Babylon; therefore it must be assumed that he was actually met in one of the remote cities of this country. See Epstein, p. 17.
55. Judah Hadassī, *Eshkōl ha-kōfer*, no. 60, 61.
56. Ibid.
57. See Epstein, p. xiv.
58. Eldad's words are reported here according to the version found in the Geniza, and published by M. Schloessinger, *The Ritual of Eldad, ha-Dani* (New York, 1908), pp. 115-16; see also the remarks of the editor, pp. 109-10.
59. See Epstein, p. 13. There are, generally speaking, differences of opinion among the scholars regarding Eldad's accounts about Ethiopia and its Jews. See, for example, Carlo Conti Rossini, "Leggende geografiche giudaiche del IX secolo," *Bulletino della Reale Societa Georgrafica Italiana,* 1925, parts 1-6, which believes that Eldad, a Jew from southern Arabia, had heard from Ethiopian slaves about Ethiopia and that the book is merely an elaboration of his tales, containing geographical concepts that appear in the literature of many generations preceding him. On the other hand, the German scholar Borchardt is of the opinion that the tales of Eldad are trustworthy, especially his account of the river Sambaṭyōn. In his view Eldad was referring to two rivers, Takazze and Abai, which separate the land of Semyen, the land of the Jews, from Tigre and Shoa. Basing his reasoning on travel descriptions from the nineteenth century, this scholar argues that these rivers do indeed make a great noise and that their color is that of sand; they are so deep as to prevent any communication for several months during the year, thus justifying Eldad's description. Furthermore, he asserts that a river in that country is called Suba or Subat, which he identifies with the Sambaṭyōn. See Paul Borchardt,

"Die Falaschajuden in Abessinien im Mittelalter," *Anthropos* 18-19 (1923/24): 261-63.

60. These tales, bearing the title *Sefer Eldad ha-Dānī,* were printed in Mantua, 1480; by Jellinek in *Bet ha-midrāsh* 2: 102-3; 3: 6-7, 17-18; and by Epstein in his above-mentioned book, together with many explanations.

Among the studies relating to the story of Eldad mention should be made of the article by L. Rabinowitz, "Eldad-ha-Dani and China," *JQR,* n. s. 36:231-38. Rabinowitz expresses the opinion that a priori we cannot deny that Eldad reached China (p. 236), and that, furthermore, he originated in one of the neighboring countries of Persia, east of Babylonia (p. 238). Against the first conjecture it can be argued that the segment dealing with his stay in the land of Asin, which is included in his account, is highly unclear; Rabinowitz's second assumption is refuted by the Arabisms in his language. Nevertheless, Rabinowitz's article deserves attention because an added conjecture is contained within it: that Eldad was one of the *Habbānis,* the Jews of southern Arabia who traced their genealogy to the tribe of Dan (p. 235). Yet earlier, Epstein had already taken this possibility into consideration (pp. xvi-xvii). However, there are many arguments that refute this view. It is unthinkable that a Jew from such a stray tribe would be as learned as was Eldad. Moreover, Eldad's relationship with the Jewish community in Babylonia is characteristic: he was drawn to it and yet apprehensive of it. A Jew who had no special reason to be afraid of them—for example, of their recognizing him—would be active principally among the Jews of Babylonia, who in those days constituted the largest center of the entire nation.

61. From this it follows that there are parallels between Eldad's *halakhōt* and legal decisions of Y'hūdae Gaon and the Jerusalem (Palestinian) Talmud. See Schloessinger, *The Ritual of Eldad,* pp. 48 ff.

62. Epstein, p. 84; cf. the version from the Geniza published by Schloessinger, p. 93; see also Epstein's comments, p. 91, and his introduction, pp. xxxviii ff., particularly, p. xliv. In addition, cf. Eshkoli, "Ha-Halākha," pp. 47-48.

63. See Epstein, p. 119, and Schloessinger p. 78; cf. Epstein's notes, p. 122.

64. See *Kitāb al-Umm* (Būlāḳ, 1321-1325), 2, p. 205; Muḥammad b. Ḳāsim al-Ghazzī, *Fatḥ al-ḳārīb* (Leiden, 1894), p. 636, as-Sarakhsī, *Al-Mabsūṭ* (Cairo, 1324-1331) 12, p. 5; the commentary of al-Kharashī on the Mukhtaṣar of al-Khalīl (Cairo, 1316-1317), 2, p. 301. Thus S. J. Rappaport and Epstein, who saw here Moslem influence upon Eldad, erred. See Epstein, p. xliii.

65. See Epstein, p. 121, and Schloessinger, p. 84; cf. Epstein's notes, pp. 130, 173.

66. The later Jewish historian Gdalya b. Yaḥyā, in *Shalshelet ha-ḳabbāla,* p. 37b, is the only one who states that they addressed themselves to Ṣemaḥ the head of the Academy of Sura, whence it follows that the one referred to is Ṣemaḥ bar Ḥayyīm (880-887).

67. This letter was published from a manuscript of Firkovich by D. H.

Müller, *Die Recensionen u. Versionen des Eldad had-Dāni* (Vienna, 1892), pp. 47 ff.; idem, "La lettre d'Eldad sur les dix tribus," *REJ* 25: 38.

68. See above, note 54. Apparently the reference here is to one person, and the name in the responsum should read Rabbana Isaac bar Mar[ana] ve-Rabbana Simḥa instead of Rabbana Isaac bar Mar *and* Rabbana Simḥa.
69. The *gaon*'s reply is included in *Eldad ha-Dānī* (Mantua, 1480).
70. The date is found in the book *Eldad* (Constantinople, 5276).
71. See *Sefer ha-shōrashīm,* p. 497.
72. See Epstein, p. 70.
73. Included in the *siddūr* printed in Venice in 1645. Cf. Scholessinger, p. 109.
74. Frankl, "Spur eines Aufenthalts des Daniten Eldad in Sura (?)," *MGWJ* 27:423 ff.

CHAPTER FIVE

1. An anonymous chronicle of 'Abdarraḥmān III (ed. Lévi-Provençal and Garcia-Gomez); *Una cronica anónima de 'Abd al-Raḥmān III al Naṣir,* pp. 37, 59; Ibn 'Idhārī, pp. 163, 174.
2. Cagigas, 2, p. 326.
3. *Shīrat Yisrāēl,* p. 63. As to the name, see Carmoly, *Litbl. des Orients,* 2, col. 584, and in particular, J. and H. Derenbourg, *Opuscules et traités d'Abou'l-walid Merwan ibn Djanah de Cordoue* (Paris, 1880), p. ii, who conjectures that Shaprūṭ-Saportas is a Hispano-Romance name.
4. Samuel David Luzzatto, *Bēt ha-ōṣar,* p. 31a.
5. See Poznanski, *REJ* 67:290.
6. Ibn Ṣā'id, *Ṭabaḳāt al-umam* (ed. Cheikho), pp. 88-89 (translated into English by Finkel, *JQR* n. s. 18:51). From this work Ibn Abī Uṣaibi'a copied his biography, 2, p. 50 (translated into French by S. Munk, *Archives israélites* 9 [1848]: 326).
7. Ibn Abī Uṣaibi'a, 2, p. 47; and he was the first in Cordova to prepare the theriaca with the correct blend of herbs contained in it.
8. Graetz is justified in his assumption that Ḥasdai was accepted into service at the court long before the end of the fifth decade of the tenth century, even though his argument, based on the word *taḳarruban,* is incorrect; see volume 5, note 21 (pp. 536-37). Fisch, *Chaszdáj ben Jicchák ben Ezrá ibn Sáprut* (Budapest, 1933), p. 6, conjectures that Ḥasdai was born around 905.
9. Ibn Abī Uṣaibi'a, 2, p. 46.
10. N.L. Leclerc, *Histoire de la médecine arabe* (Paris, 1876), 1, pp. 421, 425-26, 429.
11. See Kokowzow, p. 14.
12. Ibn Ḥauḳal, *Ṣurāt al-arḍ (Leiden,* 1938-39), 1, p. 108.
13. In the sources known to us no explanation is given as to why Ḥasdai was initially invited to serve at the royal court, but it is logical to assume that he went there as a physician.

14. Abraham b. Dā'ūd, pp. 42, 49, 68, 73 (translation, pp. 57, 67, 93, 102); *Taḥk'mōnī*, p. 179. See Luzzatto, p. 27.
15. See Luzzatto, p. 68.
16. See *Theophanes continuatus* (Bonn, 1838), pp. 454-55; see also below,
17. In order to establish with exactitude the dates of the missions, it is appropriate to depend initially on the Christian sources. The Italian writer-diplomat Liutprand relates that he was sent as an emissary to Constantinople by the king of Italy, and when he departed from there, he met in Venice with Salemon, who was about to return from his mission. Liutprand left Venice on August 25, 948, reaching the Byzantine capital on September 17. Further on he mentions that at that very time emissaries arrived there from Spain. See *Antapodosis,* bk. 6, cap. 4, 5 (Migne, 136, cols. 894, 895). (It is true that Liutprand does not specify the year, only the month and day; however, the year can be reasonably deduced from what he reports concerning the reason for his mission. See op. cit., chap. 2.) On the other hand, Constantinos Porphyrogenetos, in his book *De ceremoniis,* 1, p. 571, relates that the emissaries from Spain were received on October 24. He, too, fails to note the year, but it is reasonable to assume that this reception occurred shortly before he writing of his book and that there was no need to state the date in full. From this Reiske, in his commentaries, ibid., 2, pp. 651-52, concludes that this occurred in 948. Regarding the mission of Stephanos, who set forth with the fleet that sailed for Crete in 949, there is also a report by Constantinos Porphyrogenetos in his book, 1, p. 664.

    There are errors in the accounts of the Arabic historians, and therefore Lévi-Provençal, 2, pp. 150-51, had difficulty in understanding them. But in point of fact the information in the Arabic chronicles confirms the conclusions which flow from the Christian sources.

    The following is the information they contain: Ibn Khaldūn, 4, pp. 142-43, relates that a Byzantine mission arrived in 336 A.H. (July 23, 947–July 10, 948). Ibn Abī Uṣaibi'a, 2, pp. 47-48, relates that the emissaries of the emperor arrived in 337 A.H. (July 11, 948–June 30, 949). Ibn Ḥayyān in al-Maḳḳarī, 1, p. 235, fixed the date *ṣafar* 338 (=August 949). Ibn 'Idhārī reports the information twice, pp. 213, 215; once as occurring in 334 (945/946) and once in 338 (949/950).

    Of these, the information that is most trustworthy is in Ibn Ḥayyān who is the earliest of the above-mentioned historians; he even adds the month of the arrival of the emissaries and later the very day on which they were received. The observations of Ibn Abī Uṣaibi'a, who affirms that he is uncertain of the date, no doubt relate to this selfsame mission; the same is true of at least the second item of information in Ibn 'Idhārī. In order to understand the reports of the Arabic historians, it must be remembered that Salemon's mission was no more than an exploratory probe. He came to invite the Omayyad government to send a mission to Constantinople, inasmuch as Constantinus VII wanted to maintain the dignity of his imperial status, and not to initiate the dispatch of embassies. The resplendent Byzantine mission did not arrive until 949, and its arrival and reception were firmly engraved on the memory of the people of that generation. Ibn Khaldūn, who avowedly bases his account on Ibn Ḥayyān, tells about this reception but fixes the year as 336 A.H. This can only mean that he had information about the mission of Salemon and confused the two Byzantine missions. From this stems the duality in Ibn 'Idhārī. As for the report by Ibn Khaldūn that the emissary Hishām b. Kulaib, whom the caliph had sent after the arrival of Salemon, had departed with the emperor's emissaries and returned, after two years passed, with new emissaries—this, too, matches in part information found in other sources. Hishām returned with Stephanos in 949, after tarrying about a half year in Constantinople, as is related in a Hebrew source (see below, pp. 200-201), and we need only to emend that he did not depart with Salemon, who journeyed to central Europe. Ibn Khaldūn states that he returned after two years had passed, because he found information concerning Salemon's coming in 336 A.H. and of the arrival of the large Byzantine mission in 338 A.H.

Salemon performed in Germany the same mission he had in Andalusia. He went to invite an embassy to the royal court of his emperor, and when his request was granted, he departed with the emissary of Otto I for Constantinople. Liutprand (col. 894) reports that in 948 he met in Venice with Salemon in company with Otto I's emissary, that he had come from Saxony, and that just as the Byzantine emperor had sent a mission in 949 to Cordova, so did he send one to Otto I. See *Annales Hildesheimenses* under the year 949.

18. See Brockelmann, *Geschichte der arab. Literatur*, 1, pp. 224-25, suppl., 1, p. 369.
19. Ibn Abī Uṣaibi'a, 2, pp. 47-48, according to Ibn Djuldjul in the introduction to his book *Tafsīr asmā al-adwiya al-mufrada min Kitāb Diskūrīdīs*, which is cited in his book *Ṭabaḳāt al-aṭibbā*, p. 22, with the editor's note.
20. The biography of Johannes of Gorze was published in Philipp Labbe, *Nova Bibliotheca manuscript. librorum* (Paris, 1657), 1, pp. 741 ff.; Migne, 137, col. 239 ff.

The timetable is quite clear, even though Johannes's biographer does not fix dates.

Ibn 'Idhārī, p. 218, relates that the emissaries of Otto I arrived in Cordova in 342 A.H., which began on May 18, 953. On the other hand, it has already been mentioned that, on coming to Cordova, they complained that their official reception was being delayed and were told in reply that the caliph's emissaries who returned with them had been detained in Germany for three years (see above). From this it can be inferred that 'Abdarraḥmān sent his first mission to Otto I in 950.

As for the time during which Rabī' b. Zaid, (or, as he was designated in Latin, Recemundus) was in Frankfurt, this can be clarified from his ties with Liutprand. The two met at the royal court of Otto I, and it was Recemundus who induced Liutprand to write his *Antapodosis*. In the introduction to this historical work, Liutprand asserts that he began his book two years after meeting Recemundus. In book 3, chapters 25 and 26 (Migne, 136, cols. 844, 845) he speaks of Constantinos Porphyrogenetos as a living person, and we know that that emperor died in 959. From this we can infer that he began writing his book in 958 and met Recemundus in 956. Therefore, what is stated in the biography of Johannes concerning his stay in Cordova is quite apt. In the Migne edition, col. 308, it is reported that he tarried nearly three years in the Hispano-Moslem capital, that is, from the close of 953 to the summer of 956. (Were we to assume that the meeting of Recemundus and Liutprand occurred in 957, Johannes's stay in Cordova would add up to more than three years, since the year 342 of the *hidjra*, mentioned by Ibn 'Idhārī as the year in which he reached Cordova, ended on May 6, 954.)

In the biography of Johannes it is also related (col. 310) that the caliph discussed with him the revolt against Otto I as an event that had just occurred (*nunc*), meaning the revolt of his son Liutolf and Conrad the Red, which took place in 953/954. But it cannot be concluded from this that Recemundus returned to Cordova in 955, since in that year Otto I fought the rebels and the Hungarians but tarried in Frankfurt in 956. On this cf. *España Sagrada,* 12, p. 178, col. b, and also Migne, 136, col. 770, n. 8. It is clear, at all events, that Ḥasdai's activity occurred in 954. A survey of Johannes's mission is presented by Dozy in *ZDMG* 20 (1866): 605 ff. See also R. W. Southern, *The Making of the Middle Ages* (London, 1953), pp. 36 ff.

21. Migne, 137, col. 301.
22. Ibn 'Idhārī, p. 221. Cf. Ibn Khaldūn, 4, p. 143. In light of the information about the role of Ḥasdai in his negotiations with Johannes of Gorze, it is hard to agree with the view of Graetz, 5, p. 339, that Ḥasdai accompanied the emissary as a translator.
23. Thus in the opinion of Flores, *España Sagrada,* 34, p. 268, whereas in the view of F. Fita he died at the close of 956. See *BAH* 34: 458-61.
24. Ibn 'Idhārī, p. 221.
25. On the flight of Sancho to Pamplona, his visit to Cordova for a cure, and the military aid proffered him by the Moslems, the Christian chronicler Sampiro reports. See *España Sagrada,* 14, p. 445. But this writer does not mention that Toda also visited Cordova. This is reported by Ibn Khaldūn, 4, p. 143. We know about Ḥasdai's activities from the Hebrew sources, that is, the poems of contemporary Hebrew poets, which Luzzatto analyzed, pp. 24-25; and there, too, are cited sources and studies on the history of Navarre.

Luzzatto's conclusions were accepted by all scholars. In only one detail can they be refuted. According to Luzzatto, Toda's son García, king of Navarre, also visit Cordova with her. This is reported also by Ibn Khaldūn (according to the version cited by al-Maḳḳarī, 1, p. 235). But over against his words is the testimony of the contemporary Hebrew poet who described the royal visit. Since he mentions the "son of Ramiro," that is, Sancho, and his grandmother Toda, and describes their appearance, he would not have omitted mention of a third crowned head.

26. S. M. Stern, "Two New Data about Ḥasdai Ibn Shaprūṭ," *Zion* 11:141-42, n. 11.
27. See Kokowzow, p. 15.
28. Abraham b. Dā'ūd, p. 42 (translation, p. 57).
29. The letter was first published by E. Adler, "Un document sur l'histoire des juifs en Italie," *REJ* 67: 40-43, and Poznanski commented upon it, op. cit., pp. 288-89. Thereafter the letter was dealt with in detail by U. Cassuto, "Una lettera ebraica del secolo X," *Giornale della Società Asiatica Italiana* 29 (1918-20): 97-110; ultimately reprinted by Mann, *Texts,* 1, pp. 23-24.
30. Aronius, no. 123.
31. Ibid., no. 124. See what the editor wrote about the two letters not being identical.
32. *Sefer ha-yishshūbh,* p. 23.
33. *Ginzē Schechter,* 1, p. 320. See Ginzberg's comments there and in the introduction, p. 316. Cf. S. Krauss, "Un nouveau texte pour l'histoire judéo-byzantine," *REJ* 87: 1 ff.
34. In the opinion of Cassuto, "Una lettera," pp. 104-5, the letter was sent from the community of Bari.
35. It cannot be conjectured that the letter was written immediately after the publication of the decree in Italy, for at that time Ḥasdai did not yet occupy so important a post. There is no doubt that the emperor, Romanos I Lekapenos, did not nullify the decree until the end of his reign. In the aforementioned apocalypse it was stated that that emperor would issue a decree against the Jews and that his kingdom would speedily pass away. To be sure, this passage is not clear. But it can be taken to mean that the author of *Ḥazōn Daniel* was asserting that after the decree, the emperor's dominance would not long endure. Al-Mas'ūdī (see note 67 below) also tells about the decree issued by Romanos I Lekapenos, but does not fix its date; however, from another Hebrew source (see below), it is apparent that the decree was issued around 940. We thus have before us some items of information that offer at least a measure of substantiation for the view that the decree was in existence unil the end of the reign of Romanos I.

    But the essential point in our deliberations remains what is known to us about the biography of Ḥasdai. If they did indeed write to him from Italy around 932, we would have to suppose that he continued in the royal service at Cordova for more than forty years—which is rather unlikely.
36. Ibn 'Idhārī in M. Amari, *Biblioteca Arabo-Sicula,* 1, p. 367.
37. *Taḥk'mōnī,* ed. Castelli, p. 3. Cf. *Sefer ha-ḥasīdīm* (ed. Wistinetzki-Freimann), pp. 151-52; and emend Zolgo to read Donnolo.
38. *M'gillat aḥima'aṣ,* p. 39.
39. To be sure, the Moslems invaded southern Italy, also in 952, and a fierce battle was waged. See the sources in Amari, pp. 259-60, but it is not to be assumed that this is, in point of fact, the intent of the

letter we are considering. One reason is that the community of Oria did not return to its original locale after what happened in 925; and the second reason is all we know concerning the action that Ḥasdai took on hearing the information contained in our letter. See below and read what Cassuto has written, "Una lettera," p. 104, about Abraham b. Jehoshaphat.

40. Since the letters were not sent by means of Byzantine emissaries, there is no room for conjectures that they were written in Hebrew in order to be delivered through Jews who were attached, as it were, to this mission. Cf. Mann, *Texts,* 1, p. 5. The writing of these letters in Hebrew was, therefore, not a stratagem to hide anything but rather a way out which Ḥasdai and the caliph seized upon in order to overcome formal difficulties.
41. See below.
42. The letters were published by Mann, *Texts,* 1, pp. 12-13.
43. Michael Glycas, *Annales* (Bonn, 1836), p. 561; Cedrenus, (Bonn 1838/39) 2, p. 326; *Antapodosis,* 4 cap. 15 (Migne, 136, cols. 883-84).
44. This was the opinion of J. Mann, *Texts,* 1, p. 10. However, M. Landau, *Beiträge zum Chazarenproblem* (Breslau, 1938) p. 23, conjectured that the letter was intended for Agatha, daughter of Constantinos VII, who sometimes represented him—for example, when he was ill. But reason dictates that Ḥasdai, an Andalusian official, would write to the Byzantine emperor and empress and not to the emperor and his daughter. The conjectures of S. Krauss in connection with this letter were refuted by Mann. See *HUCA* 10:265 ff., and *MGWJ* 82; 286 ff.; see also *HUCA* 10:297-98.
45. Landau, p. 26. The reading "māṣōr" (מצור) had already been proposed by Krauss in his article, *HUCA* 10:268.
46. The link between Ḥasdai's addressing himself to the rulers of Byzantium and the letter sent him by the Jews of southern Italy is an additional reason for postdating the letter; otherwise, Ḥasdai would surely have taken action on matters that had occurred some twenty years earlier. On this Fisch, p. 17, has already commented, albeit the date he fixes for the writing of the letters to Byzantium (944-946) is incorrect.
47. See I. Lévi, "Les juifs de France du milieu du IX siècle aux Croisades," *REJ* 52:161 ff.
48. This letter, too, was published by Mann, *Texts,* 1 pp. 27-28. In order to prove that the letter was actually written in the tenth century, J. Mann points to the appellation the "communities of Fransa." He argues that in a later era they called themselves the "communities of Provence." But at that time all of what is currently France was known by this name. During the period of Omayyad rule in Spain, the Arabs, and the Jews who lived among them, gave all the land north of the Pyrenees (as well as Catalonia) the name "Frandja" or "Ifrandja." The spelling Fransa (instead of Frandja) is thus a later copyists's emendation.

We can only make a conjecture to the exact date of Joseph and Saul's visit in Spain and Provence. It is possible that they accompanied that emissary of Otto I who came to Spain in 950 (or 949), or that they joined Dudo and Rabīʻ b. Zaid when they departed for Spain in 956; but in 950 the emissary of the German king returned, together with a Mozarab bishop, and it is hard to assume that Jews who were in their company found the opportunity to call together representatives of the Provençal communities or to participate in them. Moreover, it should be noted that it appears from a second source (see below) that Saul and Joseph tarried almost a year at Cordova, and there is no ground to assume that the first emissary of Otto I was in the capital of Moslem Spain for so long a time, since there was no need to detain him. On the other hand, we must assume that these Jews, who were attached to the envoys to serve as translators or as their guides, inasmuch as they were familiar with Spain, would have to return with them.

The journey of Dudo and Rabīʻ b. Zaid in 956 was arranged with the greatest haste in order to liberate Johannes of Gorze, and it is doubtful whether Jews were in their party. They had no need of translators, because Rabīʻ b. Zaid himself was an official of the Omayyad government and Dudo of Verdun apparently was a merchant who already was in Spain. However, it is probable that Jews did join Johannes of Gorze, who made many preparations for his journey and traveled slowly. When he reached Cordova and the series of delays in his reception began, the Jews, it seems, despaired of returning together with him and set out by themselves. By this means Johannes of Gorze was able to deliver information, through them, to the king of Germany.

For the laudatory poem in honor of Joseph and Saul, see S. M. Stern, *Kirjath Sepher,* 36, p. 432.

49. Ibn Ḥauḳal, 1, p. 194; the note itself is found on the map on p. 193. See Stern, "Two New Items of Information about Ḥasdai Ibn Shaprūt," *Zion* 11:143-44. The date of Ibn Ḥauḳal's visit in Spain does not allow for conjecture that he substituted Ḥasdai for another Spanish-Jewish traveler who visited central Europe some twenty years later, according to the opinion of Baron, 3, p. 306.
50. D. M. Dunlop, *The History of the Jewish Khazars* (Princeton Univ. Press, 1954), p. 160.
51. Ibid., pp. 181-82.
52. Ibn al-Athīr, *Al-Kāmil fi 't-ta'rīkh,* ed. Tornberg (Leiden, 1851-76), 4, p. 111.
53. *De ceremoniis,* 1, p. 690.
54. See Kokowzow, p. 15.
55. See Mann, *Texts,* 1, p. 22. Cf. Landau, p. 28.
56. See Kokowzow, ibid.
57. S. Assaf discovered this passage and published it in the Berlin periodical *Jeshurun* (Heb. section) 5 (1925): 107-13 and thereafter in *M'ḳōrōt u-meḥkārīm,* pp. 91-92; and see ibid., p. 93.
58. This is the view of S. Dubnow, "Masḳānōt aḥarōnōt bi-sheēlat hakūzārīm," *Sefer zikkārōn li-kh'bhōd Poznanski,* p. 3, and of Dinaburg, *Kirjath Sepher,* 1, p. 257; this is, however, not Assaf's view; see op.

cit. (n. 57) and idem, "L'dibhrē R. Y'hūda Barzeloni 'al ha-kūzarīm," *Zion* 7:48, and the view of Mann, *Texts* 1, p. 8, which is like that of Assaf.

59. Thus Dubnow, 4, p. 482, explains it.
60. Published from a Geniza fragment by S. Schechter, "An Unknown Khazar Document," *JQR,* n.s. 3 (1912–13): 181-219; because the fragment is currently located in the library of Cambridge, it is known in scholarly literature as the Cambridge Document.
61. Thus he states in ibid., pp. 84-85: "Informing my lord of the name of our country, as we find it in books."
62. Should be read thus. See Kokowzow, p. 118.
63. Kokowzow, p. 119, conjectures that this is the title of the governor of a city. It also appears in *Theophanes,* 1, p. 571 as Βαλγίτζης Cf. Kokowzow, p. xxxvi; he conjectures that its source is *balzisei.*
64. Ch. 2, para. 1.
65. A. N. Polak, *Khazaria,* 3rd ed. (Tel Aviv, 5711/1951), pp. 34-35.
66. *De thematibus et de administrando imperio,* cap. 10 (Bonn, 1840-41), p. 80.
67. *Murūdj adh-dhahab* (ed. Paris), 2, p. 8.
68. Cedrenos, 2, pp. 316-17; *Theophanes continuatus,* pp. 423 ff; Georgios Hamartolos (Bonn, 1838), pp. 914 ff; *Antapodosis,* bk. 5, cap. 15 (Migne, 136, cols. 883-84).
69. See Landau, p. 38, and cf. idem, "The Present State of the Khazar Problem," *Zion* 7:105, where the views of the other scholars are presented.
70. Polak, p. 193.
71. Landau, p. 41. Another analysis of the events mentioned in the anonymous person's letter is given by V. Mošin, "Les Khazares et les Byzantins," *Byzantion* 6:309 ff. In his view, the author of the letter has in mind not the Russians of Kiev but a Norman dukedom in Crimea.
72. Schechter, *JQR,* n.s. 3:184.
73. Even geographical place-names such as Bagdad and Khurāsān (l. 37) are not the transliteration of a Jew from the Arabic Near East.
74. Kokowzow, pp. xxviii-ix.
75. See Krauss, *REJ* 87:14.
76. See Kokowzow, pp. 15-16.
77. Ibn al-Athīr, 8, p. 308; Ibn Ḥauḳal, 2, pp. 337-39.
78. See Kokowzow, p. 16. The Hebrew text in which this proposal is reported (see below) states: "Now, the emissaries of the king of the G'bhālīm are come . . . and they said to me: 'Give us your letters and we will see that they reach the king of the G'bhālīm, and for the sake of your honor your letter will be sent to the Jews living in the land of Hangarīn. . . .'" First, the writer of the letter numbers among the kings who sent emissaries to the Omayyad caliph "the king of the G'bhālīm, who is aṣ-Ṣiḳlāb" (Kokowzow, p. 14). The name "G'bhālīm" is unusual and leaves room for many conjectures. Many scholars have expressed the view that a Slavic people is meant, and having been trapped by a scribal error of the copyists of the

Arabic texts in which the exchange of embassies between the Omayyad caliph and Otto I is reported, a king of these Slavs, "Hūnū" or "Dūkū," was begotten. See Harkavy, *ZDMG* 21: 285-86; and cf. S. Krauss, "Die hebräischen Benennungen der modernen Völker," *Jewish Studies in Memory of George A. Kohut* (New York, 1935), pp. 390-91, and Kokowzow, pp. 62-63. In the Arabic texts the correct reading is Ṣaḳāliba; see Ibn 'Idhārī, p. 218, Ibn Khaldūn, 4, p. 143, al-Maḳḳarī, 1, p. 235.

Ibn Khaldūn mentions (loc. cit.) that even though the caliph sent Bishop Rabī' to that king of the Ṣaḳāliba, and since the subject of his mission is known from Christian sources (see above, note 20), his words resolve all doubts as to the meaning of the name Ṣaḳāliba in this passage. The Hebrew text does indeed clearly identify the G'bhālīm with the Ṣaḳāliba. As becomes clear from the timetable of the biography of Johannes of Gorze and from the information which —from the aspect of time—corresponds with it in the book of Ibn 'Idhārī what is meant is the mission to Cordova in 953, which he headed. The meaning of "King of the Ṣaḳāliba," as Otto I was designated in the aforementioned Arabic texts, is not "Slavs" but "Germans." The Arabs were not precise in speaking of the nations living in the north, and so they designated all aliens in the service of the Omayyad caliph in Spain as Ṣaḳāliba, even though many of them were members of other nations. Also the timetable, the sequence of endeavors by Ḥasdai to come into contact with the Khazars, as depicted in the Hebrew source, points to the year 953 as the date wherein the Ṣaḳāliba mission arrived. For the time being we do not know who that Alemano-German king was who also sent emissaries to 'Abdarraḥmān III. It may be assumed that this was one of the other rulers of western Europe.

79. Kokowzow, p. 65.
80. Concerning this letter, see Landau, *Zion* 7:94-95. The critical edition is that of Kokowzow, pp. 7-8; see also the introduction, pp. vi-vii.
81. Polak, pp. 87-88, 195.
82. *Al-Iṣṭakhrī, Kitāb al-masālik wa'l-mamālik* (Leiden, 1927) p. 221; Ibn Ḥauḳal, 2, p. 392; cf. Dunlop, p. 136.
83. See Landau, pp. 1-17.
84. Kokowzow, pp. 16-17; see also I. Heilperin, 1: "References to the Khazars and to the Hidden Tribes in the Letter of Ḥasdai Ibn Shaprūṭ to the King of the Khazars," *Zion* 18:80-82.
85. S. Poznanski, "Miscellen über Saadja," *MGWJ* 44:517.
86. Ibid., pp. 522-23.
87. See Büchler, "Relation d'Isaac b. Dorbelo," *REJ* 44: 237-43. On the subject of messianic longings in that era, see Landau, pp. 8-9.
88. See Landau's aforementioned article, *Zion* 7:100-1.
89. See what Landau writes on this matter, ibid., p. 101.
90. See finally Heilperin, in his article.
91. This letter, too, was published in a scientific-critical fashion by Kokowzow, pp. 19-20.
92. Polak, pp. 21-22. In the opinion of J. Marquart, *Osteuropäische u.*

Ostasiatische Streifzüge (Leipzig, 1903), p. 11, this letter was written at the end of the twelfth century.

93. These Arabisms exist in the two formulations, although the majority are in the short version. Whereas in the short version Constantinople is called Ḳūnsṭanṭina (Kokowzow, pp. 20[2], 21[4], and others), the city, in the long formation, is called Ḳūsṭandīnā (see ibid., pp. 27[6], 28[4], and see also 31[18, 21]). In the short version, the Moslem judge is called *al-Ḳāḍī* (22[23], 23[1]) and in the long version, *al-Ḳādī* (30[4/6]).
94. *Shīrat Yisrāēl*, p. 64.
95. Ibid., and Abraham b. Dā'ūd, p. 49 (translation, p. 67).
96. J. Mann, *The Jews in Egypt and in Palestine under the Fatimid Caliphs* (Oxford, 1920-22), 1, pp. 148, 150, 167, 171.
97. S. Assaf, "Mi-pinḳasa ha-'atīḳ shel Damesek," *BJPES*, pp. 42-43; see also idem, *M'ḳōrōt u-meḥḳārīm*, pp. 64-65.
98. Mann, *Jews,* 2, p. 172; cf. Assaf, ibid.
99. See Mann, *Jews,* 2, p. 334.
100. Ibid., p. 246.
101. Ibid., p. 247.
102. Bodleiana 2876[24].
103. S. Assaf, "Old Genizah Documents from Palestine, Egypt and North Africa," *Tarbiz* 9:208-9.
104. Mann, Jews, 2, p. 351.
105. S. Assaf, "T'ūdōt nōg'ot la-yishshūbh ha-y'hūdī b'Rameleh u-bash'fēla," *BJPES* 8:66.
106. See Mann, *Texts,* 1, pp. 328-29.
107. See Mann, "Responsa," *JQR,* n.s. 9:179; cf. Assaf, *M'ḳōrōt u-meḥḳārīm*, p. 142, n. 79.
108. See Yāḳūt, *Mu'djam al-buldān* (ed. Wüstenfeld), 1, pp. 552-53.
109. *JQR,* n.s. 9:150 ff. Naḥūm al-Baradānī was also a scholar who sent out responsa, but it is unlikely that he was an emissary of the academies, which is the conjecture of Mann, *Texts,* 1, p. 152.
110. Published by I. Goldziher, "Mélanges judéo-arabes 23," *REJ* 50: 182 ff.
111. *Shīrat Yisrāēl,* p. 64.
112. See Lévi-Provençal, 3, p. 229.

CHAPTER SIX

1. See Luzzatto, p. 66.
2. Mann, *Texts,* 2, pp. 25-26.
3. D. Flusser found, in a manuscript of *The Book of Yōsīphōn*, the date "885 since the Destruction," that is, 953. See his article, "The Author of the Book of Yōsīphōn, His Personality and His Age," *Zion* 18:114; he is of the opinion that this is the date of that work. If this view is correct, it is possible that Ḥasdai's emissary requested from the author who wrote in southern Italy, a draft or first edition—as was the practice of the emissaries of the Moslem nobles regarding the books of their scholars who dwelt in foreign lands—and that he made a copy of that draft. But it is also possible that our source actually refers to *The Book of Antiquities* by Josephus, since—as Flusser has shown in his

article, p. 122—in those days interest in the writings of Josephus was shown in southern Italy and copies were made of them. Cf. also Krauss, *MGWJ* 77: 58 ff.; he assumed that there existed an earlier *Book of Yōsīphōn* ("Ur-Jossipon").

4. *Shīrat Yisrāēl*, pp. 63-64, where *"me-Surya u-Babhel"* (from Syria and Babylonia) is written; it should be translated *ash-Shām-Palestine*. Cf. W. Bacher, "Schām als Name Palästinas," *JQR* 18: 564-65.
5. Ibid.
6. Cowley, "Bodleian Geniza Fragments," p. 402.
7. See J. Mann, "'Inyānīm shōnīm l'ḥēḳer t'ḳūfat ha-g'ōnīm," *Tarbiz* 5:154.
8. See the letter published by Cowley; see also below.
9. Abraham b. Dā'ūd, p. 59 (translation, p. 79).
10. See the letter published by Cowley.
11. Ibn ar-Rumāḥis was slain in 980; see Lévi-Provençal, 2, p. 262. In connection with the war in Morocco in 972, 'Abdallāh b. Rayāḥīf is mentioned by Ibn 'Idhārī, p. 245, as commander of the fleet. The editors amended it to 'Abdallāh b. Rumāḥis, even though this version is included in two manuscripts and even though the first name ('Abdallāh) also is different from that of Ibn Rumāḥis; but the author of the article "Al-Ḥakam II" in *Encyclopedia of Islam* speaks of Admiral 'Abdallāh b. Rayāḥīn, and Mann, *Texts*, 1, p. 86, follows him. In all versions of the name in the account of Abraham b. Dā'ūd, p. 46 (translation, p. 63), the Hebrew letter mem appears, and one must conclude that the Jewish historian had in mind Ibn ar-Rumāḥis.
12. Ibn al-Athīr, 7, pp. 384-85; Ibn 'Idhārī, pp. 221, 222.
13. There is no proof that Moses was taken captive in a ship seized by the Spaniards in 955. However, in the light of the data embodied in the words of Abraham b. Dā'ūd, who is the chief source for this account, it can really be assumed that he was captured at about that time (see below).

    In reality Ibn ar-Rumāḥis is not mentioned in Arabic sources except in connection with military activities after 970, but it is possible to conjecture that he served in the Omayyad navy many years before.
14. The account by Abraham b. Dā'ūd reflects the popular tradition that took shape among the Jews of Andalusia in the generation following that of Moses, around the time he came to Spain. As proof of the antiquity of the tradition there is the fact that the author of *Ḳōrē ha-dōrōt* (ed. Cassel, p. 5a) cites it in the name of Samuel ha-nagīd. The arguments refuting the tale of the four captives are cited at length by Eppenstein, "Beiträge zur Geschichte u. Literatur in gaonäischen Zeitalter," *MGWJ* 55: 324 ff., 464 ff., 614 ff.; 56: 80 ff. In spite of this, Mann maintained the view that the account was veracious; see "Responsa," *JQR* n.s. 9: 169-70; *Texts*, 1, p. 86. A summary of all the studies to his own time is given by M. Auerbach, "Die Erzählung von den vier Gefangenen," *Jahresbericht des Rabbiner-Seminars zu Berlin 1925-27*. A detailed analysis of the legendary elements is in G.D. Cohen, "The Story of the Four Captives," *PAAJR* 29: 55 ff.

    The principal argument against the tale is the time discrepancy in the incidents. From the words of Abraham b. Dā'ūd, it follows without a shadow of doubt that during the time of Ḥasdai, Moses b. Ḥanōkh was appointed as rabbi of Cordova, where he taught over the years, and that after his death, his son was also chosen as his successor, thanks to Ḥasdai's help. It may be presumed that the Jewish-Spanish historian was well versed in these matters. It must therefore be assumed that Moses came to Spain during the rule of 'Abdarraḥmān III, who died in 961. The date which, for practical purposes, was fixed by Abraham b. Dā'ūd, was transmitted in the manuscripts in various versions: 990 or 970.

At all events, his observation that the incident occurred in the days of Sh'rīra Gaon clearly refutes his accounts of the links of Moses b. Ḥanōkh with Ḥasdai Ibn Shaprūṭ; however, the contradictions in the account of Abraham b. Dā'ūd are rendered particularly conspicuous by comparison of the data about Moses and the two other captives (he did not know the name of the fourth). Sh'marya b. Elḥānān, who was, according to Abraham b. Dā'ūd, redeemed in Egypt and really did head an academy there, died in 1012, as is noted in documents of the Cairo Geniza. There also was located a letter of Ḥushiēl, the third captive, who, according to Abraham b. Dā'ūd, was redeemed in Kairawan, and in it he relates that he left a Christian country and went to a Moslem country, in order to get to Sh'marya, but he does not mention a word about their having once been captives. (This letter was published by Schechter, *JQR* 11:643 ff.) From this it can be inferred that Ḥushiēl was apparently from southern Italy, for that was the only Christian land at that time in which distinguished scholars like him could originate.

Ḥushiēl, who was captured with Moses b. Ḥanōkh, according to Abraham b. Dā'ūd, died in 1028, as we learn from the consolatory poem which the Nagid sent to his son Ḥananēl. It is hardly likely that there were two men in Kairawan called Ḥushiēl at the same time or one generation after another and that both would be important rabbis. Ḥushiēl, who died in 1028, is no doubt the same Ḥushiēl who sent the letter to Sh'marya b. Elḥānān. In this letter he mentions his son Elḥānān, whereas in the consolatory letter which the Nagid sent after his death, only his son Ḥananēl is mentioned. Just as this Ḥananēl is renowned in rabbinic literature as one of the great scholars of that epoch, so to is Elḥānān mentioned in various documents as an important rabbi. Therefore Mann maintains that at the end of the tenth century there were in Kairawan two rabbis named Ḥushiēl: Ḥushiēl the father of Elḥānān, and Ḥushiēl the father of Ḥananēl; see *JQR* n.s. 9:165 ff. In his opinion, Ḥushiēl the father of Ḥananēl was taken captive together with Moses b. Ḥanōkh in 972 and reached Kairawan, whereas Ḥushiēl the father of Elḥānān arrived there of his own will around 990. However, this conjecture is, as we have said, a remote one, and it is more likely to assume that Ḥushiēl went to Kairawan with one son, namely, Elḥānān, and that the second, Ḥananēl was born to him there and that he himself died in 1028. It therefore can be concluded that Ḥushiēl and Sh'marya lived during the generation following that of Moses b. Ḥanōkh. Cf. Assaf in his criticism of the treatise of Aptowitzer in *Kirjath Sepher,* 10, p. 356; such was also the view of S. Poznanski in "Anshē Kairawān" in *Sefer ha-zikkārōn l'-Abraham Eliyāhu* (Harkavy) (St. Petersburg, 1908) (Hebrew section), pp. 186-87.

Baron, 5, pp. 46-47, also inclines to believe the account of Abraham b. Dā'ūd and based his opinion on Z. Ya'abheṣ, *Sefer Tōl'dōt Yisrāēl,* 10, pp. 238-39. As for the existence of a similar tale in Midrash Tanḥūma, it only demonstrates that this was a common leitmotif. Again, it is unlikely that a Hispano-Omayyed admiral would visit an Egyptian port in order to sell captives. Moreover, neither Sh'marya nor Ḥushiēl came to Egypt and Kairawan as captives.

The tale was apparently fabricated on the basis of the fact that in the second half of the tenth century three scholars from southern Italy arrived in Spain, Kairawan, and Egypt, where they filled an important role as heads of an academy. Although the time element decidedly refutes the account that they were taken captive in one ship, there is no a priori impediment to the belief that Moses was really taken captive. Such occurrences were common in those days. However, it is certain that the incident relating to his wife should be erased and likewise Abraham b. Dā'ūd's account of the dispute in the *bēt ha-midrash* (Talmud school). These are additions that were designed to embellish the account.

15. *Sha'arē Ṣedeḳ,* part 3, section 2, no. 21; part 4, section 1, no. 9; *T'shūbhōt GMUM,* no. 179, 180, 181, 207, 210; *Sefer ha-'iṭṭūr,* f. 5b, 9b, 38a, 42b, 76a, 100b; *Sefer Rabiya* cited in the notes to the *T'shūbhōt GMUM,* no. 20; *Shibolē ha-leḳeṭ* by Zedekiah b. Abraham (ed. Buber), no. 32 (see all of these in an abridged German translation by Müller, no. 1-15). Add also Assaf, *T'shūbhōt ha-g'ōnīm,* in *Madā'ē ha-yahādut,* 2, no. 23.
16. See Ashēr b. Y'ḥiēl (Rosh) in the tractate Rosh Hashanah, ch. 4, no. 13, where the son of Moses b. Ḥanōkh is mentioned. It is, to be sure, a matter of course that in this he continued in the paths of his father, and he is cited only because of the reliance placed upon the authority of the Nagid, who was his disciple. Cf. I. Halevi, *Dōrōt ha-rīshōnīm* (Frankfurt, 1891-1934), 3, pp. 287-88.
17. This letter was published by J. Mann, "Gaonic Studies," *Hebrew Union College Jubilee Volume,* pp. 248 ff.
18. See J. Mann, "Misrat rosh ha-gōla b'-babhel v'-hista'afūta b'-sōf t'ḳūfat ha-g'ōnīm," *Sefer zikkārōn for S. A. Poznanski* (Warsaw, 1927), (Hebrew section), p. 20.
19. "Keep me in mind also with a donation in my behalf." According to Marx (see below), the writer of the letter wants the contribution designated for the academy to be sent in his name.
20. The letter was published by Cowley, *JQR* 18: 399 ff. See comments by A. Marx, ibid., p. 768. He identified the recipient of the letter as Ḥasdai. He later held invalid Mann's conjecture regarding the identity of the writer of this letter. See *Hebrew Union College Jubilee Volume,* pp. 229 ff.; *HUCA,* 3, pp. 309-10.

Concerning the members of the B'ne Aaron family, see Mann in his article "Inyānīm shōnīm," pp. 173-74.

21. Mann published this letter in *Hebrew Union College Jubilee Volume*, pp. 252-53. The date of this letter, which has not been fully preserved, can be assigned to the years 954-958. In the letter written to Ḥasdai in 953 he is not called *resh kalla,* whereas in 959 he is referred to by this designation in two poems. See Luzzatto, pp. 65, 67.
22. M. Z. Weiss, "S'rīdīm me-ha-g'nīza," *Ha-Ṣōfē l'ḥokhmat Yisrāēl* 10 (1925): 159-63. See also Mann, ibid. 11:147-48; H. Cowley, "Bodleian Geniza Fragments," *JQR* 19: 104-6. As for a letter that Sh'rīra, according to Mann, sent at a later period to Spain, see *Texts,* 1, p. 87. However, Assaf, in *T'ḳūfat ha-g'ōnīm,* p. 55, conjectures that the letter published by Mann, *JQR* n.s. 9: 146 ff., was sent to Spain.
23. *Taḥk'mōnī,* p. 180.
24. See above, pp. 188-89 and 215.
25. Porges, "La querelle de Menahem ben Sarouk avec Dounash ben Labrat," *REJ* 24:146 demonstrated that this is the book's name, whereas *Maḥberet* is the designation of the collection of words under every letter as Jews generally refer to it.
26. This was the arrangement in the lexicon as M'naḥem himself issued it. See Filipowski in the Hebrew introduction of the publication of the book (London, 1854), p. 17; and see D. Kaufmann, "Das Wörterbuch Menachem Ibn Saruk's nach Codex Bern 200" *ZDMG* 40 (1886): 375.
27. For an evaluation of the lexicon from a grammatical aspect, see W. Bacher, "Die Anfänge der hebräischen Grammatik," *ZDMG* 49:324 ff. Of the influence of the Karaites upon him, N. Allōnī speaks "Micah b'shibh'īm millīm bodēdōt' l'rabbenu Saadiah Gaon," *Sefer Samuel Dim* (Jerusalem, 1958), p. 364; and, in particular, his article: "Hashpā'ōt Ḳaraiyōt 'al-maḥberet M'naḥem,' *Ōṣar Y'hūdē S'farad* 5 (5725):21-54; see also note 41 below.
28. This letter supplies us with all the biographical details concerning M'naḥem discussed above. It was published by S. D. Luzzatto, *Bēt ha-ōṣar,* 1, pp. 26-27.

In this text there should be a change of f. 32a, l. 7, from *ābhīkh* (your father) to *āḥīkh,* (your brother). Yet earlier M'naḥem tells of the death of Ḥasdai's father, and it is therefore impossible that he should continue: "For from the day that I was wronged till now, except for the mercy shown me by my lord, your father . . . in whose shade I found shelter even as he spread his compassion over me, etc." Moreover, he mentions his supporter with the benediction "May his God help him," and in his notes, Luzzatto has commented that this is a benediction for the living and not for the dead. The name of this brother was, it seems, Abūn, and he was older than Ḥasdai, as is apparent from the poem in *Ginzē Schechter,* 3, pp. 297-98, upon which Stern commented in *Kirjath Sepher,* 36, p. 432 (and he adds that mention of this brother is lacking in literature; and thus we have a solution to the problem!).

The time of M'naḥem's dismissal can be set within the limits of the years 955-958, for in 954 he was still in the service of Ḥasdai and wrote for him the letter to the king of the Khazars. But the incident should not be set after 958, because in his long letter there is no hint regarding the diplomatic achievements of Ḥasdai in that year. Had M'naḥem written after 958, he would surely have mentioned them. As for the return of the manuscript, see Porges, pp. 146-47.

29. The important source regarding Dūnash's origin is Moses b. 'Ezrā, who states: *"Dūnash ben Labraṭ al-lāwī al-Baghdādī al-aṣl al-Fāsī al-mansha'a,"* which B.-Z. Halper, in *Shīrat Yisrāēl,* p. 64, translated: "Dūnash ben Labraṭ originated in Bagdad and was educated in Fez." There is a difference of opinion among scholars as to the meaning of the statement by Moses b. 'Ezrā: "Some say he was born in Bagdad and others that he was born in Fez." Decisive proof that he was indeed born in Morocco can be deduced from his name. A Jewish boy born in Bagdad would have been given a Hebrew or an Arabic name that would have clung to him throughout life, especially where the person under discussion was a Hebrew poet. The name "Adōnīm" given him by medieval writers was merely a "Hebraization" of his name, and he himself was called "Dūnash," since he did not have a Hebrew name. On the name Dūnash, see N. Allōnī in the preface to the collection of his poems (Jerusalem, 1947), pp. 23-24. See also Ibn 'Idhārī, 3, p. 98. As for the name Labraṭ, see a document from the year 1034, Cambridge Univ. Library, Or. 1080 J6 and also T.-S. 16.174, a letter from the second half of the eleventh century.
   The description of Dūnash's youth as Allōnī presents it is utterly erroneous. According to him—p. 10—Dūnash was born and studied in Irak until he was twenty years old or more; how can this description be harmonized with the statement of Moses b. 'Ezrā that he was raised in Fez? Also his conjecture that Dūnash's parents migrated to Irak is rather tenuous, for in that era the direction of Jewish migration was precisely from Irak to the Western countries.
30. Some scholars expressed the view that Dūnash was the grandson of Saadya Gaon because he applied to Saadya the appellation "grandfather," in translation of the Arabic word *shaikh,* which means both "grandfather" (ancient one) and "teacher." In fact, the appellative *zāḳēn* was customarily used at that time for *sābh* (grandfather); see the document published by Mann, *JQR,* n.s. 9; 153; and see the observations of Shabb'tai Donnolo in Geiger's *M'lō ḥofnayim* (Berlin, 1840), p. 31; cf. *Kerem ḥemed,* 8, p. 97b, n. 3. But Allōnī, p. 7, already brought a proof in refutation of this view expressed by the opponents of Dūnash. And it should be added that if Dūnash had really been Saadya's grandson, this would surely have been mentioned more than once in his own writings and in those of others.
31. Allōnī in his above-mentioned preface, pp. 8, 9.
32. Ibid., p. 11.
33. A part was published by S. Marcus, *Mizraḥ u-ma'arābh* 4 (5690): 3-9, and an additional part by M. Zulay in *Sinai* 29 (5711):35-37.
34. See H. Brody, " 'Al ha-mishḳal ha'aradhī ba-shīra ha-'bhrit," *Sefer ha-yōbhēl for S. Krauss* (Jerusalem, 1937), pp. 117-26. His view is

agreed to by N. Allōnī, *Tōrat ha-mishḳālīm* (Jerusalem, 5711), pp. 20-21.

35. See Allōnī, pp. 39-40.
36. H. Schirmann, *Ha-Shīra ha-'ibhrīt bī-S'fārād u-bi-Provence* (Jerusalem and Tel Aviv, 1955-57), 1, p. 32; ibid., pp. 34-35, is printed the poem cited above.
37. See Porges's aforementioned article. Porges's conclusions, namely, that Dūnash obtained the original manuscript of M'naḥem's lexicon (actually Porges does not state when he obtained it), are in line with the fact that in M'naḥem's long letter there is no mention of the strictures that Dūnash leveled against him. Porges's assumptions—together, of course, with the supposition that the manuscript fell into the hands of Dūnash at the time of M'naḥem's dismissal—confirm the surmise that Dūnash did indeed write his responses after M'naḥem's misfortune.
38. The book was published by Filipowski, London, 1855.
39. See Bacher, "Die Anfänge," p. 368.
40. D. Yellin, "Hitabḳut Dūnash ben Labraṭ," *Sefer zikkārōn le-Asher Gulak and Samuel Klein* [Studies in memory of A. Gulak and S. Klein] (Jerusalem, 1942), pp. 106, 110; idem, "T'shūbhōt Dūnash b. Labraṭ," *L'shōnēnu* 11:203.
41. *T'shūbhōt*, p. 73. See also N. Allōnī, "Dūnash's Preface to His Responses to the Maḥberet of M'naḥem," *Bēt ha-mikra* 1 (1965): 45-63.
42. He is mentioned by his full name in *Shīrat Yisrāēl*, p. 64 (where it is erroneously written as Isaac Abū Ḳaprōn), and also in the introduction to the *T'shūbhōt talmīdē M'naḥem*, ed. Stern (Vienna, 1870), p. 17, ll. 6-8, "Va-yeḥrad Yiṣḥāḳ ḥarāda." Therefore there is no doubt about the identification of M'naḥem's disciple and the man about whom Moses b. 'Ezra speaks. See Schirmann, 1, pp. 42-43.
43. See below, p. 453, note 52.
44. The poem, accompanied by annotations, was last published by Schirmann, op. cit.
45. See D. Yellin, "L'-hasāgat talmīdē M'naḥem Ben Sārūk," *Sefer ha-yōbhēl for S. Krauss*, pp. 127-35.
46. P. 57.
47. P. 30.
48. P. 82.
49. This treatise was published together with *T'shūbhōt talmīdē M'naḥem* as *Liber Responsionum* by Stern; see note 42 above.
50. *Shīrē Dūnash*, ed. Allōnī, pp. 88-89.

CHAPTER SEVEN

1. See Dozy, *Recherches sur l'histoire et la littérature de l'Espagne pendant le moyen âge*, 3d ed. (Paris, 1881), 1, appendixes, p. vi.
2. See Lévi-Provençal, 3, p. 207.
3. *T'shūbhōt GMUM*, no. 211.
4. Ibid., no. 178, 206.
5. Ibid., no. 196, 197, 209.
6. Ibid., no. 180.
7. Ibid., no. 199.

8. *Sefer ha-'iṭṭūr,* f. 9b.; *T'shūbhōt GMUM,* no. 195, 203.
9. *T'shūbhōt GMUM,* no. 175.
10. Ibid., no. 201.
11. *Sefer ha-'iṭṭūr,* f. 42b, *T'shūbhōt GMUM,* no. 204.
12. *T'shūbhōt GMUM,* no. 197.
13. *Sefer ha-'iṭṭūr,* f. 100b.
14. *T'shūbhōt GMUM,* no. 197, 198.
15. See above, pp. 116-17.
16. *T'shūbhōt GMUM,* no. 203.
17. Ibid., no. 208.
18. Ibid., no. 202.
19. Ibid., no. 210.
20. Ibid., no. 86; and see there the publisher's note.
21. Cf. Müller, pp. 6 ff.
22. Mann, "Responsa," *JQR,* n.s. 10: 317; Caro, *Sozial u. Wirtschaftsgeschichte der Juden,* 1, p. 141.
23. L. Levillain, *Examen critique des chartes mérovingiennes et carolingiennes de l'abbaye de Corbie* (Paris, 1902), p. 235, no. 15.
24. Ibn Ḥauḳal, 1, pp. 110, 114.
25. Al-Muḳaddasī, p. 239.
26. Ibn Ḥauḳal, 1, p. 114.
27. Lévi-Provençal, 3, p. 302.
28. González de Leon, *Noticia historica del origen de los nombres de las calles de Sevilla* (Seville, 1839), pp. 45, 145-46. Even though these names are vestiges of the era of Christian dominance, it can be assumed with certainty that these were places already designated earlier for artisans of this occupation.
29. Ibid., p. 438.
30. See the entry "Saragossa" in *The Jewish Encyclopedia,* 11, pp. 52 ff.
31. Ibid.
32. I. Loeb, "Actes de vente hébreux en Espagne," *REJ* 4:226.
33. Lévi-Provençal, 3, p. 432.
34. Abraham b. Dā'ūd, pp. 50, 58 (translation, pp. 68, 79).
35. Muhammad Imamuddin, "Historia ecónomica de España en la epoca omeya," *Revista de la Universidad de Madrid* 5 (1956): 351. Idem, *Some Aspects of the Socioeconomic and Cultural History of Muslim Spain, 711-1492 A.D.* (Leiden, 1965), pp. 119-20.
36. See note 28 above.
37. Tomas Ximenez de Embún, *Descripción histórica de la antigua Zaragoza* (Saragossa, 1901), p. 61.
38. See L. Torres Balbás, "Alcaicerías," in *Al-Andalus* 14:439. As added evidence, mention should be made of the Calle de la Alcaicería de la Seda (Street of the market hall of the silk merchants) in Seville, which was also called Calle de la Judería. Its location was fixed by King Fernando after the capture of the city. See González de Leon, pp. 161-62.
39. Al-Muḳaddasī, p. 236.
40. Ibn al-Faraḍī, *Historia virorum doctorum Andalusiae* (Madrid, 1892), nos. 181, 184, 235, 650. Cf. S.M. Imamuddin, "Commercial Relations

of Spain with Iraq, Persia, Khurasan, China and India in the Tenth Century, A.D.," *Islamic Culture* 35 (1961): 177 ff. Idem, *Some Aspects,* pp. 126 ff.

41. Mann, "Responsa," *JQR,* n.s. 10:323.
42. Ibn Ḥayyān al-Muḳtabis, ed. Antuña (Paris, 1932), p. 23; the passage was previously published by R. Dozy, *Recherches sur l'histoire et la littérature de l'Espagne,* 2, appendixes, p. lxxxviii, and was there translated into French, p. 286.
43. *Sha'arē Ṣedeḳ,* part 3, section 2, no. 11, 21.
44. Ibid., no. 15. Cf. *Geonica,* 2, p. 30, and see there p. 20. In addition, Mann, "Responsa," *JQR,* n.s. 7:482.
45. S. Assaf, *Mi-sifrūt ha-g'ōnīm* (Jerusalem 1933), p. 103.
46. See *T'shūbhōt GMUM,* no. 191; cf. Müller, p. 35.
47. *T'shūbhōt GMUM,* no. 192; cf. Müller, p. 37.
48. This is the view accepted by scholars investigating the history of Moslem and Christian Spain, although proofs for this have not yet been adduced. See Cl. Sánchez-Albornoz, *Una ciudad hispano-cristiana hace un milenio: Estampas de la vida en León* (Buenos Aires, 1947), p. 32; Lévi-Provençal, 3, p. 309.
49. *España Sagrada,* 10, p. 425.
50. Ibid., pp. 425-26.
51. H. Pirenne, *Mohammed and Charlemagne* (London, 1954), pp. 255-60.
52. Ibn Khurdādhbeh speaks of "the western sea," but it cannot be assumed that he means the Atlantic Ocean.
53. This passage, whose contents are here given in abridged form and with some changes, is found in the edition of de Goeje, p. 135.

    Later various books contained this information in translations into European languages. See the list in the book especially devoted to the Radhanites: L. Rabinowitz, *Jewish Merchant Adventurers* (London, 1948), pp. 194 ff. The text was translated for the first time by A. Sprenger in his paper "Some Original Passages on the Early Commerce of the Arabs," *Journal of the Asiatic Society of Bengal* (1844): pp. 519 ff. Before Rabinowitz a detailed and accurate description of the commerce of the Radhanites was given by J. Jacobs, *Jewish Contributions to Civilization* (Philadelphia, 1919), pp. 194 ff. An in-depth critique of the account by Ibn Khurdādhbeh was made by Cl. Cahen, "Ya-t-il eu des Rahdānites," *REJ* 123 (1964): 499-505. Although Cahen emphasizes that the authenticity of this testimony is not to be discounted simply because for the time being it stands alone, he provokes arguments regarding the trade routes of the Radhanites as they are set down in this text. But see against this paper my "Quelques observations d'un orientaliste sur la thèse de Pirenne," *JESHO* 13 (1970): 182 ff. On the name of these merchants, see J. Jacobi, "Die Rādānīya," *Der Islam* 47 (1971): pp. 261-62.
54. His book has not yet been discovered, but a digest has come down to us, made by 'Alī b. Ḥasan ash-Shaizarī in the first half of the eleventh century. The passage is found in the edition of de Goeje, pp. 270-71. Against the view that Ibn al-Faḳīh copied from Ibn Khurdādhbeh, see M. Hadj-Sadok in the introduction to *Description du Maghreb et*

de l'Europe au IIIe–IXe siècle (Algiers, 1949), p. xii, who endeavors to prove that the two writers drew from common sources.

55. See de Goeje, *Bibliotheca Geographorum Arabicorum*, 5, p. 251.
56. Rabinowitz, p. 128, has already dealt with this.
57. In the letter of Ḥasdai Ibn Shaprūṭ to the Khazar king, it is related, in Kokowzow, p. 12, that two Spanish Jews, Judah b. Meïr b. Nathan and Joseph Hagrīs, had visited a short time before in Khazaria, but it was not stated that they were merchants. On the contrary, from this letter it can be concluded that even in the ninth century Jewish merchants from Spain were not accustomed to visit the Khazar country, for if this were the case. Ḥasdai would have known about their travels and depended on their accounts.
58. H. Pirenne, *Economic and Social History of Medieval Europe* (London, 1947), pp. 11, 133; idem, *Mohammed and Charlemagne*, p. 258; and one can make additions to his proofs: see below; also cf. Marquart, p. 24.
59. Al-Muḳaddasī, p. 239.
60. See ibid., pp. 30, 225.
61. See p. 272 above (and cf. note 26); it is certain that when al'-Muḳaddasī (see n. 25), speaks of textiles that were exported from Spain, he has in mind also silk cloth.
62. The data concerning the export of Andalusian silk to oriental lands were unknown to many of the scholars who dealt with the subject of the Radhanites, and for this reason they had difficulty in understanding what was said by Ibn Khurdādhbeh; thus they maintained that the Radhanites bought the silk cloth in Greece. See W. Heyd, *Histoire du commerce du Levant* (Leipzig, 1923), 1, p. 127; Rabinowitz, p. 166.
63. Aronius, no. 83; see chapter 2, n. 12 above.
64. Migne, 104, col. 99 ff, 71. Aronius (see no. 85) fixes the date of this letter as 822–825, but Abbot Adelard died in January 823 (see col. 101, the note of the first editor); therefore the letter's date must be set earlier.
65. Migne, ibid., col. 173-74.
66. Ibid., col. 72.
67. Ibid., col. 76; cf. Aronius, no. 92, for the explanation of the last-mentioned passage. On the reconstruction of the dispute, see Caro, 1, p. 155. In particular cf. B. Blumenkranz, *Juifs et chrétiens dans le monde occidental, 430-1069* (Paris, 1960), pp. 94-95, 134-35, 193-94, 301-2.
68. Migne, 104, col. 75.
69. Ibn Ḥauḳal, 1, p. 110; al-Muḳaddasī, p. 242.
70. Assaf, *Geonic Responsa from Geniza MSS.*, p. 39. Assaf conjectures that this is perhaps a question that Naṭrōnai Gaon was asked. See op. cit., p. 36, and Assaf's article "Slavery and the Slave Trade among the Jews in the Middle Ages," *Zion* 4:100.
71. *Geonic Responsa from Geniza MSS.*, p. 77; cf. "Slavery and the Slave Trade," p. 101.
72. Aronius, no. 122.
73. *Antapodosis*, in Migne, 136, col. 896.
74. Dozy, 2, p. 154. He is the one who referred to the merchants of Verdun

as Jews, as a consequence of his dependence on that passage in Liutprand; Lévi-Provençal copied from him, *L'Espagne musulmane au Xe siècle* (Paris, 1932), p. 29. But see below.

75. Al-Maḳḳarī, 1, p. 92.
76. Ibn Ḥauḳal, 1, p. 110.
77. It cannot be assumed that he copied from Ibn Ḥauḳal.
78. Al-Muḳaddasī, p. 242. Some scholars doubt the trustworthiness of these data. See A. Harkavy, in *Ha-Maggid* 1877, no. 23:219, who maintains that Jewish law forbids castration, and therefore the words of al-Muḳaddasī are to be regarded as an anti-Semitic indictment; see also Mann, "Responsa," *JQR* n.s. 10:151. But these scholars were unaware that Ibn Ḥauḳal and al-Maḳḳarī also give the same account. People in that epoch regarded the slave trade in a different light, and Moslems, Christians, and Jews engaged in it; one of the branches of this trade dealt in castrates. The expectation of earning large profits was stronger than the conscience of the Christians, who, contrary to the wishes of the church, sold their coreligionists to Moslems. Why is it then not believable that Jews would castrate heathen youths, even as the Christian merchants of Verdun had done?

CHAPTER EIGHT

1. *Ḳ'bhūṣat ḥakhāmīm*, p. 111; the correct text is in Harkavy, "L'tōl'dōt R. Samuel Hanagīd," p. 39.
2. According to the accepted view, the wall did not run in a straight line to the river; instead, near the palace and the buildings annexed to it, it turned westward, where stood one of the gates of the city, the Sevilla Gate (Bāb Ishbīliya) or Perfumers' Gate (Bāb al-'aṭṭārīn). However, R. Castejón, *Cordoba califal* (Cordova, 1930), p. 267, refutes this view, maintaining that the urban area surrounded by a wall was widened toward the west at this site in the fourteenth century. See also Castejón, p. 277.
3. The official map of the city in 1811 still shows this gate.
4. This street is mentioned in an account of disturbances in 1391, included in a book written at the end of the seventeenth century (although it is no doubt based on old documents and records) that was not published: Antonio Moreno Marin, *Antiguedad y excelencia de la Catedral de Cordoba*. The passage can be found in the copy of Vázquez Venegas (see note 13 below).
5. At the eastern end of this street there is presently a plaza named for Judah Halevi; however, this plaza was located there just a short time ago, when a house that had collapsed was razed.
6. See Moreno, op. cit.
7. This view was expressed by Rafael Romero y Barros, "La sinagoga de Cordoba," *BAH* 5:259 as well as Castejón, p. 281; but there is no proof for it.
8. See Moreno, op. cit.
9. M. Ocaña, "Las puertas de la medina de Cordoba," *Al-Andalus* 3:149; R. Ramirez de Arrellano, *Historia de Cordoba* (Ciudad Real, 1915-18), 1, p. 131.

10. See Castejón, p. 281.
11. Samuel de los Santos, "La Ermita de San Bartolomé o Capilla del Hospital del Cardenal Salazar," *BAC* 10:46.
12. Against this tradition see Rodrigo Amador de los Rios, "La iglesia de San Bartolomé en el Hospital del Cardenal en Córdoba, vulgarmente llamada Mezquita de Almanzor," *Museo Español de Antigüedades* (Madrid, 1875), 4, pp. 167-80; idem, *Inscripciones árabes de Córdoba* (Madrid, 1879), pp. 387 ff. Castejón nevertheless maintains this view, p. 281, and according to the map drawn by him (beside p. 300), he is of the opinion that the entire palace was west of Al-Manṣūr Street.
13. Vazquez Venegas collected historical material on Cordova by order of King Carlos III. The essence of his conclusions on this matter was published by Samuel de los Santos, "La Ermita," *BAC* 9:250-51; see also particularly pp. 253, 255.
14. Al-Maḳḳarī, 1, p. 303; al-Idrīsī, p. 208; cf. also al-Muḳaddasī, p. 233, and al-Khushanī, *Al-Ḳuḍāt bi-Ḳurṭuba* (Madrid, 1914), pp. 112-13.
15. Al-Maḳḳarī, 1, p. 98.
16. Ocaña, "Las puertas." Cf. Castejón, pp. 273-74, where he converts one gate into two; that is, he speaks of the Gate of the Jews and the Talavera Gate as if they were two gates; in the end, he counts the seven gates mentioned in the authentic sources as nine. (His count is in error, inasmuch as he counts his no. 6 twice. See p. 274, l. 1 and l. 3 from the bottom.)
17. Al-Maḳḳarī, 1, p. 304. For some reason Lévi-Provençal, 3, p. 368, casts doubt on this information and holds that the Jews, too, reached the cemetery where they buried their dead by way of this gate. Ramirez de Arrellano, 1, p. 134, conjectures that this quarter was at the site of the present neighborhoods of Barrio del Matadero and Barrio de las Olerías, whereas Castejón, p. 293, thinks that it was behind the Monastery de la Merced, that is, on the northwestern side. In his opinion the mosques of Umm Salama and Kūta Rāshō were northeast of the Gate of the Jews. Alongside the Bāb al-Yahūd was a Mozarab monastery named for Eulalia. See Castejón, p. 333.
18. Abraham b. Dā'ūd, pp. 48, 52 (translation, pp. 66, 70).
19. See S. Abramson, *Sinai* 26:205-6. It should be noted that there are variant versions for the spelling of the name of the family. See in the notes of Cohen, p. 48.
20. He is mentioned in a letter published by Mann, *Hebrew Union College Jubilee Volume,* p. 255; cf. Moses Steinschneider *JQR* 9:595-96.
21. Scheiber in *Sinai* 27:217-18.
22. *Shīrat Yisrāēl,* p. 64; the Arabic source is in M. Steinschneider in Geiger's *Jüd. Zeitschrift* 1:238. Abū 'Umar Ibn Yaḳwā is cited in *Sefer ha-shōrashīm*, ed. Bacher, p. 48; cf. Moses Steinschneider, *JQR* 10:122.
23. *Shīrat Yisrāēl,* loc. cit., and also *Sefer ha-riḳmah,* p. 227; see there in the variant readings.
24. See commentary of Obadiah b. David on *Hilkhōt ḳiddūsh ha-ḥōdesh,* ch. 7, halakha a.

25. See Isaac Israeli, *Y'sōd 'ōlam* (Berlin, 1848), ch. 4, p. 28b, and see there 28a.
26. See in Abraham b. Hiya, *Sefer ha-'ibbūr,* part 2, section 7, p. 54; part 3, section 5, p. 95. Cf. *Graetz,* 5, p. 374.
27. González de Leon, p. 76.
28. Ibid., p. 390.
29. Ibid., pp. 106-7.
30. Ibid., pp. 72-73.
31. Ibid., p. 273. It was this church the Arabic writers had in mind when they reported on the location of the residence of the governor, 'Abdal'azīz, the son of Mūsā b. Nuṣair, and his wife, Egilona, the widow of the Visigothic king Roderick. In the book *Fatḥ al-Andalus,* the editor, in his comments on pp. 96-97, explains that a synagogue is intended. Still earlier, Casiri found a similar passage (2, p. 325), which he translated *Templum Salvatoris*; but Faustino de Borbón, *Cartas para ilustrar la historia de la España arabe* (n.p., 1796), p. xxxii, disclosed that it was a synagogue; and after him Pascual de Gayangos, *The History of the Mohammedan Dynasties in Spain* (London, 1840-43), p. 404, went astray, as did M. Mendez-Bejarano, *Histoire de la juiverie de Sevilla* (Madrid, 1922), p. 13. None of these scholars surmised that the meaning of the Arabic phrase كنيسة ربينة was "the Church of Ruppina," nor did they ask themselves why a Visigothic queen would find herself in a synagogue.
32. González de Leon, pp. 118-19.
33. Simonet, p. 150.
34. González de Leon, p. 213.
35. Ibid., p. 215.
36. González de Leon, p. 369, relates, however, that the quarter was called La Vieja Judería because the Jews were transferred there in 1391. How strange! It should have been called La Nueva Judería. From this it can be concluded that this was a Jewish neighborhood in an earlier period, long before the persecution of the Jews by the Christians. Cf. Méndez-Bejarano, p. 24.
37. According to Méndez-Bejarano, p. 22, the Jewish quarter included in that period a wide zone in the southern part of the city, namely, the area in which the Great Mosque (currently the cathedral) was built later, but there is no proof for this.
38. González de Leon, pp. 207-8.
39. Ibid., p. 438.
40. Ibid., p. 439.
41. Alonso Morgado, *Historia de Sevilla* (Seville, 1587), p. 44b.
42. Rodrigo Caro, *Antiguedades y principado de la illustrissima ciudad de Sevilla* (Seville, 1634), p. 20b; cf. Méndez-Bejarano, p. 58. Outside the gate was a suburb called by this name; see Torres Balbás, *Al-Andalus* 18:169.
43. See Caro, *Antiguedades.* It would seem that the Atambór Gate (see Méndez-Bejarano, p. 58) was a gate that was opened at a much later period.

44. This street was formerly called Rodrigo Alfonso (after the uncle of King Alfonso X who resided there).
45. In the opinion of González de Leon, pp. 217-18, it was so called for a Jewish family, but this is merely a conjecture.
46. See ibid., pp. 179, 374.
47. Also called Calle del Canal del Agua; see ibid., p. 250.
48. See ibid., pp. 345-46; Méndez-Bejarano, p. 63.
49. González de Leon, p. 445.
50. In the seventeenth century Hebrew inscriptions were still visible in this church. See Caro, *Antiguedades,* pp. 20a–b, 42b.
51. Formerly San Jerónimo; cf. González de Leon, p. 289.
52. It was not then on the site where it is currently located, but rather in its vicinity. The church was moved from place to place.
53. González de Leon, p. 445.
54. See ibid., pp. 268-69.
55. See Caro, p. 20b; González de Leon, pp. 337-39.
56. González de Leon, p. 156.
57. Caro, p. 20b; Méndez-Bejarano, p. 62.
58. Caro, ibid.
59. Abraham b. Dā'ūd, p. 59 (translation, p. 79).
60. See commentary of Isaac Abrabanel on Zechariah 12:7; cf. *Shebheṭ Y'hūdā* (ed. Shohet), p. 33.
61. See remarks of Isaac Abrabanel, ibid.
62. Abraham b. Dā'ūd, p. 59 (translation, p. 79). There is another version: Asāna, and Harkavy therefore conjectured in the *M'assef* (of Rabinowitz), 1, p. 41, that perhaps what is meant is the city of Ossuna. To be sure, in the days of the Omayyad caliphs, Ossuna was a flourishing town, but this conjecture is not reasonable on two counts: (1) in Arabic, Ossuna is called Ushūna, and indeed even in the version Asāna the letter alef appears after the samekh; (2) the *gaon* addresses the leading communities of various districts in southern Spain, and Ossuna is located near cities in which there were important communities listed by the *gaon.* This is not the case regarding Calsena, which was the chief community of a particular district, of which no community is mentioned by the *gaon.* Cf. Schirman, *Sefer Assaf* (Jerusalem, 5713), p. 498 (without any reasons being given).
63. See *Ar-Rauḍ al-mi'ṭār,* pp. 162-63; and Lévi-Provençal's translation, p. 195, where he added bibliographical notes.
64. See ibid. Lévi-Provençal unjustifiably offers the explanation: 'Abdarraḥmān II. In the text the reference is to 'Abdarraḥmān ben Muḥammad, who was 'Abdarraḥmān III.
65. *Ḳ'bhūṣat ḥakhāmīm,* pp. 110-11. See also *T'shūbhōt GMUM,* no. 26; "Lucena has no non-Jew who sets up prohibitions against you; why do you not establish *'ērūbhē ḥaṣērōt* [amalgamations of courtyards] etc." Cf. *Sefer ha-'ittīm,* p. 148.
66. Al-Idrīsī, p. 205.
67. See Ibn Abī Uṣaibi'a, 2, p. 76.

68. See what Joseph ben Ṣaddīḳ wrote in A. Neubauer, *Mediaeval Jewish Chronicles and Chronological Notes* (Oxford, 1887-95), 1, p. 93.
69. See al-Idrīsī, loc. cit.
70. See commentary of Isaac Abrabanel on Zechariah 12:7, and also see his commentary on Obadiah, v. 20.
71. According to local tradition, the Jews of Lucena had a synagogue in a house at Number 4 Calle Condesa Carmen Pizarro. Today one can see there two rows of columns and plain arches that divided a rather large hall into three sections. But there is no proof, nor is it reasonable to think, that these columns are remnants from the era of Moslem rule; at most it is possible to believe the tradition that this is the site where a synagogue once stood. The house in its present form was possibly built in the sixteenth century, and it is certain that it was repaired and altered many times. See F. Cantera, "La Judería de Lucena," *Sefarad* 13:343-54.
72. *Seder Rabh 'Amram,* la; the text was published by Ginzberg, *Geonica,* 2, pp. 114-17; cf. S. Assaf, *Ha-Shiloaḥ* 35:402. On the matter of the connection between the rabbis of Lucena and the *g'ōnīm* of Babylonia, see also conjectures by Mann, "Responsa," *JQR*, n.s. 11:443.
73. Abraham b. Dā'ūd, p. 59 (translation, p. 79).
74. *Shīrat Yisrāēl,* p. 65.
75. Ibid., p. 64; *Sefer ha-riḳma,* p. 175; see also Bacher, introduction to *Sefer ha-shōrashīm,* p. 11.
76. *Shīrat Yisrāēl,* loc. cit. Cf. Schirmann, *Sefer Assaf,* p. 501.
77. *Shīrat Yisrāēl,* loc. cit.; cf. Steinschneider in Geiger's *Jüd. Zeitschrift* 1:238; there the name occurs with a שׂ (sin); cf. Schirmann, op. cit. There is a poem in his honor, bearing *"Ha-sar"* as its title, among the poems of Solomon Ibn Gabirol, ed. Bialik-Rawnitzky, book 6, p. 3; and cf. Schirmann, *Tarbiz* 8:293, n. 17.
78. For the names Illiberi and Granada, see L. Eguílaz Yanguas, "Origen de las ciudades Garnata é Illiberi y de la Alhambra," *Homenaje a D. Francisco Codera* (Saragossa, 1904), pp. 333-38.
79. See Simonet, *Descripción,* p. 41, and in addition Miguel Lafuente Alcántara, *Historia de Granada* (Granada, 1904-7), 2, p. 30.
80. See L. Equílaz Yanguas, *MAH* 8:37, and see next note.
81. The passage as rendered by Yanguas is faulty; cf. Dozy, *Recherches,* 1:342 ff. The text which Leví-Provençal cites in *Al-Andalus* 18:67 is completely erroneous, inasmuch as in it the Darro is confused with the Genil River.
82. José Francisco de Luque, *Granada y sus contornos* (Granada, 1858), p. 17; Luis Seco de Lucena, *Plano de Granada arabe* (Granada, 1910), pp. 13, 30.
83. Seco de Lucena, *Plano,* p. 80.
84. Ibid., p. 48. But it should be noted that the church was formerly in a more northerly section; after a fire broke out in it, it was moved to its present location.
85. There are many who dispute the view, cited above, that ancient Illiberi was a distance of ten kilometers from Granada. Most students

of Spanish history locate Illiberi in the northern section of Granada in the quarter of Albaicín (al-Bayyāzīn). Among them should be mentioned Francisco Bermudez de Pedraza, *Antiguedad y excelencias de Granada* (Madrid, 1608), pp. 30a ff.; Simonet, *Descripción*, pp. 30 ff.; L. Eguílaz Yanguas, *Del lugar donde fue Iliberis* (Madrid, 1881), pp. 10-11; M. Gomez Moreno, "De Illiberi a Granada," *BAH* 46:44-61.

The view that Illiberi was near Atarfe, and not on the site of what is currently Granada, is maintained by L. de Marmol Carvajal, *Historia del rebelion y castigo de los moriscos del reyno de Granada* (Malaga, 1600), pp. 3b ff.; M. Lafuente Alcántara, *Historia*, 1, p. 131; de Luque, *Granada*, pp. 9-10; J. y M. Oliver Hurtado, *Granada y sus monumentos arabes* (Malaga, 1875), pp. 6, 30, 395 ff.; L. Seco de Lucena, *La Alhambra* (Granada, 1935), p. 38.

86. Ibn 'Idhārī, p. 134.
87. Abraham b. Dā'ūd, p. 59 (translation, p. 79).
88. See *Shebheṭ Y'hūdā*, p. 34.
89. Abraham b. Dā'ūd, op. cit.
90. Ibid., p. 69. Cf. Mann in *Tarbiz* 5:283; see S. Abramson, "Letters by *G'ōnīm*," *Tarbiz* 31:196.
91. Al-Muḳaddasī, p. 234.
92. Al-Idrīsī, p. 202.
93. Moses Ibn 'Ezrā, cited in Luzzatto, p. 21.
94. Fr. de Pisa, *Descripción de la imperial ciudad de Toledo* (Toledo, 1917), f. 38a; A. Martín Gamero, *Historia de la ciudad de Toledo*, p. 632.
95. Martín Gamero, p. 642.
96. M. Vallecillo Avila, "Los judíos de Castilla en la alta edad media," CHE 14 (1950): 57-58.
97. A. González Palencia, *Los Mozárabes de Toledo en los siglos XII y XIII* (Madrid, 1926-30), 1, p. 74; Torres Balbás, "Mozarabías y juderías de las ciudades hispano-musulmanas," *Al-Andalus* 19: 193.
98. See Ibn Abī 'l-Fayyāḍ in Casiri, 2, p. 320.
99. Simonet, *Historia*, p. 164.
100. M. González Simancas, *Las sinagogas de Toledo y el baño liturgico judio* (Madrid, 1929), p. 16.
101. S. Ramon Parro, *Toledo en la mano* (Toledo, 1857), 2, p. 331.
102. See the material cited by Rodrigo Amador de los Rios, "El arrabal de los judíos" in his series of articles "Reminiscencias de Toledo," *RABM* 11:265.
103. See Amador de los Rios, "El puente de S. Martin," in his series of articles "Las puentes de la antigua Toledo," *RABM* 8:439 ff.
104. Ibn 'Idhārī, p. 85; cf. Martín Gamero, p. 633 (in his opinion an ancient Visigothic palace existed there), and Amador de los Rios in the article mentioned in note 103, pp. 443-44.
105. The article on the Jewish quarter by Amador de los Rios, cited above in note 102, depicts the Jewish neighborhood within the boundaries fixed for it after the Christian reconquest in the later Middle Ages, when the northernmost neighborhoods were taken from the Jews; in the Moslem epoch, however, the Jewish quarter was almost three

times as large. Of course, it is not necessary to assume that the entire area between the eastern boundary of the Jewish quarter, as it is depicted above, and the Tagus was densely populated. It is decidedly possible, as Amador de los Rios inclines to think, that the northwestern section of the city was sparsely populated and contained many gardens or orchards.

106. See Lévi-Provençal, 3, p. 228.
107. Cf. the information on the period after Christian reconquest adduced by Amador de los Rios, "El arrabal de los judíos," pp. 256-57.
108. Such is the opinion of Amador de los Rios, ibid., pp. 259-60; but according to another view this fortress was built near the western end of the Calle del Angel. De Pisa, p. 28b, relates that in his time an old tower near the San Martin Bridge was called Castello de la Judería, and he therefore thinks that the fortress of the Jewish quarter was located there, but this view does not correspond with the historical-topographical facts referred to above. A document of a later period, from 1270, speaks of two fortresses in the Jewish quarter, the fortress on the Tagus being called the "old one." It may therefore be assumed that after the Christian reconquest, when the area of the Jewish quarter was restricted, a new fortress was erected; see Torres Balbás, p. 194.
109. See D. Kaufmann, "Les synagogues de Tolède," *REJ* 38: 251-52.
110. See Martín Gamero, pp. 644-45; but this writer does not distinguish between it and the Great Synagogue. See E. Lambert, "Les synagogues de Tolède," *REJ* 84: 24, and holding the same opinion, F. Cantera, *Sinagogas españolas* (Madrid, 1955), p. 37.
111. See Martín Gamero, loc. cit.; Ramiro F. Valbuena, "La 'Bet ham-Midras' o 'casa de estudios' de los judíos en Toledo," *RABM* 18:452; and see especially Lambert, "Les synagogues," pp. 25 ff.
112. L.G. Zelson, "Viga mudéjar con inscripción hebraica en Toledo," *BAH* 89:318-21.
113. See Rodrigo Amador de los Rios, "La Alcaná de Toledo" *RABM* 24: 48-77, in which he brings various opinions as to the meaning of the name "Alcaná." This scholar did not wish to decide whether Jews did indeed have shops there during Moslem rule (see op. cit., pp. 75-76). But it is reasonable to believe that the king of Castile who captured the city did not grant the Jews additional new quarters, but let them retain those they already had. Lambert is of the opinion that the ancient synagogue was perhaps in the Alcaná. See his above-mentioned article, p. 23, and also Cantera, *Sinagogas,* p. 41; but there, p. 40, he conjectures that the Great Synagogue was located there—which is rather unlikely.
114. See Amador de los Rios, *RABM* 11:261-62.
115. See observations of Isaac Abrabanel at the end of his commentary on the Book of Kings and in his commentary on Obadiah, v. 20; see also *Shebheṭ Y'hūdā*, p. 33.
116. See *Tarbiz* 7:308, 318.
117. Dozy, "Essai sur l'histoire des Todjibides, etc.," *Recherches,* 1, pp. 216 ff.; F. Codera, "Los Tochibíes en España," *BAH* 12:395 ff.; idem, "Nuevas noticias acerca de los Tochibíes," *BAH* 15:435 ff.

118. See [F. Fita], "Lápidas hebreas de Calatayud," *BAH* 12:15 ff.; I. Loeb, "Une inscription hébraïque de Calatayud," *REJ* 16:273-75; Cantera-Millás, no. 205. In the view of Loeb, it is also possible to read it as 208 (that is, the year 847); however, in the light of information on the development of the city according to Arabic sources, it is preferable to read 280.
119. Vicente de la Fuente, *Historia de la siempre augusta y fidelisima ciudad de Calatayud* (Calatayud, 1880-81), 1, pp. 115, 129.
120. Ibid., p. 116; de la Fuente, who relies upon a local unclear tradition, says that in the time of Moslem rule the Jewish quarter was east of the city and outside the walls. This information is refuted by the above-mentioned gravestone in the cemetery west of the city. This proves that the Jews always resided near the western wall. It cannot be supposed that they dwelt east of the city and took their dead for burial to a remote place west of the city. It is likewise not to be assumed that after their conquest of the city, the Christians settled the Jews in an area between the walls, seeing that they had from earlier times dwelt outside, or that they gave them locations in the upper city.
121. A consideration of the topography allows for the assumption that this street was not entirely within the Jewish quarter; one can assume that in the Christian era its southern portion was not occupied by Jews. There can be no doubt that the Christians saw to it that the streets which surrounded the principal church would be occupied by Christians.
122. See de la Fuente, 2, p. 231. Concerning this family, see M. Kayserling, *Christoph Columbus u. der Antheil der Juden an den spanischen u. portugiesischen Entdeckungen* (Berlin, 1894), pp. 51 ff., 65 ff.
123. De la Fuente, 1, pp. 298-99.
124. Cantera, *Sinagogas*, pp. 188-89.
125. M. Steinschneider, *JQR* 11:605.
126. Hieronimus Blancas, *Aragonensium rerum commentarii* (Saragossa, 1588), p. 11; Ricardo del Arco, *Zaragoza histórica* (Madrid, 1928), p. 18; F. Codera, "Noticias ecclesiasticas de Zaragoza," *La Lectura católica*, (Madrid, 1880), 2, pp. 187 ff. It must be admitted that the scholars who refer to a Christian quarter rely on a local tradition and that the proof offered by Codera is doubtful.
127. Ximenez de Embún, p. 61.
128. Ibid.
129. Ibid., p. 57.
130. José Blasco, *Las parroquías de la ciudad Zaragoza* (Saragossa, 1944), p. 10.
131. Formerly the San Lorenzo Church was located in it. See ibid., p. 9.
132. Ignacio de Asso, *Historia de la economia politica de Aragón* (Saragossa, 1798), p. 214.
133. Ibid., p. 331; see also Manuel Serrano y Sanz, *Origenes de la dominación espãnola en America* (Madrid, 1918), 1, p. 8; Blasco, *Las parroquías*, p. 9. Of course, there is no need to assume that throughout the entire era of Moslem rule, the Mozarabs had any connection with this neighborhood. If indeed the church was taken away from

the Christians, the area was no doubt annexed to the Jewish quarter and was not settled by Moslems.

134. Cf. Ximenez de Embún, p. 59.
135. Ricardo del Arco, "Las juderías de Jaca y Zaragoza," *Sefarad* 14:89; Torres Balbás, "La judería de Zaragoza y su baño," *Al-Andalus* 21: 178.
136. See below.
137. Serrano, *Origenes*, p. 8; Torres Balbás, p. 179.
138. Ximenez de Embún, p. 62.
139. A description of this synagogue of the end of the Middle Ages is to be found in various sources. See [F. Fita], "La sinagoga de Zaragoza," *BAH* 18: 82-85; Cantera, *Sinagogas*, pp. 357 ff.
140. Ximenez de Embún, p. 29; Blasco, *Las parroquias*, p. 10; cf. Baer, *Urkunden*, 1, p. 850, about "the synagogue in the San Gil (or Jil) neighborhood."
141. See del Arco, *Sefarad* 15:89.
142. See Simonet, pp. 168-67. The letter itself is in Migne, 88, col. 719-21.
143. Concerning a much later period, see M. Kayserling, *REJ* 28:166.
144. M. Kayserling in *Jewish Encyclopedia*, 2, p. 527 (no source is indicated).
145. Carreras Candi, *La ciudad de Barcelona (Geografía general de Cataluña)*, 3, pp. 489 ff., 492; C. Cornet y Mas, *Guía de Barcelona* (Barcelona, 1882), p. 198.
146. F. Fita, "Los Hebreos de Barcelona en el siglo IX," *BAH* 4:69-70.
147. J.M. Millás, "Epigrafía hebraicoespañola," *Sefarad* 5:295-96; Cantera-Millás, p. 184.
148. Ibn Khaldūn, 4, p. 143.
149. Migne, 137, col. 300.
150. Ibn Ḥauḳal, 1, p. 109.
151. Cantera-Millás, nos. 243, 290.
152. Ar-Razī in *Al-Andalus* 18:73.
153. J. Sánchez Real, "Los judíos de Tarragona," *Boletín arqueológico* (Tarragona) 49: 17-18.
154. Al-Idrīsī, p. 191.
155. Sánchez Real, "Los judíos," gives a comprehensive description of the Jewish quarter at the end of the Middle Ages.
156. B. Hernandez Sanahuja, *Tarragona bajo el poder de los Arabes* (Tarragona, 1882), pp. 17 ff.
157. Cantera-Millás, no. 189.
158. E. Bayerri, *Historia de Tortosa y su comarca* (Tortosa, 1954), 6, pp. 140-41.
159. In the opinion of Cantera-Millás, *Inscripciones*, no. 199 in their collection—the inscription on the gravestone of Samuel Solomon Ḳarḳosa(?)—belongs to the period here being discussed.
160. Thus wrote S. Assaf, who published the responsum (question and answer) in the collection *Madā'ē ha-yahadūt* (1927), 2, pp. 52-53. He preferred to ascribe the responsum to Moses b. Ḥanōkh rather than to Moses the *gaon* of Sura (832-842), because in his opinion both the style and the content point to this, that is, the rabbinic jurist's knowledge of the Jews of Tortosa, which is reflected in his words. See also ibid., p. 131.

161. *Shīrat Yisrāēl*, p. 64; see also above, p. 250.
162. In al-Ḳazwīnī, *Kosmographie* (ed. Wüstenfeld, Göttingen 1898), 2, p. 373, he is called Ibrāhīm b. Aḥmad, but in the book *Ar-Rauḍ al-mi'ṭār*, p. 171, Ibrāhīm b. Yūsuf; and see there in the translation, p. 206, where he is called Ibrāhīm b. Ya'ḳūb al-Isrā'īlī aṭ-Ṭurtūshī. Kowalski takes into consideration the possibility that the writers who quote him or the copyists skipped one link in the genealogical tree and that his grandfather's name was really Yūsuf. See T. Kowalski, *Relacja Ibrahīma Ibn Ja'ḳūba* (Kraków, 1946), p. 34; however, H. Z. Hirschberg indicates the possibility that Ibn Ya'ḳūb was the family name and Yūsuf, the name of his father. See his article "Abraham b. Jacob," *Sinai* 22 (1948): 280.
163. See *Murūdj adh-dhahab*, 3, pp. 69-70.
164. Al-Ḳazwīnī, 2, p. 396. Kowalski's conjecture, p. 31, as to the route chosen by Ibrāhīm is not acceptable. The inhabitants of Moslem Spain were generally not accustomed to travel on the Atlantic Ocean in order to reach northern Europe; the transit of merchants from the Omayyad kingdom to Catalonia and France was more customary (that is, during peacetime). Even Johannes of Gorze went to Spain by this route and so did the emissary whom 'Abdarraḥmān III later sent to the king of Germany.
165. This is how it should read. See Kowalski, p. 41. The fixing of this date refutes the conjecture of Lewis that Ibrāhīm was attached to the embassy with which 'Abdarraḥmān III responded to the visit of Johannes of Gorze. See B. Lewis, "The Muslim Discovery of Europe" *Bulletin of the School of Oriental and African Studies* 20 (1957): 412-13. Johannes returned to Germany in 956, and it is unlikely that the caliph would wait ten years until he sent a new embassy to respond to this visit. No convincing grounds have been advanced for the view that Ibrāhīm made his journey to the emperor in 973. See, for example, B. Spuler, "Ibrahīm ibn Ja'qūb, orientalistische Bemerkungen," *Jahrb. f. Gesch. Osteuropas* 3 (1938).
166. *Ar-Rauḍ al-mi'ṭār*, p. 171; see also al-Ḳazwīnī, 2, p. 373; however the text there is faulty.
167. Al-Ḳazwīnī, 2, pp. 387, 409.
168. Ibid., p. 404.
169. Of course, we cannot fix the route of his travels in Germany, inasmuch as we can only depend upon quotations from his words found in Arabic writings, in which Ibrāhīm b. Ya'ḳūb tells about one place or another. Therefore it is not known where he visited *before* his meeting with the emperor and where *after*. As for some studies by Slavists regarding the testimony of Ibrāhīm about Poland, see Baron, 3, p. 338; and see further C. M. Fraehn, "Beleuchtung der merkwürdigen Notiz eines Arabers aus dem XI. Jarhundert über die Stadt Maynz," *Mémoires de l'Acad. Imp. des Sciences* (Saint Petersburg) Sciences pol., hist., philol., série 6, (1834), 2, pp. 92 ff. (who replaces Ibrāhīm b. Ya'ḳūb with Abū Bakr Muḥammad b. al-Walīd Ibn Abī Randaḳa, who was also known as aṭ-Ṭurṭūshī).
170. Kowalski, p. 4.
171. This is what it should be, not Merseburg. See Kowalski, p. 46.

172. As stated, the entire treatise has not come down to us, but the Arabic geographers quote various fragments from it. The largest fragment is cited by the eleventh century Hispano-Arabic geographer ʻAbdallāh b. ʻAbdalʻazīz al-Bakrī, in his book *Kitāb al-masālik wa ʼl-mamālik*, his tale about the Slavic countries. This fragment was first published by A. Kunik and Baron Rosen in a supplement to *Bulletin of the Russian Academy for the Sciences* 32, no. 2 (Saint Petersburg, 1878). Cf. Brokkelmann, 1, p. 523, Suppl. 1, p. 410. Kowalski (see note 162, above) published it again on the basis of an ancient manuscript, clarifying in a detailed introduction all the known data concerning Ibrāhīm; he proved that we cannot speak of two Ibrāhīm b. Yaʻḳūbs, one a Moslem and one a Jew (from Africa!), as was the opinion of Georg Jacob, *Ein arabischer Berichterstatter aus dem 10. Jahrhundert* . . . (Berlin, 1891), p. 10; idem, *Arabische Berichte von Gesandten an germanische Fürstenhöfe aus dem 9. und 10. Jahrhundert* (Berlin-Leipzig, 1927), pp. 3, 6. Even though Kowalski's argument is convincing in this matter, he has not adduced an acceptable theory regarding the mission of Ibrāhīm b. Yaʻḳūb. The Polish scholar justifiably refutes the conjecture that Ibrāhīm was a slave-trader and inclines toward the view that he was attached to a diplomatic mission as a translator or a physician. H. Z. Hirschberg also conjectures that he was a physician who accompanied such a mission. See his critique of Kowalski's treatise in *Kirjath Sepher* 24:46.

Many arguments can be advanced against this conjecture: (1) Nothing is known of a diplomatic mission sent by Caliph al-Ḥakam II to Emperor Otto I. (2) If such a mission was indeed sent and Ibrāhīm was attached to it, it is hard to suppose that he would be allowed to circulate so freely in the broad reaches of the German Empire and to go from there to the Slavic countries. A member of a diplomatic mission was regarded a diplomatic envoy, and he would no doubt be regarded warily and with some suspicion. (3) From his account of his conversation with the emperor concerning the transfer of the bones of the saint of Lorca, it could be taken that Ibrāhīm was the chief envoy—but it cannot be assumed that so estimable a function would be given to the Tortosan Jew, who was an unimportant man at the Spanish court and not at all to be compared with Ḥasdai Ibn Shaprūṭ, who was a high official. For a mission to the German emperor a Christian cleric would have been preferred, as was sent by ʻAbdarraḥmān III in his time. The account given here, which is of course merely the product of conjecture, corresponds much more with the circumstances of the time, namely, the activities of the caliph who then ruled in Cordova and the data in Ibrāhīm's own travelogue.

To be sure, the view that Ibrāhīm b. Yaʻḳūb was a slave-trader still finds adherents. See M. Canard, "Ibrāhīm ibn Yaʻqūb et sa relation de voyage en Europe," *Etudes d'orientalisme dédiées à la mémoire de Lévi-Provençal* (Paris, 1962), 2, p. 506; however the Karaite scholar Jakimowicz believes that he made his journey in order to visit the Jewish communities; R. Jakimowicz, "Kilka uwag nad relacja o Slowianach Ibrahima ibn Jaʻkuba," *Slavia Antiqua* 1 (1948): 439 ff.

In the survey of Ibrāhīm's journey given above, only those places are mentioned for which we possess explicit evidence. However, Georg Jacob surmised that all the descriptions of cities and regions in central and northern Europe included in the work of al-Ḳazwīnī derive from Ibrāhīm b. Ya'ḳūb, such as the description of Utrecht (2, p. 388), Soest (ibid., p. 413), Paderborn (ibid., p. 415), and remote Ireland (ibid., pp. 388-89). And in his treatise *Arabische Berichte von Gesandten* Jacob added more details. But in the chapters devoted to these localities, Ibrāhīm b. Ya'ḳūb's name is not mentioned, except that several times mention is made of al-'Udhrī, from whom he copied—in which case Jacob offers no proof, although his conjecture cannot be discounted a priori.

173. Al-Ḳazwīnī, see note 167 above.
174. Ed. Kowalski, ll. 39-40.
175. See, in addition, al-Ḳazwīnī, 2, p. 415.
176. See preface by Lévi-Provençal to the book *Ar-Rauḍ al-mi'ṭār*, p. xxiv.
177. See *España Sagrada,* 13, pp. 249-50.
178. See al-Makkarī, 1, p. 226.
179. Abraham b. Dā'ūd, p. 59 (translation, p. 79).
180. See the account of the Bishop Massona, who lived at the end of the sixth century, Migne, 80, col. 139.
181. Cantera-Millás, *Inscripciones,* no. 289; see there p. 415, and see also nos. 287-88.
182. See the letter published by A. Marmorstein, *REJ* 70:103; cf. with note 184.
183. Cf. Abraham b. Dā'ūd, loc. cit.
184. Ibid. In this instance, also, it can be assumed that the *gaon* had in mind the Jews of the entire region, but mentioned only the principal community.
185. *Shīrat Yisrāēl,* pp. 64, 65.
186. Baer, *Urkunden,* 2, pp. 307, 348.
187. Bernabe Moreno de Vargas, *Historia de la ciudad de Mérida* (Madrid, 1633), pp. 259a f.; Pascual Madoz, *Diccionario geografico-estadistico de España* (Madrid, 1848), 11:389.
188. See Moreno de Vargas, *Historia,* according to a document in the municipal archives.
189. *Ar-Rauḍ al-mi'ṭār,* p. 36.
190. Ch. 23, p. 29a.
191. M. Kayserling, *Geschichte der Juden in Portugal* (Leipzig, 1867), p. 2.
192. Lévi-Provençal, 1, p. 49; 3, p. 196.

CHAPTER NINE

1. *Shīrat Yisrāēl,* p. 64, and see below.
2. See *Shīrat Yisrāēl,* p. 64; see also M. Steinschneider in *CB* 1437-39 and also *JQR* 11, p. 616.
3. *Sha'arē Sedeḳ,* part 3, section 1, no. 29; section 2, no. 11 (in the MS. of Halberstam the responsum is ascribed to Joseph Ibn Abītūr), section 2, no. 28; section 3, no. 9; part 4, section 4, no. 42 (cf. *T'shūbhōt R. Solomon b. Adret,* ed. Warsaw, no. 477); section 5, no. 21; section 6, no. 21;

section 8, no. 23, *T'shūbhōt GMUM*, no. 193 and perhaps also 171, 192 (see Müller's notes there); A. Marx, "Shālōsh t'shūbhōt l'rav Joseph Gaon . . . ," *Ginzē ḳedem* 3, pp. 57-64; no. 2 ff. are those of Joseph Ibn Abītūr, as was demonstrated by S. Assaf in *Kirjath Sepher*, 2, pp. 183-84. Assaf himself, in his collection, *Geonica*, p. 98, published a responsum which in his view is by Joseph Ibn Abītūr.

4. See E. Landshuth, *'Amūdē ha-'abhōda* (Berlin, 5617), pp. 12-13; L. Zunz, *Literaturgeschichte der synag. Poesie* (Berlin, 1865), pp. 178-79; H. Schirmann, *Shīrīm ḥadāshīm min ha-g'nīza* (Jerusalem, 1965), pp. 150-51.
5. *Taḥk'mōnī*, p. 41.
6. See what M. Zulay wrote in the collection *'Alī-'ayin* (*Minḥat d'bhārīm l'* S. Z. Schocken; Jerusalem, 5708-5712), p. 100; see also *Mibhḥār ha-shibh'im* published by ha-Makhōn l'ḥeḳer ha-shīra (Tel Aviv, 5708), no. 32; *Tarbiz* 20:162 (Zulay assumes, on the basis of the caption "lamed lamed resh bet," that the hymn is that of Joseph Ibn Abītūr, but see Schirmann, *Sefer Assaf*, p. 504); for his poetry in general see Schirmann, 1, pp. 53-54. Cf. M. Sachs, *Die religiöse Poesie der Juden in Spanien*, 2d ed. (Berlin, 1901), pp. 251-52; S. Bernstein, "Piyūṭē ma'mādōt of R. Joseph Ibn Abītūr," *Sinai* 31 (5712): 284-309; idem, "S'līḥōt biltī y'dū'ot of R. Joseph Ibn Abītūr," *Sura* 1 (5714): 26-47; H. Brody-K. Albrecht, *Sha'ar ha-shīr* (Leipzig, 1905), pp. 9-15; Schirmann, *Sefer Assaf*, p. 506.
7. Harkavy, *MGWJ* 34: 285-86; idem, *Magazin* 14 (1887): 32-33; idem, *Ḥadāshīm gam y'shānīm*, no. 1, pp. 3-4.
8. Saadya Ben Danan, "Ma'amar 'al seder ha-dōrōt," *Ḥemda g'nūza*, f. 29a.
9. See Cagigas, 2, p. 368. Apparently a Jewish astrologer named al-Manṣūr ben Abraham dedicated to him a book that later translated from Arabic to Latin by Plato Tiburtinus. See F. Wüstenfeld, *Die Übersetzungen arabischer Werke in das lateinische seit dem XI. Jahrhundert (Abhandl. d. Kgl. Ges. d. Wiss. zu Göttingen Bd. 22)* (Göttingen 1877), p. 41.
10. Ibn Ṣā'id, pp. 88-89.
11. Abraham b. Dā'ūd, p. 49 (translation, pp. 66-67).
12. The scholars had difficulty understanding the words of Abraham b. Dā'ūd. Graetz was of the opinion that he translated the Mishnah; see vol. 5, p. 372. Müller, p. 5, speaks of a commentary to the entire Talmud. Sachs, p. 354, conjectures that his comment was made orally.
13. See Abraham b. Dā'ūd, loc. cit.
14. Marmorstein published this letter, "Neues Material über Joseph ben Isak Satanas," in *MGWJ* 67 (1923): 59-60, and later S. Assaf published it once more, adding emendations and commentaries, as "Mikhtabh me-rabbi Josef Ibn Abītūr," *Ḥemdat Yisrāēl* (*Sefer ha-zikārōn l'rabbi Ḥayyim Ḥizḳiyahu Medīnī*, Jerusalem, 5706), pp. 24-27 and in an emended form in *M'ḳōrōt u-meḥkārīm*, pp. 115-18. Assaf surmises that the letter was sent to Sh'marya b. Elḥānān, the renowned head of the Talmud academy at Fostat. Concerning the meeting of Ibn Abītūr with Khalfa b. Ḥakmōn, see S. Abramson, *Tarbiz* 31:199.

15. *T'shūbhōt GMUM*, no. 172, and part of the same responsum, no. 3 of the responsa published by Marx, *Ginzē ḳedem,* 3 (see note 3 above); see also Mann, *JQR,* n.s. 11:465, and cf. Assaf, *Kirjath Sepher,* 2, p. 183. See also Marx, p. 6.
16. See the list of the *t'shūbhōt ha-g'ōnīm* published by S. Assaf, in *Mi-sifrūt ha-g'ōnīm*, pp. 219-20. Reference is made there to "Abū Ya'ḳūb al-Andalusī," who no doubt is Joseph Ibn Abītūr, as noted with justice by J. Mann, "Inyānīm shōnīm," pp. 284-85. "Abū Ya'ḳūb" is an appellation for Joseph; also, these responsa were sent to Fostat, and it cannot be conjectured that at the selfsame time there were two Josephs from Spain there, both having been distinguished scholars who corresponded with the *g'ōnīm* of Babylonia.
17. The letter was published by Marmorstein, *REJ* 70:101-2. Cf. the emendations by Mann, *REJ* 71:110-12. It was later published again in its entirety by Mann, *Tarbiz* 6:84-88. Abramson casts doubt on the identification of the Ḥanōkh mentioned in this letter with Ḥanōkh b. Moses; see *Tarbiz* 31:198-99, but the rarity of the name Ḥanōkh supports the identification. Can it be assumed that at that very time there were two men named Ḥanōkh who were in controversy with Joseph Ibn Abītūr?
18. Mann, *Jews,* 2, pp. 59-60.
19. *Sha'arē Ṣedeḳ*, part 3, section 1, no. 28, 29; *T'shūbhōt GMUM*, no. 182.
20. Abraham b. Dā'ūd, p. 50 (translation, pp. 66-67).
21. Ibn 'Idhārī, pp. 259, 279, 297.
22. *Sefer ha-riḳma,* p. 227; cf. K. al-Luma', ed. J. Derenbourg: *Le livres des parterres fleuris* (Paris, 1886), p. 208: *aṣḥāb al-inzāl.* According to Stern this is an appellation given to men of the court. See what he wrote in *Zion* 15:137. But this is an unlikely surmise.
23. *T'shūbhōt GMUM,* no. 172; cf. Mann, *JQR,* n.s. 11:465; Assaf, *Kirjath Sepher* 2, p. 183.
24. P. Kahle, *Masoreten des Westens* (Stuttgart, 1927-30), 1, pp. 65-66; cf. Mann, *Tarbiz* 6:283-84.
25. Zulay, in the collection *'Alī'ayin*, p. 110.
26. H. Schirmann, "Ḳīnōt 'al ha-g'zērōt be-Ereṣ Yisrāēl, Africa, Ashkenaz 'Ṣar'fat," *Ḳōbheṣ al yad* 3 (13): 27-28.
27. *Sha'arē Ṣedeḳ*, part 3, section 1, no. 28; section 5, no. 9; *Tōratan shel rishōnīm* (Frankfurt on Main, 1882), part 1, p. 48; *T'shūbhōt GMUM*, no. 175, 182, 194, 202-4, 208-9, 211; and in the opinion of Müller, also, 163, 176-78, 183-86, 191, 196-99, 201, 206; *Halākhōt P'sūḳōt* (Constantinople, 1516) according to Müller, pp. 30, 31.
28. Y'rūḥam b. M'shullam, *Sefer Tōl'dōt Adam* (Constantinople, 5281), p. 16b; H. Gross, "Aaron Hakohen u. sein Ritualwerk Orchot Chajim," *MGWJ* 18: 531; Isaac Giyyāṭ, *Hilkhōt Rosh ha-shāna* (Sha'arē Simḥa, Fürth, 5621), p. 29 (cf. the same matter in his name in Rabbēnū Ashēr, ch. 6, no. 16); *Kol Bo* (Fürth, 5542), p. 10b.
29. See the letter published by Mann, *Texts,* 1, p. 121; cf. there pp. 109-10, as well as pp. 1459-60.
30. Abraham b. Dā'ūd, p. 53 (translation, pp. 70-71). It is true that he states that Ḥanōkh died "in 4775, 13 years before the death of R. Hai,

of blessed memory," and Hai Gaon died in 1038. And also in the *Sefer ha-yoḥasīn* the date of his death is set down as 4785. However, the first date is to be preferred, for had he died in 1024, we should have to assume that he reached a ripe old age, having been appointed as rabbi of Cordova around 970, when he was no doubt a mature person. It can be surmised that the author of *Sefer ha-yoḥasīn* emended the statement of Abraham b. Dā'ūd.

31. Lévi-Provençal, 2, pp. 206, 223, 259, 261, 264, 265, 266, 271.
32. Ibn 'Idhārī, pp. 293-94.
33. Ibid., p. 279.
34. *Kitāb al-Luma'*, pp. 207 (last word), 305.
35. See B. Klar, "Ha-Shīra ve-ha-ḥayim," in the collection *Areshet* (Jerusalem, 5704), pp. 335-36; see also p. 343.
36. See J. Weiss, *Tarbūt ḥaṣrānīt ve-shīra ḥaṣranīt* (Jerusalem, 5708), especially pp. 11-12.
37. Millás Vallicrosa, *La poesia sagrada hebraicoespañola*, 2d ed. (Madrid, 1948), p. 30.
38. Kokowzow, *Novyje materialy*, p. 2; Derenbourg, *Opuscules*, p. x, believes that this is the name Yaḥyā with the Spanish diminutive *ujjo*.
39. Abraham b. Dā'ūd, p. 73 (translation, pp. 101-2); *Shīrat Yisrāēl*, p. 64.
40. This is only a conjecture, which finds itself supported by the character of the treatise mentioned below as the third of his treatises and uncertain information cited below in note 52.
41. On the names of the book, see *CB* 1301.
42. The original was published by M. Jastrow: *The Weak and Geminative Verbs in Hebrew by Abū Zakariyyà Yaḥya ibn Dawud, Known as Ḥayyuḡ* (Leiden, 1897). The translations are Ewald-Dukes, *Beiträge zur Geschichte der aeltesten Auslegung* u. *Spracherklärung des Alten Testaments*, vol. 3 (Stuttgart-Frankfurt a.M., 1844); J.W. Nutt, *Two Treatises on Verbs containing Feeble and Double Letters by R. Jehuda Ḥayug* (London-Berlin, 1870). For another translation see Porges, *MGWJ* 34:321-22. The book *S'fat yeter*, by Isaac Halevi b. El'azar, MS. Neubauer, 1458, is not a translation but a paraphrase. See M. Steinschneider in *HB* 20:10.
43. The original was published, together with the Hebrew translation, by Nutt as an appendix to the two books on the verbs (see preceding note); he added an English translation to the three treatises.
44. The manuscript found in the Saint Petersburg library was published by Kokowzow, *Novyje materialy*, 2, pp. 1-58; see the Russian section, pp. 1-74. Before the publication of this fragment, scholars were in a state of confusion as to the character, as well as the title, of the book, for the reason that writers of the Middle Ages mentioned the work without having seen it and expressed incorrect views about it. Abraham Ibn 'Ezrā, who read *Kitāb an-Nūtaf*, translated it as *Sefer ha-ḳorḥa* (in the introduction to *Sefer ha-moznāyim*), and other authors turned it into *Sefer ha-riḳḥa* and *Sefer ha-riḳma*. Tanḥūm ha-Y'rūshalmī relates that Ḥayyūdj, in this commentary, discussed verbs he had skipped in his two works on the conjugation of verbs. See Israelson,

"L'ouvrage perdu de Jehouda Hajjoudj," *REJ* 19:306 ff.; cf. Derenbourg, ibid., pp. 310-11; Harkavy, ibid. 31:288-89.

45. See Derenbourg, op. cit.; *al-Mustalḥiḳ*, p. 4.
46. K. al-Līn, p. 22.
47. Kokowzow, p. 6 (Hebrew section).
48. MS. Neubauer 223, see index, col. 951.
49. Cf. W. Bacher, *Abraham ibn Esra als Grammatiker*, p. 177.
50. MS. Neubauer 221. In his introduction to his commentary on the Song of Songs, Joseph Ibn 'Aḳnīn numbers Abū Zakariyā among the commentators who wrote commentaries based on the literal meaning of the text. See A. Neubauer, "Joseph ben Aqnin," *MGWJ* 19:306. But there the intent is not precisely the commentators of Song of Songs.
51. See sources in note 45.
52. Abraham b. Dā'ūd, p. 73 (translation, pp. 101-2); Abraham Ibn 'Ezrā, *S'fat yeter*, no. 74; David Ḳimḥī in the beginning of *Sefer mikhlōl*.

    Among the scholars who dealt with the history of Hebrew philology there were some really great and esteemed ones who identified Yaḥyā b. Dā'ūd Ḥayyūdj with the Y'hūda b. David who edited the responsa of M'naḥem's disciples. This view was expressed by W. Bacher in "Winter-Wünsche" 2:157 ff.; Derenbourg, *Opuscules*, pp. ix-x; Kokowzow, p. 3; and N. Allōnī in a special article, "Y'hūda b. David and Y'hūda Hayyūdj," *Minḥa l'Y'hūda* (Zlotnik: Jerusalem, 5710), pp. 67-83. But this view is refuted on several grounds that cannot be discounted.

    The arguments against identification of the two grammarians are advanced by Gross in his book on M'naḥem Ben Sārūḳ, p. 29, and especially by S. Poznanski in his article "New Material on the History of Hebrew and Hebrew-Arabic Philosophy during the X-XII Centuries," *JQR*, n.s. 16:247 ff. Those who support the identification of Y'hūda b. David with Ḥayyūdj point to the similarity between various passages in the responsa of M'naḥem's disciples and in the writings of Ḥayyūdj. See Bacher in "Winter-Wünsche," and Allōnī, "Y'hūda b. David," pp. 73-74; but this argument is invalid, since of course a later philologist is influenced by his predecessors, even borrowing ideas and principles, especially in a book designed for use by students.
53. The book was published by Schröter in Breslau, 1866, with the title *Sefer T'shūbhōt Dūnash Halevi b. Labraṭ 'al R. Saadya Gaon*.
54. See ibid., nos. 104, 195.
55. This incomplete critical work, which survived in a single manuscript, was ascribed by the copyist to Dūnash b. Labraṭ because he found his name in the text but failed to realize that that passage contains a quotation from the renowned poet and grammarian. Despite this consideration, this view was maintained not only by the publisher of the treatise (see the preceding note), but also by some of the esteemed writers on Judaica, such as Eppenstein; see "Studien über Dunasch's Kritik gegen Saadia," *MGWJ* 46:62 ff.; ibid., 533-34; Bacher, ibid., 478-79; Poznanski, *JQR*, n.s. 16:239, 255-56. The first to upset this theory was N. Porges, "Ueber die Echtheit der dem Dunasch b. Labrāt zugeschriebenen kritik gegen Saadja," *Gedenkbuch David Kaufmann*

(Breslau, 1900), pp. 245 ff. But he, too, halted midway and did not grasp the fact that this criticism is not of one piece. This was indicated by D. Herzog, *The Polemic Treatise against Saadya, ascribed to Dunasch ben Labrat,* Saadya Studies (Manchester, 1943), pp. 26 ff.

56. In the opinion of Schirmann, *Tarbiz* 7:296, most of the members of the "second group" listed by Moses Ibn 'Ezrā, *Shīrat Yisrāēl,* p. 64, were born between 950 and 960. This is in essence correct, but it seems that Moses Ibn 'Ezrā was not exact in the chronological order in his division of the writers of Spanish Jewry into groups according to time, Isaac Ibn Djiḳaṭilla, who is not mentioned as the first in the second group, was born, no doubt, much before 950; see above, p. 259, for the time of the writing of the responsa of M'naḥem's disciples; also, Joseph Ibn Abītūr was undoubtedly born before 950, and he was the disciple of Moses ben Ḥanōkh, who died in the days of Ḥasdai Ibn Shaprūṭ. See above ch. 6, note 13, regarding the time of his arrival in Spain.
57. *Shīrat Yisrāēl,* p. 64.
58. See *Sefer ha-shōrashīm,* ed. Bacher, p. x.
59. The *azhārōt* of Isaac Ibn Djiḳaṭilla first became known from the commentary written by Moses Ibn Tibbōn on the *azhārōt* of a later poet, in which he cites the words of Isaac Ibn Djiḳaṭilla by way of comparison. See S. Z. H. Halberstam, "Shi'urē b'rākha," *Ḳōbhes 'al yad,* 9th year, pp. 29-30; A. Neubauer, "Azhārōt on the 613 Precepts," *JQR* 6:698 ff. Later M. Zulay found, in the Geniza collections, a fragment of the *azhārōt* and published it in *Tarbiz* 20: 161-76.
60. See *Shīrat Yisrāēl,* p. 64. The family's name was Mar Saul (see below, note 65).
61. *Opuscules,* p. 333.
62. See *Sefer ha-shōrashīm,* pp. 94, 189, 366, 408; *Sefer ha-riḳma,* p. 284.
63. See Bacher, introduction to *Sefer ha-shōrashīm,* p. x. Concerning a written work, there is indication also from the quotations by Abraham Ibn 'Ezrā in connection with Deuteronomy 32:17 and Isaiah 27:3. Cf. Ewald-Dukes, *Beiträge zur Geschichte der aeltesten Auslegung,* 2, p. 168. The quotation that is first mentioned is also cited by Isaac b. El'azar in his *Sefer ha-riḳma,* MS. Paris, 1225, see L. Dukes, *Litbl. des Orients,* 7, col. 706. According to Pinsker, *Liḳḳūṭe ḳadmōniyyōt,* supplements, p. 65, the Karaite Levi b. Jephet quotes the *Iggarōn* (Lexicon) of Isaac b. Saul, and they are also cited by the Karaite 'Alī b. Sulaimān; however, as to the identification of Isaac b. Saul with our Isaac b. Levi Ben Mar Saul, doubt is expressed by Moses Steinschneider, *Arabische Literatur der Juden,* p. 120, and Schirmann (see below).
64. *Sefer ha-riḳma,* pp. 226-27.
65. H. Schirmann collected his poetry from printed copies and MSS. and evaluated them: "Isaac Ben Mar Saul, the Poet of Lucena," *Sefer Assaf* (Jerusalem, 5713), pp. 496-504; see also his collection, *New Poems from the Genizah,* pp. 157-58, and idem, "The Ephebe in Medieval Hebrew Poetry," *Sefarad* 15: 55-58, and especially pp. 58-59.

In *Shīrat Yisrāēl,* p. 64, it is asserted that Isaac Ibn Djiḳaṭilla surpassed Isaac Ben Mar Saul because his knowledge of the Arabic language was much greater. Judged on the basis of remnants of their writings, Isaac Ben Mar Saul was influenced by Arabic poetry, and it is hard to assume that he had no good mastery of their language. It seems that the author of *Shīrat Yisrāēl* had in mind their principles in relation to grammar and exegesis.

66. See *Sefer ha-riḳma,* pp. 200, 275, 278, 310 (and see note 64 above) and perhaps also 223 (col. 6). See Steinschneider, *Arabische Literatur,* p. 121, and also S. Poznanski, *Zur jüdisch-arabischen Litteratur* (Berlin, 1904), p. 60.
67. *Taḥk'mōnī,* p. 181.
68. *Shīrat Yisrāēl,* p. 64. He is not to be identified with Abū 'Umar Ibn Yaḳwā of Cordova, whom Moses Ibn 'Ezrā mentions earlier (see p. 299 above), for it cannot be supposed that in the selfsame passage the author would speak of one man as if he were two people, that is, refer to them by two separate names and not say that he is referring to one. Cf. Steinschneider, *Arabische Literatur,* p. 122.
69. The name is Arabic, and the spelling Ḥalfōn is a corruption of that name. Generally, names ending with ון are sounded as *un,* but at times our poets rhyme them with וֹן —*on* (for example, *ṣāfōn*), so it seems that they pronounced it also וֹן —*on.* See Steinschneider, *JQR* 11:127-28, and H. Schirmann, "Isaac Ibn Khalfōn," *Tarbiz* 7:294.
70. Moses Ibn 'Ezrā states that he was the youngest of the "second group" of poets in Spain. See *Shīrat Yisrāēl,* p. 64, and the Arabic source by Steinschneider in *Jüd. Zeitschrift* of Geiger, 1, p. 238. Of course the text should be emended by erasing the waw before our poet's name. As for the time of his birth, see Schirmann, "Isaac Ibn Khalfōn," p. 295.
71. *Sefer ha-riḳma,* pp. 226-27; cf. Munk, *JA,* 1850, 2, p. 43.
72. See Schirmann, "Isaac Ibn Khalfōn," pp. 296-300. However, it is not stated in any source currently known that his father-in-law was Isaac Ibn Ḳaprōn. Cf. also H. N. Bialik, *Tarbiz* 2:504, who does not identify this Ibn Ḳaprōn with Isaac Ibn Ḳaprōn.
73. See *Shīrat Yisrāēl,* pp. 64-65.
74. See Davidson, *JQR,* n.s. 1:231 ff.
75. The name should be read 'Aukal; see Assaf, in *Tarbiz* 20:177. Concerning Menasseh b. Abraham al-Ḳazzāz, see Mann, *Jews,* 1, pp. 19-20.
76. *Diwan,* ed. Mirsky, 2d ed. (Jerusalem, 1966), pp. 82-83.
77. See S. Abramson, "On the New Fragment of the Diwan of R. Isaac Ben Khalfōn," *Sinai* 28 (1951): 125.
78. *Diwan,* p. 92.

INDEX OF PERSONS AND PLACES*

Names beginning with al-, ar-, as-, etc. are listed under the second element of the name

*Prepared by Kay Powell

Mas'ūdī, Abū-al-Ḥasan 'Ali al-, 205, 345, 346
Mauritania, 30
Maurūr hill, 314, 315
M'bhassēr Gaon, 232
Mecca, 53, 85, 143, 149
Medina, 28, 54, 59, 149
Medina-Sidonia, 20, 307
Mediterranean basin, 30, 35, 46, 65, 148, 156, 157, 164, 200, 237, 280, 287, 309, 360, 367
Mediterranean Sea, 27, 65, 121, 141, 165, 189, 235, 236, 279, 281, 363
Menasseh b. Abraham al-Ḳazzāz, 397
Mérida, 57, 64, 96, 277, 350-53, 356, 359
  Christians of, 58, 68, 351
  conquest of, 21-23, 26
  Jews of, 352-53
  products of, 274
Meseta, 17
Mesopotamia, 36, 209, 221, 222, 223, 225
Metz, 170, 171, 175
Mieszko, Duke, 348
Mithridates Eupator, 161
M'naḥem, Rabbi, 184
M'naḥem Ben Sārūḳ, 244-51, 256-61, 344, 349, 383, 393
Mohammed, 54, 82, 83, 84, 85, 86, 173, 182, 402
Moisen (man of Sahagún), 116
Monte Cassino, 171
Montichel hill, 320, 326
Montiel, 18
Montjuich (Jewish Mountain), 340
Mordecai (son of Joseph Ibn Abītūr), 366
Morocco ("Far West"), 31, 32, 40, 41, 45, 46, 60-61, 62, 152, 226, 252, 318, 362, 372, 376, 387, 397
  Arabic rulers of, 8, 164, 169
  Jews of, 29, 51, 219, 220, 224, 240, 253, 381, 382, 384
Moses (brother of Aaron b. Abraham b. Aaron), 239
Moses b. Ḥanōkh, 234-37, 241, 343, 355, 357, 364, 380
Mosul, 197, 222
Mount Seir, 213
Mount Sinai, 77
Mount Zion, 186
Mozambique, 276
Mu'āwiya, 43
Mughīth ar-Rūmī, 10, 14-16
Muhādjir Ibn al-Kaṭīl, 325
Muḥammad I, 87-90, 94-102, 107, 328, 351
Muḥammad al-Anḳar, 330
Muḥammad b. al-Ḥasan as-Zubaidī, 383
Muḥammad b. Ḥusain, 177
Mu'izz, Caliph al-, 381
Muḳaddasī, al-, 272, 276, 284-85, 290, 319, 345
Muḳtadir, Caliph al-, 157, 345
Muḳtafī, Caliph al-, 220
Mundhir, Emir al-, 102-3, 330
Murcia, 21, 97, 105, 112
Mūsā b. Ḥudair, 156
Mūsā b. Mūsā, 99
Mūsā b. Nuṣair, 5, 9, 19-22, 26, 28, 29, 32, 119, 353-54
Muṣhafī, al-, *see* Dja'far b. 'Uthmān al-Muṣhafī
Mutawakkil, Caliph al-, 89

Naḥshōn bar Ṣaddōḳ, 131, 136
Naḥūm (grandson of Naḥūm al-Ḥazzān al-Baradānī), 225
Naḥūm al-Ḥazzān al-Baradānī, 225-26
Narbonne, 13, 53